D0840468

Windows Server® 2008 Server Core Administrator's Pocket Consultant

Mitch Tulloch with the
Windows Server Core Team
at Microsoft

PUBLISHED BY
Microsoft Press
A Division of Microsoft Corporation
One Microsoft Way
Redmond, Washington 98052-6399

Copyright © 2009 by Mitch Tulloch

Library of Congress Control Number: 2008935157

Printed and bound in the United States of America.

1 2 3 4 5 6 7 8 9   QWE   3 2 1 0 9 8

Distributed in Canada by H.B. Fenn and Company Ltd.

A CIP catalogue record for this book is available from the British Library.

Microsoft Press books are available through booksellers and distributors worldwide. For further information about international editions, contact your local Microsoft Corporation office or contact Microsoft Press International directly at fax (425) 936-7329. Visit our Web site at www.microsoft.com/mspress. Send comments to mspinput@microsoft.com.

Microsoft, Microsoft Press, Active Directory, BitLocker, Excel, Hyper-V, Internet Explorer, Jscript, MSDN, SharePoint, SQL Server, Visual Basic, Visual Studio, Win32, Windows, Windows Media, Windows NT, Windows PowerShell, Windows Server, and Windows Vista are either registered trademarks or trademarks of the Microsoft group of companies. Other product and company names mentioned herein may be the trademarks of their respective owners.

The example companies, organizations, products, domain names, e-mail addresses, logos, people, places, and events depicted herein are fictitious. No association with any real company, organization, product, domain name, e-mail address, logo, person, place, or event is intended or should be inferred.

This book expresses the author's views and opinions. The information contained in this book is provided without any express, statutory, or implied warranties. Neither the authors, Microsoft Corporation, nor its resellers, or distributors will be held liable for any damages caused or alleged to be caused either directly or indirectly by this book.

Acquisitions Editor: Martin DelRe
Developmental Editor: Karen Szall
Project Editor: Carol Vu
Editorial Production: ICC Macmillan, Inc.
Technical Reviewer: Bob Dean; Technical Review services provided by Content Master, a member of CM Group, Ltd.
Cover: Tom Draper Design

Body Part No. X15-12261

Contents at a Glance

Table of Contents

What do you think of this book? We want to hear from you!

Microsoft is interested in hearing your feedback so we can continually improve our books and learning resources for you. To participate in a brief survey, please visit:

www.microsoft.com/learning/booksurvey

What do you think of this book? We want to hear from you!

Microsoft is interested in hearing your feedback so we can continually improve our books and learning resources for you. To participate in a brief survey, please visit:

www.microsoft.com/learning/booksurvey

Acknowledgments

Huge thanks first of all to Andrew Mason, Principal Program Manager for the Server Core program at Microsoft, for reviewing all my chapters for technical accuracy and for patiently responding to my numerous questions.

Much thanks as well to the following individuals: to my friend and colleague Jason Miller, MVP, who assisted me in developing and testing the Hyper-V content for this book; to James O'Neill, IT Pro Evangelist at Microsoft UK, who reviewed the Hyper-V content and provided helpful advice; and to Bob Dean, the technical reviewer for this project, who went above and beyond the call of duty in helping ensure the content is accurate. Special thanks also to Bill Noonan, Mark Kitris, and the members of the CSS Global Technical Readiness Team (GTR) at Microsoft for the invaluable assistance they provided on this project.

Thanks also to Karen Szall, the development editor at Microsoft Press for this book, and Carol Vu, the project editor at Microsoft Press, both of whom I've enjoyed working with on this project and hope to do so again in the future. Thanks also to Martin DelRe, who first approached me about being involved in this project.

Thanks as well to my friend and agent, Neil Salkind of Salkind Literary Agency, which is part of Studio B Productions, Inc.

And finally, thanks to my wife, Ingrid, for her encouragement and support during this project.

Foreword

By Andrew Mason
Principal Program Manager Lead, Windows Server Core

As Windows Server has continued to evolve, increasing functionality with each release, it became apparent that there was a need for additional deployment flexibility. Windows Server is a general-purpose operating system, but it is frequently deployed to provide a fixed function on a network, such as a DNS Server, File Server, Active Directory Domain Services domain controller, and so on. In these deployments, more functionality than necessary is often installed for a single server role to run, and a common customer request has been to allow the installation of just what is needed. The result of this is the new Server Core installation option in Windows Server 2008.

Server Core is an exciting and big step forward that allows customers more flexibility in how they deploy, manage, maintain, and secure a Windows Server installation. You may have heard that Server Core is a minimal, GUI-less interface, or even that it is a Windows without windows installation of Windows Server. As you will see as you go through this book, Server Core is much more than just the removal of the Windows shell. The way I like to describe Server Core is that it is a slice off the bottom of the operating system, providing a subset of the full functionality. To that end, customers are finding a variety of ways to take advantage of the many benefits Server Core provides. Some of the benefits you will find include a reduction in the number of software updates required to maintain the operating system (OS), a smaller attack surface, its relative simplicity (there's less to configure, so there's less to misconfigure), and the fact that it can be used to extend the life of older hardware.

As you delve into Server Core in this book, you may wonder why some functionality was included while other functionality was left out of Server Core. The best way to explain that in the limited space I have is to state the goal we had in designing Server Core: to provide customers with a minimal installation option that reduces management, maintenance, and the security attack surface while running the network infrastructure server roles and still being manageable with the same set of tools. To achieve this, a lot of time was spent on the management side to ensure Server Core is manageable and fits seamlessly in with the management infrastructures that customers are already using with Windows Server. We included functionalities such as Windows Installer, so that the Microsoft Windows Installer (.msi) packages for management agents can be used to install the agents the same way they are on a full Windows Server installation. However, including functionality in Server Core while trying to maintain these goals is very much a tightrope walk that requires some hard decisions and some omissions until dependencies can be changed.

This book will be an invaluable resource for administrators wanting to understand how to install, configure, and manage a Server Core installation. It is a resource that you can refer to for end-to-end deployments of Server Core, as well as for guidance on using specific server roles and useful tips for working with Server Core.

The Server Core team is very proud of what we were able to accomplish and hope you will take advantage of its benefits in your environment.

Introduction

Welcome to the *Windows Server 2008 Server Core Administrator's Pocket Consultant*. Server Core is a new installation option available for Windows Server 2008 that has a reduced servicing footprint and is designed for running a specific set of server roles for dedicated use. Enterprises have been asking for a book like this for a while, because Server Core can help branch offices, data centers, and other environments significantly reduce the cost involved with deploying and managing servers running Microsoft Windows. I hope you find that this book meets your needs and answers any questions you may have about Server Core; feel free to use my personal contact info found later in this Introduction to send me questions.

Who Is This Book For?

The target audience for the *Windows Server 2008 Server Core Administrator's Pocket Consultant* is administrators and staff of enterprise IT departments who need to learn how to deploy, configure, manage, and maintain Server Core computers in various roles, including domain controllers, infrastructure servers, Web servers, and other supported roles. The book assumes that you have at least a couple of years' experience managing servers running Windows in various roles, that you are familiar with most of the administrative tools used to manage servers running Windows, and that you have at least some experience trying to administer such servers from the command line.

Because most administrators who work with servers running Windows tend to be comfortable using administrative tools like Microsoft Management Console (MMC) consoles for managing their servers, this book focuses to a large extent on showing how you can perform many administrative tasks from the command line. This choice of focus was obvious for two reasons. First, when you log on to Server Core, all you see is a command prompt—there's no desktop! That means no MMC consoles either, but of course, you can use most MMC consoles remotely to manage Server Core from another computer, and that's covered too. But second, I didn't want to reinvent the wheel because über-author William Stanek has already published an excellent book called the *Windows Server 2008 Administrator's Pocket Consultant,* which explains in detail how to use these various MMC consoles to manage different roles and features on servers running Windows Server 2008. The result is that this present book is intended to complement Stanek's book instead of supplant it, and I encourage you to buy both books and use them together as a comprehensive quick reference for administering all aspects of the Windows Server 2008 platform.

How This Book Is Organized

Although this book is intended mainly as a quick lookup reference of how to perform administrative tasks, you can also read the book from cover to cover and gain a good understanding of the capabilities, features, and occasional quirks of Server Core. Whatever way you use it—as a task reference or for learning purposes—you'll benefit from using the most comprehensive resource available on administering Server Core.

The overall flow of this book looks like this:

- Chapter 1 provides a brief introduction to the platform and should be read in its entirety if you are new to Server Core.

- Chapters 2 and 3 cover manual and unattended deployment methods and various post-deployment configuration tasks that you may need to perform.

- Chapter 4 looks at the various roles and features that you can install on Server Core and explains how to deploy them both manually and during unattended installation.

- Chapters 5 and 6 explain the various tools and methods that you can use to administer Server Core, including using the local command line, Remote Desktop, the Windows Remote Shell, MMC consoles, Group Policy, and, to a limited extent, Windows PowerShell.

- Chapters 7 through 12 examine in detail each of the server roles that you can install on Server Core and how to install, configure, and manage each role using the tools and methods described in Chapters 5 and 6.

- Finally, Chapter 13 describes how to maintain various aspects of Server Core, including managing services, devices, processes, scheduled tasks, event logs, software updates, and management agents.

Conventions Used in This Book

Many elements have been used in this book to help keep the text clear and easy to follow. Commands within text that you can type to perform different tasks are styled in **bold** type. Commands with their command output are styled in `monospace` type to make them more visible, and I've included typical output of many commands so you can know what to expect when you use them. And new terms being introduced are styled in *italic* type.

I've also included the following elements where they can be helpful:

- **Note**   Provides additional detail or a sidelight on the topic under discussion

- **Caution**   Informs you of things to be aware of so you can avoid potential pitfalls

- **Tip**   Gives you some pointers that you'll probably want to know because it will make your job easier

- **Best Practices** Offers advice that you should follow to maintain supportability for your configuration

- **More Info** Directs you to where you can get more information about the subject being discussed

Other Server Core Resources

While this book is intended as a comprehensive resource on administering Server Core, there are several other resources out there that you can use if this book doesn't provide you with all the information you need. I've already mentioned the *Windows Server 2008 Administrator's Pocket Consultant,* which complements this book—Stanek's book focuses on GUI administration, while this book concentrates on how you can do things from the command line. Another book you may find useful is the *Windows Command-Line Administrator's Pocket Consultant, Second Edition,* also by William Stanek, which explains the syntax of different Windows commands. Both these books are published by Microsoft Press and are available from booksellers everywhere.

For a quick introduction to administering Server Core, you can read the "Server Core Installation Option of Windows Server 2008 Step-By-Step Guide" in the Windows Server 2008 Technical Library on Microsoft TechNet at *http://technet.microsoft.com/en-us/windowsserver/default.aspx*

There are also several blogs that contain some excellent posts on administering Server Core. The two I've found most useful are Andrew Mason's "Server Core" blog on TechNet *(http://blogs.technet.com/server_core/)* and the Server Core posts on Sander Berkouwer's "The Things That Are Better Left Unspoken" blog *(http://blogs.dirteam.com/blogs/sanderberkouwer/).*

Finally, if you want to interact with other administrators who are working with Server Core, the best place to do so is the Server Core forum on TechNet at *http://forums.technet.microsoft.com/en-US/winservercore/threads/.* Feel free to post your questions and comments there, or better yet, answer questions posted by others.

Contact the Author

You may feel free to contact me if you have comments, questions, or suggestions regarding anything in this book. While I respond to all queries from readers and will do my best to answer your question to your satisfaction, I cannot provide readers with technical support. Please send your questions to the alias *sc@mtit.com,* where they will be queued for my attention; expect a reply within one or two days. You can also check my Web site *http://www.mtit.com* for links to numerous articles and tips I've written. Please check these out because the answer to your question or problem may already be published in one of these.

Support

Every effort has been made to ensure the accuracy of this book. Microsoft Press provides corrections for books through the World Wide Web at the following address: *http://www.microsoft.com/mspress/support.*

If you have comments, questions, or ideas about this book, please send them to Microsoft Press using either of the following methods:

Postal mail:

Microsoft Press

Attn: *Windows Server 2008 Server Core Administrator's Pocket Consultant* Editor

One Microsoft Way

Redmond, WA 98052-6399

E-mail:

mspinput@microsoft.com

Please note that product support isn't offered through the mail addresses. For support information, visit Microsoft's Web site at *http://support.microsoft.com/.*

Chapter 1
Examining Server Core

Server Core is an exciting new installation option available in Windows Server 2008 that enables branch offices, data centers, and other networking environments to greatly reduce the total cost of ownership (TCO) involved with deploying and managing Windows servers. This chapter explains the rationale behind the design of Server Core, the benefits that organizations can gain by deploying Server Core, and how a Server Core installation differs from a Full installation of Windows Server 2008.

What Is Server Core?

The Server Core option is a new minimal installation option that is available when you are deploying the Standard, Enterprise, or Datacenter edition of Windows Server 2008[1]. Server Core provides you with a minimal installation of Windows Server 2008 that supports installing only certain server roles, as described later in this chapter. Contrast this with the Full installation option for Windows Server 2008, which supports installing all available server roles and also other Microsoft or third-party server applications, such as Microsoft Exchange Server or SAP.

Before we go any further, the phrase "installation option" needs to be explained. Normally, when you purchase a copy of Windows Server 2008, you purchase a license to use certain editions or stock-keeping units (SKUs). Table 1-1 lists the various editions of Windows Server 2008 that are available. The table also indicates which installation options (Full, Server Core, or both) are available for each edition.

Table 1-1 Windows Server 2008 Editions and Their Support for Installation Options

Edition	Full	Server Core
Windows Server 2008 Standard (x86 and x64)	✓	✓
Windows Server 2008 Enterprise (x86 and x64)	✓	✓
Windows Server 2008 Datacenter (x86 and x64)	✓	✓
Windows Web Server 2008 (x86 and x64)	✓	✓

---

1. Windows Web Server 2008, which is designed to be used as a single-purpose or scale-out front-end Web server, also supports both the Full and Server Core installation options. However, Windows Web Server 2008 is available only on preinstalled systems through system builder and original equipment manufacturer (OEM) channels. For more information about Windows Web Server 2008 licensing, see *http://www.microsoft.com/ windowsserver2008/en/us/licensing-web-server.aspx*. This book focuses on supporting only Server Core installations of Standard, Enterprise, and Datacenter editions.

Table 1-1   Windows Server 2008 Editions and Their Support for Installation Options

Edition	Full	Server Core
Windows Server 2008 for Itanium-Based Systems	✓	
Windows HPC Server 2008 (x64 only)	✓	
Windows Server 2008 Standard without Hyper-V (x86 and x64)	✓	✓
Windows Server 2008 Enterprise without Hyper-V (x86 and x64)	✓	✓
Windows Server 2008 Datacenter without Hyper-V (x86 and x64)	✓	✓

To understand what an "installation option" is, let's say you've purchased a volume license that lets you install a copy of Windows Server 2008 Enterprise Edition. When you insert your volume-licensed media into a system and begin the installation process, one of the screens you'll see, as shown in Figure 1-1, presents you with a choice of editions and installation options.

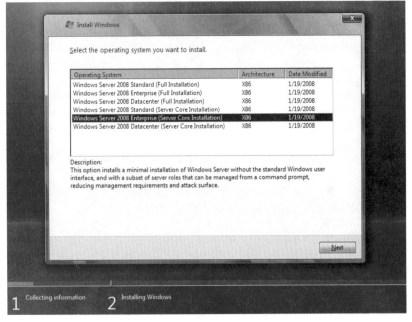

Figure 1-1   Selecting a Server Core installation option to install

In Figure 1-1, your volume license (or product key, for retail media) gives you two installation options you can choose between: the second option (a Full Installation of Windows Server 2008 Enterprise) and the fifth option (a Server Core Installation of Windows Server 2008 Enterprise), with the latter selected in this example. You'll learn more about installing Server Core in Chapter 2, "Deploying Server Core."

Full vs. Server Core

Since the early days of the Microsoft Windows platform, Windows servers were essentially "everything" servers that included all kinds of features, some of which you might never actually use in your networking environment. For instance, when you installed Windows Server 2003 on a system, the binaries for Routing and Remote Access Service (RRAS) were installed on your server even if you had no need for this service (although you still had to configure and enable RRAS before it would work). Windows Server 2008 improves earlier versions by installing the binaries needed by a server role only if you choose to install that particular role on your server. However, the Full installation option of Windows Server 2008 still installs many services and other components that are often not needed for a particular usage scenario.

That's the reason Microsoft created a second installation option—Server Core—for Windows Server 2008: to eliminate any services and other features that are not essential for the support of certain commonly used server roles. For example, a Domain Name System (DNS) server really doesn't need Windows Internet Explorer installed on it because you wouldn't want to browse the Web from a DNS server for security reasons. And a DNS server doesn't even need a graphical user interface (GUI), because you can manage virtually all aspects of DNS either from the command line using the powerful Dnscmd.exe command, or remotely using the DNS Microsoft Management Console (MMC) snap-in.

To avoid this, Microsoft decided to strip everything from Windows Server 2008 that was not absolutely essential for running core network services like Active Directory Domain Services (AD DS), DNS, Dynamic Host Configuration Protocol (DHCP), File and Print, and a few other server roles. The result is the new Server Core installation option, which can be used to create a server that supports only a limited number of roles and features.

The Server Core GUI

When you finish installing Server Core on a system and log on for the first time, you're in for a bit of a surprise. Figure 1-2 shows the Server Core user interface after first logon.

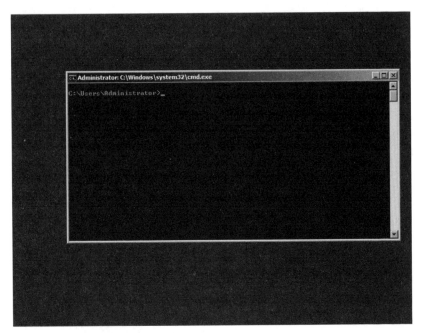

Figure 1-2   Server Core user interface

There's no desktop! That is, there is no Windows Explorer shell, with its Start menu, Taskbar, and the other features you may be used to seeing. All you have is a command prompt, which means that you have to do most of the work of configuring a Server Core installation either by typing commands one at a time, which is slow, or by using scripts and batch files, which can help you speed up and simplify your configuration tasks by automating them. You can also perform some initial configuration tasks using answer files when you perform an unattended installation of Server Core.

For administrators who are experts in using command-line tools like Netsh.exe, Dfscmd.exe, and Dnscmd.exe, configuring and managing a Server Core installation can be easy, even fun. For those who are not experts, however, all is not lost—you can still use the standard Windows Server 2008 MMC tools for managing a Server Core installation. You just need to use them on a different system running either a full installation of Windows Server 2008 or Windows Vista with Service Pack 1.

You'll learn more about configuring and managing a Server Core installation in Chapters 3 to 6 of this book, while later chapters deal with how to manage specific server roles and other components. Meanwhile, if you think you need to learn more about the various Windows command-line tools and how to use them, there are two good resources to consult:

- The Command Reference section of the Windows Server 2008 Technical Library (*http://technet2.microsoft.com/windowsserver2008/en/library/69baa34b-d4b3-40ec-bd2f-12d98f7802d51033.mspx?mfr=true*)

- The *Windows Command-Line Administrator's Pocket Consultant* by William R. Stanek (Microsoft Press, 2008)

Table 1-2 lists the main GUI applications, together with their executables, that are available in a Server Core installation.

Table 1-2   GUI Applications Available in a Server Core Installation

GUI Application	Executable with Path
Command prompt	%WINDIR%\System32\Cmd.exe
Microsoft Support Diagnostic Tool	%WINDIR%\System32\Msdt.exe
Notepad	%WINDIR%\System32\Notepad.exe
Registry Editor	%WINDIR%\System32\Regedt32.exe
System Information	%WINDIR%\System32\Msinfo32.exe
Task Manager	%WINDIR%\System32\Taskmgr.exe
Windows Installer	%WINDIR%\System32\Msiexec.exe

That's a pretty short list! Now here's a list of user interface elements that are not included in Server Core:

- The Windows Explorer desktop shell (Explorer.exe) and any supporting features such as Themes

- All MMC consoles

- All Control Panel utilities, with the exception of Regional And Language Options (Intl.cpl) and Date And Time (Timedate.cpl)

- All Hypertext Markup Language (HTML) rendering engines, including Internet Explorer and HTML Help

- Windows Mail

- Windows Media Player

- Most accessories such as Paint, Calculator, and Wordpad

The .NET Framework is also not present in Server Core, which means there's no support for running managed code on a Server Core installation. Only native code—code written using Windows application programming interfaces (APIs)—can run on Server Core. In summary, any GUI applications that depend on either the .NET Framework or on the Explorer.exe shell won't run on Server Core. You'll learn more about running applications on Server Core in Chapter 13, "Maintaining Server Core."

Note Because Windows PowerShell requires the .NET Framework, you cannot install Windows PowerShell onto Server Core. You can, however, manage a Server Core installation remotely using Windows PowerShell so long as you use only PowerShell WMI commands. For more information on managing Server Core using Windows PowerShell, see Chapter 6, "Remote Management."

Supported Server Roles

A Server Core installation includes only a limited number of server roles compared with a Full installation of Windows Server 2008. Table 1-3 compares the roles available for both Full and Server Core installations of Windows Server 2008 Enterprise Edition.

Table 1-3   Comparison of Server Roles for Full and Server Core Installations of Windows Server 2008 Enterprise Edition

Server Role	Available in Full Installation	Available in Server Core
Active Directory Certificate Services (AD CS)	✓	
Active Directory Domain Services (AD DS)	✓	✓
Active Directory Federation Services (AD FS)	✓	
Active Directory Lightweight Directory Services (AD LDS)	✓	✓
Active Directory Rights Management Services (AD RMS)	✓	
Application Server	✓	
DHCP Server	✓	✓
DNS Server	✓	✓
Fax Server	✓	
File Services	✓	✓
Hyper-V	✓	✓
Network Policy and Access Services	✓	
Print Services	✓	✓
Streaming Media Services	✓	✓
Terminal Services	✓	
UDDI Services	✓	
Web Server (IIS)	✓	✓
Windows Deployment Services	✓	

While the roles available for Server Core are generally the same regardless of architecture (x86 or x64) and product edition, there are a few exceptions:

- The Hyper-V (virtualization) role is available only if you purchased Windows Server 2008 with Hyper-V product media (Hyper-V is available only for x64 versions). If you do not need this role, you can purchase Windows Server 2008 without Hyper-V product media instead. For more information about installing Hyper-V on Server Core, see Chapter 12, "Hyper-V and Other Roles."

- The File Services role on Standard Edition is limited to one standalone Distributed File System (DFS) root and does not support Cross-File Replication (DFS-R). For more information about this, see Chapter 10, "File and Print Services Roles."

- Before you can install the Streaming Media Services role on Server Core, you need to download and install the appropriate Microsoft Update Standalone Package (.msu file) for your server's architecture (x86 or x64) from the Microsoft Download Center. For more information concerning this, see Chapter 12.

- The Web Server (IIS) role does not support ASP.NET. This is because the .NET Framework is not supported on Server Core, which limits what you can do with a Server Core Web server.

See Chapter 4, "Installing Roles and Features," to learn about different ways of installing and removing roles on Server Core. Also see Chapters 7 through 12 for specific information concerning installing and managing each server role.

Supported Optional Features

A Server Core installation also supports only a limited subset of the features available on a Full installation of Windows Server 2008. Table 1-4 compares the features available for both Full and Server Core installations of Windows Server 2008 Enterprise Edition.

Table 1-4   Comparison of Features for Full and Server Core Installations of Windows Server 2008 Enterprise Edition

Feature	Available in Full Installation	Available in Server Core
.NET Framework 3.0 Features	✓	
BitLocker Drive Encryption	✓	✓
BITS Server Extensions	✓	
Connection Manager Administration Kit	✓	
Desktop Experience	✓	
Failover Clustering	✓	✓

Table 1-4   Comparison of Features for Full and Server Core Installations of Windows Server 2008 Enterprise Edition

Feature	Available in Full Installation	Available in Server Core
Group Policy Management	✓	
Internet Printing Client	✓	
Internet Storage Name Server	✓	
LPR Port Monitor	✓	
Message Queuing	✓	
Multipath IO	✓	✓
Network Load Balancing	✓	✓
Peer Name Resolution Protocol	✓	
Quality Windows Audio Video Experience	✓	
Remote Assistance	✓	
Remote Differential Compression	✓	
Remote Server Administration Tools	✓	
Removable Storage Manager	✓	✓
RPC Over HTTP Proxy	✓	
Simple TCP/IP Services	✓	
SMTP Server	✓	
SNMP Services	✓	✓
Storage Manager for SANs	✓	
Subsystem for UNIX-based Applications	✓	✓
Telnet Client	✓	✓
Telnet Server	✓	
TFTP Client	✓	
Windows Internal Database	✓	
Windows PowerShell	✓	
Windows Product Activation Service	✓	
Windows Server Backup Features	✓	✓
Windows System Resource Manager	✓	
WINS Server	✓	✓
Wireless LAN Service	✓	

Again, there are some points you need to know about concerning the features available on Server Core:

- Some features may require special hardware to function properly (or at all) on Server Core. These features include BitLocker Drive Encryption, Failover Clustering, Multipath IO, Network Load Balancing, and Removable Storage.

- Failover Clustering is not available on Standard Edition.

Server Core Architecture

Digging deeper into Server Core, let's briefly look at the architecture of a Server Core installation of Windows Server 2008 by comparing it with that of a Full installation. First, remember that Server Core is not a different version of Windows Server 2008 but simply an installation option that you can select when installing Windows Server 2008 onto a system. This implies the following:

- The kernel on a Server Core installation is the same one found on a Full installation of the same hardware architecture (x86 or x64) and edition.

- If a binary is present on a Server Core installation, a Full installation of the same hardware architecture (x86 or x64) and edition has the same version of that particular binary (with two exceptions discussed later).

- If a particular setting (for example, a specific firewall exception or the startup type of a particular service) has a certain default configuration on a Server Core installation, that setting is configured exactly the same way on a Full installation of the same hardware architecture (x86 or x64) and edition.

Figure 1-3 shows a simplified view of the architecture of both a Full installation and a Server Core installation of Windows Server 2008. The dotted line indicates the architecture of Server Core, while the entire diagram represents the architecture of a Full installation.

The diagram illustrates the modular architecture of Windows Server 2008, with Server Core being constructed upon a subset of the core operating system features. For the same hardware architecture and edition, every file present on a clean install of Server Core is also present on a Full installation, with the exception of two special files (Scregedit.wsf and Oclist.exe), which are present only on Server Core. These special files were included on Server Core to simplify the initial configuration of a Server Core installation and the addition or removal of roles and optional components. For more information concerning Scregedit.wsf, see Chapter 3, "Initial Configuration," and for more information concerning Oclist.exe, see Chapter 4.

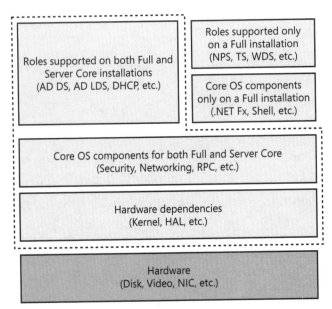

Figure 1-3   The architectures of Server Core and Full installations

Driver Support

The architectural diagram of Server Core shown in Figure 1-3 is obviously simplified; one thing it doesn't show is the difference in device driver support between Server Core and Full installations. A Full installation of Windows Server 2008 contains thousands of in-box drivers for different types of devices, which enable you to install products on a wide variety of different hardware configurations. (Client operating systems like Windows Vista include even more drivers to support devices such as digital cameras and scanners that are normally not used with servers.)

If a new device is connected to (or installed in) a Full installation of Windows Server 2008, the Plug and Play (PnP) subsystem first checks whether an in-box driver for the device is present. If a compatible in-box driver is found, the PnP subsystem automatically installs the driver and the device then operates. On a Full installation of Windows Server 2008, a balloon popup notification may be displayed, indicating that the driver has been installed and the device is ready for use.

On a Server Core installation, the driver installation process is the same (the PnP subsystem is present on Server Core) with two qualifications. First, Server Core includes only a minimal number of in-box drivers, and only for the following types of devices:

- A standard Video Graphics Array (VGA) video driver
- Drivers for storage devices
- Drivers for network adapters

Note that for each of the three device categories shown here, Server Core includes the same in-box drivers that are found on a corresponding Full installation (for the same hardware architecture).

Also, when the PnP subsystem automatically installs a driver for a new device, it does so silently—no balloon popup notification is displayed. Why not? Because there is no GUI on Server Core—there's no taskbar, so there's no notification area on the taskbar!

So what do you do when you add the Print Services role to a Server Core installation and you want to install a printer? You add the printer driver manually to the server—Server Core has no in-box print drivers. For more information on installing device drivers on Server Core, see Chapter 13.

Service Footprint

Because Server Core is a minimal installation, it has a smaller system service footprint than a corresponding Full installation of the same hardware architecture and edition. For example, about 75 system services are installed by default on a Full installation of Windows Server 2008, of which approximately 50 are configured for automatic startup. By contrast, Server Core has only about 70 services installed by default, and fewer than 40 of these start automatically.

Table 1-5 lists the services that are installed by default on a Server Core installation, with the startup mode for and account used by each service.

Table 1-5   System Services Installed by Default on Server Core

Service Name	Display Name	Startup Mode	Account
AeLookupSvc	Application Experience	Auto	LocalSystem
AppMgmt	Application Management	Manual	LocalSystem
BFE	Base Filtering Engine	Auto	LocalService
BITS	Background Intelligent Transfer Service	Auto	LocalSystem
Browser	Computer Browser	Manual	LocalSystem
CertPropSvc	Certificate Propagation	Manual	LocalSystem
COMSysApp	COM+ System Application	Manual	LocalSystem
CryptSvc	Cryptographic Services	Auto	Network-Service
DcomLaunch	DCOM Server Process Launcher	Auto	LocalSystem
Dhcp	DHCP Client	Auto	LocalService
Dnscache	DNS Client	Auto	Network-Service
DPS	Diagnostic Policy Service	Auto	LocalService

Table 1-5   System Services Installed by Default on Server Core

Service Name	Display Name	Startup Mode	Account
Eventlog	Windows Event Log	Auto	LocalService
EventSystem	COM+ Event System	Auto	LocalService
FCRegSvc	Microsoft Fibre Channel Platform Registration Service	Manual	LocalService
gpsvc	Group Policy Client	Auto	LocalSystem
hidserv	Human Interface Device Access	Manual	LocalSystem
hkmsvc	Health Key and Certificate Management	Manual	LocalSystem
IKEEXT	IKE and AuthIP IPsec Keying Modules	Auto	LocalSystem
iphlpsvc	IP Helper	Auto	LocalSystem
KeyIso	CNG Key Isolation	Manual	LocalSystem
KtmRm	KtmRm for Distributed Transaction Coordinator	Auto	Network-Service
LanmanServer	Server	Auto	LocalSystem
LanmanWorkstation	Workstation	Auto	LocalService
lltdsvc	Link-Layer Topology Discovery Mapper	Manual	LocalService
lmhosts	TCP/IP NetBIOS Helper	Auto	LocalService
MpsSvc	Windows Firewall	Auto	LocalService
MSDTC	Distributed Transaction Coordinator	Auto	Network-Service
MSiSCSI	Microsoft iSCSI Initiator Service	Manual	LocalSystem
msiserver	Windows Installer	Manual	LocalSystem
napagent	Network Access Protection Agent	Manual	Network-Service
Netlogon	Netlogon	Manual	LocalSystem
netprofm	Network List Service	Auto	LocalService
NlaSvc	Network Location Awareness	Auto	Network-Service
nsi	Network Store Interface Service	Auto	LocalService
pla	Performance Logs & Alerts	Manual	LocalService
PlugPlay	Plug and Play	Auto	LocalSystem
PolicyAgent	IPsec Policy Agent	Auto	Network-Service

Table 1-5   System Services Installed by Default on Server Core

Service Name	Display Name	Startup Mode	Account
ProfSvc	User Profile Service	Auto	LocalSystem
ProtectedStorage	Protected Storage	Manual	LocalSystem
RemoteRegistry	Remote Registry	Auto	LocalService
RpcSs	Remote Procedure Call (RPC)	Auto	Network-Service
RSoPProv	Resultant Set of Policy Provider	Manual	LocalSystem
sacsvr	Special Administration Console Helper	Manual	LocalSystem
SamSs	Security Accounts Manager	Auto	LocalSystem
SCardSvr	Smart Card	Manual	LocalService
Schedule	Task Scheduler	Auto	LocalSystem
SCPolicySvc	Smart Card Removal Policy	Manual	LocalSystem
seclogon	Secondary Logon	Auto	LocalSystem
SENS	System Event Notification Service	Auto	LocalSystem
SessionEnv	Terminal Services Configuration	Manual	LocalSystem
slsvc	Software Licensing	Auto	Network-Service
SNMPTRAP	SNMP Trap	Manual	LocalService
swprv	Microsoft Software Shadow Copy Provider	Manual	LocalSystem
TBS	TPM Base Services	Manual	LocalService
TermService	Terminal Services	Auto	Network-Service
TrustedInstaller	Windows Modules Installer	Auto	LocalSystem
UmRdpService	Terminal Services UserMode Port Redirector	Manual	LocalSystem
vds	Virtual Disk	Manual	LocalSystem
VSS	Volume Shadow Copy	Manual	LocalSystem
W32Time	Windows Time	Auto	LocalService
WcsPlugInService	Windows Color System	Manual	LocalService
WdiServiceHost	Diagnostic Service Host	Manual	LocalService

Table 1-5 System Services Installed by Default on Server Core

Service Name	Display Name	Startup Mode	Account
WdiSystemHost	Diagnostic System Host	Manual	LocalSystem
Wecsvc	Windows Event Collector	Manual	Network-Service
WinHttpAuto-ProxySvc	WinHTTP Web Proxy Auto-Discovery Service	Auto	LocalService
Winmgmt	Windows Management Instrumentation	Auto	LocalSystem
WinRM	Windows Remote Management (WS-Management)	Auto	Network-Service
wmiApSrv	WMI Performance Adapter	Manual	LocalSystem
wuauserv	Windows Update	Auto	LocalSystem

For information on managing services on a Server Core installation, see Chapter 13.

Why Is Server Core Useful?

To decide whether and how to implement Server Core in your environment, you need to understand the benefits that Server Core can provide and some possible usage scenarios for the platform.

Benefits of Server Core

Before we look at the benefits of Server Core, let's debunk a misconception: Improved performance is not one of the benefits of running Server Core instead of a Full installation of Windows Server 2008. This may seem paradoxical until you realize that most of the elements that are part of a Full installation but not Server Core are idle unless a user is logged onto the server. And because servers usually don't have users logged onto them except when they're being administered, the result is that the performances of a Server Core installation and a Full installation are about equal if they are both running identical roles.

So what are the benefits of running Server Core instead of a Full installation? There are many, including the following:

- **Greater stability**   Because a Server Core installation has fewer running processes and services than a Full installation, the overall stability of Server Core is greater. Fewer things can go wrong, and fewer settings can be configured incorrectly.

- **Simplified management**   Because there are fewer things to manage on a Server Core installation, it's easier to configure and support a Server Core installation than a Full one—once you get the hang of it.

■ **Reduced maintenance**   Because Server Core has fewer binaries than a Full installation, there's less to maintain. For example, fewer hot fixes and security updates need to be applied to a Server Core installation. Microsoft analyzed the binaries included in Server Core and the patches released for Windows Server 2000 and Windows Server 2003 and found that if a Server Core installation option had been available for Windows Server 2000, approximately 60 percent of the patches required would have been eliminated, while for Windows Server 2003, about 40 percent of them would have.

■ **Reduced memory and disk requirements**   A Server Core installation on x86 architecture, with no roles or optional components installed and running at idle, has a memory footprint of about 180 megabytes (MB), compared to about 310 MB for a similarly equipped Full installation of the same edition. Disk space needs differ even more—a base Server Core installation needs only about 1.6 gigabytes (GB) of disk space compared to 7.6 GB for an equivalent Full installation. Of course, that doesn't account for the paging files and disk space needed to archive old versions of binaries when software updates are applied. See Chapter 2 for more information concerning the hardware requirements for installing Server Core.

■ **Reduced attack surface**   Because Server Core has fewer system services running on it than a Full installation does, there's less attack surface (that is, fewer possible vectors for malicious attacks on the server). This means that a Server Core installation is more secure than a similarly configured Full installation.

Possible Usage Scenarios

Consider again the nine server roles you can install on Server Core:

■ AD DS

■ AD LDS

■ DNS

■ DHCP

■ File Services

■ Print Services

■ Streaming Media Services

■ Web Server (IIS)

■ Hyper-V

This list of roles should immediately suggest some possible usage scenarios for Server Core within your organization. Here are some ways that you could use Server Core to make your network more secure, more reliable, easier to manage, and easier to maintain:

- **Infrastructure servers**   Domain controllers, DHCP servers, and DNS servers are the backbone of your network. Running these roles on Server Core can strengthen this backbone in every way.

- **Branch office servers**   Because Server Core installations are more secure and require fewer software updates than Full installations, they are ideal for use in remote locations, such as branch offices where you have few (or no) information technology (IT) staff and less physical security than at your head office location. For example, you might deploy a Server Core installation as a read-only domain controller with BitLocker for added security at a branch office.

- **Server consolidation and testing**   Because Hyper-V is a supported role on Server Core, you can use Server Core to consolidate multiple servers onto a single system while still keeping them isolated. This can help lower your TCO by reducing your hardware requirements and your power, cooling, and management costs. Server Core running Hyper-V also provides a convenient environment for deployment testing.

- **Extending hardware life**   Because Server Core has lower disk and memory requirements than Full installations, you may be able to get more life out of old systems. For example, when you need to upgrade your e-mail or database servers, those boxes could be moved down the line to become network infrastructure servers running Server Core.

Non-Usage Scenarios

What *shouldn't* you use Server Core for? The main thing to understand is that Server Core is intended to run only the nine server roles listed previously. *Nothing else.* In other words, Server Core can't be used as a platform for running server applications such as Exchange Server, Microsoft SQL Server, or third-party server applications like SAP. You also can't use it for running Microsoft Office System applications or Microsoft Office SharePoint Server. And you can't (or at least shouldn't) use it to run custom applications you've developed in-house. In short, Server Core is not an application hosting platform.

This doesn't mean you can't install some applications on Server Core—you can, provided the applications have no dependency on the GUI. For example, you can install many of the following types of server applications onto Server Core:

- Antivirus agents
- Backup agents
- System management agents

You'll learn more about installing applications on Server Core in Chapter 13. But that's about it as far as what else you can install on Server Core is concerned.

Chapter 2
Deploying Server Core

Windows Server Core can be deployed using the same tools and methods as in a full installation of Windows Server 2008. These deployment methods can include manual installs, unattended installs using the Windows Automated Installation Kit (Windows AIK), unattended installs using Windows Deployment Services, and unattended installs using the Microsoft Deployment Toolkit (MDT). You'll briefly examine these various deployment solutions in this chapter.

One important point is that you can use answer files to ease much of the headache of performing the initial configuration of a Server Core installation. However, rather than cover answer file settings for initial configuration of Server Core here, you'll examine these settings in Chapter 3, "Initial Configuration." The focus of this present chapter, therefore, is on understanding and using different tools and methods for deploying Server Core, as well as configuring the minimal answer file settings that are needed to automate the installation process fully.

Planning for Installation

Successful deployment always begins with careful planning, and this section summarizes the following necessary information concerning deploying Server Core:

- Hardware requirements

- Upgrade constraints

System Requirements

Before you deploy Server Core onto a system, ensure that the hardware requirements are met or exceeded. Table 2-1 shows the minimum, recommended, and optimal system requirements for Server Core installations.

Table 2-1   System Requirements for a Server Core Installation

Hardware	Minimum	Recommended	Optimal
Processor	1 GHz (x68 processor) 1.4 GHz (x64 processor)	2 GHz or faster	3 GHz
Memory	512 MB		1 GB
Disk	8 GB	8 to 10 GB	40 GB

The disk requirements need some further explanation. The disk footprint for a Server Core installation is only about 1.5 GB for x86 systems, but this figure doesn't include any room needed for the paging file or a memory dump file (if one is generated). It also doesn't include any space to accommodate earlier versions of system binaries when service packs, hot fixes, and security updates have been applied to your server. Windows Server 2008 stores such binaries in the Windows Side-by-Side (WinSxS) directory found under %Windir%, and the more updates you apply to your server, the bigger this directory grows.

Important   Because of the need to accommodate such additional files, Microsoft recommends that you install Server Core on a partition that is at least 8 to 10 GB in size. But even this might not be enough space if you plan to install multiple roles on your server. To be safe, you should ensure that the partition on which you install Server Core is at least 40 GB in size.

Upgrade Constraints

Server Core is unique among Windows platforms in that it has limited upgrade options. For example, here is a list of upgrade paths that are *not* supported with Server Core:

- You can't upgrade any previous version of Windows Server to a Server Core installation. For example, you can't upgrade Windows Server 2003 to Windows Server 2008 Server Core.

- You can't convert a Server Core installation to a full installation of Windows Server 2008.

- You can't convert a full installation of Windows Server 2008 to a Server Core installation.

In fact, the only supported upgrade path for Server Core is upgrading a Windows Server 2008 Server Core installation to Windows Server 2008 R2 Server Core. Windows Server 2008 R2 is scheduled to be available sometime in 2009.

The Windows Server 2008 Product Roadmap can be found at http://www.microsoft.com/windowsserver2008/en/us/roadmap.aspx.

Manually Installing Server Core

Server Core can be installed manually in two ways:
- From the DVD
- Over the network

Performing a Manual Install from DVD

To manually install Windows Server 2008 from DVD media, you need a Windows Server 2008 product DVD, a product key, and licenses. You can acquire these items from one of three locations:

■ **Retail**   If you are a small business or an individual, you can purchase Windows Server 2008 products with five or more client access licenses (CALs) from a retail store that sells computer hardware, software, and services. Each copy comes with a unique product key that can be found on the product packaging, and during installation, you are prompted to supply this key. Once installation is finished, Windows also uses the product key to complete activation of the product.

■ **Volume Licensing**   Depending on the size and needs of your business, you can use Microsoft Volume Licensing programs such as Open License, Select License, and Enterprise Agreements to acquire installation media and licenses for installing Windows Server 2008 products. Volume-licensed versions of Windows Server 2008 do not require you to enter a product key during installation. However, you still have to obtain either Multiple Activation Key (MAK) or Key Management Service (KMS) product keys from the Volume Licensing Service Center (VLSC) found at *https://www.microsoft.com/licensing/servicecenter/home.aspx*. In addition, activation is still required after installation is complete.

■ **Original Equipment Manufacturer (OEM)**   If you are an OEM or a system builder, you would typically create a customized installation of Windows Server 2008 and then perform OEM activation of your system by associating the installation with the system's firmware.

Performing a Manual Install Using Retail DVD Media

To install Server Core manually using retail DVD product media, follow these steps:

1. Configure your system's firmware to boot first from the DVD.

2. Insert your product DVD and restart the system.

3. Follow the prompts to specify regional and language settings, accept the End User Licensing Agreement (EULA), enter your product key, select the Server Core installation option you want to install (Standard, Enterprise, or Datacenter), choose a partition to install to, and follow the other steps of the installation.

Performing a Manual Install Using Volume-Licensed DVD Media

The procedure here is the same as described previously, except you won't be prompted to enter a product key during the installation process. This is because volume-licensed editions of Windows Server 2008 install as KMS clients that attempt activation with a KMS host by default. If you are using MAK activation instead of KMS, however, you must activate your installation using your assigned MAK key.

To change from KMS to MAK activation using the command prompt, type the following in your Server Core command prompt:

```
slmgr.vbs -ipk xxxxx-xxxxx-xxxxx-xxxxx-xxxxx
```

In this command, the 25-character string *xxxxx-xxxxx-xxxxx-xxxxx-xxxxx* should be your MAK product key.

For more information about activating Server Core, see Chapter 3.

If you don't activate your Server Core installation within the 60-day grace period, your desktop background turns black and a dialog box indicating that your server is not activated is displayed when you interactively log onto your server. This dialog box can delay the interactive logon process for a period of time ranging from 15 seconds to 2 minutes. More important, Windows Update only allows you to install critical updates until you activate your server, which you should do immediately.

For detailed information concerning how Volume Activation works, see "Volume Activation 2.0 for Windows Vista and Windows Server 2008," found at http://technet.microsoft.com/en-us/library/bb892849.aspx.

Performing a Manual Install over the Network

To manually install Server Core over the network, perform the following steps:

1. Create a shared folder on a file server (for example, \\FILESRV6\Install) and ensure that the share permissions are Everyone has Read access and the NTFS permissions include Everyone has Read & Execute permission.

2. Copy the entire contents of your Windows Server 2008 product DVD to the share you created.

3. Boot the destination system using one of the following methods:

   ❑ Using a bootable Windows Preinstallation Environment (Windows PE) image, which is the preferred method.

   ❑ Using a previously installed Windows installation such as Windows Server 2003. When you install Server Core onto a partition that has a previous version of Microsoft Windows installed on it, the folders and files of the previous installation are moved to a folder named %SystemDrive%\Windows.old, which can be deleted afterward if these files and folders aren't needed.

   ❑ Using a third-party network boot disk or CD.

4. Run \\FILESRV6\Install\Setup.exe with the desired optional parameters to start Windows Setup and begin the installation process.

5. Respond to the prompts as needed.

For information on how to create a bootable Windows PE image, see the section "Creating a Bootable Windows PE CD," later in this chapter. To find a list of optional parameters you can use when running Windows Setup (Setup.exe), see the topic "Windows Setup Command-Line Options" within the Deployment Tools Technical Reference section of the Windows AIK User's Guide (Waik.chm), which can be accessed from the Start menu on a system on which you have installed the Windows AIK.

Deploying Server Core Using the Windows AIK

Manually installing operating systems can wear you out quickly. It's much better in all but the smallest business environments to perform unattended installations. The foundation for performing all unattended installations of Windows Server 2008 and Windows Vista is the Windows AIK, a collection of tools and supporting documentation designed to help you automate the process of installing Windows on bare-metal systems (computers that have no operating system installed).

The four key tools in the Windows AIK are as follows:

- **Windows PE** Windows PE is a minimal version of the operating system with limited services that can be used to begin the process of installing Windows on bare-metal systems. Once you create a bootable Windows PE image (.iso file), you burn this image onto CD media and then use your Windows PE CD to boot a bare-metal system and install Windows on it.

- **Windows System Image Manager (Windows SIM)** Windows SIM can be used to create answer files that can be used to automate the installation process. It also can be used to create distribution shares from which you perform your installations.

- **System Preparation Tool (Sysprep)** Sysprep can be used to prepare a Windows installation for disk imaging by removing system-specific information from it, such as security identifiers (SIDs) and event logs. Once a system has been generalized like this, you can use ImageX to capture an image of the installation for deployment onto other systems.

- **ImageX** ImageX is a command-line tool that can be used to capture, modify, and apply file-based disk images. Using ImageX, you can apply a Windows image that has been generalized and captured on destination systems quickly and easily.

The sections that follow in this chapter demonstrate how to use these tools; however, for more detailed information concerning the capabilities and usage of each tool, see the Windows AIK User's Guide (Waik.chm).

Types of Unattended Installs

Your business needs should determine the method you use to deploy Windows in your organization. Based on the number of servers you need to deploy, one can categorize deployment methods as follows:

- **Low-volume deployment** Small businesses generally have only a couple of servers that need deploying, and therefore, an *unattended install from DVD method* is usually the best approach in these environments. This method can be fully automated and does not require a network. It is essentially a type of manual deployment.

- **Medium-volume deployment**   Enterprises that have more than a handful of servers that need deploying can use the *install from configuration set method,* which uses either a Windows DVD or a Windows PE CD to boot the destination systems, and uses either a network file server or a removable medium such as a USB flash drive to host the shared folder containing the Windows source files.

- **Large-volume deployment**   Large datacenters where hundreds of servers need to be deployed can use the *install from image method* to create images of Windows installations, customize these images, and deploy them on destination systems.

Before you employ any of these three unattended installation methods, you need to install the Windows AIK so you can use its tools to deploy Server Core.

Installing the Windows AIK

Before you go further, you should understand these two terms:

- **Technician computer**   This is the computer on which you install the Windows AIK tools and documentation. If you need to create configuration sets, distribution shares for your deployments, or both, you usually do it on this computer as well.

  Your technician computer can run Windows Server 2008, Windows Server 2003, Windows Vista, or Windows XP, depending on your environment and deployment needs. It's a good idea to have at least one other hard drive on your technician computer as a dedicated location for storing your Windows image files. It's also a good idea to have a DVD burner on your technician computer and third-party CD-burning or DVD-burning software. That way, you can easily use your technician computer for burning Windows PE boot disks.

- **Destination computer**   This is a bare-metal system on which you are going to deploy Windows.

The Windows AIK can be obtained from the Microsoft Download Center. To deploy Server Core, however, you must download "Automated Installation Kit (AIK) for Windows Vista SP1 and Windows Server 2008" (*http://go.microsoft.com/fwlink/ ?LinkId=79385*), which contains version 1.1 of the Windows AIK. Do not download previous versions of the Windows AIK, as they cannot be used for deploying Windows Server 2008.

The Windows AIK is downloaded as an .iso DVD image file, and you need to burn it to writable DVD media before you can use it to install the Windows AIK on your technician computer. Alternatively, you can use third-party .iso image-mounting software, such as DAEMON Tools (*http://www.daemon-tools.cc*), to mount the image on your technician computer and install it.

Once you've burned your DVD, you install the Windows AIK as follows:

1. Select the .NET Framework Setup on the Windows AIK splash screen and follow the prompts to install the .NET Framework 2.0 on your technician computer. (If your technician computer is running Windows Vista or Windows Server 2008, skip to step 3.)

2. Select the MSXML 6.0 Setup option on the splash screen and follow the prompts to install MSXML 6.0 on your technician computer.

3. Select the Windows AIK Setup option on the splash screen and follow the prompts to complete the installation of the Windows AIK on your technician computer.

4. Click Start, All Programs, Microsoft Windows AIK, and finally Windows PE Tools Command Prompt. This opens a command prompt window with C:\Program Files\Windows AIK\Tools\PETools> as the current directory, and it updates your system path to include the directories that contain your Windows PE tools.

5. Click Start, All Programs, Microsoft Windows AIK, and then Documentation to open the various Windows AIK Help files and the Getting Started guide.

Creating a Basic Answer File for Unattended Installs

A key tool for performing unattended installs is Windows SIM, which is used to write answer files, create configuration sets, and create distribution shares for deploying Windows.

As shown in Figure 2-1, the Windows SIM user interface has five panes:

- **Distribution Share pane**   Where you create, select, and work with distribution share folders and add items from a distribution to an answer file

- **Windows Image pane**   Where you open Windows Imaging (.wim) files and the components and packages that are available for installation

- **Answer File pane**   Where you create, configure, and save answer files for automating Windows Setup

- **Properties pane**   Where you configure the properties of a component or package that you have added to an answer file

- **Messages pane**   Displays any errors or warnings that result when you validate an answer file

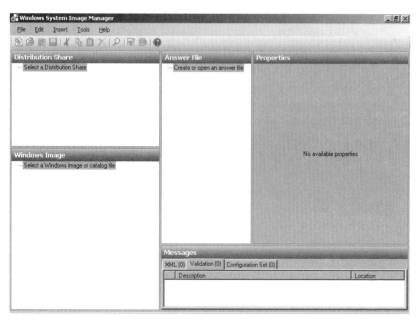

Figure 2-1   Windows SIM

In general, to create an answer file for unattended installation of Windows, you perform the following steps:

1. Open a Windows image from a .wim file and generate a catalog of the image.

2. Create a new answer file.

3. Add the necessary components from your image to the appropriate configuration pass of your answer file to automate Windows Setup as desired.

4. Configure the properties of each component as needed.

5. Save your answer file onto a removable medium such as a floppy disk or USB key, or to a network share.

Before going on, here are a few more terms you should be familiar with:

- **Windows Imaging (.wim) file**   A binary file that contains one or more compressed, file-based images of Windows Vista or later operating systems

- **Catalog**   A binary file that contains the state of all the components and packages in a Windows image

- **Answer file**   An Extensible Markup Language (XML) file that contains settings that will be applied to a Windows image during installation

■ **Configuration pass**   One of seven different phases of Windows Setup (see
Table 2-2 for details)

Table 2-2   Configuration Passes of Windows Setup

Configuration Pass	Description
windowsPE	Runs at the beginning of the installation process when Windows PE boots the system. Answer file settings for this configuration pass can be used to configure disks, specify a product key, specify boot-critical drivers, and perform other tasks.
offline-Servicing	Runs during the installation process immediately after the Windows image has been applied to the system. Answer file settings for this configuration pass can be used to apply packages including updates, hotfixes, and language packs.
specialize	Runs during the installation process immediately after the offlineServicing pass. Answer file settings for this configuration pass can be used to configure machine-specific information such as network settings and international settings.
oobeSystem	Runs at the end of the installation process just before Windows Welcome starts. Answer file settings for this configuration pass can be used to configure the Windows Welcome experience for first user logon.
generalize	Runs only when the sysprep /generalize command is used. This config-uration pass removes machine-specific information from the system to create a master installation whose image can be captured and installed on destination computers.
auditSystem	Runs only when you boot to audit mode, which happens when you use the sysprep /audit command. Answer file settings for this configuration pass can be used to configure system-specific settings, such as assigning a computer name or adding device drivers to the system.
auditUser	Runs only when you boot to audit mode, which happens when you use the sysprep /audit command. Answer file settings for this configuration pass can be used to configure user-specific settings such as executing RunSynchronous or RunAsynchronous commands or scripts on the system. The auditUser configuration pass happens immediately after the auditSystem pass.

Minimal Answer File Settings for an Unattended Install

To create a basic answer file for a completely unattended installation of Server Core,
you must at least configure your answer file to supply values for the following groups
of settings:

■ Regional settings, including keyboard layout, user locale, and default user
interface language

■ The disk, partition, and file system on which to install Windows

■ The operating system image (edition and installation option) to install (such as Server Core Enterprise)

■ Acceptance of the EULA

Note that all these answer file settings should be specified in the windowsPE configuration pass of Windows Setup.

Preparing to Create an Answer File

To prepare to use Windows SIM to create an answer file for a completely unattended installation of Server Core, follow these steps:

1. Log on to your technician computer as an administrator and insert your Windows Server 2008 product DVD media into the DVD drive and create a folder for storing your Windows image files. There are two types of image files:

   ❏ A *boot image* is an image you can use to boot a bare-metal system to begin the process of installing Windows onto the system. The Boot.wim file in the \Sources folder on your Windows Server 2008 product DVD is a default boot image that you can customize further if needed.

   ❏ An *install image* is a captured image of the installed Windows Vista or Windows Server 2008 operating system that can be applied onto your system. The Install.wim file in the \Sources folder on your Windows Server 2008 product DVD is a default install image that you can use as a basis for creating custom install images.

   For example, if your second hard drive is W:, you could create a folder named W:\Sources and then a subfolder named W:\Sources\WS08 for storing your default Windows Server 2008 images. Then copy the Boot.wim and Install.wim files from the \Sources folder on your product DVD to the W:\Sources\WS08 folder on your hard drive.

2. Click Start, All Programs, Microsoft Windows AIK, and then Windows System Image Manager to open Windows SIM.

3. In the Windows Image page, right-click Select A Windows Image Or Catalog File and choose Select Windows Image. Then browse to W:\Sources\WS08, select Install.wim, and click OK.

4. In the Select An Image dialog box, choose Windows Longhorn SERVERENTER-PRISECORE, or any other Server Core image for which you want to create an answer file, as shown here.

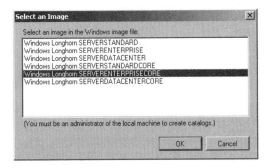

Note If your image names have a "V" in them (for example, SERVERENTER-PRISEVCORE), your product DVD is for Windows Server 2008 without Hyper-V.

5. Click OK. If you are prompted to create a catalog file for your selected image, click Yes. (Creating a catalog file can take a few minutes.)

6. In the Windows Image pane, expand the Components node to display the various components listed under it.

7. In the Answer File pane, right-click Create Or Open An Answer File and choose New Answer File to create a new (blank) answer file, as shown here.

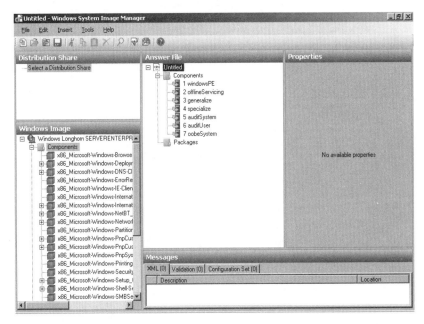

Note The procedure described here uses an x86 image for illustrative purposes; however, the steps are the same when using an x64 image.

Configuring Minimal Answer File Settings for a Completely Automated Install

You are now ready to create your answer file for a completely unattended installation of Server Core. To proceed, follow these steps (this procedure assumes the destination computer's hard drive has no partitions on it):

1. Expand the Microsoft-Windows-International-Core-WinPE node to display the SetupUILanguage node beneath it. Then right-click on the SetupUILanguage node and select Add Settings To Pass 1 windowsPE. This adds the configurable settings for the Microsoft-Windows-International-Core-WinPE\SetupUILanguage component to your answer file and displays the configurable settings for this component in the Properties pane, as shown here.

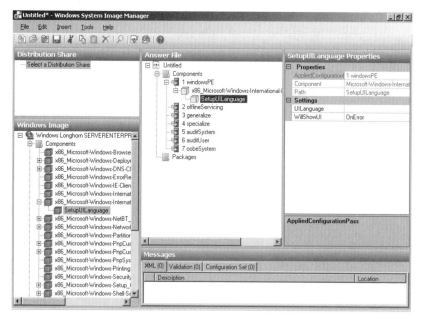

2. Type **en-US** or some other language identifier as the value for the UILanguage setting in the Properties pane, as shown here.

3. In the Answer Pane, select the Microsoft-Windows-International-Core-WinPE node in your answer file to display its configurable properties and type **en-US** or some other language identifier as the value for all the settings shown here.

4. In the Windows Image pane, select the Microsoft-Windows-Setup component, expand this component, right-click UserData beneath it, and select Add Setting To Pass 1 windowsPE. This adds the configurable settings for the Microsoft-Windows-Setup\UserData component to your answer file and displays the configurable settings for this component in the Properties pane.

5. In the Properties pane, click the blank value box to the right of the AcceptEula setting so that a down arrow appears. Then click the down arrow and select True, as shown here.

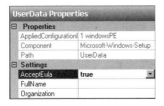

Note If you are creating an answer file for retail media instead of volume-licensed media, you also need to add the Microsoft-Windows-Setup\User-Data\ProductKey component to your answer file and type your 25-character product key (including dashes) into the value box for the Key setting.

6. In the Windows Image pane, expand to Microsoft-Windows-Setup\DiskConfig-uration\Disk\CreatePartitions\CreatePartition, right-click CreatePartition, and

select Add Setting To Pass 1 windowsPE. Then, in the Properties pane, type **1** as the value for Order, **20000** for Size, and use the drop-down arrow for Type to select Primary.

7. Select the DiskID component under Microsoft-Windows-Setup\DiskConfiguration\ Disk in your answer file and type **0** as the value for DiskID in the Properties pane.

8. In the Windows Image pane, expand to Microsoft-Windows-Setup\Image-Install\OSImage\InstallFrom\MetaData, right-click MetaData, and select Add Setting To Pass 1 windowsPE. Then, in the Properties pane, type **/image/name** as the value for Key and **Windows Longhorn SERVERENTERPRISECORE** as the value for Value. This specifies that your answer file installs the Server Core installation option of Windows Server 2008 Enterprise Edition.

9. In the Windows Image pane, expand to Microsoft-Windows-Setup\ImageInstall\ OSImage\InstallTo, right-click InstallTo, and select Add Setting To Pass 1 windowsPE. Then, in the Properties pane, type **0** as the value for DiskID and **1** for PartitionID.

10. Right-click the top node ("Untitled") in the Answer File pane, select Close Answer File, and click Yes to save your changes. When the Save As dialog box appears, type either **Autounattend.xml** or **Unattend.xml** as the name for your answer file, as follows:

   ❑ Name your answer file Autounattend.xml if you are planning on using it to automate your install using the install from DVD or install from configuration set method.

   ❑ Name your answer file Unattend.xml if you are planning on using it to automate your install using the install from image method.

You now have an answer file that you can use for performing a completely unattended install of Server Core, but before you use your answer file, you should validate it to make sure its settings are configured properly.

To validate an answer file, select Validate Answer File from the Tools menu of Windows SIM. If there are any errors or warnings concerning your answer file, they are displayed in the Message pane at the bottom right of Windows SIM as shown in Figure 2-2.

Tip   The procedures described in this section create a minimal answer file for performing unattended installation of Server Core. Many additional Server Core settings can be configured using an answer file; some of these additional settings are described in Chapter 3 and later chapters.

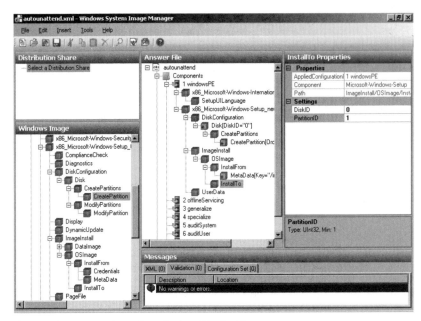

Figure 2-2   Errors and warnings displayed in the Message pane

Performing an Unattended Install from a DVD

Once you've created a valid answer file for automating Windows Setup, you can use that answer file to deploy Server Core onto bare-metal hardware. The simplest deployment method is the manual-but-automated unattended install from a DVD. However, because this method doesn't scale well, it can be used only for low-volume deployments.

To perform an unattended install from DVD of Server Core, perform these steps:

1. Copy the answer file you created in the previous section of this chapter to a removable medium such as a floppy disk or USB flash drive. Make sure your answer file is named Autounattend.xml.

2. Insert your Windows Server 2008 product DVD into the DVD drive of your system and insert the floppy or flash drive.

3. Restart your system. Windows Setup uses your answer file to perform a completely unattended install of Server Core.

Once you have completed your install, you can do either of the following:

■ Finish the initial configuration of your server, add roles and optional components, and perform other customizations, and then add the server to your production network. For more information about configuring and customizing a Server Core installation, see Chapter 3 and Chapter 4, "Installing Roles and Features."

■ Configure and customize the server and then run **sysprep /generalize /oobe /shutdown** to create a master installation whose image you can capture and deploy onto multiple destination computers. For more information, see the section "Performing an Install from Image," later in this chapter.

Performing an Install from a Configuration Set

A *configuration set* is a subset of what's contained on a *distribution share*, which is an optional set of folders that contain additional files used to control an unattended installation.

Configuration sets are more portable than distribution shares because they can be stored either on a network share or on removable media such as floppy disks and USB flash drives. By using a configuration set with an answer file, you can further automate the process of installing Server Core on bare-metal hardware.

The install from configuration set method of deploying Windows can be performed in two ways:

■ Manually (without a network) by storing the configuration set on removable media

■ Over the network by storing the configuration set on a network share

The second method is more scalable, so it is recommended. Before you can use this method to deploy Server Core, however, you need to create a bootable Windows PE CD so you can boot your bare-metal system, connect to the network, and install Windows.

Creating a Bootable Windows PE CD

As mentioned previously, Windows PE is a minimal version of Windows that can be used to boot bare-metal systems so you can install an operating system on them. If you are going to use Windows PE for deploying Server Core, you should use Windows PE 2.1, which is based upon the Windows Server 2008 and Windows Vista SP1 kernel and servicing stack.

> **Note**   Windows PE also runs when you perform a completely manual install of Server Core from your product DVD. The entire first phase of Windows Setup—from booting off the DVD until files are beginning to be copied to your hard drive—takes place within the windowsPE configuration pass of Setup.

When you boot a system using a Windows PE CD, you'll see a command-prompt window against a gray background, as shown in Figure 2-3.

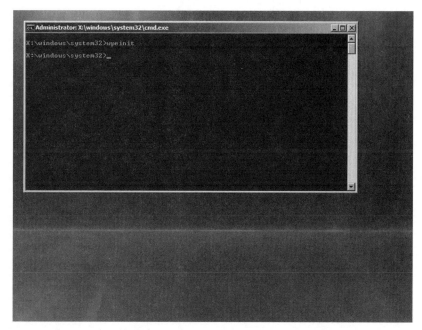

Figure 2-3   Windows PE user interface

The X: drive in the Windows PE command prompt is a RAM disk (a writable disk volume in volatile memory) that is created and used when Windows PE boots from read-only media (a CD or DVD). Using this command prompt, you can run Windows PE command-line tools such as diskpart and BCDEdit. You can also copy additional tools like Imagex.exe to your Windows PE CD when creating it so that you can run them with the default Windows PE tools.

To create a bootable 32-bit Windows PE 2.1 CD from x86 product media, follow these steps:

1. On your technician computer (assumed here to be running Windows Server 2003 and with the Windows Server 2008 Boot.wim and Install.wim files located in the W:\Sources\WS08 directory) click Start, All Programs, Microsoft Windows AIK, and then Windows PE Tools Command Prompt. A command prompt opens with C:\Program Files\Windows AIK\Tools\PETools as the current directory.

2. Type **copype.cmd x86 W:\winpe_x86** to create a Windows PE build folder structure under the W:\Winpe_x86 folder.

   Note   If your W:\Sources\WS08 folder contains x64 images of Windows Server 2008, type **copype.cmd x64 W:\winpe_x64** instead and adjust the paths in the commands that follow accordingly.

3. Copy the ImageX tool to your Windows PE build folder structure by typing the following command:

    copy "C:\Program Files\Windows AIK\Tools\x86\imagex.exe" W:\winpe_x86\iso\imagex.exe

    > **Tip**   You won't need ImageX on your Windows PE CD to perform an install from a configuration set, but you will need it for performing an install from image (as described later in this chapter), so it's best to add it now to your Windows PE CD.

4. Type the following command to create an .iso file named Winpe_x86.iso in the root of the W: drive from your Windows PE build folder structure:

    oscdimg –n –bW:\winpe_x86\etfsboot.com W:\winpe_x86\iso W:\winpe_x86.iso

5. Use third-party CD-burning software to burn W:\Winpe_x86.iso onto writable CD media.

Creating a Configuration Set

Next you need to create your configuration set and store it on a network share so you can perform your install. To do this, you'll first create a distribution share as follows:

1. On your technician computer, open Windows SIM. Then in the Distribution Share pane, right-click Select A Distribution Share and choose Create Distribution Share. Browse to the W: drive, click New Folder, and name your new folder **DistShare** or some other name.

2. Click Open. A new distribution share is created that has three subfolders under it, as shown here.

These subfolders are as follows:

❑ **OEM Folders**   This is a legacy folder for adding custom applications to your Windows installation. The new way of doing this with the Windows AIK is to create a data image for your installation. A *data image* is an additional .wim file that contains applications, files, and additional resources that supplement the contents of your Install.wim file. For more information about data images, see the Windows AIK Help file (Waik.chm).

❏ **Out-of-Box Drivers** This folder can contain any additional .inf-based device drivers that may be needed for Windows Setup to complete on the hardware that you are installing Windows on if the wide variety in-box drivers aren't sufficient. If any of these drivers are boot-critical (such as for the mass storage device on which you will be installing Windows), then you must add the Microsoft-Windows-PnPCustomizationsWindowsPE component of your answer file (specifying the windowsPE configuration pass) and configure these settings accordingly. For an example of how to add an out-of-box driver to a distribution share, see the next procedure.

❏ **Packages** This folder can contain software updates, language packs, and other types of packages you want to add to your Windows installation. To add a package, you first import it using Windows SIM and then add it to your answer and configure its settings. For more information about adding packages to an installation, see the Windows AIK Help file (Waik.chm).

Now you're ready to create your configuration set, as follows:

1. On your technician computer, create two shared folders (for example, \\Filesrv6\Install and \\Filesrv\Configsets) that map to the folders W:\Install and W:Configsets on your computer. Share these two folders with shared folder permissions Everyone has Read permissions and NTFS permissions Everyone has Read & Execute permissions.

2. Copy the entire contents of your Windows Server 2008 product DVD to the Install folder.

3. Use Windows SIM to open the answer file Autounattend.xml that you previously created. Then, from the Tools menu, select Explore Distribution Share to open W:\DistShare in Windows Explorer.

4. Create a subfolder named Driver1 under W:\DistShare\Out-of-Box Drivers and copy the .inf file for your driver to the Driver1 folder.

5. In the Answer File pane, right-click the top node (Autounattend.xml) and select Insert Driver Path To Pass 1 windowsPE. Browse to your W:\DistShare\Out-of-Box Drivers\Driver1 folder and click Open. Doing this adds Microsoft-Windows-PnPCustomizationsWinPE component to the windowsPE pass of your answer file, as shown here.

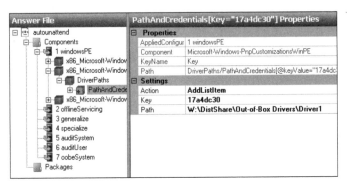

6. Validate your answer file by selecting Validate Answer File from the Tools menu. Then save your answer file by clicking Save on the toolbar.

7. Select Create Configuration Set from the Tools menu of Windows SIM.

8. Type **W:\configsets** in the target folder text box of the Create Configuration Set dialog box, as shown here.

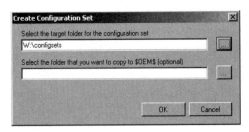

9. Click OK twice to create your configuration set, as shown here.

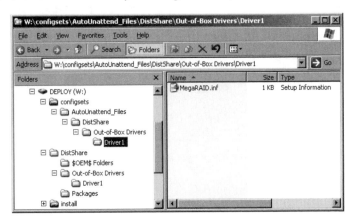

Performing an Install from a Configuration Set Using a Network Share

You're finally ready to perform an install from configuration set deployment of Server Core. To do this, you'll need your bootable Windows PE CD and a DHCP server to assign an Internet Protocol (IP) address and subnet mask to Windows PE so you can connect to Filesrv6 over the network and install Server Core.

Perform the following steps for this installation method:

1. Boot your bare-metal system using your Windows PE CD.

2. When the Windows PE command prompt is displayed, type **net use y:** **\\FILESRV6\Install** and **net use z: \\FILESRV6\Configsets** to map drives to the shares where your installation source files and configuration set are located. You may need to specify credentials to connect to your technician computer, such as the user name Filesrv6\Administrator and the password for this account.

3. Type **y:\setup.exe /unattend:z:\autounattend.xml**, and Server Core installs with no further user intervention.

Performing an Install from Image

The install from image method is most useful when you need to deploy a large number of servers that have the same underlying hardware, such as in a large data-center environment. A key tool for this type of deployment is the ImageX command-line utility that is installed as part of the Windows AIK. Using ImageX, you can capture a Windows image (.wim file) of an existing master computer, work with this image in various ways, and apply the image to a specified drive on a destination computer.

The following sections show how to perform an install from image deployment of Server Core. Before doing this, however, make sure you have a DHCP server available on your network so Windows PE can pick up an IP address. For simplicity, this section breaks down the install from image method into two high-level steps:

1. Create a master installation of Server Core and capture its image to a network share.

2. Deploy the captured image onto bare-metal destination computers using ImageX and answer files.

Creating and Capturing the Master Installation

To create and capture your master installation, follow these steps:

1. Begin by installing Server Core on a system and customize the installation as desired by choosing configuration settings, adding roles and optional components, and making any other changes to your master installation that you want.

   Not all roles can be installed on a master computer. See Chapter 4 for more information.

2. Open an elevated command prompt on your master computer, browse to the %Windir%\System32\Sysprep directory, and **type sysprep /audit /generalize /shutdown** to remove all machine-specific information from your master installation of Server Core. The **/audit** switch allows you to boot into audit mode in the future should you need to configure your master installation further.

3. On your technician computer, create a new folder named W:\Images and share the folder as \\Filesrv6\Images with shared folder permissions Everyone has Full Control and NTFS permissions Everyone has Full Control.

4. Boot your master computer using a Windows PE CD created using the instructions given in the section "Creating a Bootable Windows PE CD," earlier in this chapter.

5. Type **d:\imagex.exe /compress fast /capture c: c:\myimage.wim "Master Installation" /verify** at the Windows PE command prompt. This command captures an image of the C: drive on your server and saves the captured image back onto the C: drive as Myimage.wim. The capture may take some time to complete; it is finished when the message "Successfully imaged c:\" displays.

6. Type **net use y: \\FILESRV6\Images** to connect to the Images share on your technician computer. You may need to specify credentials to connect to your technician computer, such as the user name Filesrv6\Administrator and the password for this account.

7. Type **copy c:\myimage.wim y:** to copy the image of your master installation from the master computer to the Images share on your technician computer. The copy operation may take a few moments to complete. Verify that Myimage.wim is present in the W:\Install folder on your technician computer before proceeding further.

8. Remove the Windows PE CD from your master computer and turn the machine off using its power switch.

Applying the Captured Image to a Destination Computer

You are now ready to deploy the image you captured of your master installation on a destination computer. The steps for doing this are as follows:

1. Boot your destination computer using your Windows PE CD. When the command prompt appears, create a new primary partition, set the partition as active, and format it using NTFS by typing the following commands:

diskpart

select disk 0

clean

create partition primary size=20000

select partition 1

active

format

assign letter=C:

exit

The following window illustrates the result of these commands:

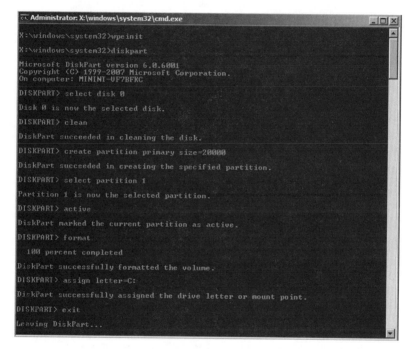

2. Type **net use y: \\FILESRV6\Images** to map a drive to the share where the image of your captured master installation is located. You may need to specify credentials in order to connect to your technician computer, such as the user name Filesrv6\Administrator and the password for this account.

3. Type **copy y:\myimage.wim c:** to copy the captured image to the local hard drive of the destination computer. This may take a few moments to complete.

4. Type **d:\imagex.exe /apply c:\myimage.wim 1 c:** to apply the captured image to the destination computer. This will take a few minutes to complete; it is finished when the message "Successfully applied image" displays.

Tip   You can also automate the previous series of commands by adding them to your Windows PE build folder structure and editing Startnet.cmd to run the batch file automatically when Windows PE boots. For more information, see the topic "Include a Custom Script in a Windows PE Image" in the Windows Preinstallation Environment User's Guide (WinPE.chm), which is installed as part of the Windows AIK documentation.

5. Remove the Windows PE CD from your destination computer and type **exit** to reboot the computer. When the system restarts, the specialize pass of Windows Setup runs, and a few minutes later you'll be prompted to run the machine out-of-box-experience (OOBE) to specify your locale/language and a name for your server. After that, you log on and are presented with the Server Core command prompt.

For more information about different methods of deploying Windows using the Windows AIK, see the Windows AIK User's Guide (WAIK.chm), which is installed as part of the Windows AIK documentation.

Deploying Server Core Using Windows Deployment Services

The Windows AIK tools are a powerful platform for performing various types of deployments, but they don't let you store and manage Windows images centrally. For such purposes, you can use Windows Deployment Services, which is a server-based solution for deploying Windows onto bare-metal hardware.

Windows Deployment Services is the successor to Remote Installation Services (RIS), which was introduced in Microsoft Windows 2000 Server. Using Windows Deployment Services, you can store, manage, and deploy your images using a central MMC console. Windows Deployment Services is available in two ways:

■ As an option when you install the Windows AIK onto Windows Server 2003 SP2

■ As a server role that you can add to a full installation of Windows Server 2008

Windows Deployment Services is a server-based solution that includes a Pre-Boot Execution Environment (PXE) server. This means that when you boot a bare-metal computer, the computer automatically downloads the Windows Deployment Services client, runs Windows PE, and downloads and applies a Windows image to its hard drive.

Windows Deployment Services includes two management tools you can use for configuring the server, managing images, and performing other tasks. These two tools are the Windows Deployment Services MMC console and the WDSUTIL command-line utility.

A full treatment of how to use Windows Deployment Services is beyond the scope of this book, but this section gives a basic walkthrough of how to use it to deploy Server Core.

The deployment scenario described here assumes that you have two servers running Windows Server 2008:

- A domain controller named DC.contoso.com that is also a DHCP server
- A separate Windows Deployment Services server named WDS.contoso.com

To use Windows Deployment Services to deploy Server Core onto bare-metal hardware, log onto server WDS using domain administrator credentials and perform the following steps:

1. Install the Windows Deployment Services role on server WDS either by using Server Manager or by typing **ServerManagerCmd –install WDS** at the command prompt.

2. Create a store for your boot and install images on the W: drive of server WDS by typing **WDSUTIL /Initialize-Server /reminst:"W:\RemoteInstall"** at the command prompt.

3. Configure the WDS server to respond to requests from any destination computers (both known and unknown) by typing **WDSUTIL /Set-Server /Answer-Clients:all** at the command prompt.

   Tip If you installed Windows Deployment Services on a single computer that is also a domain controller and a DHCP server, you'll need to run the command **WDSUTIL /Set-Server /UseDHCPPorts:no /DHCPoption60:yes** at a command prompt after step 3.

4. Add the default boot image from your Windows Server 2008 product DVD to your image store by typing **WDSUTIL /Add-Image /ImageFile:"<drive>\ sources\boot.wim" /ImageType:boot** at the command prompt, where <drive> is your DVD-ROM drive. The default boot image should be visible in the Windows Deployment Services MMC console, as shown here.

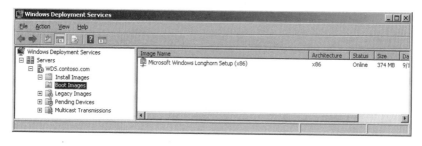

5. Add a new image group to your store by typing **WDSUTIL /Add-ImageGroup /ImageGroup:ImageGroup1** at the command prompt. An *image group* is used to store related images in the store of a Windows Deployment Services server. Single-instance storage makes image groups a more effective way of storing images than keeping them separate.

6. Add the default install image of Server Core Enterprise from your Windows Server 2008 product DVD to ImageGroup1 in your image store by typing **WDSUTIL /Add-Image /ImageFile:"<*drive*>\sources\install.wim" / ImageType:install /ImageGroup:ImageGroup1 /SingleImage:"Windows Longhorn SERVERENTERPRISECORE"** at the command prompt, where <*drive*> is your DVD-ROM drive. The default install image should be visible in the console, as shown here.

7. Create a capture image from your default boot image by typing **WDSUTIL / New-CaptureImage /Image:"Capture Boot Image" /Filepath:W:\ TEMP\cap.wim** at a command prompt. A *capture image* is a boot image that you can use to boot a master computer so you can capture an install image of your master installation. Then, you can deploy this install image onto your destination computers later.

8. Add your capture image to the Boot Images folder of your image store by typing **WDSUTIL /Add-image /ImageFile:W:\TEMP\cap.wim /imageType:boot** at a command prompt. Your capture image should be visible in the console, as shown here.

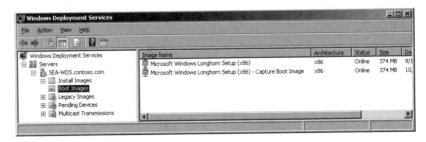

9. Now manually install Server Core on your master computer and customize the server as desired. Configure the BIOS on the server so that the first option in the boot order is PXE boot.

10. Open a command prompt and type **cd %WINDIR%\system32\sysprep** followed by **sysprep /oobe /generalize /shutdown** to remove all machine-specific information from the computer. Then shut it down.

11. When you restart the master computer, it should acquire an address from the PXE server (that is, from server WDS). Your master computer should download Wdsnbp.com from server WDS. Wdsnbp.com validates the DHCP/PXE response packet and then downloads PXEBoot.com from server WDS using Trivial File Transfer Protocol (TFTP). PXEBoot.com then prompts you to press F12 to download the capture image from server WDS, as follows:

```
CLIENT MAC ADDR: 00 03 FF 1D 88 8C   GUID: 0819402C-D2E4-2D44-B439-1E7DF16926F5
CLIENT IP: 10.10.0.101  MASK: 255.255.0.0  DHCP IP: 10.10.0.10
GATEWAY IP: 10.10.0.1

Downloaded WDSNBP...

Architecture: x86
Contacting Server: 10.10.0.20.
TFTP Download: boot\x86\pxeboot.com

Press F12 for network service boot
```

12. A menu of available boot images will display. Select your capture image from the menu to download the capture image to your master computer. Once this is finished, the Capture Image wizard starts and prompts you to select the volume you want to capture (specify the C: drive) and to specify a name and description for the captured install image that will be created. When the captured install image is created, it should initially be saved on the local hard drive of the master computer so that the capture process won't abort if network connectivity fails during the capture process. During the Capture Image wizard, you also need to specify which image group on server WDS the wizard should upload the captured install image (.wim file) to once the capture process is finished.

13. Now you are ready to use server WDS to deploy the captured image of your master installation onto your destination computers. To do this, your destination computers need to be configured in their BIOS so that PXE boot is first in the boot order. Begin by booting a destination computer and press F12 when prompted.

14. When the menu of available boot images appears, select the one that you want to use (you can use your default boot image for this purpose). Once the boot image has been downloaded from server WDS, the destination computer boots into Windows PE and prompts you to specify a locale/language and your administrator credentials for the domain.

15. A list of available install images (including the captured image of your master installation) displays. Select the image of your master computer that you previously captured and specify which drive you want to install onto. The installation then completes.

> **Note** You can also automate the prompts in the last step of this procedure (and automate the configuration of other settings) by using Windows SIM to create an Unattend.xml answer file for the Windows Deployment Services client and storing this answer file in the W:\RemoteInstall\WDSClientUnattend folder on your Windows Deployment Services server. If you do this, you need to perform some additional configuration of your Windows Deployment Services server so that unattended installs will be performed, but details concerning this are beyond the scope of this book.

For a detailed walkthrough of how to configure and use Windows Deployment Services, see the "Step-by-Step Guide for Windows Deployment Services in Windows Server 2008" in the Windows Deployment Services topic of the Windows Server 2008 Technical Library (http://technet.microsoft.com/bb250589). For more information on the syntax of the WDSUTIL command, see the "WDSUTIL" entry in the Command Reference section of the Windows Server 2008 Technical Library.

Deploying Server Core Using Microsoft Deployment

Microsoft Deployment Toolkit (MDT) 2008 is the next version of the Microsoft Solution Accelerator for Business Desktop Deployment (BDD) 2007. BDD 2007 is a set of tools, documentation, scripts, and templates designed to integrate all the various Microsoft deployment technologies (such as the Windows AIK tools and Windows Deployment Services) into a single common deployment console called the Deployment Workbench. MDT takes this further by supporting installation of the following platforms and products:

- 32-bit and 64-bit versions of Windows Vista Business, Enterprise, and Ultimate editions (both RTM and SP1)

- 32-bit and 64-bit versions of all editions of Windows Server 2008 (both Full and Server Core)

- 32-bit and 64-bit versions of all editions of Windows Server 2003 SP2 and Windows Server 2003 R2

- 32-bit and 64-bit versions of Windows XP Professional SP2 and Windows XP Tablet PC Edition

- Microsoft Office 2007 Professional, Professional Plus, Enterprise, and Ultimate editions

MDT is built upon other Microsoft deployment tools, and after installing it, you can choose to download and install the following tools automatically from the Deployment Workbench:

- Windows AIK
- Application Compatibility Toolkit 5.0.2
- User State Migration Tool 3.0.1
- MSXML 6.0

A discussion of how to use MDT to deploy Server Core is beyond the scope of this book. However, you can learn the latest information concerning MDT from the Microsoft Deployment Toolkit Team Blog (http://blogs.technet.com/msdeployment/), *and you can download MDT 2008 from* http://go.microsoft.com/fwlink/?LinkId=103947. *In addition, full documentation for MDT 2008 can be found at* http://technet.microsoft.com/en-us/library/bb456439.aspx.

Chapter 3
Initial Configuration

Once you've deployed Server Core, your next task is to perform an initial configuration of your servers. Initial configuration tasks for Server Core include setting a password for the Administrator account, changing the name of the server, configuring date and time settings, configuring Internet Protocol (IP) address settings, enabling Remote Desktop, configuring Windows Firewall with Advanced Security, activating the server, and other actions. This chapter examines how to perform these various tasks for configuring a Server Core installation.

Because the distinction between initial configuration tasks and general configuration tasks may depend upon your own business needs, the list of tasks covered in this chapter should not be considered comprehensive. If you can't find a particular task in this chapter, check the index of this book—the task is likely to be covered in another chapter.

Methods for Performing Initial Configuration

There are two ways of performing initial configuration tasks for a Server Core installation:

■ Locally, using the command prompt

■ During unattended installation, by configuring answer file settings

The following sections use one or both of these methods (where applicable) to configure various aspects of a Server Core installation.

For additional answer files that you can configure to customize an unattended installation of Windows Server 2008, see the Unattended Windows Setup Reference Help file (Unattend.chm), which is installed as part of the Windows AIK 1.1 documentation. For an overview of how to use Windows System Image Manager (Windows SIM) to create and configure answer files, see the section "Creating a Basic Answer File for Unattended Installs," in Chapter 2, "Deploying Server Core."

Setting the Local Administrator Password

You must set a password for the local Administrator account the first time you log on to a newly installed Server Core installation. You can also set this password during unattended installation using an answer file, and you can reset the password later from the command prompt.

Setting the Local Administrator Password During First Logon

To set the password for the local Administrator account when the installation is complete and the screen displays "Press CTRL+ ALT+DELETE to log on," perform the following steps:

1. Press Ctrl+Alt+Del and then click Other User.

2. Type **Administrator** for the user name, leave the password blank, and press Enter.

3. The message "The user's password must be changed before logging on the first time." displays.

4. Click OK, type and confirm your new password, and press Enter. Be sure your new password complies with the password complexity requirements of a default Windows Server 2008 installation (shown in Table 3-1).

5. When the message "Your password has been changed" appears, click OK. The logon process completes.

Table 3-1   Password Strength Requirements of a Default Windows Server 2008 Installation

Password Policy Setting	Default Value
Enforce password history	0 (disabled)
Maximum password age	42
Minimum password age	0
Minimum password length	0
Password must meet complexity requirement	1 (enabled)
Store passwords using reversible encryption for all users in the domain	0 (disabled)

> **Tip**   You can use the Secedit command to view and modify local password policies on your server. For example, to verify the information in Table 3-1, type **secedit / export /cfg stuff.txt** to export the local security policy on your server to a file named stuff.txt, and then type **notepad stuff.txt** to display the result in Notepad. Type **secedit /?** for more information on how to use the Secedit command.

Setting the Local Administrator Password Using an Answer File

You can use Windows SIM to set the password for the local Administrator account using an AutoUnattend.xml or Unattend.xml answer file as follows:

1. Add the following component to the oobeSystem configuration pass of your answer file:

    Microsoft-Windows-Shell-Setup\UserAccounts\AdministratorPassword

2. In the Properties pane of Windows SIM, type **Pa$$w0rd** (or another password) for Value under Settings.

By default, Windows SIM obfuscates the value of the Administrator password in your answer file. This is because the Hide Sensitive Data setting on the Tools menu is enabled by default. The obfuscated value will be displayed the next time you open your answer file in Windows SIM (see Figure 3-1).

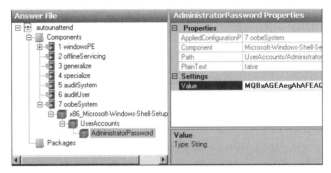

Figure 3-1   The password for the local Administrator account, obfuscated within an answer file

Resetting the Local Administrator Password from the Command Prompt

After you have logged on to Server Core for the first time as the local administrator, you can reset the password for this account by using the Net User command as follows:

```
C:\Users\Administrator>net user administrator *
Type a password for the user:Pa$$w0rd2
Retype the password to confirm:Pa$$w0rd2
The command completed successfully.
```

Changing the Local Administrator Password

You can change the password for the local Administrator account after you have logged on to Server Core in two ways:

■ Press Ctrl+Alt+Del, click Change Password, and type your old and new passwords as indicated.

■ Type **net user administrator *** at the command prompt and then type your new password twice when prompted.

Managing Local Users and Groups

During initial configuration, you may need to add or remove new local users or groups on your Server Core installation. This section covers mainly the administration of local users and groups, although some procedures also apply to domain users. For additional information on managing domain users and groups, see Chapter 7, "Active Directory Domain Services Role."

Managing Local Users and Groups from the Command Prompt

Examples of tasks for managing local users and groups from the command prompt include displaying a list of users, adding users, removing users, and adding users to the Administrators local group.

Displaying a List of Local User Accounts   You can view a list of all local user accounts on your server by typing **net user** at the command prompt as follows:

```
C:\Users\Administrator>net user
User accounts for \\WIN-86SKBDBRWDP

-------------------------------------------------------------------------------
Administrator               Guest
The command completed successfully.
```

Adding a Local User Account   To add a new local user account for user Tony Allen (whose user name is tallen) and assign this account the password Pa$$w0rd, type **net user tallen Pa$$w0rd /fullname:"Tony Allen" /add** at the command prompt. You can then type **net user** to confirm that the account was created.

Removing a Local User Account   To remove Karen Berg's local user account, type **net user kberg /remove** at the command prompt. Type **net user** to verify the action.

Adding a User to the Local Administrators Group   To add Tony Allen to the local Administrators group on the server, type **net localgroup Administrators /add tallen** at the command prompt. To verify the action, type **net localgroup Administrators** as follows:

```
C:\Users\Administrator>net localgroup Administrators
Alias name       administrators
Comment          Administrators have complete and unrestricted access to the
computer/domain
Members

-------------------------------------------------------------------------------
Administrator
tallen
The command completed successfully.
```

Another way of verifying the previous action is to log off as Administrator, log on as user Tony Allen, and type **net user test /add**. At this point, you should see the message "Access is denied," indicating that Tony cannot perform this action because his account is still only a member of the local Users group, not the Administrators group.

> **Note**   Server Core supports Fast User Switching (FUS). This means that in the previous example, you could remain logged on as Administrator while using FUS to also log on as Tony Allen. Press Ctrl+Alt+Del and select Switch User to use FUS on Server Core.

To remove Tony from the local Administrators group, type **net localgroup Administrators /delete tallen** at the command prompt.

You can also use the net localgroup command to add a domain user account to the local Administrators group on your server. To do this, type **net localgroup Administrators /add** *domain\username,* where *domain* is the NetBIOS name of the Active Directory domain where the user account resides. The /delete option also works for domain accounts.

For more information on using net commands like net user and net localgroup on Server Core, search the Microsoft Download Center at http://www.microsoft.com/downloads *for the latest version of the "Windows Command Reference," download WinCmdRef.exe, and unzip the file WinCmdRef.chm to a folder on your computer. This Help file describes how to use the included command-line tools to perform various tasks on Windows Vista, Windows Server 2003, and Windows Server 2008.*

Managing Users and Groups Using an Answer File

You can use Windows SIM to create a new local user account and add it to the local Administrators group using an AutoUnattend.xml or Unattend.xml answer file as follows:

1. Add the following component to the oobeSystem configuration pass of your answer file:

   Microsoft-Windows-Shell-Setup\UserAccounts\LocalAccounts\LocalAccount

2. Type **Karen Berg** (or another user's full name) for DisplayName, type **Administrators** for Group, and type **kberg** (the logon name of the user) for Name, all in the Properties pane of Windows SIM.

3. In the Answer File pane, expand LocalAccount, select Password beneath it, and type **Pa$$w0rd** (or another password) in the box beside Value.

4. Repeat steps 1-3 for each additional local user account you want to create.

You can also create new domain user accounts during unattended setup by adding the following component under Microsoft-Windows-Shell-Setup to the oobeSystem configuration pass of your answer file:

\UserAccounts\DomainAccounts\DomainAccountList\DomainAccount

Changing the Computer Name

During initial configuration, you should assign a NetBIOS computer name to your computer. Computer names must be no more than 15 characters long and should comply with Domain Name System (DNS) naming conventions. That is, they should contain only alphabetic characters (A-Z), numeric characters (0-9), and the minus sign (<;$MI>). In addition, computer names cannot be composed only of numbers.

Best Practices It's a good idea to use server names that are as descriptive and specific as possible. For example, SEA-SC1 could be the name of the first Server Core installation deployed in Seattle, VAN-DC2 could be the name of the second domain controller in Vancouver, and so on. See *http://www.microsoft.com/technet/ solutionaccelerators/wssra/ve/WSSRA-VEPG_7.mspx* for additional suggestions on naming servers in enterprise environments.

Changing the Computer Name from the Command Prompt

Unless a computer name is specified in an answer file, Windows Setup automatically generates a random computer name when Server Core is installed. After installation, you can rename your server by using the Netdom Renamecomputer command. For example, to display your server's current computer name, use the Hostname command as follows:

```
C:\Users\Administrator>hostname
WIN-86SKBDBRWDP
```

To change your server's name to SEA-SC1, follow these steps:

```
C:\Users\Administrator>netdom renamecomputer %computername% /newname:sea-sc1
This operation will rename the computer WIN-86SKBDBRWDP to sea-sc1.

Certain services, such as the Certificate Authority, rely on a fixed
machine name. If any services of this type are running on WIN-
86SKBDBRWDP, then a computer name change would have an adverse impact.

Do you want to proceed (Y or N)?y
The computer needs to be restarted in order to complete the operation.

The command completed successfully.
```

To restart your server and complete the action of changing its computer name, use the Shutdown /r /t 0 command. After the server restarts, you can verify the name changing using either the Hostname command or by typing **set c** to display all environment variables beginning with the letter *c*, like this:

```
C:\Users\Administrator>set c
CommonProgramFiles=C:\Program Files\Common Files
COMPUTERNAME=SEA-SC1
ComSpec=C:\Windows\system32\cmd.exe
```

Changing the Computer Name of a Domain-Joined Computer

To change the name of a Server Core installation that has been joined to a domain, use the Netdom Rename command with the following syntax:

netdom rename %computername% /newname:*newname* /userd:*domain\ username* /passwordd:*

Type the password when prompted and reboot the computer to make the change take effect.

Specifying the Computer Name in an Answer File

You can use Windows SIM to specify the computer name using an Autounattend.xml or Unattend.xml answer file as follows:

1. Add the Microsoft-Windows-Shell-Setup component to the specialize configuration pass of your answer file.

2. In the Properties pane, type **SEA-SC1** (or another computer name) for ComputerName.

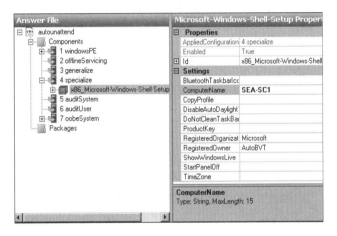

Note   Specifying an asterisk (*) or a null string causes a random computer name to be generated during Setup.

Configuring TCP/IP Networking Settings

Unless configured otherwise in an answer file for unattended installation, a new Server Core installation is configured for dynamic addressing to acquire its Transmission Control Protocol/Internet Protocol (TCP/IP) networking settings from a Dynamic Host Configuration Protocol (DHCP) server. You can change the TCP/IP settings either from the command line using the Netsh command or by specifying them in an answer file.

Configuring IPv4 Networking Settings from the Command Prompt

To display the current IPv4 configuration of your server, use the Ipconfig command. You can also use the Netsh Interface Ipv4 Show Config command to display the IPv4 configuration of a specified interface (or all interfaces) on the computer as follows:

```
C:\Users\Administrator>netsh interface ipv4 show config

Configuration for interface "Local Area Connection"
    DHCP enabled:                         Yes
    IP Address:                           169.254.98.13
    Subnet Prefix:                        169.254.0.0/16 (mask 255.255.0.0)
    InterfaceMetric:                      10
    DNS servers configured through DHCP:  None
    Register with which suffix:           Primary only
    WINS servers configured through DHCP: None

Configuration for interface "Loopback Pseudo-Interface 1"
    DHCP enabled:                         No
    IP Address:                           127.0.0.1
    Subnet Prefix:                        127.0.0.0/8 (mask 255.0.0.0)
    InterfaceMetric:                      50
    Statically Configured DNS Servers:    None
    Register with which suffix:           Primary only
    Statically Configured WINS Servers:   None
```

The fact that the IP address of the server is in the form *169.254.y.z* indicates that the server is configured to use dynamic addressing but there is no DHCP server available on the network. As a result, the server's address has been auto-assigned using Automatic Private IP Addressing (APIPA).

To display all IPv4 interfaces on the computer, use the following command:

```
C:\Users\Administrator>netsh interface ipv4 show interfaces

Idx  Met    MTU   State        Name
---  ---  -----   -----------  --------------------
  2   10   1500   connected    Local Area Connection
  1   50 4294967295 connected    Loopback Pseudo-Interface 1
```

From this, you can see that the interface number (IDX) for the Local Area Connection network interface is 2. You need this information to configure static addressing for the interface. For example, say you want to assign the following static IPv4 settings to your server:

IP address = 172.16.11.190

Subnet mask = 255.255.255.0

Default gateway = 172.16.11.1

To assign these settings to the Local Area Connection interface on your computer, type the following command:

```
C:\Users\Administrator>netsh interface ipv4 set address name=2 source
=static 172 .16.11.190 255.255.255.0 172.16.11.1
```

Tip   You could also use *name="Local Area Connection"* in the previous command and the result would be the same.

To specify 172.16.11.161 as the address of your primary DNS server for this interface, type the following:

```
C:\Users\Administrator>netsh interface ipv4 add dnsserver name=2
address=172.16.11.161 index=1
```

If you want to specify a secondary DNS server for this interface, repeat the previous command using the IP address of the secondary server, but change the index to 2.

You can verify your static address configuration using Ipconfig as follows:

```
C:\Users\Administrator>ipconfig /all

Windows IP Configuration

    Host Name . . . . . . . . . . . . : sea-sc1
    Primary Dns Suffix  . . . . . . . :
    Node Type . . . . . . . . . . . . : Hybrid
    IP Routing Enabled. . . . . . . . : No
    WINS Proxy Enabled. . . . . . . . : No

Ethernet adapter Local Area Connection:

    Connection-specific DNS Suffix  . :
    Description . . . . . . . . . . . : SiS 900 PCI Fast Ethernet Adapter
    Physical Address. . . . . . . . . : 00-11-D8-60-ED-D4
    DHCP Enabled. . . . . . . . . . . : No
    Autoconfiguration Enabled . . . . : Yes
    Link-local IPv6 Address . . . . . : fe80::50d0:4c17:d149:620d%2(Preferred)
    IPv4 Address. . . . . . . . . . . : 172.16.11.190(Preferred)
    Subnet Mask . . . . . . . . . . . : 255.255.255.0
    Default Gateway . . . . . . . . . : 172.16.11.1
    DNS Servers . . . . . . . . . . . : 172.16.11.161
    NetBIOS over Tcpip. . . . . . . . : Enabled

Tunnel adapter Local Area Connection*:

    Media State . . . . . . . . . . . : Media disconnected
    Connection-specific DNS Suffix  . :
    Description . . . . . . . . . . . : Microsoft ISATAP Adapter
    Physical Address. . . . . . . . . : 00-00-00-00-00-00-00-E0
    DHCP Enabled. . . . . . . . . . . : No
    Autoconfiguration Enabled . . . . : Yes
```

To change back to using dynamic addressing instead of static addressing for this interface, use the following two commands:

```
C:\Users\Administrator>netsh interface ipv4 set address name=2 source=dhcp
C:\Users\Administrator>ipconfig /renew
```

The first command switches the interface from static to dynamic addressing. The second command attempts to acquire an IP address from a DHCP server.

Configuring IPv4 Networking Settings Using an Answer File

You can use Windows SIM to specify IPv4 networking settings using an Autounattend.xml or Unattend.xml answer file as follows:

1. Add the following component to the specialize configuration pass of your answer file to identify the network interface to which you are going to assign an address:

   Microsoft-Windows-TCPIP\Interfaces\Interface

2. In the Properties pane, type **Local Area Connection** for Identifier.

3. Add the following component to the specialize pass to disable automatic addressing:

   Microsoft-Windows-TCPIP\Interfaces\Interface\IPv4Settings

4. Click the box to the right of the DhcpEnabled setting and select False using the drop-down arrow.

5. Add the following component to the specialize pass to specify an IP address and subnet mask for your interface:

   Microsoft-Windows-TCPIP\Interfaces\Interface\UnicastIpAddresses\IpAddress

6. Type **1** in the box to the right of Key and type **172.16.11.20/24** or another IPv4 address in the box to the right of Value. Note that you must specify an address for your network adapter using Classless Inter-Domain Routing (CIDR) notation.

7. Add the following component to the specialize pass to specify the default gateway:

   Microsoft-Windows-TCPIP\Interfaces\Interface\Routes\Route

8. Type **1** in the box to the right of Identifier, type **172.16.11.1** or another default gateway address in the box to the right of NextHopAddress, and type **0.0.0.0/0** in the box to the right of Prefix:

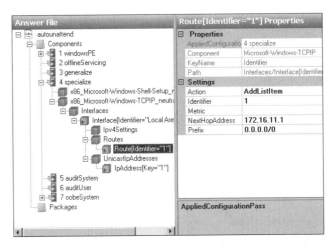

9. Add the following component to the specialize pass to specify a DNS server:

   Microsoft-Windows-DNS-Client\Interfaces\Interface

10. Type **Local Area Connection** in the box to the right of Identifier.

11. Add the following component to the specialize pass to specify a DNS server:

    Microsoft-Windows-DNS-Client\Interfaces\Interface\DNSServerSearch-Order\IpAddress

12. Type **1** in the box to the right of Key and type **172.16.11.161** or another DNS server address in the box to the right of Value.

13. To add a second DNS server address, repeat steps 11 and 12, but type **2** instead of **1** for Key.

Configuring IPv6 Networking Settings

To configure IPv6 settings from the command prompt, use the interface ipv6 context of the Netsh command. For more information about using Netsh on Windows Server 2008, download the Windows Server 2008 Network Shell (Netsh) Technical Reference from the Microsoft Download Center (*http://www.microsoft.com/downloads*). This download is a .zip file that contains the Netsh.chm Help file for the Netsh command in Windows Server 2008.

To configure IPv6 settings using an answer file, add the following component to the specialize pass of your answer file and configure the settings for this component accordingly:

Microsoft-Windows-TCPIP\Interfaces\Interface\IPv6Settings

For more information about IPv6 on Microsoft platforms, see *Understanding IPv6, Second Edition* by Joseph Davies (Microsoft Press, 2008).

Configuring Date and Time Settings

Date and time settings include the current date, time, time zone, and Internet time synchronization settings for your server.

Configuring Date and Time Settings from the Command Prompt

You can use the Date And Time item in the Control Panel to configure date and time settings for a Server Core installation. To do this, type **control timedate.cpl** at the command prompt to open the Date And Time user interface (shown in Figure 3-2) and configure the settings as desired. Note that an Internet Time tab is present only on stand-alone servers belonging to a workgroup.

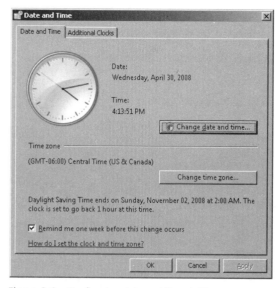

Figure 3-2   Configuring date and time settings

Configuring Date and Time Settings Using an Answer File

The only date and time setting you can configure using an answer file is the time zone. You can use Windows SIM to specify the time zone using an Autounattend.xml or Unattend.xml answer file as follows:

1. Add the following component to either the specialize or oobeSystem configuration pass of your answer file:

   Microsoft-Windows-Shell-Setup

2. In the Properties pane, type **Central Standard Time** (or another time zone identifier string) in the box to the right of the TimeZone.

For a list of time zone identifier strings, see the "TimeZone" entry in the Unattended
Windows Setup Reference (Unattend.chm) Help file that is installed with the
Windows AIK.

Configuring Regional and Language Settings

Regional and language settings include the following:

- The format used to display dates, times, numbers, and currencies

- The current location (country)

- The current keyboard language and other input languages

- The system locale

Configuring Regional and Language Settings from the Command Prompt

You can use the Regional And Language Options item in Control Panel to configure
location, keyboard and input language, and other localization settings. To do this, type
control intl.cpl at a command prompt to open the Regional And Language Options
user interface (shown in Figure 3-3) and then configure the settings as desired. You
can also use the Keyboards And Languages tab to install or uninstall additional languages on your computer.

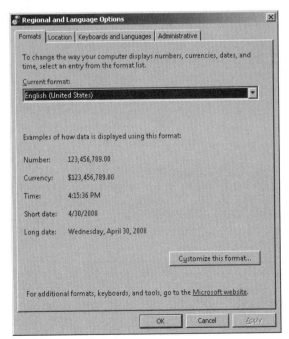

Figure 3-3   Configuring regional and language settings

Configuring Regional and Language Settings in an Answer File

Regional and language settings can be configured in two ways when performing an unattended install:

- By configuring the answer file settings for the following component during the windowsPE configuration pass of Windows Setup:

  Microsoft-Windows-International-Core-WinPE

  Configuration of these settings is required to perform an automated install; see the section "Configuring Minimal Answer File Settings for a Completely Automated Install," in Chapter 2, for more information.

- By configuring the answer file settings for the following component during the specialize or oobeSystem configuration pass:

  Microsoft-Windows-International-Core

  Settings applied during these passes override corresponding settings applied during the windowsPE pass.

Configuring Automatic Updates

You can configure settings for Automatic Updates on a Server Core installation by using the built-in Scregedit.wsf script. This script is unique to Server Core (it's not present on Full installations of Windows Server 2008) and modifies Automatic Update settings by using Windows Management Instrumentation (WMI) to create several registry keys and values under the following registry key:

HKLM\SOFTWARE\Policies\Microsoft\Windows\CurrentVersion\Windows-Update\Auto Update

You must use the Scregedit.wsf script with Cscript.exe as follows:

- If your current directory is %Windir%\System32, type **cscript scregedit.wsf <options>**

- From any other current directory, type **cscript C:\Windows\System32\ scregedit.wsf <options>**

Configuring Automatic Updates from the Command Prompt

To view the current Automate Update settings on your server, use the following command:

```
C:\Users\Administrator>cscript C:\Windows\System32\scregedit.wsf /AU /v
Microsoft (R) Windows Script Host Version 5.7
Copyright (C) Microsoft Corporation. All rights reserved.

SOFTWARE\Microsoft\Windows\CurrentVersion\WindowsUpdate\Auto Update
AUOptions Value not set.
```

The output "Value not set" indicates that Automatic Updates has not yet been configured on your server. To enable Automatic Updates to download and install updates automatically when they become available, use the following command:

```
C:\Users\Administrator>cscript C:\Windows\System32\scregedit.wsf /AU 4
Microsoft (R) Windows Script Host Version 5.7
Copyright (C) Microsoft Corporation. All rights reserved.

Registry has been updated.
```

If you need to disable Automatic Updates temporarily, use the following command:

```
C:\Users\Administrator>cscript C:\Windows\System32\scregedit.wsf /AU 1
```

For help about using the /AU option with Scregedit.wsf to configure Automatic Updates, use the /? switch like this:

```
C:\Users\Administrator>cscript C:\Windows\System32\scregedit.wsf /AU /?
Microsoft (R) Windows Script Host Version 5.7
Copyright (C) Microsoft Corporation. All rights reserved.

Automatic Updates - Manage Automatic Windows Updates These settings can be
used to configure how Automatic Updates are applied to the Windows system.
It includes the ability to disable automatic updates and to set the
installation schedule.

/AU [/v][value]

        /v      View the current Automatic Update settings
        value   value you want to set to.

        Options:
        4 - Enable Automatic Updates
        1 - Disable Automatic Updates
```

For general help concerning all options available for Scregedit.wsf, type **cscript C:\Windows\System32\scregedit.wsf /?** at a command prompt.

> **Note**   The Scregedit.wsf script was created to enable administrators to configure certain aspects of Server Core that would be difficult to configure otherwise. These aspects include configuring Automatic Updates, configuring Remote Desktop, enabling remote management of IPSec Monitor, and changing the priority for DNS SRV records.

Configuring Automatic Update Settings Using an Answer File

You can use Windows SIM to configure Automatic Updates using an Autounattend.xml or Unattend.xml answer file as follows:

1. Add the following component to the oobeSystem configuration pass of your answer file:

   Microsoft-Windows-Shell-Setup\FirstLogonCommands\SynchronousCommand

2. In the Properties pane, type **cscript C:\Windows\system32\scregedit.wsf /AU 4** in the box beside CommandLine and type **1** in the box beside Order, as shown here:

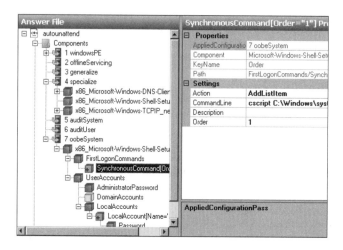

Caution   You cannot use %Windir% instead of C:\Windows in the previous procedure because environment variables are not initialized until the logon process completes.

Tip   Commands specified in FirstLogonCommands\SynchronousCommand run the first time a user logs onto the computer and execute after logon but before the desktop appears. You can configure multiple commands to run by repeating steps 1 and 2 in the previous procedure for up to 500 commands. Multiple commands run synchronously; that is, the next command executes only after the previous command has completed. If you run multiple commands, you must type a different unique number for Order so that the commands run in the desired order. You can also specify a Description for each command as a mnemonic device.

Configuring Windows Error Reporting

Windows Error Reporting (WER) is a feature of Windows Server 2008 that monitors for exceptions and sends problem reports to Microsoft for trending and analysis. WER can be configured to send either summary or detailed reports to Microsoft. In addition, WER stores error reports that have been generated in the following directories:

- **WER user store**   Users\Username\AppData\Local\Microsoft\Windows\WER
- **WER machine store**   ProgramData\Microsoft\Windows\WER

You can configure WER on a Server Core installation by using the Server-WEROptin.exe utility, which is found in the %Windir%\System32 directory.

Configuring Windows Error Reporting from a Command Prompt

To view the current configuration for WER on your server, use the following command:

```
C:\Windows\System32>serverweroptin /query

Current Windows Error Reporting Setting: Disabled

Windows can send descriptions of problems on this server to Microsoft. If
you choose to automatically send generic information about a problem,
Microsoft will use the information to start working on a solution.
```

To configure WER to send summary reports to Microsoft, use the following command:

```
C:\Windows\System32>serverweroptin /summary

You have chosen to enable Windows Error Reporting to automatically send
summary reports to Microsoft.
```

To configure WER to send detailed reports, use the following command:

```
C:\Windows\System32>serverweroptin /detailed

You have chosen to enable Windows Error Reporting
to automatically send detailed reports to Microsoft.
```

To disable sending of WER reports to Microsoft, use the following command:

```
C:\Windows\System32>serverweroptin /disable

You have chosen to disable Windows Error Reporting
```

Configuring Windows Error Reporting on Domain-Joined Computers

In a domain environment, you can also configure WER settings using the following Group Policy settings:

- Computer Configuration\Administrative Templates\Policies\Windows Components\Windows Error Reporting
- User Configuration\Administrative Templates\Policies\Windows Components\Windows Error Reporting

Note that WER policy settings relating to notifications and user interface items are not applicable to Server Core installations.

Configuring WER Settings Using an Answer File

You can use Windows SIM to configure WER settings using an Autounattend.xml or Unattend.xml answer file. For example, to enable WER and configure it to send detailed reports to Microsoft automatically, perform the following steps:

1. Add the following component to the oobeSystem configuration pass of your answer file:

   Microsoft-Windows-Shell-Setup\FirstLogonCommands\SynchronousCommand

2. In the Properties pane, type **C:\Windows\system32\serverweroptin /detailed** in the box beside CommandLine and type **1** (or another number if you are running multiple FirstLogonCommands) in the box beside Order.

Participating in the Customer Experience Improvement Program

The Customer Experience Improvement Program (CEIP) can be used to collect information about how you use Microsoft products and about any problems you encounter while using these products. Microsoft then uses the collected information to improve these products and to help solve problems when they occur. Participation in CEIP is voluntary and no personally identifying information is sent to Microsoft. For more information, see *http://www.microsoft.com/products/ceip/EN-US/default.mspx.*

You can opt into or out of CEIP on a Server Core installation by using the Server-CEIPOptin.exe utility, which is found in the %Windir%\System32 directory.

Configuring CEIP Settings from the Command Prompt

To view the current configuration for CEIP on your server, use the following command:

```
C:\Windows\system32>serverceipoptin /query
Current Customer Experience Improvement participation: not participating

If you join the Windows Server Customer Experience Improvement Program
(CEIP), we will collect statistical information about your system, and
Windows will periodically upload a small file to Microsoft that contains
a summary of the information collected.

The uploaded data contains no information that allows us to identify you or
your company. If you participate and then decide to use imaging technology
on this server to build other servers, those servers will be included in
the CEIP program.
```

To opt into CEIP, use the following command:

```
C:\Windows\system32>serverceipoptin /enable
```

And to opt out, use the following command:

```
C:\Windows\system32>serverceipoptin /disable
```

> **Tip** In a domain environment, you can redirect CEIP uploads to Microsoft Operations Manager (MOM) or System Center Operations Manager by configuring the following Group Policy setting: Computer Configuration\Administrative Templates\Policies\Windows Components\Customer Experience Improvement Program\Allow Corporate redirection of Customer Experience Improvement uploads

Configuring CEIP Settings Using an Answer File

You can use Windows SIM to opt into CEIP using an Autounattend.xml or Unattend.xml answer file as follows:

1. Add the following component to the oobeSystem configuration pass of your answer file:

   Microsoft-Windows-Shell-Setup\FirstLogonCommands\SynchronousCommand

2. In the Properties pane, type **C:\Windows\system32\serverceipoptin /detailed** in the box beside CommandLine and type **1** (or another number if you are running multiple FirstLogonCommands) in the box beside Order.

Activating Windows

To activate a Server Core installation, use the Slmgr.vbs script found in the %Windir%\System32 directory. This script should be used with Cscript.exe and can take different parameters.

Activating Windows from the Command Prompt

To display the current licensing information for your server, use the following command:

```
C:\Windows\system32>cscript slmgr.vbs /dli
Microsoft (R) Windows Script Host Version 5.7
Copyright (C) Microsoft Corporation. All rights reserved.

Name: Windows Server(R), ServerEnterpriseCore edition
Description: Windows Operating System - Windows Server(R),
VOLUME_KMSCLIENT channel
Partial Product Key: XXXXX
License Status: Initial grace period
Time remaining: 83640 minute(s) (58 day(s))

Key Management Service client information
    Client Machine ID (CMID): 3d1b4af6-1854-48a2-afe6-2e205c8074ef
    DNS auto-discovery: KMS name not available
    KMS machine extended PID:
    Activation interval: 120 minutes
    Renewal interval: 10080 minutes
```

To view the date when your grace period expires, use the following command:

```
C:\Windows\system32>cscript slmgr.vbs /xpr
Microsoft (R) Windows Script Host Version 5.7
Copyright (C) Microsoft Corporation. All rights reserved.

Initial grace period ends 6/13/2008 3:05:04 PM
```

To install a product key on your server, such as a Multiple Activation Key (MAK) for an installation from volume-licensed media, use the following command (replacing the *x*'s with your product key):

```
C:\Windows\system32>cscript slmgr.vbs /ipk XXXXX-XXXXX-XXXXX-XXXXX-XXXXX
Microsoft (R) Windows Script Host Version 5.7
Copyright (C) Microsoft Corporation. All rights reserved.

Installed product key XXXXX-XXXXX-XXXXX-XXXXX-XXXXX successfully.
```

To activate your installation using the product key you installed, use the following command:

```
C:\Windows\system32>cscript slmgr.vbs /ato
Microsoft (R) Windows Script Host Version 5.7
Copyright (C) Microsoft Corporation. All rights reserved.

Activating Windows Server(R), ServerEnterpriseCore edition (bb1d27c4-959d-
4f82-bb0fd-c02a7be54732) ...
Product activated successfully.
```

> **Note** On many corporate networks, Internet connectivity is provided through a proxy server. If this is the case for your environment, you need to configure a proxy server for your Server Core installation before activation can succeed. For information on how to do this, see the section "Configuring Proxy Server Settings," later in this chapter.

You can verify activation using the /xpr switch as follows:

```
C:\Windows\system32>cscript slmgr.vbs /xpr
Microsoft (R) Windows Script Host Version 5.7
Copyright (C) Microsoft Corporation. All rights reserved.

The machine is permanently activated.
```

For a list of the different parameters Slmgr.vbs can take, type **cscript slmgr.vbs /?** at a command prompt.

For more information concerning Volume Activation (VA) 2.0 for Windows Server 2008 and Windows Vista SP1, see http://technet.microsoft.com/en-us/library/bb892849.aspx.

Activating Windows Using an Answer File

You can use Windows SIM to activate Server Core using an Autounattend.xml or Unattend.xml answer file. For example, to activate a volume-licensed version of Server Core using a MAK product key, use the following command:

1. Add the Microsoft-Windows-Shell-Setup component to the specialize configuration pass of your answer file.

2. In the Properties pane, type your 25-character product key (**XXXXX-XXXXX-XXXXX-XXXXX-XXXXX**) in the box beside Product Key.

3. Add the following component to the oobeSystem configuration pass of your answer file:

   Microsoft-Windows-Shell-Setup\FirstLogonCommands\Synchronous-Command

4. In the Properties pane, type **cscript C:\Windows\system32\slmgr.vbs /ato** in the box beside CommandLine and type **1** (or another number if you are running multiple FirstLogonCommands) in the box beside Order.

After you log on to your server for the first time, be sure to verify that your server has been activated by typing **cscript C:\Windows\system32\slmgr.vbs /xpr** at a command prompt.

Enabling Remote Desktop

You can enable Remote Desktop on a Server Core installation using the Scregedit.wsf script, which is found in the %Windir%\System32 directory. Enabling Remote Desktop allows you to connect remotely to a Server Core installation and manage it as if you were sitting at the local console of the server.

Enabling Remote Desktop from the Command Prompt

To see whether Remote Desktop is currently enabled on your Server Core installation, use the following command:

```
C:\Windows\System32>cscript scregedit.wsf /ar /v
Microsoft (R) Windows Script Host Version 5.7
Copyright (C) Microsoft Corporation. All rights reserved.

System\CurrentControlSet\Control\Terminal Server fDenyTSConnections
View registry setting. 1
```

A value of 1 for the fDenyTSConnections registry value indicates that Remote Desktop is disabled (the default). To enable Remote Desktop, change this registry value from 1 to 0 as follows:

```
C:\Windows\System32>cscript scregedit.wsf /ar 0
Microsoft (R) Windows Script Host Version 5.7
```

Copyright (C) Microsoft Corporation. All rights reserved.

Registry has been updated.

> **Note**   Enabling Remote Desktop by using Scregedit.wsf also opens the necessary Windows Firewall ports to enable your Server Core installation to accept incoming connections from Remote Desktop Connection (RDC) clients.

After fDenyTSConnections has been set to 0, you can use RDC 6.0 or later to connect to your Server Core installation from a different computer by pressing Windows Key+R on the other computer, typing **mstsc**, specifying the name or IP address of your Server Core installation, specifying credentials (either *domain\username* or *server\username*), clicking Connect, and typing the password for your credentials when prompted.

Configuring Remote Desktop to Require Network Level Authentication

By default, when Remote Desktop is enabled on a Server Core installation, clients running earlier versions of RDC, such as RDC 5.x, are allowed to connect. By requiring Network Level Authentication (NLA), however, you can enhance the security of your Server Core installation by ensuring that user authentication is completed before you establish a full Remote Desktop connection and your logon screen appears. NLA is supported by RDC 6.x, which is included by default in Windows Vista and Windows Server 2008.

> **Note**   RDC 6.1 is included in Service Pack 3 for Windows XP; see *http://support.microsoft.com/kb/951616* for details. You can download an RDC 6.0 client for Windows Server 2003 by going to *http://support.microsoft.com/kb/925876*.

To view the current security configuration of Remote Desktop on your server, use the following command:

```
C:\Windows\System32>cscript scregedit.wsf /cs /v
Microsoft (R) Windows Script Host Version 5.7
Copyright (C) Microsoft Corporation. All rights reserved.

System\CurrentControlSet\Control\Terminal Server\WinStations\
RDP-Tcp UserAuthentication
View registry setting.
0
```

A value of 0 (the default) means that earlier RDC 5.x clients are allowed to connect to your server. To require clients to use NLA for enhanced security, use the following command:

```
C:\Windows\System32>cscript scregedit.wsf /cs 1
```

For more information about using Remote Desktop to manage Server Core remotely, see Chapter 6, "Remote Management."

Enabling Remote Desktop Using an Answer File

You can use Windows SIM to enable Remote Desktop using an Autounattend.xml or Unattend.xml answer file as follows:

1. Add the following component to the specialize configuration pass of your answer file:

   Microsoft-Windows-TerminalServices-LocalSessionManager

2. In the Properties pane, click the text box to the right of the fDenyTSConnections setting until a drop-down arrow appears. Click the arrow and select False.

3. Add the following component to the oobeSystem configuration pass of your answer file:

   Microsoft-Windows-Shell-Setup\FirstLogonCommands\SynchronousCommand

4. In the Properties pane, type **C:\Windows\system32\netsh advfirewall firewall set rule group="Remote Desktop" new enable=yes** in the box beside CommandLine and type **1** (or another number if you are running multiple First-LogonCommands) in the box beside Order.

If you also want to require Remote Desktop clients to use NLA to connect to your Server Core installation, perform the following additional steps for configuring your answer file:

1. Add the following component to the specialize configuration pass of your answer file:

   Microsoft-Windows-TerminalServices-RDP-WinStationExtensions

2. In the Properties pane, type **1** in the box beside UserAuthentication.

Enabling Remote Administration of Windows Firewall

Windows Firewall is enabled by default on Server Core for all profiles (public, private, and domain). However, before you can use the Windows Firewall With Advanced Security MMC snap-in on a remote computer to manage Windows Firewall on your Server Core installation, you must enable remote firewall management on your Server Core installation. If you don't do this, the only way you will be able to configure Windows Firewall on your server is locally, by using the advfirewall context of the Netsh command.

Enabling Remote Administration of Windows Firewall from the Command Prompt

To enable remote firewall management of your Server Core installation for all firewall profiles, type the following command:

netsh advfirewall firewall set rule group="Windows Firewall Remote Management" new enable=yes

You can verify that remote management has been enabled as follows:

```
C:\Windows\System32>netsh advfirewall firewall show rule name="Windows
Firewall Remote Management (RPC)"
Rule Name:                           Windows Firewall Remote Management (RPC)
----------------------------------------------------------------------
Enabled:                    Yes
Direction:                  In
Profiles:                   Private
Grouping:                   Windows Firewall Remote Management
LocalIP:                    Any
RemoteIP:                   Any
Protocol:                   TCP
LocalPort:                  RPC
RemotePort:                 Any
Edge traversal:             No
Action:                     Allow
```

Configuring Windows Firewall from the Command Prompt

You can use the advfirewall context of the Netsh command to configure many aspects of Windows Firewall on your Server Core installation. For example, to turn off Windows Firewall temporarily for testing purposes, type the following command:

netsh advfirewall set allprofiles state off

Or, to create a new firewall rule that allows inbound connections on TCP port 2100, type the following command:

netsh advfirewall firewall add rule name="Allow Inbound TCP port 2100" protocol=TCP dir=in localport=2100 action=allow

For more information about using netsh on Windows Server 2008, download the Windows Server 2008 Network Shell (Netsh) Technical Reference from the Microsoft Download Center (http://www.microsoft.com/downloads).

Enabling Remote Administration of Windows Firewall Using an Answer File

You can use Windows SIM to enable Remote Desktop using an Autounattend.xml or Unattend.xml answer file as follows:

1. Add the following component to the oobeSystem configuration pass of your answer file:

   Microsoft-Windows-Shell-Setup\FirstLogonCommands\SynchronousCommand

2. In the Properties pane, type **C:\Windows\system32\netsh advfirewall firewall set rule group="Windows Firewall Remote Management" new enable=yes** in the box beside CommandLine and type **1** (or another number if you are running multiple FirstLogonCommands) in the box beside Order.

Joining a Domain

You can join your Server Core installation to an Active Directory domain by using the Netdom command. Joining or leaving a domain requires domain administrator credentials.

> **Important**   If your Server Core installation has a static IP address assigned to it instead of using DHCP, be sure that the DNS server address points to a domain controller before attempting to join the domain. See the section "Configuring TCP/IP Networking Settings," earlier in this chapter, for information on how to configure TCP/IP settings on Server Core installations.

Joining a Domain from the Command Prompt

To join a Server Core computer named SEA-SC1 to the CONTOSO domain using the domain administrator credentials of Tony Allen (tallen@contoso.com), use the netdom command as follows:

```
C:\Windows\system32>netdom join SEA-SC1 /domain:CONTOSO /userd:tallen /
passwordd :*
Type the password associated with the domain user:Pa$$w0rd

The computer needs to be restarted in order to complete the operation.

The command completed successfully.
```

Use the **shutdown −r −t 0** command to reboot your server for the domain join operation to complete. Verify that a computer account has been created for your server in the Computers container using the Active Directory Users And Computers MMC console on your domain controller.

> **Tip**   You can also prestage computer accounts in Active Directory provided that you know the globally unique identifier (GUID) of the computer you want to join to Active Directory. To determine your computer's GUID, check for a label on the inside or outside of your computer's case. You can also obtain the GUID by viewing your BIOS information, by using the WMI interface to display the UUID value of the Win32_ComputerSystemProduct class, or by sniffing network traffic for DHCP-Discover packets from your computer. For more information on using the Active Directory Users And Computers MMC console to manage Server Core, see Chapter 7.

You can also use the Netdom command to disjoin your Server Core installation from the domain to which it belongs. To remove server SEA-SC1 from the CONTOSO domain, type the following command:

netdom remove SEA-SC1 /domain:CONTOSO /userd:tallen /passwordd:*

Joining a Domain Using an Answer File

You can use Windows SIM to join your Server Core installation to a domain during an unattended install automatically by configuring your Autounattend.xml or Unattend.xml answer file as follows:

1. Add the following component to the specialize configuration pass of your answer file:

   Microsoft-Windows-UnattendedJoin\Identification

2. In the Properties pane, type **CONTOSO** (or the name of another domain) in the box to the right of the JoinDomain setting.

3. In the Answer File pane, expand Microsoft-Windows-UnattendedJoin\Identification and select the Credentials component beneath it.

4. In the Properties pane, type the domain administrator credentials that Windows Setup will use to join the computer to the domain. For example, if Tony Allen (tallen@contoso.com) is a Domain Admin in the CONTOSO domain, you can type **CONTOSO** for Domain, **tallen** for Username, and **Pa$$w0rd** (or another password) for Password, as shown here.

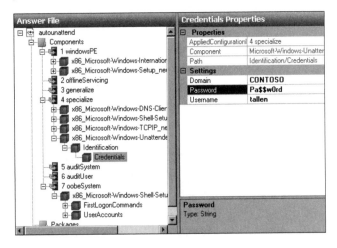

Note   The password for the credentials used to perform a domain join are stored in clear text in your answer file, so be sure to safeguard any removable media on which your answer file is stored.

Other Initial Configuration Tasks

The following are a few other tasks you may want to perform right away on a new Server Core installation. All these tasks can be performed from the command line, either locally from the console or remotely using an RDC (provided that Remote Desktop has been enabled). Many of these tasks can also be automated using the Microsoft-Windows-Shell-Setup\FirstLogonCommands\SynchronousCommand component of an Autounattend.xml or Unattend.xml answer file. See the section "Configuring Automatic Update Settings Using an Answer File," earlier in this chapter, for an example of how to configure FirstLogonCommands.

Configuring the Paging File

You can use the Windows Management Instrumentation Command-line (WMIC) to configure the paging file on a Server Core installation. By default, Windows Server 2008 automatically manages the size of its paging file. To disable auto-management of the paging file on server SEA-SC1, type the following command:

wmic computersystem where name="SEA-SC1" set AutomaticManagedPagefile=False

To create a new paging file on the E: drive with an initial size of 1,000 megabytes (MB) and a maximum size of 2,000 MB, type the following command:

wmic pagefileset where name="E:\pagefile.sys" set InitialSize=1000,Maximum-Size=2000

Configuring Display Settings

You can configure display settings on your Server Core installation by directly modifying the registry using Regedit.exe.

Caution   Serious problems can occur if you incorrectly modify the registry, so be sure to back up the registry before you modify it so you can restore it if a problem occurs. For information on how to back up and restore the registry, see Microsoft Knowledge Base article KB322756 at *http://support.microsoft.com/kb/322756/*.

To change your current display resolution settings, follow these steps:

1. Type **regedit** at the command prompt to open the Registry Editor.

2. Browse to the following registry key:

   HKLM\SYSTEM\CurrentControlSet\Control\Video

   You will see several subkeys under this key of the form {GUID}\0000, representing different logical and physical video adapters on your computer.

3. Find the {GUID}\0000 subkey that has the values DefaultSettings.XResolution and DefaultSettings.YResolution under it, double-click these two values, and assign them different values as desired. For example, you could set Default-Settings.XResolution to 1280 (decimal) and DefaultSettings.YResolution to 1024 (decimal) to change your display resolution to 1280 x 1024 pixels.

4. Log off and on again for the changes to take effect.

You can also change other display settings by modifying the registry. For example, you can change the color depth from the default 8-bit (256 colors) to 16-bit or 32-bit by modifying the following value:

HKEY_LOCAL_MACHINE\System\CurrentControlSet\Control\Video\GUID\
0000\DefaultSettings.BitsPerPel

And you can change the video refresh rate by modifying this value to be your new refresh rate in hertz (Hz):

HKEY_LOCAL_MACHINE\System\CurrentControlSet\Control\Video\
GUID\0000\DefaultSettings.VRefresh

> **Caution**   If you make changes to display settings that are not supported by your video card, your liquid crystal display (LCD) monitor will not display a signal—and if you are using a cathode ray tube (CRT) monitor, you can damage your monitor!

You can also configure display settings by using an Autounattend.xml or Unattend.xml answer file as follows:

1. Add the following component to the oobeSystem configuration pass of your answer file:

   Microsoft-Windows-Shell-Setup\Display

2. In the Properties pane, type values for each display setting as desired. For example:

   ❑ Type **1280** for HorizontalResolution

   ❑ Type **1024** for VerticalResolution

   ❑ Type **16** for ColorDepth

> **Caution**   Be careful not to configure a value for RefreshRate that is not supported by your monitor.

Configuring Screen Saver Timeout

By default, Server Core is configured to display a password-protected screen saver if there is no mouse or keyboard activity for a period of time. You can configure screen saver settings on your Server Core installation by directly modifying registry values found under the key HKEY_CURRENT_USER\Control Panel\Desktop. Table 3-2 summarizes the names of each value, their use, and the default setting for a Server Core installation. These registry changes take effect immediately.

Table 3-2   Registry Values for Modifying Screen Saver Settings

Value	Description	Default
ScreenSaveActive	1 for enabled, 0 for disabled	1
ScreenSaverIsSecure	1 for password-protected, 0 for not password-protected	1
ScreenSaveTimeOut	Number of seconds of inactivity until screen saver appears	600
SCRNSAVE.EXE	Path and filename of screen saver	C:\Windows\System32\Logon.scr

You can use Windows SIM to configure screen saver settings by modifying the registry using an Autounattend.xml or Unattend.xml answer file. For example, to disable the screen saver, perform the following steps:

1. Add the following component to the oobeSystem configuration pass of your answer file:

   Microsoft-Windows-Shell-Setup\FirstLogonCommands\Synchronous-Command

2. In the Properties pane, type **reg add "HKCU\Control Panel\Desktop" /v ScreenSaveActive /t REG_SZ /d 0 /f** in the box beside CommandLine and type **1** (or another number if you have multiple FirstLogonCommands) in the box beside Order.

   Caution   You can use **reg add** with FirstLogonCommands in an answer file to change almost any registry setting automatically during an unattended install. Be careful, though—modifying the registry incorrectly can lead to system instability or even an unbootable system!

Configuring Proxy Server Settings

You can use the winhttp context of the Netsh command to configure proxy server settings on your Server Core installation. This is useful because Server Core does not include Windows Internet Explorer (proxy server settings are configured on the Connections tab of Internet Options).

For example, to configure Server Core to use a proxy server named proxysrv.contoso.com over port 80, type the following command:

netsh winhttp set proxy proxysrv.contoso.com:80

And to configure Server Core to bypass this proxy server for local (intranet) addresses, type the following command:

netsh winttp set proxy proxysrv.contoso.com:80 bypass-list="<local>"

To view your current proxy server settings, type **netsh winhttp show proxy** at the command prompt.

> **Note** Server Core cannot access the Internet through a proxy that needs a password to allow connections.

Chapter 4
Installing Roles and Features

A key task connected with administrating Windows Server Core is installing the various roles and features supported by this platform. This chapter looks at how to install and uninstall a role or feature and how to enumerate the currently installed roles and features on a Server Core computer. Also discussed are how to install roles and features automatically during unattended Setup and how you can reduce the disk footprint of Server Core by permanently removing binaries for unneeded roles and features.

Understanding Roles and Features

A *role* is a set of software programs that, when properly installed and configured, enables a computer running Windows Server 2008 to perform a specific function for multiple users or other computers within a network. An example of a role is the DNS Server role, which enables client computers to perform name lookups to access various resources on a network.

You can run only a limited number of roles on a Server Core installation. Specifically, the following roles are available in-box on a Server Core installation:

- Active Directory Domain Services (AD DS)
- Active Directory Lightweight Directory Services (AD LDS)
- DHCP Server
- DNS Server
- File Services
- Print Services
- Web Server (IIS)

In addition, the following two roles can be installed on Server Core, but their binaries must be downloaded from Microsoft before the roles can be added to the server:

- Streaming Media Services
- Hyper-V (virtualization)

For information on how to administer a particular role, see the chapter where that role is covered.

A *feature* is a set of software components that are designed to provide supporting functionality to roles, to the administrator, and to server management. An example of a feature is Failover Clustering, which is designed to provide high availability on Windows Server 2008 computers running business-critical server roles.

You can install only a limited number of features on Server Core. Specifically, the following roles are available on a Server Core installation (items marked with an asterisk require appropriate hardware to be implemented as well):

- Backup
- Bitlocker Drive Encryption*
- Failover Clustering*
- Multipath IO*
- Network Load Balancing*
- Quality Windows Audio Visual Experience (QWAVE)
- Removable Storage*
- Simple Network Management Protocol (SNMP)
- Subsystem for UNIX-based Applications (SUA)
- Telnet client
- Windows Internet Name Service (WINS)

Additional information concerning features available on Server Core can be found in later chapters. Note that some features, like SUA and Multipath IO, are not covered in this book—see the Windows Server 2008 Resource Kit from Microsoft Press for more information concerning these features.

Tools for Installing Roles and Features

On a full installation of Windows Server 2008, you have several different tools and methods you can use to install roles and features on your server. These tools and methods include the following:

- Initial Configuration Tasks page
- Server Manager MMC console
- ServerManagerCmd.exe command-line tool
- Ocsetup.exe command-line tool
- Unattended install using an answer file

On a Server Core installation, however, only two of these tools and methods can be used, namely:

- Ocsetup.exe command-line tool
- Unattended install using an answer file

In addition, Server Core includes Oclist.exe, a command-line tool that is not present on Full installations of Windows Server 2008. Oclist.exe is implemented with

Ocsetup.exe and can be used to enumerate the list of installed roles and features on a Server Core installation.

For more information on using Ocsetup.exe to add roles and features to a Server Core installation, see the section "Installing and Uninstalling Roles and Features Using Ocsetup," later in this chapter. For information concerning using Oclist.exe for enumeration of roles and features on a Server Core installation, see the section "Enumerating Installed Roles and Features Using Oclist," later in this chapter. Finally, for information on how to add roles and features to a Server Core installation during an unattended install, see the section "Unattended Installation of Roles and Features," later in this chapter.

Note   You cannot add roles and features to a Server Core installation remotely by using Server Manager running on a Full installation of Windows Server 2008.

Understanding Packages

To install roles and features on Server Core, you must understand what packages are and the dependencies that can exist between them. A *package* is a group of files that modify optional Microsoft Windows components such as roles and features. Packages can also include items such as service packs, security updates, language packs, hot fixes, and even device drivers, but for the purposes of this book, we'll focus on packages as in-box optional components of Windows.

Packages are installed or removed using a tool called Package Manager (Pkgmgr.exe), which is found in the %Windir%\System32 folder on a Windows Server 2008 installation. And because Windows Server 2008 is a completely componentized operating system, Package Manager can also be used to enable or disable roles and features on an offline Windows Server 2008 image. The process of installing or removing packages on a Windows image is called *servicing* the image.

To install or remove packages from a running Windows Server 2008 installation, however, you should use Ocsetup.exe instead of Pkgmgr.exe. Ocsetup.exe can be used to perform two kinds of actions:

- Installing or removing Microsoft System Installer (.msi files) online by calling the Windows Installer service (MSIExec.exe)

- Passing packages to Package Manager for online installation or removal

When adding or removing roles and features on Server Core, Ocsetup.exe performs the latter function, which means that Ocsetup.exe effectively acts as a "wrapper" for Pkgmgr.exe functionality on running installations of Windows. For instance, the command

```
C:\Windows\system32>start /w ocsetup FailoverCluster-Core
```

invokes Package Manager as follows:

```
C:\Windows\system32>"C:\Windows\system32\pkgmgr.exe" "/iu:FailoverCluster-
Core" "/ocs:C:\Windows\ocsetup_cbs_install_FailoverCluster-Core."
```

For more information on using Ocsetup.exe for installing and removing packages on Server Core, see the section "Installing and Uninstalling Roles and Features Using Ocsetup," later in this chapter.

Understanding Package Names

Before you can install a package on Server Core, you must know the package name for the package. A *package name* is a unique string that identifies the package internally to Windows. Package names can be different from the displayed "friendly" names of roles and services. For example, the package name for the DHCP Server services is DHCP-ServerCore, while the package name for the Bitlocker feature is simply Bitlocker.

Important   Package names are case sensitive when used with Ocsetup.exe.

Table 4-1 lists Server Core roles and their corresponding package names that you can use when installing or uninstalling roles using Ocsetup. Note that some roles in this table have multiple role services that you can install or remove separately for the role. In addition, this table does not provide sufficient information for installation of the following roles:

- AD DS, which is installed by using the Dcpromo command instead of Ocsetup.exe (this is explained further in Chapter 7, "Active Directory Domain Services Role")

- Web Server (IIS), which includes dozens of role services and features that depend on each other in various ways (this is explained further in Chapter 11, "Web Services Role")

Table 4-1   Server Core Roles and Their Package Names

Role	Role Service	Package Name
Active Directory Domain Services (AD DS)		DirectoryServices-Domain-Controller-ServerFoundation
Active Directory Lightweight Directory Services (AD LDS)		DirectoryServices-ADAM-ServerCore
DHCP Server		DHCPServerCore
DNS Server		DNS-Server-Core-Role
File Services	DFS Namespaces	DFSN-Server
	DFS Replication	DFSR-Infrastructure-ServerEdition
	Services for Network File System	ServerForNFS-Base
	File Replication Service	FRS-Infrastructure

Table 4-1   Server Core Roles and Their Package Names

Role	Role Service	Package Name
Print Services	Print Server	Printing-ServerCore-Role
	LPD Service	Printing-LPDPrintService
Web Server (IIS)		IIS-WebServerRole
Streaming Media Services		MediaServer
Hyper-V (virtualization)		Microsoft-Hyper-V

Table 4-2 lists similar information for Server Core features. In this table, note that there are two BitLocker packages:

- BitLocker, which installs the BitLocker Drive Encryption feature, a hard-drive encryption tool that protects data on stolen hardware

- BitLocker-RemoteAdminTool, the BitLocker Drive Encryption Remote Administration Tool, which you can use to enable and configure BitLocker on other computers without enabling BitLocker on the Server Core installation itself

Table 4-2   Server Core Features and Their Package Names

Feature	Package Name
Backup	WindowsServerBackup
BitLocker Drive Encryption	BitLocker
BitLocker Drive Encryption Remote Administration Tool	BitLocker-RemoteAdminTool
Failover Clustering	FailoverCluster-Core
Multipath IO	MultipathIo
Network Load Balancing	NetworkLoadBalancingHeadlessServer
Quality Windows Audio Visual Experience	QWAVE
Removable Storage	Microsoft-Windows-RemovableStorage-ManagementCore
SNMP	SNMP-SC
SUA	SUACore
Telnet client	TelnetClient
WINS	WINS-SC

Understanding Package Dependencies

Some role services and features in Windows Server 2008 (particularly those relating to Microsoft Internet Information Services, or IIS) have dependencies on other role services and features. For example, the following tree diagram shows the hierarchy of dependencies for the IIS-ASP role service:

```
IIS-WebServerRole
+ IIS-WebServer
+ + IIS-ApplicationDevelopment
+ + + IIS-ASP
+ + + IIS-CGI
+ + + IIS-ISAPIExtensions
+ + + + IIS-ASP
```

The tree diagram shows that the IIS-ASP role service depends upon the IIS-Application-Development role service, which in turn depends upon the IIS-WebServer role service, which in turn depends upon the IIS-WebServerRole role service. This means, for example, that if you want to install the IIS-ApplicationDevelopment role service, you first must install both the IIS-WebServer role service and its parent, the IIS-WebServer-Role role service. You would not need to install the IIS-ASP role service, however—only the parent elements of the IIS-ApplicationDevelopment role service within the hierarchy must be installed. On the other hand, the tree diagram shows that if you want to install the IIS-ASP role service, you must install the IIS-Application Development role service and its parent elements, plus the IIS-ISAPIExtensions role service and its parent elements. In fact, you even have to install other role services not shown in the diagram.

Below is a complete tree diagram (with the exception of IIS-WebServerRole and WAS-WindowsActivationService, where only child elements are shown and not grandchildren or further) showing all the dependences between Server Core roles, role services, and features. This diagram is useful when you plan on installing role services or features to ensure that all required parent elements are installed. For a complete list of dependencies for the IIS-WebServer role, see Chapter 11.

```
BitLocker
BitLocker-RemoteAdminTool
ClientForNFS-Base
DFSN-Server
DFSR-Infrastructure-ServerEdition
DHCPServerCore
DirectoryServices-ADAM-ServerCore
DirectoryServices-DomainController-ServerFoundation
DNS-Server-Core-Role
FailoverCluster-Core
FRS-Infrastructure
IIS-WebServerRole
+ IIS-FTPPublishingService
+ IIS-WebServer
```

```
+ IIS-WebServerManagementTools
Microsoft-Windows-RemovableStorageManagementCore
MultipathIo
NetworkLoadBalancingHeadlessServer
Printing-ServerCore-Role
+ Printing-LPDPrintService
QWAVE
ServerForNFS-Base
SNMP-SC
SUACore
TelnetClient
WAS-WindowsActivationService
+ WAS-ProcessModel
WindowsServerBackup
WINS-SC
```

> **Tip**   You can also use Oclist.exe to display a full diagram showing the dependencies between different roles, role services, and features in Server Core. See the next section for more information.

Enumerating Installed Roles and Features

Oclist.exe is a special tool that is included only in Server Core installations of Windows Server 2008. It allows you to display the current state (Installed or Not Installed) of all roles, role services, and features that are available for installation on Server Core. Oclist.exe uses lower-level application programming interfaces (APIs) than ServerManager-Cmd.exe, and the result is that Oclist.exe does not display items using the same hierarchical arrangement used by ServerManagerCmd.exe and the Server Manager console. For example, in Server Manager on a Full installation of Windows Server 2008, the HTTP Logging role service shows the following dependencies in the Add Roles Wizard:

```
Web Server (IIS)
+ Web Server
+ + Health and Diagnostics
+ + + HTTP Logging
```

On a Server Core installation, however, the HTTP Logging role service shows the following additional dependencies:

```
WAS-WindowsActivationService
+ WAS-ProcessModel
+ + IIS-HttpLogging
```

This means that on Server Core, IIS-HttpLogging could be considered a feature (or a subfeature of the Windows Process Activation Service feature) instead of a role service. However, the distinction is irrelevant to the functionality.

Enumerating Installed Roles and Features Using Oclist

To view a list of currently installed roles, role services, and features using Oclist.exe, type **oclist** at a command prompt:

```
C:\Users\Administrator>oclist
Use the listed update names with Ocsetup.exe to install/uninstall a
server role or optional feature.
 Adding or removing the Active Directory role with OCSetup.exe is not
supported. It can leave your server in an unstable state. Always use
DCPromo to install or uninstall Active Directory.


============================================================================
Microsoft-Windows-ServerCore-Package
Not Installed:BitLocker
Not Installed:BitLocker-RemoteAdminTool
Not Installed:ClientForNFS-Base
Not Installed:DFSN-Server
Not Installed:DFSR-Infrastructure-ServerEdition
         Installed:DHCPServerCore
Not Installed:DirectoryServices-ADAM-ServerCore
Not Installed:DirectoryServices-DomainController-ServerFoundation
Not Installed:DNS-Server-Core-Role . . .
```

This truncated command output shows that the DHCP Server role is installed on the Server Core installation.

Using Find to Simplify the Output of Oclist

The raw output of Oclist.exe is quite long, but you can make it easier to read by piping the command output to the Find command. For example, to display all installed roles, role services, and features that are currently installed, run this command:

```
C:\Users\Administrator>oclist | find "  Installed"
    Installed:DHCPServerCore
    Installed:IIS-WebServerRole
    |---      Installed:IIS-WebServer
    |         |---      Installed:IIS-ApplicationDevelopment
    |         |---      Installed:IIS-CommonHttpFeatures
    |         |---      Installed:IIS-HealthAndDiagnostics
    |         |---      Installed:IIS-Performance
    |         |---      Installed:IIS-Security
    |---      Installed:IIS-WebServerManagementTools
```

And to display all non-IIS roles, role services, and features that are installed, use the following command:

```
C:\Users\Administrator>oclist | find "  Installed" | find /v "IIS"
    Installed:DHCPServerCore
```

Note the additional spaces before the word *Installed* in the previous command.

> **Tip**   You can also type **oclist | more** to pipe the command output of Oclist into the More command so you can view the command output one page at a time (by repeatedly pressing the spacebar) or one line at a time (by repeatedly pressing Enter) within your command window.

Enumerating Installed Roles and Features Using WMI

You can also use Windows Management Instrumentation (WMI) to determine which roles and features are installed on your Server Core installation. The script ListRoles-AndFeatures.vbs, shown here, uses the Win32_ServerFeature class to enumerate all roles and features installed on the local Server Core installation:

ListRolesAndFeatures—Enumerates roles and features installed on Server Core

```
strComputer = "."

Set objWMIService = GetObject("winmgmts:\\" & strComputer & "\root\cimv2")

Set colFeatureList = objWMIService.ExecQuery _
    ("SELECT Name FROM Win32_ServerFeature")

For Each objFeature In colFeatureList
  WScript.Echo objFeature.Name

Next
```

For example, if you run script on a Server Core installation that has the DHCP Server and Print Services roles and the SNMP and Windows Server Backup features, the result is the following:

```
C:\Windows\System32>cscript C:\scripts\ListRolesAndFeatures.vbs
Microsoft (R) Windows Script Host Version 5.7
Copyright (C) Microsoft Corporation. All rights reserved.

Print Services
DHCP Server
Windows Server Backup Features
SNMP Services
Print Server
SNMP Service
Windows Server Backup
```

WMI provides information about the installed roles and features that Oclist.exe does not. For more information about the possible values that can be returned by the Win32_ServerFeature class, see http://msdn.microsoft.com/en-us/library/cc280268(VS.85).aspx on MSDN.

Installing and Uninstalling Roles and Features Using Ocsetup

You can use Ocsetup.exe to install or remove roles, role services, and features on Server Core. Ocsetup.exe syntax is case sensitive, so you must type package names exactly as shown previously in Tables 4-1 and 4-2 (or exactly the same as in the output of the Oclist command).

Installing a Role or Feature Using Ocsetup

To install a role, role service, or feature on Server Core, use this command syntax:

start /w ocsetup *package_name*

The Start command is required to be used with Ocsetup.exe to open the Ocsetup.exe process in its own window. The /w switch causes Start to wait for the spawned process to finish running before returning to the command prompt.

Installing the DHCP Server Role

For example, to install the DHCP Server role on Server Core, run the following command:

```
C:\Users\Administrator>start /w ocsetup DHCPServerCore
```

Verifying Installation of the Role

To verify that the role was installed successfully, you can use Oclist.exe with Find as follows:

```
C:\Users\Administrator>oclist | find /i "dhcp"
    Installed:DHCPServerCore
```

The /i switch in the Find command means that the search string is case insensitive.

Uninstalling the DHCP Server Role

To uninstall the previously installed DHCP Server role, use the /uninstall switch of Ocsetup.exe as follows:

```
C:\Users\Administrator>start /w ocsetup DHCPServerCore /uninstall
```

Verify that the role has been uninstalled as follows:

```
C:\Users\Administrator>oclist | find /i "dhcp"
Not Installed:DHCPServerCore
```

Installing the Web Server (IIS) Role

Check whether any IIS role services have been installed on the server as follows:

```
C:\Users\Administrator>oclist | find /i "iis" | find /i " installed"

C:\Users\Administrator>
```

No IIS role services are currently installed.

Now install the Web Server (IIS) role as follows:

```
C:\Users\Administrator>start /w ocsetup IIS-WebServerRole
```

Verify the addition of the role as follows:

```
C:\Users\Administrator>oclist | find /i "iis" | find /i " installed"
    Installed:IIS-WebServerRole
    |---       Installed:IIS-WebServer
    |          |---       Installed:IIS-ApplicationDevelopment
    |          |---       Installed:IIS-CommonHttpFeatures
    |          |---       Installed:IIS-HealthAndDiagnostics
    |          |---       Installed:IIS-Performance
    |          |---       Installed:IIS-Security
    |---       Installed:IIS-WebServerManagementTools
```

Note Installing the Web Server (IIS) role results in several role services being installed by default. See Chapter 11 for more information concerning this.

Adding HTTP Logging to the Web Server (IIS) Role

Attempt to add the HTTP Logging role service to your Web server as follows:

```
C:\Users\Administrator>start /w ocsetup "IIS-HttpLogging"
```

Check whether the HTTP Logging service has been successfully installed as follows:

```
C:\Users\Administrator>oclist | find /i "httplogging"
    |          |   |--- Not Installed:IIS-HttpLogging
    |          |--- Not Installed:IIS-HttpLogging
```

You can see from the code that the service wasn't installed. The reason for this is that the service installation also depends on the Windows Process Activation Service (WAS). Consult the section "Understanding Package Dependencies," earlier in this chapter, to see the dependencies of this role service on other components.

Installing Roles and Features That Have Dependencies

Use the following command to install the Windows Process Activation Service (WAS) feature, then install the WAS Process Model subfeature (which depends upon WAS).

So now you can install the HTTP Logging role service, which depends upon both the WAS Process Model and the IIS-HealthAndDiagnostics role service, as follows:

```
C:\Users\Administrator>start /w ocsetup WAS-WindowsActivationService
&& start /w ocsetup WAS-ProcessModel && start /w ocsetup IIS-HttpLogging
```

Verify that the HTTP Logging service is now installed as follows:

```
C:\Users\Administrator>oclist | find /i "httplogging"
    |        |       |---      Installed:IIS-HttpLogging
    |        |---      Installed:IIS-HttpLogging
```

For more information on using && to execute multiple commands in sequence, see Chapter 5, "Local Management."

Removing Roles and Features That Have Dependencies

To remove WAS and other services and features that depend on WAS, like the WAS Process Model and HTTP Logging, run the following command:

```
C:\Users\Administrator>start /w ocsetup WAS-WindowsActivationService
/uninstall
```

At this point, you are prompted to reboot the system to complete the uninstallation of this feature.

Note Installing some roles and features, such as the Print Services role (Printing-ServerCore-Role), requires rebooting the system. Uninstalling certain roles and features may also require a reboot.

After rebooting, verify that all WAS components and the HTTP Logging service have been removed as follows:

```
C:\Users\Administrator>oclist | find /i "WAS-"
Not Installed:WAS-WindowsActivationService
    |--- Not Installed:WAS-ProcessModel

C:\Users\Administrator>oclist | find /i "httplogging"
    |        |       |--- Not Installed:IIS-HttpLogging
    |        |--- Not Installed:IIS-HttpLogging
```

Installing Multiple Roles and Features Using Ocsetup with an Answer File

Use an Extensible Markup Language (XML) answer file to the HTTP Logging service, with the WAS and WAS Process Model features upon which the logging service depends, as follows:

```
C:\Users\Administrator>start /w ocsetup IIS-HttpLogging
/unattendfile:"C:\unattend.xml"
```

Verify that the HTTP Logging service and its parent WAS features have been installed as follows:

```
C:\Users\Administrator>oclist | find /i "WAS-"
    Installed:WAS-WindowsActivationService
    |---      Installed:WAS-ProcessModel

C:\Users\Administrator>oclist | find /i "httplogging"
    |         |       |---       Installed:IIS-HttpLogging
    |         |---     Installed:IIS-HttpLogging
```

The answer file used here and specified using the /unattendfile switch for Ocsetup looks like this:

```
<?xml version="1.0" encoding="utf-8"?>
<unattend xmlns="urn:schemas-microsoft-com:unattend">
    <servicing>
        <package action="configure">
            <assemblyIdentity name="Microsoft-Windows-ServerCore-Package"
version="6.0.6001.18000" processorArchitecture="x86" publicKey
Token="31bf3856ad364e35" language="" />
            <selection name="IIS-HttpLogging" state="true" />
            <selection name="WAS-ProcessModel" state="true" />
            <selection name="WAS-WindowsActivationService" state="true" />
            <selection name="IIS-HealthAndDiagnostics" state="true" />
            <selection name="IIS-WebServer" state="true" />
            <selection name="IIS-WebServerRole" state="true" />
        </package>
    </servicing>
    <cpi:offlineImage cpi:source="wim:w:/sources/ws08/install.wim#Windows
Longhorn SERVERENTERPRISEVCORE" xmlns:cpi="urn:schemas-microsoft-com:cpi" />
</unattend>
```

You can use the Windows System Image Manager (Windows SIM) to create an answer file for installing multiple roles and features from the command line using Ocsetup. For more information concerning this, see the next section of this chapter, "Unattended Installation of Roles and Features," and also see Chapter 2, "Deploying Server Core," and Chapter 3, "Initial Configuration," for instructions on how to create answer files using Windows SIM.

> **Tip**   Type **ocsetup /?** at a command prompt for a list of command-line switches that you can use with Ocsetup.exe.

Unattended Installation of Roles and Features

You can add roles and features to a Server Core installation during an unattended installation. To do this, first create your basic answer file using the procedures outlined in Chapters 2 and 3. Then follow the steps described in this section to configure your answer file to add roles and features automatically at the end of the installation process. For example, to configure your answer file to install the Windows Server Backup feature and the DNS Server role automatically, follow these steps:

1. Open your answer file using Windows SIM. Your answer file should have already been configured to automate the deployment of Server Core using the techniques outlined in Chapters 2 and 3.

2. In the Windows Image pane of Windows SIM, make sure your Server Core install image is open and then expand Packages, Foundation, and finally Microsoft-Windows-ServerCore-Package.

3. Right-click Microsoft-Windows-ServerCore-Package and choose Add To Answer File from the shortcut menu, as shown here.

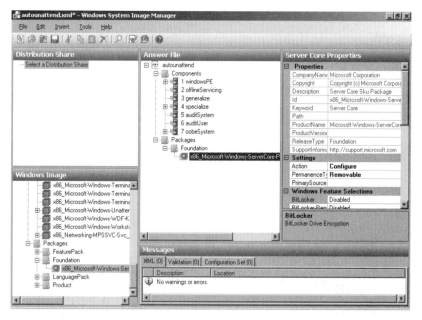

4. In the Properties pane, scroll down until the setting DNS-Server-Core-Role becomes visible, and then click in the box to the right of this setting to display a drop-down arrow. Click the arrow and change the value of this setting to Enabled.

5. Click in the box to the right of the WindowsServerBackup setting to display a drop-down arrow, and then click the arrow and change the value of this setting to Enabled, as shown here.

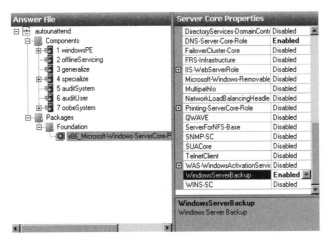

6. Validate your answer file and save it onto a USB flash drive as Autounattend.xml.

7. Insert your Windows Server 2008 product DVD into the DVD drive of the system on which you will be installing Server Core. Insert the USB flash drive containing your answer file into the system as well.

8. Reboot the system and install Server Core in unattended mode using the settings contained in your answer file.

9. Log on to your new installation and verify that the DNS Server role and Windows Server Backup feature have been successfully installed, as shown here.

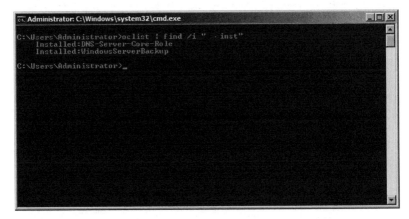

Note   If you install a particular role service or feature during an unattended install, you must also configure your answer file to install all roles, role services, and features that your particular role service or feature depends upon.

The *<servicing>* section of the answer file used in the previous scenario looks like this:

```
<servicing>
    <package action="configure">
        <assemblyIdentity name="Microsoft-Windows-ServerCore-Package"
version="6.0.6001.18000" processorArchitecture="x86" publicKeyToken="31bf3
856ad364e35" language="" />
        <selection name="DNS-Server-Core-Role" state="true" />
        <selection name="WindowsServerBackup" state="true" />
    </package>
</servicing>
```

As mentioned in the section "Installing Multiple Roles and Features Using Ocsetup with an Answer File," earlier in this chapter, you can also use Windows SIM to create answer files that you can use with the /unattendfile switch of Ocsetup. These answer files contain only a *<servicing>* section and are thus different than answer files used to automate Windows Setup. However, answer files for both purposes are created the same way using Windows SIM as demonstrated in the previous procedure.

Sysprep Support for Server Roles

As shown in Table 4-3, not all server roles support Sysprep. If you run the Sysprep /Generalize command against a Server Core installation that has certain server roles installed, those roles may not continue to function after imaging and deployment. For server roles that don't support Sysprep, you must install and configure the roles after imaging and deployment using either Ocsetup.exe.

Table 4-3   Sysprep Support for Server Roles in Server Core

Role	Sysprep Support?
Active Directory Domain Services (AD DS)	No
Active Directory Lightweight Directory Services (AD LDS)	No
DHCP Server	Yes
DNS Server	No
File Services	No
Hyper-V (virtualization)	No
Print Services	No
Streaming Media Services	No
Web Server (IIS)	Yes (in most scenarios)

Permanently Removing Unneeded Roles and Features

You can reduce the disk footprint of a Server Core installation by permanently removing the binaries for unneeded server roles and features from your hard drive. Another reason for doing this is to ensure that an administrator doesn't accidentally add a role or feature to a Server Core computer that is supposed to perform a fixed function.

> **Caution**   Permanently removing the binaries for installing unneeded server roles and features is a one-way operation. Once you remove the binaries for a particular role or feature, there is no way to bring these binaries back and thus no way to install that role or feature. So if you realize later that you need that particular role or feature, your only option is to uninstall and reinstall your entire Server Core installation.

To remove the binaries for unneeded server roles and features from your hard drive permanently, follow these steps:

1. Type **pkgmgr /up:*package_name*** at a command prompt, where *package_name* is the package name of the role or feature you want to remove.

2. Repeat step 1 for each role or feature you want to remove.

3. Reboot the system to complete the removal of the roles and features that you specified in the previous steps. You may need to wait some time for the removal process to finish.

Now when you type **oclist**, you no longer see the roles or features you removed.

To remove a package permanently using Package Manager, you must specify its full package name rather than the short version used by Ocsetup. The full package names of the role and feature packages available for permanent removal on 64-bit versions of Server Core are as follows:

- Microsoft-Hyper-V-Package~31bf3856ad364e35~amd64~~6.0.6001.18000

- Microsoft-Windows-BLB-Package~31bf3856ad364e35~amd64~~6.0.6001.18000

- Microsoft-Windows-DFSN-ServerCore~31bf3856ad364e35 ~amd64~~6.0.6001.18000

- Microsoft-Windows-DFSR-ServerEdition-Package~31bf3856ad364e35 ~amd64~~6.0.6001.18000

- Microsoft-Windows-DhcpServerCore-Package~31bf3856ad364e35 ~amd64~~6.0.6001.18000

- Microsoft-Windows-DirectoryServices-ADAM-SrvFnd-Package~31bf3856ad364e35 ~amd64~~6.0.6001.18000

- Microsoft-Windows-DirectoryServices-DomainController-SrvFnd-Package
  ~31bf3856ad364e35~amd64~~6.0.6001.18000

- Microsoft-Windows-DNS-Server-Core-Role-Package
  ~31bf3856ad364e35~amd64~~6.0.6001.18000

- Microsoft-Windows-FailoverCluster-Core-Package
  ~31bf3856ad364e35~amd64~~6.0.6001.18000

- Microsoft-Windows-FileReplication-Package
  ~31bf3856ad364e35~amd64~~6.0.6001.18000

- Microsoft-Windows-IIS-WebServer-Core-Package
  ~31bf3856ad364e35~amd64~~6.0.6001.18000

- Microsoft-Windows-Internet-Naming-Service-SC-Package
  ~31bf3856ad364e35~amd64~~6.0.6001.18000

- Microsoft-Windows-MultipathIo-Package~31bf3856ad364e35
  ~amd64~~6.0.6001.18000

- Microsoft-Windows-NetworkLoadBalancingHeadlessServer-Package
  ~31bf3856ad364e35~amd64~~6.0.6001.18000

- Microsoft-Windows-NFS-ServerFoundation-Package~31bf3856ad364e35
  ~amd64~~6.0.6001.18000

- Microsoft-Windows-Printing-ServerCore-Package~31bf3856ad364e35
  ~amd64~~6.0.6001.18000

- Microsoft-Windows-QWAVE-Package~31bf3856ad364e35
  ~amd64~~6.0.6001.18000

- Microsoft-Windows-RemovableStorageManagementCore-Package
  ~31bf3856ad364e35~amd64~~6.0.6001.18000

- Microsoft-Windows-SecureStartup-OC-Package~31bf3856ad364e35
  ~amd64~~6.0.6001.18000

- Microsoft-Windows-SNMP-SC-Package~31bf3856ad364e35
  ~amd64~~6.0.6001.18000

- Microsoft-Windows-SUA-Core-Package~31bf3856ad364e35
  ~amd64~~6.0.6001.18000

- Microsoft-Windows-Telnet-Client-Package~31bf3856ad364e35
  ~amd64~~6.0.6001.18000

Note If you are working with a 32-bit version of Server Core and want to remove the previously listed packages permanently using Package Manager, you can do so by just changing *amd64* to *x86* in each of the package names.

Chapter 5
Local Management

Local management of a Server Core installation is primarily performed from the command prompt. Server Core does include a few graphical user interface (GUI) tools, such as Registry Editor and Notepad, but you have to perform most configuration and management tasks using command-line tools and scripts when you are managing a Server Core installation locally. This chapter covers starting and customizing the command prompt, running multiple commands, performing conditional processing, and working with environment variables. The chapter also includes a command reference so you can know what commands can be performed to manage a given role or feature or to perform a specific task. Finally, the chapter briefly covers managing Server Core locally using Windows Management Instrumentation (WMI) scripting.

Using the Command Prompt

The Windows Command Prompt (Cmd.exe) is the shell presented to an administrator the first time he or she logs on to a newly installed Server Core installation. You can perform most administrative tasks locally from the command prompt. However, many tasks are much easier to perform remotely using Microsoft Management Console (MMC) consoles. For more information on remotely managing Server Core, see Chapter 6, "Remote Management." To use the command prompt effectively when locally managing a Server Core installation, you must be familiar with various aspects of the Windows Command Prompt.

Starting the Command Prompt

When you log on to a Server Core installation, a command prompt window automatically opens with the user's profile directory (C:\Users*username* or %USERPROFILE%) as the current directory. This means, for example, that if you log on using the local Administrator account, the following prompt is displayed:

```
C:\Users\Administrator>
```

Changing the Current Directory of the Default Command Prompt

You can change the current directory of the default command prompt (that is, the one that opens when you log on to Server Core) by editing the Shell registry value, a REG_SZ type value found in the location HKLM\SOFTWARE\Microsoft\Windows NT\CurrentVersion\Winlogon.

By default, the data for this registry value is set to the following string:

```
cmd.exe /c "cd /d "%USERPROFILE%" & start cmd.exe /k runonce.exe /
AlternateShellStartup"
```

If you change "%USERPROFILE%" to "%WINDIR% in this value data, Server Core automatically opens a command prompt with C:\Windows as its current directory when you log on to your server.

Using the Run and RunOnce Registry Keys

The reason to have Runonce.exe /AlternateShellStartup in the data for the Shell registry key described in the previous section is to enable processing of the Run and RunOnce registry keys on Server Core. These registry keys are found in the following locations:

- HKLM\Software\Microsoft\Windows\CurrentVersion\Run

- HKCU\Software\Microsoft\Windows\CurrentVersion\Run

- HKLM\Software\Microsoft\Windows\CurrentVersion\RunOnce

Any commands specified by the RunOnce registry key are run the first time a user logs on to Server Core but not for subsequent logons. Any commands specified by the Run key are run every time the user logs on. For example, to cause Notepad to run every time users log on to Server Core, open the Default value under the Run key and type **notepad.exe** as the data for the value.

> **Note** There is no RunOnce registry key in the HKCU hive on Server Core. There are also no RunServices registry keys.

Start a Command Prompt When No Command Prompt Is Visible

If you accidentally close the initial command prompt, you can get it back again as follows:

1. Open Task Manager by pressing Ctrl+Shift+Esc.
2. Click New Task to display the Create New Task dialog box.
3. Type **cmd** and click OK.
4. Close Task Manager if it's no longer needed.

A new command prompt that is opened in this way has the system folder (C:\Windows\System32 or %SystemRoot%\System32) as its current directory.

Another way you can re-open a command prompt is to press Ctrl+Alt+Del and log off your server and then log back on again by entering your credentials. You can also start Task Manager by pressing Ctrl+Alt+Del to display the Microsoft Windows logon screen and then clicking Start Task Manager.

Tip   You can also type **logoff** at the command prompt to log off your Server Core installation.

Starting Additional Command Prompt Windows

You can open a second command prompt by typing **start cmd** from within your first command prompt. Then you can open additional command prompt windows if needed. Any new command prompts that are opened in this way are sometimes called *nested command prompts*, and they automatically have the system folder as their current directory. Normally, when you use the Start Cmd command to open additional command prompts, the windows are tiled, as shown in Figure 5-1.

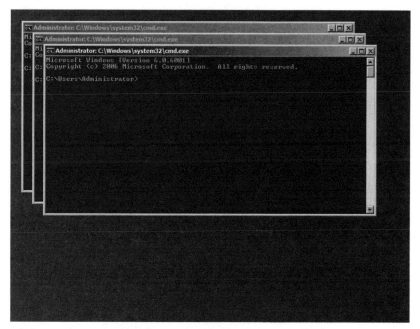

Figure 5-1   Tiled command prompt windows

Starting a Command Prompt at a Specified Drive or Directory

You can start a command prompt at a specific drive or directory by using the /k switch for Cmd.exe. For example, to open a command prompt with C:\Windows\Temp as its current directory, type this:

start cmd /k "cd C:\Windows\Temp"

This command starts a second command prompt and changes the current directory to C:\Windows\Temp by running the command **cd C:\Windows\Temp** within the second command prompt. The /k switch means that the second command prompt remains open after the Cd command executes. Another way of doing this is to use an environment variable as follows:

start cmd /k "cd %WINDIR%\Temp"

Note that using %TEMP% instead of %WINDIR%\Temp in this command opens the new command prompt at the user's Temp directory, not the system Temp directory.

Another example is to open a new command prompt with the E: drive as its current directory, as follows:

start cmd /k E:

> **Note** When you open a new command prompt at the root of a volume as just described, the new command prompt is positioned directly on top of the old one rather than being tiled.

Starting a Command Prompt Using Parameters

Cmd.exe has other parameters besides the /k switch used in the previously described procedures. Here's the general syntax of Cmd.exe on Windows Server 2008:

cmd [{/c | /k}] [/s] [/q] [/d] [{/a | /u}] [/t:FG] [/e:{on | off}] [/f:{on | off}] [/v:{on | off}] [String]

Table 5-1 provides more information concerning each of these parameters.

Table 5-1   Parameters for Cmd.exe

Parameter	Description
/c	Carries out the command specified by String and then stops.
/k	Carries out the command specified by String and then continues.
/s	Modifies the treatment of String after /c or /k.
/q	Turns the echo off.
/d	Disables execution of AutoRun commands.
/a	Formats internal command output to a pipe or a file as American National Standards Institute (ANSI).
/u	Formats internal command output to a pipe or a file as Unicode.

Table 5-1   Parameters for Cmd.exe

Parameter	Description
/t:FG	Sets the foreground F and background G colors. Valid hexadecimal digits that can be used as the values for F and G are: 0 = Black 1 = Blue 2 = Green 3 = Aqua 4 = Red 5 = Purple 6 = Yellow 7 = White 8 = Gray 9 = Light blue A = Light green B = Light aqua C = Light red D = Light purple E = Light yellow F = Bright white
/e:on	Enables command extensions.
/e:off	Disables commands extensions.
/f:on	Enables file and directory name completion.
/f:off	Disables file and directory name completion.
/v:on	Enables delayed environment variable expansion.
/v:off	Disables delayed environment variable expansion.
String	Specifies the command you want to carry out.
/?	Displays help at the command prompt.

Working with Multiple Command Prompts

You can move command prompts around on the Server Core background by dragging their title bars in the usual fashion. You can also maximize and minimize command prompts as needed, but you have to tile them manually. Because Server Core does not have a taskbar, minimized command prompts look different on Server Core than on a Full installation of Windows Server 2008 (as shown in Figure 5-2). Readers who recall using Windows 3.1 will see the difference.

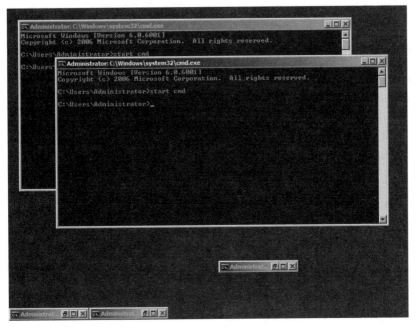

Figure 5-2 Minimized command prompt windows in Server Core

Closing a Command Prompt

If you no longer need a particular command prompt window, just type **exit** from within it to close it.

Customizing the Command Prompt

You can customize your Server Core command prompt to make it easier to use or read. Customization can be performed by editing the properties of Cmd.exe (as shown in Figure 5-3), which can be accessed by clicking in the command prompt window and pressing Alt+Spacebar+P.

Customizations made to Cmd.exe are retained across reboots and apply to any command prompt windows you open. The following sections cover some suggested customizations to make it easier to administer Server Core locally from the command prompt.

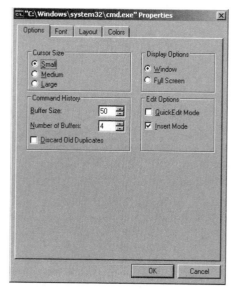

Figure 5-3   Configuring the properties of Cmd.exe

Increasing the History Buffer

If you want, you can increase the command history buffer to almost 5,000 commands, which means you can access previously typed commands easily by using the up and down arrows to select them from the buffer. To increase the buffer capacity, on the Options tab, under Command History, type **999** for Buffer Size and type **5** for Number Of Buffers.

Simplifying Cut and Paste

To simplify the process of using cut and paste functions in Server Core, on the Options tab, under Edit Options, select both the Quick Edit Mode and Insert Mode check boxes. Doing this allows you to copy and paste within the command prompt window (and between command prompt windows) simply by doing the following:

- To copy text, hold down your left mouse button and drag over the text to select it. Then right-click anywhere in the command window to copy the selected text to the clipboard.

- To paste text from the clipboard into the command prompt, right-click anywhere in the command prompt window and the text is pasted at the location of the cursor.

Increasing the Screen Buffer

Another performance enhancement you can configure can make it easier for you to scroll and view the output of previously executed commands. To do this, on the Layout tab, under Screen Buffer Size, type **9999** for Height.

Additional Customizations

Other customizations you may want to make to improve readability (for example, for accessibility reasons) include the following:

- On the Layout tab, under Screen Buffer Size, increase Width as desired.

- On the Font tab, increase the size of the font as desired.

- On the Layout tab, under Window Size, increase Height, Width, or both as desired.

- On the Colors tab, change the color of the text and background as desired.

Tip You can also select Full Screen under Display Options on the Options tab to have the command prompt always open in Full Screen mode instead of as a window. If you do this and later want to switch to Window mode, press Alt+Enter while in Full Screen mode. You can use Alt+Enter to toggle between Full Screen mode and Window mode.

Customizing the Background

You can also change the default background color of Server Core by using Registry Editor to modify the Background value found in the location HKCU\Control Panel\Colors.

Note After making this registry change, you need to log off and then log back on again for the change to take effect.

The data for Background specifies the Red-Green-Blue (RGB) value for the background. The default value is the string "29 95 122", and this can be changed to anything from "0 0 0" (black) to "255 255 255" (white). Table 5-2 lists some common RGB values you can use for customizing the background.

Table 5-2   RGB Values for Common Colors

Color	RGB Value
Red	255 0 0
Green	0 255 0
Blue	0 0 255
Cyan	0 255 255
Magenta	255 0 255
Yellow	255 255 0
White	255 255 255
Black	0 0 0

Note   The maximum length of a string that you use at the command prompt is 8,191 characters. This limitation applies to the command line, to individual environment variables (such as the PATH variable) that are inherited by other processes, and to all environment variable expansions. In addition, this limitation also applies to batch file processing if you use the command prompt to run batch files.

Running Multiple Commands

There are several ways that you can run multiple commands by typing a single command line. These methods include the following:

■ Using the ampersand (&) symbol to separate multiple commands on a single command line. For example, typing **notepad & regedit** at the command prompt opens both Notepad and Registry Editor. When you use single ampersands like this, Cmd.exe runs the first command, then the second command, and so on until all the commands have been executed. All the commands specified are executed even if one or more of them fail.

■ Using a double ampersand (&&) symbol to separate multiple commands on a single command line. For example, the following command can be used to install a Multiple Activation Key (MAK) key for a volume-licensed Server Core installation and then activate the installation using this key:

cscript C:\Windows\system32\slmgr.vbs /ipk XXXXX-XXXXX-XXXXX-XXXXX-XXXXX && cscript C:\Windows\system32\slmgr.vbs /ato

When you use &&, a command following a && executes only if the command preceding that && executes successfully.

■ Using a double bar (||) symbol to separate multiple commands on a single command line. When you use double bars like this, a command following a || executes only if the command preceding that || fails.

You can also use parentheses to group chains of commands together in various ways if desired.

Command Redirection

You can use redirection operators to redirect command input and output streams as desired. Table 5-3 describes some commonly used operators you can use to perform command redirection.

Table 5-3   Command Redirection Operators

Operator	Description
>	Writes the command output to a file or device
<	Reads the command input from a file instead of the keyboard
> >	Appends the command output to the end of a file without deleting information already in the file

In addition, you can use the bar (|) operator to pipe the output of one command to use it as input for another command. For example, you can enumerate the installed roles and features on a Server Core installation, save it to a text file, and open that file in Notepad using a single command line, as follows:

oclist | find " Installed" > installed.txt & notepad installed.txt

Working with Environment Variables

Environment variables define the behavior of the command shell or operating system. There are two types of environment variables:

- **System environment variables**   These define the global behavior of the operating system and are available to all system processes. System environment variables are predefined and can be modified only by administrators.

- **Local environment variables**   These define the behavior of the environment for the currently running instance of Cmd.exe. Local environment variables are available only when the current user is logged on.

You can use environment variables in commands to represent their value. For example, typing **cd %WINDIR%** changes the current directory to C:\Windows.

Table 5-4 lists all predefined environment variables on Windows Server 2008 with their type (system or local) and function.

Table 5-4   Predefined Environment Variables on Server Core

Variable	Type	Description
%ALLUSERSPROFILE%	Local	Returns the location of the All Users Profile
%APPDATA%	Local	Returns the default location where applications store data
%CD%	Local	Returns the current directory
%CMDCMDLINE%	Local	Returns the exact command line used to start the current command prompt window
%CMDEXTVERSION%	System	Returns the version number of the current Command Processor Extensions
%COMPUTERNAME%	System	Returns the computer's name

Table 5-4   Predefined Environment Variables on Server Core

Variable	Type	Description
%COMSPEC%	System	Returns the exact path to Cmd.exe
%DATE%	System	Returns the current date
%ERRORLEVEL%	System	Returns the error code for the most recently used command (non-zero generally means error)
%HOMEDRIVE%	System	Returns the drive letter for the user's home directory
%HOMEPATH%	System	Returns the full path of the user's home directory
%HOMESHARE%	System	Returns the network path to the user's shared home directory
%LOGONSERVER%	Local	Returns the name of the domain controller that validated the current logon session
%NUMBER_OF_PROCESSORS%	System	Returns the number of processors installed on the computer
%OS%	System	Returns the operating system name
%PATH%	System	Specifies the search path for executable files
%PATHEXT%	System	Returns a list of file extensions that Windows considers executable
%PROCESSOR_ARCHITECTURE%	System	Returns the processor chip architecture
%PROCESSOR_IDENTIFIER%	System	Returns the processor description
%PROCESSOR_LEVEL%	System	Returns the processor model number
%PROCESSOR_REVISION%	System	Returns the processor revision number
%PROMPT%	Local	Returns the command prompt settings for the current interpreter
%RANDOM%	System	Returns a random decimal number between 0 and 32767
%SYSTEMDRIVE%	System	Returns the drive containing the operating system root directory
%SYSTEMROOT%	System	Returns the location of the operating system root directory
%TEMP% and %TMP%	System and User	Returns the default temporary directories used by applications available to the logged on user
%TIME%	System	Returns the current time

Table 5-4 Predefined Environment Variables on Server Core

Variable	Type	Description
%USERDOMAIN%	Local	Returns the domain of the user's account
%USERNAME%	Local	Returns the name of the currently logged on user
%USERPROFILE%	Local	Returns the location of the current user's profile
%WINDIR%	System	Returns the location of the operating system directory

Displaying Environment Variables

You can use the Set command to display the value of an environment variable. For example, to return the value of the current logon server, execute this command:

```
C:\Users\Administrator>set logonserver
LOGONSERVER=\\SEA-SC1
```

You can also just type **set l** to display all environment variables that begin with the letter *L*, as follows:

```
C:\Users\Administrator>set l
LOCALAPPDATA=C:\Users\Administrator\AppData\Local
LOGONSERVER=\\SEA-SC1
```

> **Tip** To display all environment variables defined on the computer, type **set** at a command prompt.

Defining New Environment Variables

To define a new environment variable named XYZ and assign it the value Hello World, run the following command:

```
C:\Users\Administrator>set XYZ=Hello World
```

Verify the variable exists:

```
C:\Users\Administrator>set x
XYZ=Hello World
```

Remove the variable as follows:

```
C:\Users\Administrator>set XYZ=
```

Using Environment Variables

To use an environment variable in a command or script, you must enclose it with percent signs (%). For example, the first command listed here defines an environment variable named INS; and then the second command uses this variable to display all currently installed roles and features:

set IN=" Installed"

oclist | find %IN%

You can also use the Setx command to set persistent System and User environment variables. For example, to perform the previous action but make %IN% a persistent system environment variable, replace the first command with the following:

setx IN "\" Installed\""

> **Note**   After running Setx, you must open a new command prompt window using Task Manager for the new variable to be defined. Using Start Cmd to open a child window won't do this.

Commands for Common Tasks

To become an expert in administering Server Core from the command prompt, you need the following:

- Familiarity with using the command-line tools included in Windows Server 2008

- Knowledge of which tools can be used to administer a particular role or feature, or to perform a particular type of task

Familiarity with using command-line tools is gained only through experience, but the best place to get started learning about these tools is the Windows Server 2008 Command-Line Reference, a comprehensive listing of command-line tools. You can access this as a zipped Windows Help file named WinCmdRef.chm that you can download from the Microsoft Download Center at http://www.microsoft.com/downloads/ *(just search for "Windows Command Reference"). This command reference is also available online as part of the Windows Server 2008 Technical Library on Microsoft TechNet.*

Another good reference for Windows Server 2008 commands is the book Windows Command-Line Administrator's Pocket Consultant, Second Edition *by William Stanek (Microsoft Press, 2008).*

Table 5-5 provides a quick guide to some of the more useful command-line tools you can use for performing specific types of administrative tasks in Server Core. The table is not meant to be complete and the task areas in it are not ordered in any particular way. Also, while most of the tools listed in this table are command-line tools, a few of them are scripts or GUI tools. For information concerning tools used for administering specific roles or features, see the chapter in this book that covers that particular role or feature.

Table 5-5   Tools for Performing Common Types of Tasks

Task	Tools
View system information	■ Msinfo32
	■ Set
	■ Systeminfo
View user information	■ Whoami
Manage users and groups	■ Net accounts
	■ Net group
	■ Net localgroup
	■ Net user
View or change computer name	■ Hostname
	■ Netdom renamecomputer
Join or leave a domain	■ Netdom join
Log off or shut down	■ Logoff
	■ Shutdown
Configure networking	■ Ipconfig
	■ Netsh interface
	■ Netsh routing
	■ Route
Configure Windows Firewall	■ Netsh advfirewall
Configure Internet Protocol security (IPsec)	■ Netsh ipsec
	■ Scregedit.wsf
Activate Windows	■ Slmgr.vbs
Manage services	■ Net continue
	■ Net pause
	■ Net start
	■ Net stop
	■ Sc
	■ Tasklist
Manage processes	■ Taskkill
	■ Tasklist
	■ Taskmgr
Manage tasks	■ At
	■ Schtasks
Collect and analyze performance data	■ Logman
	■ Relog
	■ Typeperf

Table 5-5   Tools for Performing Common Types of Tasks

Task	Tools
View events and manage event logs	■ Wevtutil
Manage disks and storage	■ Compact ■ Defrag ■ Diskpart ■ Diskraid ■ Mountvol
Manage Volume Shadow Copy Service (VSS)	■ Vssadmin
Manage file systems and file permissions	■ Cacls ■ Convert ■ Fsutil ■ Icacls ■ Takeown
Manage files	■ Openfiles ■ Sigverif
Manage shares and share permissions	■ Net share
Manage the registry	■ Reg ■ Regedit
Install and manage drivers	■ Driverquery ■ Pnputil ■ Sc
Install and manage updates	■ Pkgmgr ■ Scregedit.wsf ■ Systeminfo ■ Wuauclt ■ Wusa
Install roles and features	■ Oclist ■ Ocsetup
Install applications	■ Msiexec
Manage Group Policy	■ Gpresult ■ Gpupdate ■ Secedit
Manage certificates	■ Certreq ■ Certutil

Table 5-5   Tools for Performing Common Types of Tasks

Task	Tools
Manage Terminal Services (Remote Desktop for Administration)	■ Change
	■ Logoff
	■ Msg
	■ Mstsc
	■ Qappsrv
	■ Qprocess
	■ Query
	■ Qwinsta
	■ Reset session
	■ Rwinsta
	■ Shadow
	■ Tscon
	■ Tsdiscon
	■ Tskill

Most Windows Sysinternals tools, such as Process Explorer and Process Monitor, also work on Server Core. For more information about Windows Sysinternals, see http://technet.microsoft.com/en-us/sysinternals/default.aspx.

Using Scripts

You can administer a Server Core installation locally using scripts. *Scripts* provide a way of automating complex or repetitive administration tasks to simplify the job of managing servers in your environment.

Server Core includes a number of administration scripts written in Visual Basic Scripting Edition (VBScript), including Slmgr.vbs, which is used for activating Windows, and Prncnfg.vbs and Prnmngr.vbs, which are used for configuring and managing printers. Server Core also includes a Windows Script (.wsf) file named Scregedit.wsf, which can be used to perform several initial server configuration tasks that otherwise would require editing the registry. To look at some examples of using this script, see Chapter 3, "Initial Configuration."

You can also write your own custom scripts to administer Server Core. These custom scripts could be any of the following:

■ Batch (.bat) files

■ VBScript (.vbs) scripts

■ Windows Script File (.wsf) files

VBScript or Windows Script files can also use the built-in Windows Management Instrumentation (WMI) providers in Server Core to automate the administration of many aspects of Server Core using scripts.

Note   Windows PowerShell cannot be installed on Server Core because of its dependencies upon the .NET Framework. However, PowerShell can be used to manage a Server Core installation remotely, provided that the PowerShell commands you use rely only on WMI. For more information on managing Server Core remotely using PowerShell, see Chapter 6.

WMI Support in Server Core

Server Core supports a subset of WMI functionality found in a Full installation of Windows Server 2008. To examine WMI support in Server Core, we must consider WMI providers, namespaces, and classes.

For information about the architecture and operation of WMI, see the topic "Windows Management Instrumentation," which can be found on MSDN at http://msdn.microsoft.com/en-us/library/aa394582(VS.85).aspx.

WMI Provider Support in Server Core

A *WMI provider* is a Component Object Model (COM) server that communicates with managed objects to access data and event notifications, such as the registry or a Simple Network Management Protocol (SNMP) device. A default installation of Server Core includes all the WMI providers found on a Full installation of Windows Server 2008 except for Win32_OfflineFilesProvider (the Offline Files WMI provider), which isn't found on Server Core because Server Core doesn't support the Offline Files feature.

The script ListProviders.vbs, shown here, can be used to display a list of all WMI providers installed in the root\CIMV2 namespace:

ListProviders.vbs
```
strComputer = "."

Set objWMIService=GetObject("winmgmts:{impersonationLevel=impersonate}!\\" & _
    strComputer & "\root\cimv2")

Set colWin32Providers = objWMIService.InstancesOf("__Win32Provider")

For Each objWin32Provider In colWin32Providers
    WScript.Echo objWin32Provider.Name
Next
```

Here is the result of running this script on a new installation of Server Core that has no roles or features installed:

```
C:\Users\Administrator>Cscript ListProviders.vbs

Microsoft (R) Windows Script Host Version 5.7
Copyright (C) Microsoft Corporation. All rights reserved.
```

```
ProviderSubSystem
Msft_ProviderSubSystem
MS_NT_EVENTLOG_EVENT_PROVIDER
MS_Power_Management_Event_Provider
RegPropProv
WmiPerfInst
RegProv
Microsoft|ServerComponentProvider|V1.0
MS_NT_EVENTLOG_PROVIDER
SoftwareLicensingProduct_Provider
WmiPerfClass
VolumeChangeEvents
Standard Non-COM Event Provider
MSVSS__PROVIDER
WMIPingProvider
WMI Self-Instrumentation Event Provider
RegistryEventProvider
Cimwin32A
NamedJobObjectLimitSettingProv
RouteProvider
SCM Event Provider
WhqlProvider
DFSProvider
MS_Shutdown_Event_Provider
CIMWin32
NamedJobObjectActgInfoProv
WBEMCORE
RouteEventProvider
MSVDS__PROVIDER
NamedJobObjectSecLimitSettingProv
UserProfileProvider
MSIProv
Win32_WIN32_TERMINALSERVICE_Prov
SessionProvider
NamedJobObjectProv
WMI Kernel Trace Event Provider
SECRCW32
SystemConfigurationChangeEvents
SoftwareLicensingService_Provider
DskQuotaProvider
Win32ClockProvider
Win32_OsBaseline
```

Note Installing roles or services on Server Core may install additional WMI
providers and make additional WMI namespaces and classes available.

WMI Namespace Support in Server Core

A *WMI namespace* is a logical database of WMI classes and their instances. A default installation of Server Core includes all the WMI namespaces found on a Full installation of Windows Server 2008 except for the following namespaces:

```
root\Microsoft
root\Microsoft\HomeNet
root\aspnet
```

The script ListNamespaces.vbs, shown here, can be used to display a list of all WMI namespaces on a computer:

ListNamespaces.vbs
```
strComputer = "."
Call EnumNameSpaces("root")

Sub EnumNameSpaces(strNameSpace)
    WScript.Echo strNameSpace
    Set objWMIService=GetObject _
        ("winmgmts:{impersonationLevel=impersonate}\\" & _
            strComputer & "\" & strNameSpace)

    Set colNameSpaces = objWMIService.InstancesOf("__NAMESPACE")

    For Each objNameSpace In colNameSpaces
        Call EnumNameSpaces(strNameSpace & "\" & objNameSpace.Name)
    Next
End Sub
```

Here is the result of running this script on a new installation of Server Core that has no roles or features installed:

```
C:\Users\Administrator>Cscript ListNamespaces.vbs

Microsoft (R) Windows Script Host Version 5.7
Copyright (C) Microsoft Corporation. All rights reserved.

root
root\subscription
root\subscription\ms_409
root\DEFAULT
root\DEFAULT\ms_409
root\CIMV2
root\CIMV2\Security
root\CIMV2\Security\MicrosoftTpm
root\CIMV2\ms_409
root\CIMV2\TerminalServices
root\CIMV2\TerminalServices\ms_409
root\Cli
root\Cli\MS_409
```

```
root\nap
root\SECURITY
root\RSOP
root\RSOP\User
root\RSOP\User\S_1_5_21_4263854795_656447682_2170832392_500
root\RSOP\User\S_1_5_21_3602272388_85614491_4261325587_500
root\RSOP\User\ms_409
root\RSOP\Computer
root\RSOP\Computer\ms_409
root\WMI
root\WMI\ms_409
root\directory
root\directory\LDAP
root\directory\LDAP\ms_409
root\Policy
root\Policy\ms_409
root\Hardware
root\Hardware\ms_409
```

> **Note** Installing roles or features on Server Core can also install additional WMI namespaces. For example, if you install the DNS Server role on the computer, the root\MicrosoftDNS namespace is also installed.

WMI Classes Supported by Server Core

A *class* is a template for a type of object that you can manage using WMI. For example, the Win32_LogicalDisk class is a template for logical disks on Windows machines, and WMI uses this class to generate one instance of Win32_LogicalDisk for each installed disk.

The primary classes for working with Windows-based operating systems are the Win32 classes included in the Root\Cimv2 namespace. A default installation of Server Core includes all the Win32 classes found on a Full installation of Windows Server 2008 except for the following classes:

```
Win32_OfflineFilesAssociatedItems
Win32_OfflineFilesCache
Win32_OfflineFilesChangeInfo
Win32_OfflineFilesConnectionInfo
Win32_OfflineFilesDirtyInfo
Win32_OfflineFilesFileSysInfo
Win32_OfflineFilesItem
Win32_OfflineFilesPinInfo
Win32_OfflineFilesSuspendInfo
Win32_PerfFormattedData_NETCLRData_NETCLRData
Win32_PerfFormattedData_NETCLRNetworking_NETCLRNetworking
Win32_PerfFormattedData_NETDataProviderforOracle_NETDataProviderforOracle
Win32_PerfFormattedData_NETDataProviderforSqlServer_NETDataProvider
forSqlServer
Win32_PerfFormattedData_NETFramework_NETCLRExceptions
```

```
Win32_PerfFormattedData_NETFramework_NETCLRInterop
Win32_PerfFormattedData_NETFramework_NETCLRJit
Win32_PerfFormattedData_NETFramework_NETCLRLoading
Win32_PerfFormattedData_NETFramework_NETCLRLocksAndThreads
Win32_PerfFormattedData_NETFramework_NETCLRMemory
Win32_PerfFormattedData_NETFramework_NETCLRRemoting
Win32_PerfFormattedData_NETFramework_NETCLRSecurity
Win32_PerfFormattedData_RemoteAccess_RASPort
Win32_PerfFormattedData_RemoteAccess_RASTotal
Win32_PerfFormattedData_Spooler_PrintQueue
Win32_PerfFormattedData_TapiSrv_Telephony
Win32_PerfFormattedData_TermService_TerminalServicesSession
Win32_PerfRawData_NETCLRData_NETCLRData
Win32_PerfRawData_NETCLRNetworking_NETCLRNetworking
Win32_PerfRawData_NETDataProviderforOracle_NETDataProviderforOracle
Win32_PerfRawData_NETDataProviderforSqlServer_NETDataProviderforSqlServer
Win32_PerfRawData_NETFramework_NETCLRExceptions
Win32_PerfRawData_NETFramework_NETCLRInterop
Win32_PerfRawData_NETFramework_NETCLRJit
Win32_PerfRawData_NETFramework_NETCLRLoading
Win32_PerfRawData_NETFramework_NETCLRLocksAndThreads
Win32_PerfRawData_NETFramework_NETCLRMemory
Win32_PerfRawData_NETFramework_NETCLRRemoting
Win32_PerfRawData_NETFramework_NETCLRSecurity
Win32_PerfRawData_RemoteAccess_RASPort
Win32_PerfRawData_RemoteAccess_RASTotal
Win32_PerfRawData_Spooler_PrintQueue
Win32_PerfRawData_TapiSrv_Telephony
Win32_PerfRawData_TermService_TerminalServicesSession
```

Note   Some of the classes listed here become available once you install roles on Server Core. For example, the Win32_PerfFormattedData_Spooler_PrintQueue class becomes available when you install the Print Services role.

The script ListClasses.vbs, shown here, can be used to display a list of all classes (potentially manageable objects) for the Root\Cimv2 namespace:

ListClasses.vbs

```
strComputer = "."
strWMINamespace = "\root\CIMV2"

Set objWMIService = GetObject("winmgmts:\\" & strComputer & strWMINamespace)
Set colClasses = objWMIService.SubclassesOf()

For Each objClass In colClasses
            WScript.Echo objClass.Path_.Path
Next
```

The output from running this script on a Server Core installation is too long to include in this book.

Installing roles or features on Server Core can make additional classes available if additional WMI namespaces are installed. For example, if you install the DNS Server role, the following two classes also become available for the Root\Cimv2 namespace:

```
Win32_PerfFormattedData_DNS_DNS
Win32_PerfRawData_DNS_DNS
```

Additional sample scripts for retrieving information about the kinds of objects that can be used in WMI scripts can be found in the Script Repository on Microsoft TechNet at http://www.microsoft.com/technet/scriptcenter/scripts/misc/wmi/ default.mspx?mfr=true.

Using WMIC

You can also use the Windows Management Instrumentation Command-line (WMIC) to administer a Server Core installation from the command prompt. WMIC provides an interactive command prompt for directly accessing and modifying system configuration using WMI. WMI can be run in one of two modes:

■ Interactively, by typing **wmic** to display the wmic:root\cli> prompt, which allows you to type a series of WMIC commands

■ Non-interactively, by typing a single WMIC command

The following are two examples of using WMIC in non-interactive mode to manage various aspects of a Server Core installation:

■ To determine whether your computer has the Server Core or Full installation installed, use the following command:

```
C:\Windows\system32>wmic path win32_operatingsystem get
OperatingSystemSKU /value
OperatingSystemSKU=41
```

To determine from this output if Server Core is installed, first convert decimal 41 to its hexadecimal value, 29. Then, look this value up in the table on *http://msdn.microsoft.com/en-us/library/ms724358.aspx,* and you'll find that you are running Server Core Enterprise Without Hyper-V Edition.

■ To view a list of software updates that have been applied to your computer, use the following command:

```
C:\Windows\system32>wmic qfe list
No Instance(s) Available.
```

The command output indicates that no updates have been installed on the computer.

For more information on WMIC, see the article "WMIC– Take Command-line Control over WMI," which can be found on Microsoft Technet at http://technet.microsoft.com/ en-us/library/bb742610.aspx, *or consult the "WMIC" entry on MSDN at* http://msdn.microsoft.com/en-us/library/aa394531(VS.85).aspx.

Chapter 6
Remote Management

Server Core can be managed remotely using a variety of approaches, including using Remote Desktop or TS Remote App, using Microsoft Management Console (MMC) snap-ins and the Remote Server Administration Tools (RSAT), using Windows Remote Shell (WinRS), using Group Policy, and, to some extent, using Windows PowerShell. This chapter examines each of these remote administration methods and demonstrates how to set them up and use them to manage Server Core.

Using Remote Desktop

You can use Remote Desktop (also known as Terminal Services for Administration) to administer a Server Core installation remotely in exactly the same way you would administer it from the local console of the server. By default, Remote Desktop is disabled on Server Core, so before you can use Remote Desktop to manage a Server Core installation remotely, you must first enable Remote Desktop on the server. This can be done in several ways, as the next sections illustrate.

Enabling Remote Desktop Using Scregedit.wsf

You can use the Scregedit.wsf script to enable Remote Desktop on your Server Core installation by logging on locally to your server and doing the following:

```
C:\Users\Administrator> cscript %windir%\system32\scregedit.wsf /ar 0
Microsoft (R) Windows Script Host Version 5.7
Copyright (C) Microsoft Corporation. All rights reserved.

Registry has been updated.
```

To verify that the registry change has been made, do this:

```
C:\Users\Administrator>cscript %windir%\system32\scregedit.wsf /ar /v
Microsoft (R) Windows Script Host Version 5.7
Copyright (C) Microsoft Corporation. All rights reserved.

System\CurrentControlSet\Control\Terminal Server fDenyTSConnections
View registry setting.
0
```

A value of 0 for the fDenyTSConnections registry value means that Remote Desktop is enabled on the system, while a value of 1 means that Remote Desktop is disabled. If you later decide you want to disable Remote Desktop on your Server Core installation, type **cscript %windir%\system32\scregedit.wsf /ar 1** at a command prompt.

Tip If your current directory is C:\Windows\System32, you can shorten these commands by omitting the %Windir%\System32\ portion of them.

Enabling Remote Desktop using Scregedit.wsf also automatically enables the Remote Desktop rule group in Windows Firewall.

Enabling Remote Desktop Using an Answer File

You can use an answer file to enable Remote Desktop during an unattended install of Server Core. You do this as follows:

1. Add the following component to the specialize configuration pass of your answer file:

   Microsoft-Windows-TerminalServices-LocalSessionManager

2. In the Properties pane, click the box to the right of the fDenyTSConnections setting; a drop-down arrow appears. Click the drop-down arrow and select False, as shown here.

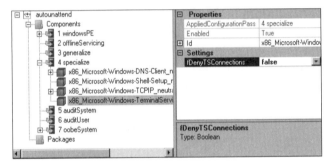

3. Add the following component to the oobeSystem configuration pass of your answer file:

   Microsoft-Windows-Shell-Setup\FirstLogonCommands\SynchronousCommand

4. In the Properties pane, type **C:\Windows\system32\netsh advfirewall firewall set rule group="Remote Desktop" new enable=yes** in the box beside CommandLine and type **1** (or another number if you are running multiple FirstLogonCommands) in the box beside Order.

Tip You can also use WinRS to enable Remote Desktop remotely on a Server Core installation. See the section "Using WinRS to Administer Server Core in a Domain," later in this chapter, for more information.

Using Scregedit.wsf to Require Network Level Authentication for Remote Desktop

By default, when Remote Desktop is enabled on Server Core, computers running versions of Microsoft Windows earlier than Windows Vista are allowed to connect. You can use the Scregedit.wsf script to prevent computers running versions earlier than Windows Vista from connecting to Server Core using Remote Desktop by logging on locally to your server and doing the following:

```
C:\Users\Administrator>cscript %windir%\system32\scregedit.wsf /cs 1
Microsoft (R) Windows Script Host Version 5.7
Copyright (C) Microsoft Corporation. All rights reserved.

Registry has been updated.
```

Doing this increases the security of your Server Core installation by requiring that the client you are using to administer Server Core uses Network Level Authentication. For more information, see the section "Configuring Remote Desktop to Require Network Level Authentication," in Chapter 3, "Initial Configuration."

Using an Answer File to Require Network Level Authentication for Remote Desktop

You can use an answer file to require that Network Level Authentication be used for Remote Desktop connections. You do this as follows:

1. Add the following component to the specialize configuration pass of your answer file:

   Microsoft-Windows-TerminalServices-RDP-WinStationExtensions

2. In the Properties pane, click the box to the right of the UserAuthentication setting and type **1** to require Network Level Authentication, as shown here.

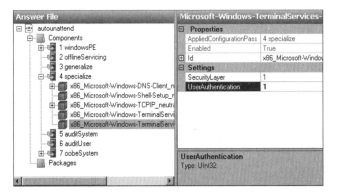

You can also configure the SecurityLayer setting to specify how your server and Remote Desktop clients authenticate each other prior to a Remote Desktop connection being established. The possible values for this setting are shown in Table 6-1.

Table 6-1   The SecurityLayer Setting Values

SecurityLayer	Result
0	Remote Desktop Protocol (RDP) is used by the server and the client for authentication prior to a Remote Desktop connection being established. Use this setting if you are working in a heterogeneous network environment.
1	The server and the client negotiate the method for authentication prior to a Remote Desktop connection being established (this is the default value). Use this setting if all your client computers are running Windows.
2	Transport Layer Security (TLS) is used by the server and the client for authentication prior to a Remote Desktop connection being established. Use this setting for maximum security.

Using Remote Desktop to Administer Server Core

To use Remote Desktop to administer a Server Core installation, log on to a computer running Windows Vista or Windows Server 2008 and do the following:

1. Press the Windows key+R to open the Run text box.

2. Type **mstsc** and press Enter to open Remote Desktop Connection.

3. Type the name, either NetBIOS or Fully Qualified Domain Name (FQDN), or the Internet Protocol (IP) address of your Server Core installation in the Computer text box.

4. Click Options and type the name of a user account that has administrative privileges on the Server Core installation. Be sure to type this user name in the form *servername\username* (if the server belongs to a workgroup) or *domainname\username* (if the server belongs to a domain), as shown here.

5. Click Connect. When the Windows Security dialog box appears, type the password for the user account you are using to administer Server Core, as shown here.

6. Select Remember My Credentials if you want Credential Manager to save the credentials for this user.

7. Click OK. After a few moments, Remote Desktop Connection should connect to your remote Server Core installation (as shown here), and you then can administer your server using the same methods described in Chapter 5, "Local Management."

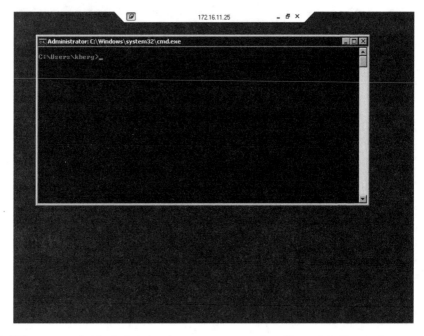

8. When you are finished administering your server, type **logoff** to end the Terminal Services session with the remote server.

Note Like the Full installation option of Windows Server 2008, the Server Core installation option supports two simultaneous Terminal Services connections for remote administration.

Using TS Remote App for Publishing Cmd to Administer Server Core

You don't have to use the full version of Remote Desktop to administer Server Core remotely. Instead, you can use Terminal Services RemoteApp to publish the Server Core command interpreter (Cmd) so that it can be started on another computer. That way, the command prompt running on Server Core programs can be accessed remotely using Terminal Services and appear as if it is running on your local administrator workstation. TS RemoteApp programs run side by side with local programs and can be maximized or minimized just as local programs can be.

To use TS Remote App to publish Cmd running on Server Core, do the following:

1. On the Server Core installation you want to manage, enable Remote Desktop using one of the methods described earlier in this chapter. Then enable the Remote Administration rule group in Windows Firewall by typing the following command:

   netsh advfirewall firewall set rule group="Remote Administration" new enable=yes

2. Now install the Terminal Server role service of the Terminal Services role on a computer running Windows Server 2008. Alternatively, you can install the Terminal Server Tools component of RSAT on a computer running Windows Server 2008, which you can then use as a Terminal Services management station.

3. On your terminal server (or on your Terminal Services management station), click Start, Administrative Tools, Terminal Services, and finally TS RemoteApp Manager to open the TS RemoteApp console on your terminal server.

4. Click Connect To Computer in the right Actions pane to open a Select Computer dialog box. Select the Another Computer option and type or browse to the name of your Server Core computer. Click OK. Your TS RemoteApp Manager console is now connected to the Server Core computer.

5. In the Actions pane, click Add RemoteApp Programs, Next, and Browse to open the Choose A Program dialog box. Browse the local file system of the Server Core computer using the connection to the C$ administrative share on that computer until you find and select the C$\Windows\System32\Cmd.exe file. Click Open, Next, and finally Finish.

6. In the RemoteApp Programs list, right-click Cmd.exe and select Create .rdp File from the drop-down menu to start the RemoteApp Wizard. Click Next twice and then click Finish. The folder C:\Program Files\Packaged Programs opens on your Server Core computer, displaying the .rdp file for Cmd.

7. Double-click the .rdp file and click Connect. The Windows Security dialog box appears. Type credentials that have administrative privileges on the remote Server Core installation and then click OK.

8. Click Run to run Cmd.exe on the remote Server Core installation and display the remote command interpreter as a command-prompt window on your desktop. You can also copy the .rdp file to any computer using the RDC 6.0 client or later and use it to connect to your Server Core installation and open the command prompt on the Server Core computer.

Managing Terminal Services on Server Core

You can use the following two MMC snap-ins for remotely managing Terminal Services (Remote Desktop for Administration) on Server Core:

- Terminal Services Manager

- Terminal Services Configuration

You can use these snap-ins on a Full installation of Windows Server 2008 that has the Terminal Services role installed, or you can use them on a computer running Windows Vista or Windows Server 2008 that has the RSAT installed.

You can also manage Terminal Services (Remote Desktop for Administration) from the command prompt on a Server Core installation. Table 6-2 lists the commands that you can use to manage Terminal Services locally on Server Core.

Table 6-2 Commands Available for Locally Managing Terminal Services on Server Core

Command	Description
Change logon	Enables or disables logons to a terminal server
Logoff	Logs a user off a session and deletes the session
Msg	Sends a message to a user or group of users
Query process	Displays information about processes running on a terminal server
Query session	Displays information about sessions on a terminal server
Query user	Displays information about user sessions on a terminal server
Tscon	Connects to another existing terminal server session
Tsdiscon	Disconnects a client from a terminal server session
Tskill	Ends a process
Shutdown	Shuts down a terminal server

For example, to display all Terminal Services sessions on a Server Core installation named SEA-SC2, do this:

```
C:\Users\tallen>query session /server:SEA-SC2
 SESSIONNAME       USERNAME            ID  STATE   TYPE      DEVICE
 services                               0  Disc
 console           tallen               1  Active
 rdp-tcp#0         Administrator        2  Active  rdpwd
 rdp-tcp                             65536  Listen
```

The output of the Query Session command shows that administrator Tony Allen (tallen@contoso.com) is logged on locally to the Server Core installation, while the default Administrator account (either a built-in local or a domain account) is logged on remotely using a Remote Desktop session.

To log the remote Administrator off of the Server Core installation forcibly, log off session 2 as follows:

```
C:\Users\tallen>logoff 2 /server:SEA-SC2
```

Verify the result:

```
C:\Users\tallen>query session /server:SEA-SC2
 SESSIONNAME       USERNAME            ID  STATE   TYPE      DEVICE
 services                              0  Disc
 console           tallen             1  Active
 rdp-tcp                           65536  Listen
```

Using WinRS

You can use WinRS to administer a Server Core installation remotely from the command line. WinRS is a command-line tool included in both Windows Vista and the Full installation of Windows Server 2008, which relies on Windows Remote Management (WinRM) to execute remote commands, especially for headless servers. WinRM is Microsoft's implementation of the WS-Management protocol, a standard Simple Object Access Protocol (SOAP)–based, firewall-friendly protocol that enables hardware and operating systems from different vendors to interoperate. You can think of WinRM as the server side and WinRS the client side of WS-Management.

Configuring WinRM on Server Core

To enable WinRM on a Server Core installation, you need to run a configuration command that creates a "listener" that can respond to WinRS commands issued from other computers. The configuration command also opens an exception for WinRM in Windows Firewall. To enable WinRM, do the following:

```
C:\Users\tallen>winrm quickconfig
WinRM is not set up to allow remote access to this machine for management.
The following changes must be made:

Create a WinRM listener on HTTP://* to accept WS-Man requests to any IP
on this machine.
Enable the WinRM firewall exception.

Make these changes [y/n]? y

WinRM has been updated for remote management.

Created a WinRM listener on HTTP://* to accept WS-Man requests to any IP
on this machine.
WinRM firewall exception enabled.
```

Note For more information on configuring WinRM, type **winrm help config** at a command prompt.

Using WinRS to Administer Server Core in a Domain

The basic syntax for WinRS commands is as follows:

winrs -r:*target command*

where *target* is the name (NetBIOS or FQDN) of the Server Core installation that has had WinRM enabled on it, and *command* is any command string that you want to execute on the Server Core installation. For example, to use WinRS to enable Remote Desktop remotely on a Server Core installation named SEA-SC2, type the following command on any computer running Windows Vista or on a Full installation of Windows Server 2008:

winrs -r:SEA-SC2 cscript %WINDIR%\system32\scregedit.wsf /ar 0

When you type this command on a computer running Windows Vista, for example, the command is executed remotely on the targeted Server Core installation and the command output is piped back to the command shell on your computer running Windows Vista:

```
C:\Users\Administrator>winrs -r:SEA-SC2 cscript %windir%
\system32\scregedit.wsf /ar 0
Microsoft (R) Windows Script Host Version 5.7
Copyright (C) Microsoft Corporation. All rights reserved.

Registry has been updated.
```

You can do anything using WinRS that you can do at the local command prompt on Server Core. For example, you can perform the initial configuration of your Server Core installation, install and uninstall roles and features on your server, and perform other tasks.

Note For more information on the syntax of WinRS commands, type **winrs /?** at a command prompt.

Using WinRS to Administer Server Core in a Workgroup

You can use WinRS to administer a Server Core installation that belongs to a workgroup. Before you can do this, however, you must add the name of your computer to the TrustedHosts table of WinRM on your Server Core installation. For example, to enable a computer running Windows Vista named SEA-DESK155 to execute commands remotely on your Server Core installation using WinRM, type the following on your Server Core computer:

```
C:\Users\Administrator>winrm set winrm/config/client @{TrustedHosts=
"SEA-DESK155"}
Client
    NetworkDelayms = 5000
    URLPrefix = wsman
    AllowUnencrypted = false
    Auth
        Basic = false
        Digest = true
        Kerberos = true
        Negotiate = true
        Certificate = true
    DefaultPorts
        HTTP = 80
        HTTPS = 443
    TrustedHosts = SEA-DESK155
```

Requirements for Using WinRS

To use WinRS to administer a Server Core installation remotely, each of the following must be true:

- Your local computer must be running either Windows Vista or a Full installation of Windows Server 2008.

- You must enable a WinRM listener on the Server Core installation, and you must open the WinRM exception in Windows Firewall on the Server Core installation; the Winrm quickconfig command can be used to do this.

- You must execute your WinRS commands using administrator credentials on the Server Core installation. If you are not currently logged on to your computer using such credentials, you can use the Net use command to connect to the Server Core computer using such credentials. For example, to connect to a Server Core installation named SEA_SC2 using the credentials of administrator Tony Allen (tallen@contoso.com), type **net use \\SEA-SC2\IPC$ /u:CONTOSO\ tallen** at a command prompt. Type Tony's password when prompted to do so, and then you can execute commands remotely on the Server Core installation using WinRS.

- Commands or scripts that are executed using WinRS must have no user interface dependencies. This means that you cannot execute commands that prompt you to Press Any Key when they are typed at the local console or require any other interactive response.

Configuring WinRM and WinRS Using Group Policy

You can use Group Policy to configure security for both WinRM and WinRS. The relevant policy settings are found in the following locations:

- Computer Configuration\Policies\Administrative Templates\Windows Components\Windows Remote Management (WinRM)

- Computer Configuration\Policies\Administrative Templates\Windows Components\Windows Remote Shell

Using MMC Snap-ins and RSAT

You can use Microsoft Management Console (MMC) snap-ins to administer a Server Core installation remotely from a Full installation of Windows Server 2008. You can also install RSAT on either Windows Vista or a Full installation of Windows Server 2008 and use these tools to administer Server Core. The advantage of using RSAT is that it gives you the full complement of MMC consoles; by comparison, on a Full installation of Windows Server 2008, you may be missing some consoles because of certain roles and features not being installed on your server. Using MMC snap-ins or RSAT allows you to administer a Server Core installation the same way that you administer a Full installation—without the need of learning the syntax of many command-line utilities.

Using MMC Consoles to Administer Server Core in a Domain

When you install a server role on a Server Core installation, the appropriate firewall ports needed to manage that role remotely using MMC snap-ins are opened automatically. This means that when you type **start /w ocsetup DNS-Server-Core-Role** at a command prompt on a Server Core installation, the command installs the DNS Server role and enables the Windows Management Instrumentation (WMI) and DNS Service rule groups to allow the DNS snap-in running on another computer to connect to Server Core.

For example, to use the DNS console found under Administrative Tools on a domain controller named FULL161 to administer a Server Core DNS server named SEA-SC2, perform the following steps:

1. On the domain controller, click Start, Administrative Tools, and then DNS to open the DNS Manager console.

2. Right-click the root node of the console and select Connect To DNS Server.

3. In the Connect To DNS Server dialog box, select The Following Computer and type **SEA-SC2** in the text box. Click OK.

4. The DNS Manager console connects to DNS server SEA-SC2. Expand the console tree to display the configuration of DNS server SEA-SC2, as shown here.

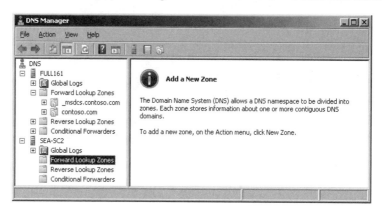

Changing the Focus of an MMC Console

Most (but not all) MMC consoles found under Administrative Tools can have their focus changed to administer a different computer than the local one on which they are being used. Examples of consoles that can have their focus changed include Active Directory Users And Computers, Computer Management, DHCP, DNS, and Event Viewer. Examples of consoles whose focus cannot be changed include Server Manager, Windows Firewall With Advanced Security, and Windows Server Backup.

Using MMC Snap-ins to Administer Server Core

You can also add MMC snap-ins to a new MMC console to administer Server Core remotely. For example, to use the Windows Firewall With Advanced Security snap-in to manage the firewall remotely on a Server Core installation named SEA-SC2, do the following:

1. Press the Windows key+R, type **mmc**, and click OK to open an empty MMC console.

2. Click File, and then click Add/Remove Snap-in. Scroll down the list of snap-ins and double-click Windows Firewall With Advanced Security to select it. When the Select Computer dialog box appears, choose Another Computer and type **SEA-SC2** in the text box, as shown here.

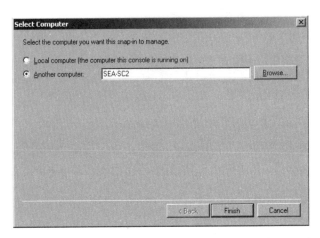

3. Click Finish, and then click OK to add the snap-in to the console. Expand the console tree to view the configuration of Windows Firewall on your Server Core installation.

Some MMC snap-ins require that you also open ports in the firewall on Server Core to use these snap-ins to administer Server Core remotely. For example, for the previous procedure to work, you must first enable the Windows Firewall Remote Management rule group in the firewall on your Server Core installation. This can be done by typing the following command at your Server Core command prompt:

netsh advfirewall firewall set rule group="Windows Firewall Remote Management" new enable=yes

Table 6-3 lists some of the more commonly used MMC snap-ins and the firewall rule group that must be enabled to use these snap-ins to manage Server Core remotely. The general syntax for enabling a rule group in Windows Firewall is as follows:

netsh advfirewall firewall set rule group="*Name of rule group*" new enable=yes

Table 6-3   Rule Groups You Must Enable in Windows Firewall to Allow Remote Management by an MMC Snap-in

MMC Snap-in	Rule Group
Event Viewer	Remote Event Log Management
Services	Remote Service Management
Shared Folders	File And Printer Sharing
Task Scheduler	Remote Scheduled Tasks Management
Reliability And Performance	Performance Logs And Alerts File And Printer Sharing
Windows Firewall With Advanced Security	Windows Firewall Remote Management

Best Practices   The simplest way to configure Windows Firewall on Server Core is to enable remote management of Windows Firewall and then use the Windows Firewall With Advanced Security snap-in on a computer running Windows Vista to make further configuration changes to your firewall. You can also use Group Policy to configure Windows Firewall once the Windows Firewall Remote Management rule group is enabled on your Server Core installation. For more information on using the Windows Firewall With Advanced Security snap-in, see *http://technet .microsoft.com/en-us/network/bb545423.aspx.*

Some MMC snap-ins require further configuration of your Server Core installation before you can use them to administer your server. The following sections describe several of these snap-ins and the additional configuration that they require on the server before they will work remotely against it.

Using the Device Manager Snap-in

To allow the Device Manager snap-in to administer Server Core remotely, perform the following steps:

1. On your Server Core computer, enable the Remote Administration rule group in Windows Firewall.

2. On a Full installation of Windows Server 2008, open a new MMC console by pressing the Windows key+R, typing **mmc**, and clicking OK.

3. Click File, and then Add/Remove Snap-in to open the Add Or Remove Snap-ins dialog box.

4. Double-click Group Policy Object Editor to display the Group Policy Wizard.

5. Click Browse, select Another Computer, and type or browse to the name of your Server Core computer. Then click OK, Finish, and finally OK again. The Group Policy Object Editor is now connected to your Server Core computer.

6. Browse the console tree to find and enable the following policy setting:

   Computer Configuration\Policies\Administrative Templates\System\Device Installation\Allow Remote Access To The PnP Interface.

7. Close the Group Policy Object Editor. Then, on your Server Core computer, type **shutdown -r -t 0** at the command prompt to restart the server.

Note   Device Manager can operate only in "view only" mode when run from a remote computer as described here.

Using the Disk Management Snap-in

To allow the Disk Management snap-in to administer Server Core remotely, perform the following steps:

1. Enable the Remote Volume Management rule group in Windows Firewall on your Server Core installation.

2. Start the Virtual Disk Service (VDS) by typing **sc start vds** at the command prompt. You can also type **sc config vds start= auto** to configure the service to start automatically each time the computer boots.

Using the IP Security Policy Management Snap-in

To allow the IP Security Policies snap-in to administer Server Core remotely, type the following command at the command prompt of your Server Core installation:

cscript %windir%\system32\scregedit /im 1

Using the Reliability And Performance Snap-in

No additional configuration is needed to use the Reliability And Performance snap-in, but it can monitor only performance data, not reliability data, on a remote Server Core installation.

Enabling Any MMC Snap-in to Administer Server Core

You can allow any MMC snap-in to administer Server Core remotely by enabling the Remote Administration rule group in Windows Firewall on your Server Core installation. To do this, type the following command:

netsh advfirewall firewall set rule group="Remote Administration" new enable=yes

As described in the section "Using MMC Consoles to Administer Server Core in a Domain," earlier in this chapter, some snap-ins require additional configuration to get them to work properly for remotely administering Server Core.

Using MMC Snap-ins to Administer Server Core in a Workgroup

To use MMC snap-ins to administer a Server Core installation that belongs to a workgroup, you need to perform the following actions on your Server Core installation:

1. Enable the required rule groups in Windows Firewall (see the previous section for details).

2. Use Cmdkey to specify different credentials for MMC connections.

For example, to use the Services snap-in on a computer running Windows Vista to administer the services on a Server Core installation named SEA-SC1 that belongs to a workgroup, perform the following steps:

1. On your Server Core installation, type the following command to enable the Remote Service Management rule group in Windows Firewall:

   netsh advfirewall firewall set rule group="Remote Service Management" new enable=yes

2. Open a command prompt on your computer running Windows Vista and type the following command:

   cmdkey /add:SEA-SC1 /user:Administrator /pass:Pa$$w0rd

   In this command, the local Administrator account on SEA-SC1 has the password **Pa$$w0rd.**

3. Open the Services console under Administrative Tools (or add the Services snap-in to an empty MMC console), right-click the root node, and select Connect To Another Computer. Type **SEA-SC1** in the dialog box and then click OK.

You can now manage services remotely on your stand-alone Server Core installation from either a stand-alone or domain-joined computer running Windows Vista or Windows Server 2008.

Note   Cmdkey is not needed for certain consoles, including Event Viewer and Scheduled Tasks.

Using RSAT to Administer Server Core in a Domain

Windows Server 2003 included the Administration Tools Pack (Adminpak.msi), which provided server management tools that allowed administrators to manage Windows 2000 Server and Windows Server 2003 family servers remotely. The Administration Tools Pack could be installed on workstations running Windows XP to provide administrators with a full set of MMC consoles on their workstations for administering servers across their network.

With Windows Server 2008, however, the Administration Tools Pack has been replaced with the Remote Server Administration Tools (RSAT), which enables administrators to manage Windows Server 2008 roles and features remotely from a computer running Windows Vista with Service Pack 1 (SP1). RSAT is included as an optional feature on all editions of Windows Server 2008, and versions of RSAT for installing on 32-bit and 64-bit versions of Windows Vista SP1 Business, Enterprise, and Ultimate editions are available for download from the Microsoft Download Center at *http://www.microsoft.com/downloads/*. For detailed information concerning the downloadable version of RSAT and the administrative tools it includes, see *http://support.microsoft.com/kb/941314*.

Using RSAT on either Windows Vista or a Full installation of Windows Server 2008, you can administer roles and features remotely on a Server Core installation the same way that you would administer them on a Full installation of Windows Server 2008.

Note RSAT cannot be installed on Server Core.

Installing RSAT on a Full Installation of Windows Server 2008

To install RSAT on a Full installation of Windows Server 2008, perform the following steps:

1. Start the Add Features Wizard from either Server Manager or Initial Configuration Tasks.

2. Expand the Remote Server Administration Tools check box and select the check boxes under it for the specific role and feature administration tools that you want to install on your server. Alternatively, you can select the Remote Server Administration Tools check box to install all the role and feature administration tools on your server.

Installing RSAT on Windows Vista SP1

To install RSAT on Windows Vista with Service Pack 1, perform the following steps:

1. Download the appropriate Windows Installer (.msi) package (either 32-bit or 64-bit) by using the links found at *http://support.microsoft.com/kb/941314*.

2. Double-click the downloaded Windows Update Standalone Installer package (Windows6.0-KB941314-x86.msu or Windows6.0-KB941314-x64.msu) to start the Setup wizard. Follow the prompts to complete the installation.

3. Open Control Panel and click Programs.

4. Under Programs And Features, click Turn Windows Features On Or Off. Respond to the User Account Control prompt as required.

5. In the Windows Features dialog box, scroll down and expand the Remote Server Administration Tools check box, then select the check boxes under it to install the remote administration snap-ins and tools that you want to install. You can also install all role and feature administration tools by selecting the Remote Server Administration Tools check box. Click OK when finished.

6. Configure your Start menu to display the Administration Tools shortcut by right-clicking Start and clicking Properties. Then on the Start Menu tab, click Customize, scroll down to System Administrative Tools, and select Display On The All Programs Menu And The Start Menu. Click OK when finished.

Note   Installing RSAT also provides additional snap-ins that you can add to a blank MMC console.

Using RSAT to Administer Server Core Remotely in a Domain

You can use the RSAT tools to administer roles and features remotely on a Server Core installation that belongs to the same domain as your management workstation. As described in the section "Using MMC Snap-ins to Administer Server Core," earlier in this chapter, you may need to configure Windows Firewall on your remote Server Core installation for some RSAT tools to be able to connect.

For example, to use RSAT on a computer running Windows Vista in the contoso.com domain to manage the DNS Server role on a Server Core installation named SEA-SC2 that belongs to the same domain, follow these steps:

1. On your Server Core installation, begin by enabling the necessary rule groups in Windows Firewall to allow remote administration of roles and features on the server. To allow remote administration of all roles and features on the server, type the following command:

   netsh advfirewall firewall set rule group="Remote Administration" new enable=yes

   As described in the section "Using MMC Consoles to Administer Server Core in a Domain," earlier in this chapter, some snap-ins require additional configuration to get them to work properly for remotely administering Server Core.

2. Click Start, Administrative Tools, and then DNS to open the DNS Manager console. Before the console opens, a Connect To DNS Server dialog box appears. Select the The Following Computer option, type **SEA-SC1**, and click OK. DNS Manager opens and lets you remotely manage your Server Core DNS server.

Tip   When you install RSAT using the procedures outlined earlier in this section, some MMC consoles found under Administrative Tools (such as the Windows Firewall With Advanced Security) cannot have their focus changed. To administer Windows Firewall remotely on a Server Core installation, you can open a blank MMC, add the Windows Firewall With Advanced Security snap-in, and change the focus of the snap-in so you can manage Windows Firewall on the remote Server Core installation.

Using RSAT to Administer Server Core Remotely in a Workgroup

You can use the RSAT tools to administer roles and features remotely on a Server Core installation that belongs to a workgroup. As described in the section "Using MMC Snap-ins to Administer Server Core," earlier in this chapter, you may need to configure Windows Firewall on your remote Server Core installation for some RSAT tools to be able to connect.

For example, to use RSAT on a computer running Windows Vista to manage the DNS Server role on a stand-alone Server Core installation named SEA-SC1, do this:

1. On your Server Core installation, begin by enabling the necessary rule groups in Windows Firewall to allow remote administration of roles and features on the server. To allow remote administration of all roles and features on the server, type the following command:

   netsh advfirewall firewall set rule group="Remote Administration" new enable=yes

   As described in the section "Using MMC Consoles to Administer Server Core in a Domain," earlier in this chapter, some snap-ins require additional configuration to get them to work properly for remotely administering Server Core.

2. Open a command prompt on your Windows Vista computer and type the following command:

   cmdkey /add:SEA-SC1 /user:Administrator /pass:Pa$$w0rd

   In the previous command, the local Administrator account on SEA-SC1 has the password Pa$$w0rd.

3. Click Start, Administrative Tools, and then DNS to open the DNS Manager console. Before the console opens, a Connect To DNS Server dialog box appears. Select the The Following Computer option, type **SEA-SC1**, and click OK. DNS Manager opens and lets you remotely manage your Server Core DNS server.

Using Other GUI Tools

You can use other graphical user interface (GUI) tools besides MMC snap-ins to manage certain aspects of Server Core remotely. These tools include the following:

- Windows Explorer
- Task Scheduler
- Registry Editor

The following procedures assume that your remote Server Core installation belongs to the same domain as your Windows Vista management workstation. If your Server Core installation belongs to a workgroup, type the command **cmdkey /add:***servername*

/**user:***username* /**pass:***password* to provide administrator credentials (that is, *username* and *password*) for these tools to be able to manage your Server Core installation (*servername*) remotely.

Using Windows Explorer Remotely

You can use Windows Explorer on a computer running Windows Vista or a computer running a Full installation of Windows Server 2008 to manage the file system remotely on a Server Core installation. To do this, follow these steps:

1. On the Server Core installation, enable the Remote Administration rule group in Windows Firewall by typing the following command:

    netsh advfirewall firewall set rule group="File and Printer Sharing" new enable=yes

2. On the computer from which you want to manage your Server Core installation's file system remotely, press the Windows key+R, type *servername*\C$ (where *servername* is the name of your Server Core installation), and click OK. Specify credentials that have administrative privileges on the Server Core installation if you are prompted to do so.

3. Windows Explorer opens a new window focused on the root of the system drive on your Server Core installation. You now can browse the system drive on your remote server, create or delete files and folders, and perform other operations depending upon your level of privileges.

You can use the previous procedure with any share, whether administrative or user-created. You can also use the Net use command to map persistent network drives to shares on your remote Server Core installation. For example, you can type **net use** Z: *servername*\C$ /**persistent:yes** at the command prompt, where *servername* is the name of your remote Server Core installation.

Using Task Scheduler Remotely

You can use Task Scheduler on a computer running Windows Vista or a computer running a Full installation of Windows Server 2008 to create, delete, configure, and manage tasks remotely on a Server Core installation. To do this, follow these steps:

1. Click Start, All Programs, Accessories, and then System Tools, and open Task Manager on your computer running Windows Vista.

2. Right-click the root node in Task Scheduler and select Connect To Another Computer.

3. Type the name of the remote Server Core installation and click OK.

Using Registry Editor Remotely

You can use Registry Editor on a computer running Windows Vista or a computer running a Full installation of Windows Server 2008 to edit the registry on a Server Core installation remotely. To do this, follow these steps:

1. Press the Windows key+R, type **regedit**, and click OK to open Registry Editor on your computer running Windows Vista.

2. Select File, and then Connect Network Registry.

3. Type the name of the remote Server Core installation and click OK.

Using Group Policy

You can use Group Policy to manage Server Core remotely the same way that you manage any other computer running Windows. You cannot install Group Policy MMC consoles on Server Core; you must manage Server Core remotely using Group Policy MMC consoles on another computer, such as a Full installation of Windows Server 2008 or a computer running Windows Vista with RSAT installed.

For more information on using Group Policy to manage Active Directory–based networks, see http://technet.microsoft.com/en-us/windowsserver/grouppolicy/default.aspx.

Group Policy Tools on Server Core

Server Core does include two command-line Group Policy tools:

- **Gpupdate** Used to refresh local Group Policy settings and Group Policy settings stored in Active Directory Domain Services. Detailed syntax for using this command can be found at *http://technet.microsoft.com/en-us/library/bb490983.aspx* or by typing **gpupdate /?** at a command prompt.

- **Gpresult** Used to display Resultant Set of Policy (RSoP) information. Detailed syntax for using this command can be found in the Windows Server 2008 Command Reference (available from the Microsoft Download Center, as cited earlier in this chapter) or by typing **gpresult /?** at a command prompt.

Using WMI Filters to Administer Server Core with Group Policy

You can use WMI filters to ensure that the policy settings contained in a particular Group Policy Object (GPO) are applied only to Server Core installations. WMI filters are used to determine the scope of Group Policy based on computer attributes such as operating system and free hard disk space.

To create a WMI filter that will cause the Seattle SC GPO to be applied only to Server Core computers, perform the following steps:

1. On your domain controller, open Group Policy Management from Administrative Tools.

2. Right-click the WMI Filters node in the console tree and select New.

3. Click Add and type the information in the screenshot shown here to create a WMI Query Language (WQL) query that uses the OperatingSystemSKU property of the Win32_OperatingSystem WMI class to determine whether a given computer is running Server Core Standard (13), Enterprise (14), or Datacenter (15) edition.

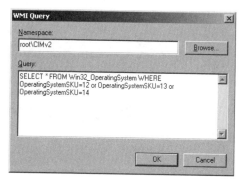

4. Click OK to add the WQL query to your WMI filter and type a name and description for your filter, as shown here.

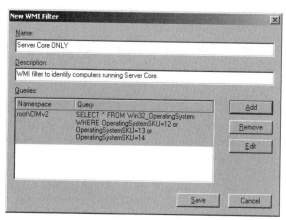

5. Click Save to save your WMI filter.

6. Under Group Policy Objects, select Seattle SC GPO.

7. On the Scope tab, under WMI Filtering, select Server Core ONLY and click Yes when the dialog box appears, as shown here. The WMI filter is now linked to the GPO.

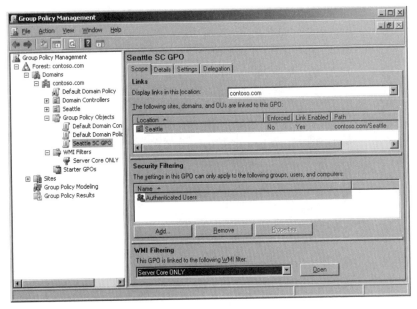

When Group Policy is processed by a computer targeted by the GPO, the WQL query contained in the WMI filter is evaluated against the WMI repository on the targeted computer. If the query evaluates as True, the GPO is applied; if the query evaluates as False, the GPO is not applied.

Note GPOs can have only one WMI filter, but you can link a single WMI filter to multiple GPOs.

Managing Local Group Policy on Server Core

You can manage local Group Policy on Server Core by using the Group Policy Object Editor running on a Full installation of Windows Server 2008 or on a computer running Windows Vista SP1. To do this, follow these steps:

1. Open a new MMC console by pressing the Windows key+R, typing **mmc**, and clicking OK.

2. Click File, and then Add/Remove Snap-in to open the Add Or Remove Snap-ins dialog box.

3. Double-click Group Policy Object Editor to display the Group Policy Wizard.

4. Click Browse, select Another Computer, and type or browse to the name of the remote Server Core computer.

5. Click OK, Finish, and finally OK again. Group Policy Object Editor is now connected to your remote Server Core computer, and you can browse local policy on the computer and configure it as desired.

Using Windows PowerShell

You can use Windows PowerShell to administer Server Core remotely, but only if you use WMI in your PowerShell commands. PowerShell WMI commands typically take the following form:

Get-WMIObject *WMIclass* -computername *servername*

where *WMIclass* is the WMI class you want to access and *servername* is the name of the remote Server Core installation.

> **Tip**   To display a list of all WMI classes supported on a remote Server Core installation, type **Get-WMIObject –list –computername** *servername* at the PowerShell command prompt.

Here is an example of using PowerShell (running on a computer running Windows Vista on which PowerShell 1.0 has been installed) to display a list of services installed on a Server Core installation named SEA-SC2 that belongs to the same domain. Perform the following steps:

1. On the Server Core installation, enable the Windows Management Instrumentation (WMI) rule group in Windows Firewall by typing the following command:

   netsh advfirewall firewall set rule group="Windows Management Instrumentation (WMI)" new enable=yes

2. On the computer running Windows Vista, open the PowerShell command prompt by clicking Start, All Programs, Windows PowerShell 1.0, and finally Windows PowerShell.

3. Use the command shown here to display a list of services installed on SEA-SC2:

```
PS C:\Users\tallen> Get-WMIObject Win32_Service -computername SEA-SC2


ExitCode  : 0
Name      : AeLookupSvc
ProcessId : 964
StartMode : Auto
State     : Running
Status    : OK

ExitCode  : 1077
```

```
Name       : AppMgmt
ProcessId  : 0
StartMode  : Manual
State      : Stopped
Status     : OK
. . .
```

Note You cannot install Windows PowerShell 1.0 locally on Server Core.

For a quick introduction to using Windows PowerShell, see the Windows PowerShell Getting Started Guide on MSDN at http://msdn.microsoft.com/en-us/library/ aa973757(VS.85).aspx.

Chapter 7

Active Directory Domain Services Role

Active Directory Domain Services (AD DS) is a central component of the Microsoft Windows platform and provides the means and tools to manage the identities and relationships that make up enterprise network environments. This chapter covers key tasks such as installing the AD DS role on Server Core, managing domain controllers running on Server Core, and working with Read-Only Domain Controllers (RODCs) running on Server Core.

Installing AD DS on Server Core

You cannot use Ocsetup to install the AD DS role on Server Core. Instead, you must use the Dcpromo utility with an answer file to install the role and promote your Server Core installation to a domain controller. You do this by typing the following command at your Server Core command prompt:

dcpromo /unattend:_unattendfile_

where _unattendfile_ is an answer file formatted in standard .ini file format that begins with the heading [DCINSTALL] and in which the remaining lines use the _option=value_ syntax used by .ini files.

Using unattended Dcpromo, you can install the AD DS role on Server Core in various ways, including the following:

- Installing the first domain controller for a new forest

- Installing a replica domain controller into a domain that has an existing domain controller

- Installing the first domain controller for a new domain tree within an existing forest

- Installing the first domain controller for a new child domain within an existing domain tree

You can also use unattended Dcpromo to remove a domain controller from an existing domain, including removal of the last domain controller within a forest. For more information, see the section "Removing a Domain Controller Using Unattended Dcpromo," later in this chapter. In addition, you can use unattended Dcpromo to install or remove an RODC within an existing domain. For more information, see the section "Installing an RODC on Server Core," later in this chapter.

Important   If you are installing a Server Core domain controller into an existing Windows 2000 Server or Windows Server 2003 domain or forest, you must prepare that domain or forest using the Adprep command. See the section "Preparing an Existing Active Directory Environment for Windows Server 2008 Domain Controllers," later in this chapter, for more information.

Creating a New Forest Using Unattended Dcpromo

You can use Dcpromo with an unattend file to create a new forest that has your Server Core installation as its forest root domain controller. For example, to create a new forest root domain named fabrikam.com that has its forest functional level set to Windows Server 2008 level and Pa$$w0rd as its Directory Services Restore Mode administrator account password, perform the following steps:

1. Use Notepad to create an unattend file containing the lines of text shown here and name the file NewForest.txt:

   ```
   [DCINSTALL]
   InstallDNS=yes
   NewDomain=forest
   NewDomainDNSName=fabrikam.com
   DomainNetBiosName=FABRIKAM
   ReplicaOrNewDomain=domain
   ForestLevel=3
   DomainLevel=3
   RebootOnCompletion=yes
   SafeModeAdminPassword=Pa$$w0rd
   ```

2. On the Server Core installation on which you want to install the AD DS role, type **dcpromo /unattend:<*path*>\NewForest.txt**, where <*path*> is the path to your unattend file. If your path contains spaces, you must enclose <*path*>\ *NewForest.txt* in quotes. Typical output from running this command is as follows:

   ```
   C:\Windows>dcpromo /unattend:F:\NewForest.txt
   Checking if Active Directory Domain Services binaries are installed...
   Active Directory Domain Services binaries are being installed.
   Please wait...
   Active Directory Domain Services Setup

   Validating environment and parameters...

   A delegation for this DNS server cannot be created because the
   authoritative parent zone cannot be found or it does not run Windows
   DNS server. If you are integrating with an existing DNS
   infrastructure, you should manually create a delegation to this
   DNS server in the parent zone to ensure reliable name resolution
   from outside the domain fabrikam.com. Otherwise, no action is required.
   ```

```
----------------------------------------
The following actions will be performed:
Configure this server as the first Active Directory domain
controller in a new forest.

The new domain name is fabrikam.com. This is also the name of
the new forest.

The NetBIOS name of the domain is FABRIKAM

Forest Functional Level: Windows Server 2008

Domain Functional Level: Windows Server 2008

Site: Default-First-Site-Name

Additional Options:
  Read-only domain controller: No
  Global catalog: Yes
  DNS Server: Yes

Create DNS Delegation: No

Database folder: C:\Windows\NTDS
Log file folder: C:\Windows\NTDS
SYSVOL folder: C:\Windows\SYSVOL

The DNS Server service will be installed on this computer.
The DNS Server service will be configured on this computer.
This computer will be configured to use this DNS server as its
preferred DNS server.

The password of the new domain Administrator will be the same
as the password of the local Administrator of this computer.
----------------------------------------

Starting...

Performing DNS installation...

Press Ctrl-C to: Cancel

Waiting for DNS installation to finish
...
Waiting for DNS Server service to be recognized... 0

Waiting for DNS Server service to start... 0
```

```
Checking if Group Policy Management Console needs to be installed...
..
Configuring the local computer to host Active Directory Domain Services
....
Creating directory partition: CN=Schema,CN=Configuration,
DC=fabrikam,DC=com; 1585 objects remaining

Creating directory partition: CN=Configuration,DC=fabrikam,DC=com;
1377 objects remaining
.
Creating directory partition: CN=Configuration,DC=fabrikam,DC=com;
1149 objects remaining

Creating directory partition: CN=Configuration,DC=fabrikam,DC=com;
980 objects remaining
.
Creating directory partition: CN=Configuration,DC=fabrikam,DC=com;
853 objects remaining

Creating directory partition: CN=Configuration,DC=fabrikam,DC=com;
702 objects remaining
.
Creating directory partition: CN=Configuration,DC=fabrikam,DC=com;
569 objects remaining

Creating directory partition: CN=Configuration,DC=fabrikam,DC=com;
442 objects remaining
.
Creating directory partition: CN=Configuration,DC=fabrikam,DC=com;
311 objects remaining

Creating directory partition: CN=Configuration,DC=fabrikam,DC=com;
215 objects remaining
.
Creating directory partition: CN=Configuration,DC=fabrikam,DC=com;
92 objects remaining

Creating directory partition: CN=Configuration,DC=fabrikam,DC=com;
0 objects remaining
.
Creating directory partition: DC=fabrikam,DC=com; 0 objects remaining

Creating Active Directory Domain Services objects on the local
Active Directory Domain Controller
.
Configuring service NETLOGON


Configuring service NtFrs
```

```
.
Setting the LSA policy information


Securing SamSs
....
Securing Kerberos Policy
..
The attempted domain controller operation has completed


Configuring the DNS Server service on this computer...
...
```

3. Once your Server Core installation reboots, press Ctrl+Alt+Del and log on as the default Domain Administrator account FABRIKAM\Administrator by typing **Pa$$w0rd** as the password for this account.

Verifying the Unattended Dcpromo Operation

You can verify the result of installing AD DS by using Dcdiag, a command-line utility that analyzes the state of domain controllers and reports any problems. For example, to verify the previous unattended Dcpromo operation, do the following:

```
C:\Users\administrator>dcdiag

Directory Server Diagnosis

Performing initial setup:
   Trying to find home server...
   Home Server = SEA-SC1
   * Identified AD Forest.
   Done gathering initial info.

Doing initial required tests

   Testing server: Default-First-Site-Name\SEA-SC1
      Starting test: Connectivity
         ........................ SEA-SC1 passed test Connectivity

Doing primary tests

   Testing server: Default-First-Site-Name\SEA-SC1
      Starting test: Advertising
         ........................ SEA-SC1 passed test Advertising
      Starting test: FrsEvent
         ........................ SEA-SC1 passed test FrsEvent
      Starting test: DFSREvent
         There are warning or error events within the last 24 hours after the
```

```
SYSVOL has been shared.  Failing SYSVOL replication problems may cause
Group Policy problems.
........................ SEA-SC1 failed test DFSREvent
Starting test: SysVolCheck
........................ SEA-SC1 passed test SysVolCheck
Starting test: KccEvent
........................ SEA-SC1 passed test KccEvent
Starting test: KnowsOfRoleHolders
........................ SEA-SC1 passed test KnowsOfRoleHolders
Starting test: MachineAccount
........................ SEA-SC1 passed test MachineAccount
Starting test: NCSecDesc
........................ SEA-SC1 passed test NCSecDesc
Starting test: NetLogons
........................ SEA-SC1 passed test NetLogons
Starting test: ObjectsReplicated
........................ SEA-SC1 passed test ObjectsReplicated
Starting test: Replications
........................ SEA-SC1 passed test Replications
Starting test: RidManager
........................ SEA-SC1 passed test RidManager
Starting test: Services
........................ SEA-SC1 passed test Services
Starting test: SystemLog
........................ SEA-SC1 passed test SystemLog
Starting test: VerifyReferences
........................ SEA-SC1 passed test VerifyReferences


Running partition tests on : ForestDnsZones
Starting test: CheckSDRefDom
........................ ForestDnsZones passed test CheckSDRefDom
Starting test: CrossRefValidation
........................ ForestDnsZones passed test
CrossRefValidation

Running partition tests on : DomainDnsZones
Starting test: CheckSDRefDom
........................ DomainDnsZones passed test CheckSDRefDom
Starting test: CrossRefValidation
........................ DomainDnsZones passed test
CrossRefValidation

Running partition tests on : Schema
Starting test: CheckSDRefDom
........................ Schema passed test CheckSDRefDom
Starting test: CrossRefValidation
........................ Schema passed test CrossRefValidation
```

```
Running partition tests on : Configuration
   Starting test: CheckSDRefDom
      ........................ Configuration passed test CheckSDRefDom
   Starting test: CrossRefValidation
      ........................ Configuration passed test
CrossRefValidation

Running partition tests on : fabrikam
   Starting test: CheckSDRefDom
      ........................ fabrikam passed test CheckSDRefDom
   Starting test: CrossRefValidation
      ........................ fabrikam passed test CrossRefValidation

Running enterprise tests on : fabrikam.com
   Starting test: LocatorCheck
      ........................ fabrikam.com passed test LocatorCheck
   Starting test: Intersite
      ........................ fabrikam.com passed test Intersite
```

You can also use Dcdiag to perform specific kinds of tests. For example, to test the Domain Name System (DNS) configuration of your domain controller, type **dcdiag / test:DNS** at the command prompt. For more information about using Dcdiag, type **dcdiag /?** at the command prompt.

Customizing the Dcpromo Unattend File for Domain Controller Promotion

You can customize your Dcpromo unattend file in various ways to control how a Server Core installation is promoted to a domain controller. For example, since unattend files are not encrypted, including the password for the Directory Services Restore Mode administrator account in them is not recommended. To resolve this issue, remove the following line from your answer file:

```
SafeModeAdminPassword=Pa$$w0rd
```

Then run Dcpromo and type the password for the DSRM administrator account at the command line as follows:

dcpromo /unattend:E:\newforest.txt SafeModeAdminPassword=Pa$$w0rd

You can control other aspects of your AD DS installation using additional answer file settings not used in the previous scenario. For example, by default the AD DS database is installed in the location %SystemRoot%\Ntds, but you can change this—for example, to another disk volume—by including the following line in your answer file:

```
DatabasePath=E:\ntds
```

Table 7-1 lists the different options you can include in a Dcpromo unattend file used for domain controller promotion, an explanation of what they mean, their possible values, and their default value (if any) when the option is not included in the unattend file.

Table 7-1   Options for Dcpromo Unattend Files Used for Domain Controller Promotion on Windows Server 2008

Option	Explanation	Possible Values	Default Value
AllowDomainReinstall	Specifies whether to recreate an existing domain.	Yes or No	No
AllowDomain-ControllerReinstall	Specifies whether to continue installing this domain controller even though an active domain controller account having the same name is detected. Be sure to specify Yes for this option only if you are certain that the existing account is no longer in use.	Yes or No	No
ApplicationPartitions-ToReplicate	Specifies application partitions to be replicated in the form of space-separated distinguished names, and encloses the entire string in quotation marks. If an asterisk (*) is specified, all application partitions will be replicated.	"*partition_DN_1 partition_DN_2 ...partition_DN_n*"	No default
ChildName	Specifies the DNS name of the child domain in single-label form. For example, specify *headquarters* when the fully qualified domain name (FQDN) is headquarters.con-toso.com.	*child_domain_na me*	No default
ConfirmGc	Specifies whether the domain controller should be designated as a global catalog (GC) server.	Yes or No	Yes (unless you are creating the first domain controller in a new child domain or new domain tree)

Table 7-1   Options for Dcpromo Unattend Files Used for Domain Controller Promotion on Windows Server 2008

Option	Explanation	Possible Values	Default Value
CreateDNSDelegation	Specifies whether to create a DNS delegation referencing this new DNS server. This option can be used only with AD DS–integrated DNS.	Yes or No	Varies depending on your environment
CriticalReplicationOnly	Specifies whether the promotion operation performs only critical replication before reboot and noncritical replication after role installation is completed and the computer reboots.	Yes or No	No
DatabasePath	Specifies the fully qualified path to the directory that contains the AD DS database. This directory must be on a fixed disk on the local computer, and it cannot be specified as a Universal Naming Convention (UNC) path.	*path_to_database _files*	%SystemRoot%\ NTDS
DelegatedAdmin	Specifies the name of the user or group that installs and administers the RODC. If unspecified, only members of the Domain Admins and Enterprise Admins groups can install and administer the RODC.	*username* or *group*	No default
DNSDelegation-Password	Specifies the password of the user name used for creating the DNS delegation. To prompt the user to enter credentials, specify an asterisk (*).	*password* or *	No default

Table 7-1   Options for Dcpromo Unattend Files Used for Domain Controller
Promotion on Windows Server 2008

Option	Explanation	Possible Values	Default Value
DNSDelegationUser-Name	Specifies the user name to be used for creating the DNS delegation. If unspecified, the credentials that you specified for AD DS installation are used.	*username*	No default
DNSOnNetwork	Specifies whether a DNS server already exists on the network. If you specify Yes, the network adapter on your computer must already be configured for name resolution with a DNS server name. Specify No if you want the DNS Server role to be installed on this computer.	Yes or No	Yes
DomainLevel	Specifies the domain functional level to assign when creating a new domain in an existing forest. The meaning of the possible values are: ■ 0 = Windows 2000 Server Native ■ 2 = Windows Server 2003 Native ■ 3 = Windows Server 2008	0, 2, or 3	Varies based on levels existing in the forest
DomainNetBiosName	Specifies the NetBIOS name for the new domain.	*NetBIOS_name*	The left-most label of the FQDN of the domain

Table 7-1   Options for Dcpromo Unattend Files Used for Domain Controller
Promotion on Windows Server 2008

Option	Explanation	Possible Values	Default Value
ForestLevel	Specifies the forest functional level to assign when creating a new domain in a new forest. The possible values are: ■ 0 = Windows 2000 Server Native ■ 2 = Windows Server 2003 Native ■ 3 = Windows Server 2008 Do not use this option if you are installing a domain controller into an existing forest.	0, 2, or 3	0
InstallDNS	Specifies whether DNS should be configured for a new domain if DNS dynamic update is not available or if there are insufficient DNS servers for the existing domain.	Yes or No	Varies based on your environment
LogPath	Specifies the fully qualified path to the directory that contains the AD DS log files. This directory must be on a fixed disk on the local computer, and it cannot be specified as a UNC path.	*path_to_log_files*	%SystemRoot%\ NTDS

Table 7-1 Options for Dcpromo Unattend Files Used for Domain Controller
Promotion on Windows Server 2008

Option	Explanation	Possible Values	Default Value
NewDomain	Specifies the type of new domain to be created. The possible values are: ■ Forest – the root domain of a new forest ■ Tree – the root domain of a new tree in an existing forest ■ Child – the child domain of an existing parent domain This option is *required* when installing AD DS on Server Core.	Forest, Tree, or Child	Forest
NewDomain-DNSName	Specifies the FQDN for the new domain.	*FQDN_of_domain*	No default
ParentDomain-DNSName	Specifies the FQDN of the existing parent domain when you are installing a child domain.	*FQDN_of_parent_domain*	No default
Password	Specifies the password of the domain admin user account used to promote the domain controller. To prompt the user to enter credentials, specify an asterisk (*).	*password* or *	No default
PasswordReplication-Allowed	Specifies names of user and computer accounts whose passwords should be replicated to this RODC. By default, no user credentials are cached on an RODC. To specify multiple security principals, add this option multiple times to your unattend file. If you want to keep this value empty, specify NONE.	*security_principal* or NONE	No default

Table 7-1   Options for Dcpromo Unattend Files Used for Domain Controller Promotion on Windows Server 2008

Option	Explanation	Possible Values	Default Value
PasswordReplication-Denied	Specifies names of user and computer accounts whose passwords should not be replicated to this RODC. To specify multiple security principals, add this option multiple times to your unattend file. If you want to keep this value empty, specify NONE.	*security_principal* or NONE	No default
RebootOnCompletion	Specifies whether to reboot the computer upon completion regardless of whether the Dcpromo operation was a success.	Yes or No	Yes
RebootOnSuccess	Specifies whether to reboot the computer upon completion but only if Dcpromo was a success.	Yes, No	Yes
ReplicaDomain-DNSName	Specifies the FQDN of the domain into which you want to promote your computer as an additional (replica) domain controller.	*FQDN_of_domain*	No default
ReplicaOrNewDomain	Specifies whether to install the domain controller as a replica DC, an RODC, or the first domain controller in a new domain. The possible values are: ■ Replica – Make this an additional domain controller in an existing domain ■ ReadOnlyReplica – Make this an RODC in an existing domain ■ Domain – Make this the first domain controller in a new domain	Replica, ReadOnlyReplica, or Domain	Replica

Table 7-1 Options for Dcpromo Unattend Files Used for Domain Controller Promotion on Windows Server 2008

Option	Explanation	Possible Values	Default Value
ReplicationSourceDC	Specifies the FQDN of the partner domain controller from which AD DS data should be replicated to the new domain controller.	*FQDN_of_DC*	No default
ReplicationSourcePath	Specifies the location of installation media used to install the new domain controller.	*path_to_installation_media*	No default
SafeModeAdmin-Password	Specifies the password for the Directory Service Restore Mode administrator account. Null passwords are not allowed.	*password*	No default
SiteName	Specifies the name of an existing site into which the new domain controller will be placed. The site name must be specified if you are installing an RODC.	*site_name*	Varies depending on the type of installation as follows: ■ For a new forest, the default value is Default-First-Site-Name. ■ For any other writable domain controller, the default value is the site associated with the subnet indicated by Internet Protocol (IP) address of the computer. If no such site exists, the default value is the site of the replication source domain controller.

Table 7-1   Options for Dcpromo Unattend Files Used for Domain Controller Promotion on Windows Server 2008

Option	Explanation	Possible Values	Default Value
SkipAutoConfigDNS	Specifies that DNS installation should skip automatic configuration of client settings, forwarders, and root hints. This option is intended for advanced uses only and can be used only if the DNS Server role is already installed on the server.	No required value	No default
Syskey	Specifies the system key for the media from which you will replicate the directory database data.	NONE or *system_key*	No default
SysVolPath	Specifies the fully qualified path to the SYS-VOL directory. This directory must be on a fixed disk on the local computer, and it cannot be specified as a UNC path.	*path_to_SYSVOL*	%System-Root%\sysvol
TransferIMRole-IfNeeded	Specifies whether Dcpromo should transfer the infrastructure master (IM) role to this domain controller. You should do this if this role is currently hosted on a GC server and you do not want this domain controller to be a GC server. If you specify Yes, you should also specify ConfirmGC=No.	Yes or No	No
UserDomain	Specifies the FQDN of the user account used for promoting the domain controller.	*FQDN*	No default

Table 7-1   Options for Dcpromo Unattend Files Used for Domain Controller Promotion on Windows Server 2008

Option	Explanation	Possible Values	Default Value
UserName	Specifies the user name of the user account that promotes the domain controller (in the form domain_name\ username, where domain_name is the single-label domain name of the domain).	domain_name\ username	No default

Tip   You can also create a Dcpromo unattend file by running Dcpromo graphically on a Full installation of Windows Server 2008 and then, on the last page of the Active Directory Installation Wizard, select the Export Configuration option. This exports the Dcpromo options that you selected when running the wizard to a properly formatted Dcpromo unattend file, which you can use to add the AD DS role to a Server Core installation. However, creating a Dcpromo unattend file manually using the options listed in Table 7-1 provides additional configuration options not available from the wizard.

Creating a New Domain Tree Using Unattended Dcpromo

You can use Dcpromo with an unattend file to create a new domain tree within an existing forest. For example, to create a new domain tree named contoso.com within an existing forest whose root domain is fabrikam.com, perform the following steps:

1. Use Notepad to create an unattend file containing the lines of text shown here and name the file NewTree.txt:

```
[DCINSTALL]
ParentDomainDNSName=fabrikam.com
UserName=FABRIKAM\Administrator
Password=Pa$$w0rd
NewDomain=tree
NewDomainDNSName=contoso.com
DomainNetBiosName=CONTOSO
ReplicaOrNewDomain=domain
DomainLevel=3
InstallDNS=yes
DNSDelegation=yes
DNSDelegationUserName=Administrator
DNSDelegationPassword=Pa$$w0rd
SafeModeAdminPassword=Pa$$w0rd
RebootOnCompletion=yes
```

2. On the Server Core installation on which you want to install the AD DS role, make sure that the Primary DNS Server setting is configured with the IP address of the forest root domain controller. For example, if the forest root domain controller of fabrikam.com has an IP address of 172.16.11.30, type the following commands on your Server Core installation to remove its existing DNS Server settings and assign the correct Primary DNS server setting:

netsh interface ipv4 delete dnsserver "Local Area Connection" all

netsh interface ipv4 add dnsserver "Local Area Connection" 172.16.11.30

3. Now type **dcpromo /unattend:*<path>*\NewTree.txt**, where *<path>* is the path to your unattend file. If your path contains spaces, you must enclose *<path>\NewTree.txt* in quotes.

4. To customize your unattend file further, see Table 7-1, earlier in this chapter.

Important   If you plan on installing a Server Core domain controller to create a new domain tree within an existing Active Directory forest running Windows 2000 Server or Windows Server 2003, first you must update your Active Directory forest schema. For more information, see the section "Preparing an Existing Active Directory Environment for Windows Server 2008 Domain Controllers," later in this chapter.

Creating a New Child Domain Using Unattended Dcpromo

You can use Dcpromo with an unattend file to create a new child domain under an existing domain in an existing forest. For example, to create a new child domain named research.fabrikam.com under the parent domain fabrikam.com, perform the following steps:

1. Use Notepad to create an unattend file containing the lines of text shown here and name the file NewChild.txt:

```
[DCINSTALL]
ParentDomainDNSName=fabrikam.com
UserName=FABRIKAM\Administrator
Password=Pa$$w0rd
NewDomain=child
ChildName=research
DomainNetBiosName=RESEARCH
ReplicaOrNewDomain=domain
DomainLevel=3
InstallDNS=yes
DNSDelegation=yes
DNSDelegationUserName=Administrator
DNSDelegationPassword=Pa$$w0rd
SafeModeAdminPassword=PA$$w0rd
RebootOnCompletion=yes
```

2. On the Server Core installation on which you want to install the AD DS role, make sure that the Primary DNS Server setting is configured with the IP address of the domain controller in the parent domain. For example, if the domain controller of the parent domain has an IP address of 172.16.11.30, type the following commands on your Server Core installation to remove its existing DNS Server settings and assign the correct Primary DNS server setting:

   netsh interface ipv4 delete dnsserver "Local Area Connection" all

   netsh interface ipv4 add dnsserver "Local Area Connection" 172.16.11.30

3. Now type **dcpromo /unattend:<*path*>\NewChild.txt**, where <*path*> is the path to your unattend file. If your path contains spaces, you must enclose <*path*>*NewChild.txt* in quotes.

4. To customize your unattend file further, see Table 7-1, earlier in this chapter.

Important If you plan on installing a Server Core domain controller to create a new child domain within an existing Active Directory forest running Windows 2000 Server or Windows Server 2003, first you must update your Active Directory forest schema. For more information, see the section "Preparing an Existing Active Directory Environment for Windows Server 2008 Domain Controllers," later in this chapter.

Installing a Replica Domain Controller into an Existing Domain Using Unattended Dcpromo

You can use Dcpromo with an unattend file to install a replica (additional) domain controller within an existing domain in an existing forest. For example, to install a replicate domain controller named SEA-SC2 within the fabrikam.com domain, which already has a domain controller named SEA-SC1, perform the following steps:

1. Use Notepad to create an unattend file containing the lines of text shown here and name the file AddReplica.txt:

```
[DCINSTALL]
UserName=FABRIKAM\Administrator
UserDomain=fabrikam.com
Password=Pa$$w0rd
ReplicaOrNewDomain=replica
ReplicaDomainDNSName=fabrikam.com
ReplicationSourceDC = SEA-SC1.fabrikam.com
InstallDNS=yes
ConfirmGC=yes
SafeModeAdminPassword=Pa$$w0rd
RebootOnCompletion=yes
```

2. On the Server Core installation on which you want to install the AD DS role, make sure that the Primary DNS Server setting is configured with the IP address of the first domain controller in the domain you want to add your new domain controller to as a replica domain controller. For example, if the first domain controller of fabrikam.com has an IP address of 172.16.11.30, type the following commands on your Server Core installation to remove its existing DNS Server settings and assign the correct Primary DNS server setting:

netsh interface ipv4 delete dnsserver "Local Area Connection" all

netsh interface ipv4 add dnsserver "Local Area Connection" 172.16.11.30

3. Now type **dcpromo /unattend:<*path*>\AddReplica.txt**, where <*path*> is the path to your unattend file. If your path contains spaces, you must enclose <*path*>*AddReplica.txt* in quotes. Typical output from running this command is as follows:

```
C:\Windows\system32>dcpromo /unattend:F:\AddReplica.txt
Checking if Active Directory Domain Services binaries are installed..
.
Active Directory Domain Services Setup

Validating environment and parameters...

A delegation for this DNS server cannot be created because the
authoritative parent zone cannot be found or it does not run
Windows DNS server. To enable reliable DNS name resolution from
outside the domain fabrikam.com, you should create a
delegation to this DNS server manually in the parent zone.


----------------------------------------
The following actions will be performed:
Configure this server as an additional Active Directory domain
controller for the domain fabrikam.com.

Site:

Additional Options:
  Read-only domain controller: No
  Global catalog: Yes
  DNS Server: Yes

Update DNS Delegation: No

Source domain controller: any writable domain controller

Database folder: C:\Windows\NTDS
Log file folder: C:\Windows\NTDS
SYSVOL folder: C:\Windows\SYSVOL
```

```
The DNS Server service will be configured on this computer.
This computer will be configured to use this DNS server as its
preferred DNS server.
----------------------------------------

Starting...

Checking if Group Policy Management Console needs to be installed...

Changing domain membership of this computer...
.
Press CTRL-C to: Cancel
.
Stopping service NETLOGON


Examining an existing forest...
.
Configuring the local computer to host Active Directory Domain Servic
es
....
Replicating the schema directory partition
.
Replicating CN=Schema,CN=Configuration,DC=fabrikam,DC=com:
received 1000 out of approximately 1578 objects
.
Replicated the schema container.

Replicating the configuration directory partition
.
Replicating CN=Configuration,DC=fabrikam,DC=com: received 1000 out
of approximately 4143 objects
.
Replicating critical domain information...
.
Completing Active Directory Domain Services installation
.
Configuring service NETLOGON


Setting the computer's DNS computer name root to fabrikam.com

.

Setting security on the domain controller and Directory Service
files and registry keys

..
Securing S-1-5-11
.
```

Securing S-1-5-32-550

Securing machine\software\microsoft\windows
.
Securing SamSs
...
Securing Kerberos Policy
.
Replicating the domain directory partition...

Press CTRL-C to: Finish Replication Later
.
Replicating DC=DomainDnsZones,DC=fabrikam,DC=com: received 42 out of approximately 42 objects
..
The attempted domain controller operation has completed

Configuring the DNS Server service on this computer...
.
Active Directory Domain Services is now installed on this computer for the domain fabrikam.com.

This Active Directory domain controller is assigned to the site Default-First-Site-Name. You can manage sites with the Active Directory Sites and Services administrative tool.

Windows Server 2008 domain controllers have a new more secure default for the security setting named "Allow cryptography algorithms compatible with Windows NT 4.0." This setting prevents Microsoft Windows and non-Microsoft SMB "clients" from using weaker NT 4.0 style cryptography algorithms when establishing security channel sessions against Windows Server 2008 domain controllers. As a result of this new default, operations or applications that require a security channel serviced by Windows Server 2008 domain controllers might fail.

Platforms impacted by this change include Windows NT 4.0, as well as non-Microsoft SMB "clients" and network-attached storage (NAS) devices that do not support stronger cryptography algorithms. Some operations on clients running versions of Windows earlier than Vista with Service Pack 1 are also impacted, including domain join operations performed by the Active Directory Migration Tool or WindowsDeployment Services.

For more information about this setting, see Knowledge Base article 942564 (http://go.microsoft.com/fwlink/?LinkId=104751).

This computer does not have static IP addresses assigned to the

IP Properties of any of its network adapters. If both IPv4 and
IPv6 are enabled for a network adapter, both IPv4 and IPv6 static
IP addresses should be assigned to both IPv4 and IPv6 Properties
of the physical network adapter. Otherwise, either an IPv4 or
an IPv6 static IP address should be assigned. You should assign
static IP address(es) for reliable Domain Name System (DNS)
operation. If you do not assign static IP address(es), then
clients may not be able to contact this domain controller and any
delegations that currently point to the dynamically assigned IP
address will stop working when the IP address changes.

Note that the last paragraph of this command output typically indicates that
your server does not have a statically assigned IPv6 address. This warning can
safely be ignored in most circumstances.

4. Use the Repadmin command to verify that the new replica domain controller
SEA-SC2 has successfully replicated its Active Directory directory database
with the first domain controller in the fabrikam.com domain, which is named
SEA-SC1:

```
C:\Users\administrator.FABRIKAM>repadmin /showrepl

Repadmin: running command /showrepl against full DC localhost
Default-First-Site-Name\SEA-SC2
DSA Options: IS_GC
Site Options: (none)
DSA object GUID: 8152d09b-c2e3-47c7-9e5e-ecc55a130c2b
DSA invocationID: e224240b-6e3c-45e4-8c59-5dd149d8cc67

==== INBOUND NEIGHBORS ======================================

DC=fabrikam,DC=com
    Default-First-Site-Name\SEA-SC1 via RPC
        DSA object GUID: a412fd6d-d01d-4fe9-b147-f41b04fba688
        Last attempt @ 2008-05-19 17:53:56 was successful.

CN=Configuration,DC=fabrikam,DC=com
    Default-First-Site-Name\SEA-SC1 via RPC
        DSA object GUID: a412fd6d-d01d-4fe9-b147-f41b04fba688
        Last attempt @ 2008-05-19 17:50:59 was successful.

CN=Schema,CN=Configuration,DC=fabrikam,DC=com
    Default-First-Site-Name\SEA-SC1 via RPC
        DSA object GUID: a412fd6d-d01d-4fe9-b147-f41b04fba688
        Last attempt @ 2008-05-19 17:50:59 was successful.

DC=DomainDnsZones,DC=fabrikam,DC=com
    Default-First-Site-Name\SEA-SC1 via RPC
        DSA object GUID: a412fd6d-d01d-4fe9-b147-f41b04fba688
        Last attempt @ 2008-05-19 17:51:01 was successful.
```

```
DC=ForestDnsZones,DC=fabrikam,DC=com
    Default-First-Site-Name\SEA-SC1 via RPC
        DSA object GUID: a412fd6d-d01d-4fe9-b147-f41b04fba688
        Last attempt @ 2008-05-19 17:51:01 was successful.
```

5. To customize your unattend file further, see Table 7-1, earlier in this chapter.

Important   If you plan on installing a Server Core domain controller as a replicate (additional) domain controller within an existing domain of an existing Active Directory forest running Windows 2000 Server or Windows Server 2003, first you must prepare your existing domain and forest. For more information, see the section "Preparing an Existing Active Directory Environment for Windows Server 2008 Domain Controllers," later in this chapter.

Removing a Domain Controller Using Unattended Dcpromo

You can use Dcpromo with an unattend file to remove a domain controller from a domain, including removing the last domain controller from a domain or forest.

Removing a Replica Domain Controller from a Domain

You can use Dcpromo with an unattend file to remove a replica domain controller from an existing domain. If your domain controller hosts any Active Directory–integrated DNS zones, those zones are removed and any DNS delegations for those zones that point to your domain controller also are removed.

For example, to remove a replicate domain controller named SEA-SC2 from fabrikam.com domain, which has SEA-SC1 as its first domain controller, perform the following steps:

1. Use Notepad to create an unattend file containing the lines of text shown here and name the file RemoveReplica.txt:

```
[DCINSTALL]
UserName=FABRIKAM\Administrator
UserDomain=fabrikam.com
Password=Pa$$w0rd
AdministratorPassword=Pa$$w0rd
RemoveApplicationPartitions=Yes
RemoveDNSDelegation=Yes
DNSDelegationUserName=FABRIKAM\Administrator
DNSDelegationPassword=Pa$$w0rd
```

2. On the Server Core installation from which you want to remove the AD DS role, type **dcpromo /unattend:<*path*>\RemoveReplica.txt**, where <*path*> is the path to your unattend file. If your path contains spaces, you must enclose <*path*>*RemoveReplica.txt* in quotes.

3. Type the following command to verify that SEA-SC2 is no longer a domain controller in the fabrikam.com domain:

```
C:\Users\administrator.FABRIKAM>netdom query dc
List of domain controllers with accounts in the domain:

SEA-SC1
The command completed successfully.
```

This command output indicates that the only domain controller remaining in the domain is SEA-SC1.

Customizing the Dcpromo Unattend File for Domain Controller Demotion

You can customize your Dcpromo unattend file in various ways to control how a domain controller running Server Core is demoted. Table 7-2 lists the different options you can include in a Dcpromo unattend file used for domain controller demotion, an explanation of what they mean, their possible values, and their default value (if any) when the option is not included in the unattend file.

Table 7-2 Options for Dcpromo Unattend Files Used for Domain Controller Demotion on Windows Server 2008

Option	Explanation	Possible Values	Default Value
AdministratorPassword	Specifies the password for the local Administrator account the computer uses after demotion.	*password*	No default
DemoteFSMO	Specifies that a forced removal should continue even if the domain controller holds an operations master role.	Yes or No	No
DNSDelegationPassword	Specifies the password of the user name used for removing the DNS delegation. To prompt the user to enter credentials, specify an asterisk (*).	*password* or *	No default
DNSDelegationUserName	Specifies the user name to be used for removing the DNS delegation. If unspecified, the credentials that you specified for AD DS removal are used.	*username*	No default

Table 7-2   Options for Dcpromo Unattend Files Used for Domain Controller Demotion on Windows Server 2008

Option	Explanation	Possible Values	Default Value
IgnoreIsLastDcInDomainMismatch	Specifies that the demotion should continue when either the option IsLastDCInDomain=Yes is specified and Dcpromo detects another active domain controller in the domain, or when the option IsLastDCInDomain=No is specified and Dcpromo cannot contact any other domain controller in the domain.	Yes or No	No
IgnoreIsLastDNSServerForZone	Specifies that the demotion should continue even if the domain controller is the last DNS server for one or more AD DS–integrated DNS zones that it hosts.	Yes or No	No
IsLastDCInDomain	Specifies that the domain controller being demoted is the last domain controller in the domain.	Yes or No	No
Password	Specifies the password of the user name used to demote the domain controller. To prompt the user to enter credentials, specify an asterisk (*).	*password* or *	No default
RebootOnCompletion	Specifies whether to reboot the computer upon completion regardless of whether the Dcpromo operation was a success.	Yes or No	Yes

Table 7-2   Options for Dcpromo Unattend Files Used for Domain Controller Demotion on Windows Server 2008

Option	Explanation	Possible Values	Default Value
RebootOnSuccess	Specifies whether to reboot the computer upon completion, but only if Dcpromo was a success.	Yes, No	Yes
RemoveApplicationPartitions	Specifies that the application directory partitions should be removed during the demotion process.	Yes or No	No
RemoveDNSDelegation	Specifies that the DNS delegations that point to this DNS server from the parent DNS zone should be removed during the demotion process.	Yes or No	Yes
RetainDCMetadata	Specifies that domain controller metadata should be retained in the domain after the demotion process. Specify this option when you have a delegated administrator removing AD DS from an RODC.	Yes or No	No
UserDomain	Specifies the FQDN of the user account used for promoting the domain controller.	*FQDN*	No default
UserName	Specifies the user name of the user account that promotes the domain controller (in the form *domain_name\username*, where *domain_name* is the single-label domain name).	*domain_name \username*	No default

Removing the Last Domain Controller from a Domain

To remove the last domain controller from a domain, follow the same instructions as in the section "Removing a Replica Domain Controller from a Domain," earlier in this chapter, but add the following additional line to your unattend file at any point:

```
IsLastDCInDomain=yes
```

Removing the Last Domain Controller from a Forest

To remove the last domain controller from a forest, follow the same instructions as in the previous section "Removing the Last Domain Controller from a Domain."

Performing a Forced Removal of a Domain Controller

You can remove a Server Core domain controller forcibly from a domain even if the domain controller is hosting one or more Flexible Single Master Operation (FSMO) roles. To remove a domain controller forcibly, follow the same instructions as in the section "Removing a Replica Domain Controller from a Domain," earlier in this chapter, but be sure to add the following additional line to your unattend file at any point:

```
DemoteFSMO=yes
```

If you forcibly remove a domain controller that hosts FSMO roles, you must update the forest metadata manually afterwards. For information on how to do this, see Knowledge Base article 216498 at *http://support.microsoft.com/kb/216498*. As an alternative to the procedure outlined there, you can delete the computer account of the removed domain controller from Active Directory, but you still have to clear out DNS records manually for the removed domain controller.

Note   You can remove a Server Core domain controller forcibly even when it is started in Directory Services Restore Mode.

Preparing an Existing Active Directory Environment for Windows Server 2008 Domain Controllers

Before you add the AD DS role to a Server Core installation that belongs to an existing Active Directory environment based on Windows 2000 Server or Windows Server 2003, you must prepare that environment by running the Adprep command. You can use Adprep to perform two kinds of actions:

- Preparing an existing Windows 2000 Server or Windows Server 2003 forest by upgrading the forest schema to the Windows Server 2008 level

- Preparing an existing Windows 2000 Server or Windows Server domain so you can add domain controllers running Windows Server 2008 to the domain

Tip If the Adprep operation fails to run successfully, view the contents of the Adprep debug logs found under the %SystemRoot%\System32\Debug\Adprep folder to troubleshoot.

Preparing an Existing Active Directory Forest

You must prepare an existing Windows 2000 Server or Windows Server 2003 forest by upgrading the forest schema to the Windows Server 2008 level before you install your first Windows Server 2008 domain controller into your forest. To do this, perform these steps:

1. Be sure that your existing Windows 2000 Server and Windows Server 2003 domain controllers are at the appropriate service pack levels. Specifically:

   ❏ All Windows 2000 Server domain controllers must be running at Service Pack 4 level or later.

   ❏ All Windows Server 2003 domain controllers must be running at Service Pack 1 level or later.

2. Upgrade any existing Microsoft Windows NT 4.0 domain controllers to Windows 2000 Server or Windows Server 2003. You must do this because Windows NT 4.0 domain controllers cannot participate in an Active Directory forest that includes Windows Server 2008 domain controllers.

3. Log on to the domain controller running Windows 2000 Server or Windows Server 2003 that hosts the schema master FSMO role using a user account that belongs to the following security groups:

   ❏ Enterprise Admins

   ❏ Schema Admins

   ❏ Domain Admins for the domain where the schema master resides

4. Insert your Windows Server 2008 product DVD into the DVD drive on your schema master.

5. Open a command prompt and type **<DVD_drive>:\sources\adprep\adprep /forestprep**, where <DVD_drive> is the letter for your DVD drive.

6. Let the schema update operation finish and then allow the schema changes to replicate to all domain controllers in your forest before you prepare any domains for a Windows Server 2008 domain controller.

Note If you plan on having RODCs in your forest, you must make additional changes to your forest using Adprep. See the section "Preparing a Forest for RODCs," later in this chapter, for more information. Note that the first Windows Server 2008 domain controller in a forest must be a GC server and it cannot be an RODC.

Preparing an Existing Active Directory Domain

You must prepare an existing Windows 2000 Server or Windows Server 2003 domain before you install your first Windows Server 2008 domain controller into your domain. To do this, perform these steps:

1. Be sure that your existing Windows 2000 Server and Windows Server 2003 domain controllers are at the appropriate service pack levels. Specifically:

   ❏ All Windows 2000 Server domain controllers must be running at Service Pack 4 level or later.

   ❏ All Windows Server 2003 domain controllers must be running at Service Pack 1 level or later.

2. Upgrade any existing Windows NT 4.0 domain controllers to Windows 2000 Server or Windows Server 2003. You must do this because Windows NT 4.0 domain controllers cannot participate in an Active Directory forest that includes Windows Server 2008 domain controllers.

3. Make sure that the domain functional level of your domain is running at a Windows 2000 native or later level. You cannot run Adprep /Domainprep if your Windows 2000 Server and Windows Server 2003 domain is running at Windows 2000 mixed functional level. To raise the domain functional level, open Active Directory Domains And Trusts, right-click the domain, select Raise Domain Functional Level, and raise the functional level of your domain to the desired level.

4. Log on to the domain controller running Windows 2000 Server or Windows Server 2003 that hosts the infrastructure master FSMO role using a user account that belongs to the following security groups:

   ❏ Enterprise Admins

   ❏ Domain Admins for the domain

5. Insert your Windows Server 2008 product DVD into the DVD drive on your infrastructure master.

6. The next step depends on whether your domain is a Windows 2000 Server domain or a Windows Server 2003 domain, as follows:

   ❏ For a Windows 2000 Server domain, open a command prompt and type *<DVD_drive>*:\sources\adprep\adprep /domainprep /gpprep, where *<DVD_drive>* is the letter for your DVD drive.

   ❏ For a Windows Server 2003 domain, open a command prompt and type *<DVD_drive>*:\sources\adprep\adprep /domainprep, where *<DVD_drive>* is the drive letter for your DVD drive.

7. Let the domain preparation operation finish and allow the changes to replicate to all domain controllers in the domain.

Note If you plan on having RODCs in your domain, you must make additional changes to your forest using Adprep. See the section "Preparing a Forest for RODCs," later in this chapter, for more information. Note that the first Windows Server 2008 domain controller in a forest must be a GC server and it cannot be an RODC.

New Functionality Provided by Windows Server 2008 Forest Functional Level

Raising the forest functional level to Windows Server 2008 level provides no additional functionality for replica domain controllers running Windows Server 2008. However, it does provide additional security protection for RODCs to prevent them from being hijacked and having rogue RODCs substituted for them.

New Functionality Provided by Windows Server 2008 Domain Functional Level

Raising the domain functional level to Windows Server 2008 level provides the following new functionalities:

- Kerberos authentication can support 128-bit and 256-bit Advanced Encryption Standard (AES) encryption.

- SYSVOL replication can take place using DFS Replication (DFSR) instead of File Replication Service (FRS).

- Last Interactive Logon Information can be used to display the time of the last successful interactive logon for a user, the workstation that the user logged on to, and the number of failed logon attempts since the last logon.

- Fine-grained password policies can be implemented.

Managing Server Core Domain Controllers

You can manage domain controllers running Server Core the same way you manage domain controllers running a Full installation of Windows Server 2008. You can use the same tools—namely, Microsoft Management consoles (MMCs) and command-line utilities—to manage both types of domain controllers. The only difference is that if you want to manage Server Core domain controllers using MMC consoles, you must do so remotely.

Managing Server Core Domain Controllers Using MMC Consoles

You can manage Server Core domain controllers remotely using MMC consoles in several different ways:

- Using the Active Directory MMC consoles on a domain controller running a Full installation of Windows Server 2008

- Using the Remote Server Administration Tools (RSAT) installed on a domain controller or member server running Windows Server 2008

- Using RSAT installed on an administrative workstation in the domain that is running Windows Vista with Service Pack 1

For example, to manage Server Core domain controllers SEA-SC1 and SCA-SC2 remotely in the fabrikam.com domain from a computer running Windows Vista with SP1, perform the following steps:

1. Log on to the computer running Windows Vista with SP1 using administrative credentials for the domain.

2. Install RSAT on the computer running Windows Vista with SP1 using the procedure described in the section "Using RSAT to Administer Server Core in a Domain," in Chapter 6, "Remote Management."

3. Click Start, Administrative Tools, and then select one of the AD DS MMC consoles (such as Active Directory Users And Computers).

4. Expand the console tree and administer AD DS as desired, as shown here:

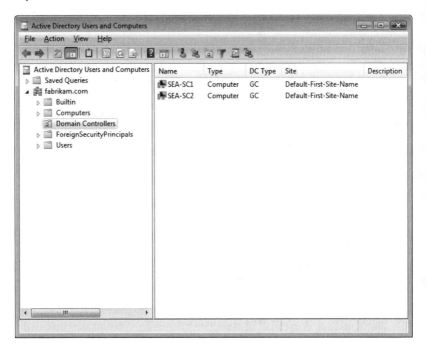

The MMC consoles and snap-ins available for administering Active Directory include the following:

- **Active Directory Users And Groups**   Used to administer users, groups, computers, and organizational units

- **Active Directory Domains And Trusts**   Used to administer domains, domain trees, forests, and trusts

- **Active Directory Sites And Services**   Used to administer sites, site links, and subnets

You can use either these MMC consoles, which are installed by default on domain controllers or as part of RSAT, or you can create a new (empty) MMC console and add these snap-ins to your console to create a custom console for administering Active Directory.

Managing Server Core Domain Controllers Using Command-Line Utilities

You can manage Server Core domain controllers using various command-line utilities. You can do this in several ways:

- By using the Server Core command prompt either locally, via a Remote Desktop connection, or via the Windows Remote Shell (WinRS).

- From the command prompt on a domain controller or member server running a Full installation of Windows Server 2008.

- From an elevated command prompt on an administrative workstation running Windows Vista with SP1. To open an elevated command prompt on Windows Vista, click Start, type **cmd**, right-click cmd under Programs, and select Run As Administrator. Respond to the User Account Control (UAC) prompt as needed.

Table 7-3 lists some of the command-line utilities that you can use for administering Active Directory. Other tools, such as Dnscmd, which is used for administering DNS (an essential part of an Active Directory environment), are discussed in other chapters of this book. For detailed syntax of each command, type the command followed by /? at a command prompt.

Table 7-3   Command-Line Utilities for Administering Active Directory

Tool	Function
dsacls	Used to display and change permissions (access control entries) in the access control list (ACL) of Active Directory objects
dsadd	Used to add objects such as user or computer accounts to the directory
dcdiag	Used to analyze the state of domain controllers in a forest and report any problems for help in troubleshooting Active Directory issues

Table 7-3   Command-Line Utilities for Administering Active Directory

Tool	Function
dsget	Used to display selected properties of the specified directory object
dsmgmt	Used to manage FSMO roles and clean up metadata left behind by abandoned domain controllers
dsmod	Used to modify selected attributes of the specified directory object
dsmove	Used to move a directory object from its current location to a new location
dsquery	Used to find directory objects that match the specified search criteria
dsrm	Used to remove a directory object, the complete subtree under the object, or both
ldifde	Used to create, modify, or delete directory objects, extend the schema, export user and group information to other applications or services, and populate Active Directory with data from other directory services
netdom	Used to join computers to a domain, manage computer accounts of domain members, reset the secure channel between a domain member and the domain, manage trusts, and view a list of domain controllers, member servers, workstations, organizational units, or FSMO roles
ntdsutil	Used to perform directory database maintenance, manage FSMO roles, remove metadata left when domain controllers are removed forcibly from the network, and other Active Directory maintenance tasks
repadmin	Used to diagnose replication problems between domain controllers, view or modify the replication topology as seen from the perspective of each domain controller, force replication between domain controllers, view replication metadata and up-to-dateness vectors, and monitor the general health of an Active Directory forest

Performing Common Active Directory Management Tasks

Covering even the most common Active Directory management tasks would require an entire book of its own, but we can cover the basics here. The following sections show how to perform a selection of common administration tasks that you are likely to need to perform in a Windows Server 2008 Active Directory environment. These sections focus on tasks that you can perform from the command prompt because this book is mainly about Server Core, and the primary way of administering Server Core is from the command prompt. When using these commands, you should be logged on as a domain administrator.

Some of the command-line tools listed in Table 7-3 include switches for running them against remote computers. For example, typing the command **dsadd user cn=kberg, ou=Seattle,dc=fabrikam,dc=com -disabled yes -pwd Pa$$w0rd -u FABRIKAM\ tallen -p *** creates a disabled user account named kberg (for Karen Berg) in the Seattle organizational unit (OU) of the fabrikam.com domain using the credentials of administrator tallen (Tony Allen) to connect to the domain. (You are prompted to enter

Tony's password after you run this command.) If you are logged on to your adminis-trator workstation using domain admin credentials, however, you usually don't have to specify credentials using the –u and –p switches used here for connecting to the domain. Alternatively, you can connect to a Server Core domain controller using Remote Desktop to run such commands directly on your domain controller. Or you can use Windows Remote Management (WinRM) to run commands remotely on the domain controller from your administrator workstation.

For additional information about performing Active Directory management tasks, includ-ing examples of managing Active Directory using MMC consoles, see the Windows Server 2008 Administrator's Pocket Consultant *by William Stanek (Microsoft Press, 2008).*

Managing FSMO Roles

To determine which domain controller holds the infrastructure master role, use the Dsquery command from your administrator workstation running Windows Vista SP1 while logged on as a domain administrator, as follows:

```
C:\Users\tallen>dsquery server -hasfsmo infr
"CN=SEA-SC1,CN=Servers,CN=Default-First-Site-
Name,CN=Sites,CN=Configuration,DC=f
abrikam,DC=com"
```

You can see that the domain controller SEA-SC1 currently holds the infrastructure master role.

To transfer the infrastructure master role from SEA-SC1 to SEA-SC2, use the Ntdsutil command as follows:

1. Type **ntdsutil** to enter the ntdsutil: prompt.

2. Type **roles** to enter the fsmo maintenance: prompt.

3. Type **connections** to enter the server connections: prompt.

4. Type **connect to server SEA-SC2** to connect to the domain controller to which you want to transfer the infrastructure master role.

5. Type **quit** to return to the fsmo maintenance: prompt.

6. Type **transfer infrastructure master** to transfer the infrastructure role from SEA-SC1 to SEA-SC2. Click Yes when a dialog box asks you if you are sure you want to do this.

7. Type **quit** twice to leave the ntdsutil: prompt and then type **dsquery server -hasfsmo infr** to verify that the infrastructure master role has been transferred successfully to SEA-SC2:

```
C:\Users\tallen>dsquery server -hasfsmo infr
"CN=SEA-SC2,CN=Servers,CN=Default-First-Site-
Name,CN=Sites,CN=Configuration,DC=f
abrikam,DC=com"
```

You can also use the Netdom command to display all FSMO role holders as follows:

```
C:\Users\tallen>netdom query /domain:FABRIKAM fsmo
Schema master               SEA-SC1.fabrikam.com
Domain naming master        SEA-SC1.fabrikam.com
PDC                         SEA-SC1.fabrikam.com
RID pool manager            SEA-SC1.fabrikam.com
Infrastructure master       SEA-SC2.fabrikam.com
The command completed successfully.
```

Managing User Accounts

To list the members of the Domain Admins security group, use the Dsget command from your administrator workstation running Windows Vista SP1 while logged on as a domain administrator, as follows:

```
C:\Users\tallen>dsget group "cn=Domain Admins,cn=
Users,dc=fabrikam,dc=com" -members
"CN=Tony Allen,OU=Seattle Users,OU=Seattle,DC=fabrikam,DC=com"
"CN=Administrator,CN=Users,DC=fabrikam,DC=com"
```

To create user Karen Berg (kberg) in the Seattle Users OU and make her a member of the Domain Admins security group, use the Dsadd command like this:

```
C:\Users\tallen>dsadd user "cn=Karen Berg,ou=Seattle Users,ou=
Seattle,dc=fabrikam,dc=com" -upn kberg@fabrikam.com -samid kberg
-fn Karen -ln Berg -display "Karen Berg" -memberof "cn=Domain
Admins,cn=Users,dc=fabrikam,dc=com" -pwd Pa$$w0rd - mustchpwd
yes -disabled no
dsadd succeeded:cn=Karen Berg,ou=Seattle Users,ou=Seattle,
dc=fabrikam,dc=com
```

This command also assigns the following properties to Karen's account:

- **-upn kberg@fabrikam**   Assigns kberg as the user logon name

- **-samid kberg**   Assigns kberg as the pre–Windows 2000 user logon name

- **-pwd Pas$$w0rd**   Assigns the account an initial password of Pa$$w0rd

- **-mustchpwd yes**   Forces the user to change the password on first logon

- **-disabled no**   Creates the account and enables it immediately

As Figure 7-1 shows, you can verify the result of running this command easily by opening the properties sheet for the user's account using Active Directory Users And Computers on a remote computer that has RSAT installed.

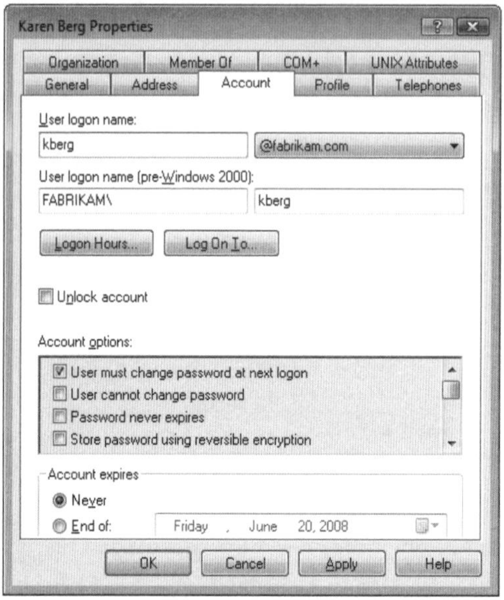

Figure 7-1   Properties of user Karen Berg

If Karen logs on, changes her password, and later forgets her password, you can reset her password to Pa$$w0rd again and make her change it by using the Dsmod command like this:

```
C:\Users\tallen>dsmod user "cn=Karen Berg,ou=Seattle Users,ou=Seattle,
dc=fabrikam,dc=com" -pwd Pa$$w0rd -mustchpwd yes
dsmod succeeded:cn=Karen Berg,ou=Seattle Users,ou=Seattle,dc=fabrikam,dc=com
```

Tip   You can also use the Net user command to create domain user accounts by using the /domain switch, and the Net group command to create domain local groups by using the /domain switch.

Managing Computer Accounts

To list all computers in your forest whose names include "-SC" (which you would be using as a naming convention for computers using Server Core), use the Dsquery command from your administrator workstation running Windows Vista SP1 while logged on as a domain administrator, as follows:

```
C:\Users\tallen>dsquery computer forestroot -name "*-SC*"
"CN=SEA-SC1,OU=Domain Controllers,DC=fabrikam,DC=com"
"CN=SEA-SC2,OU=Domain Controllers,DC=fabrikam,DC=com"
"CN=SEA-SC3,CN=Computers,DC=fabrikam,DC=com"
"CN=SEA-SC4,CN=Computers,DC=fabrikam,DC=com"
"CN=SEA-SC5,CN=Computers,DC=fabrikam,DC=com"
```

To list all domain controllers in the fabrikam.com domain, use the Netdom command like this:

```
C:\Users\tallen>netdom query dc
List of domain controllers with accounts in the domain:

SEA-SC1
SEA-SC2
The command completed successfully.
```

To display the security identifier (SID) of computer SEA-SC1, use the Dsget command like this:

```
C:\Users\tallen>dsget computer "CN=SEA-SC1,OU=Domain Controllers,
DC=fabrikam,DC=com" -sid
 sid
 S-1-5-21-3788796310-154918285-226766575-1000
dsget succeeded
```

To display the globally unique identifier (GUID) of computer SEA-SC1, use the Repadmin command like this:

```
C:\Users\tallen>repadmin /showsig SEA-SC1
Default-First-Site-Name\SEA-SC1

Current DSA invocationID: a412fd6d-d01d-4fe9-b147-f41b04fba688

No retired signatures.
```

Note The GUID shown here is the retired invocation ID of the domain controller. A domain controller changes its invocation ID whenever it is restored or when it re-hosts an application partition.

To create a computer account for a computer named SEA-DESK144 in the Seattle Computers OU of the fabrikam.com domain and make the computer a member of the Domain Computers security group, use the Dsadd command like this:

```
C:\Users\tallen>dsadd computer "cn=SEA-DESK144,
ou=Seattle Computers,ou=Seattle,dc=fabrikam,dc=com"
dsadd succeeded:cn=SEA-DESK144,ou=Seattle Computers,
ou=Seattle,dc=fabrikam,dc=com
```

To display the NetBIOS names of all computers in the Seattle Computers OU, pipe the output of the Dsquery command into the Dsget command as follows (ignore the dollar signs after the computer names):

```
C:\Users\tallen>dsquery computer "ou=Seattle Computers,
ou=Seattle,dc=fabrikam,dc=com" | dsget computer -samid
 samid
 SEA-DESK144$
 SEA-DESK143$
```

```
SEA-DESK142$
SEA-DESK141$
dsget succeeded
```

Manage Organizational Units

To list all organizational units in your forest, use the Dsquery command from your administrator workstation running Windows Vista SP1 while logged on as a domain administrator, as follows:

```
C:\Users\tallen>dsquery ou forestroot
"OU=Domain Controllers,DC=fabrikam,DC=com"
"OU=Seattle,DC=fabrikam,DC=com"
"OU=Seattle Users,OU=Seattle,DC=fabrikam,DC=com"
"OU=Seattle Computers,OU=Seattle,DC=fabrikam,DC=com"
```

To create a new OU named Vancouver and two OUs beneath it named Vancouver Users and Vancouver Computers, string three Dsadd commands together using double ampersands (&&) like this:

```
C:\Users\tallen>dsadd ou "OU=Vancouver,DC=fabrikam,DC=com" && dsadd ou
"OU=Vanco uver Users,OU=Vancouver,DC=fabrikam,DC=com" && dsadd ou
"OU=Vancouver Computers,OU=Vancouver,DC=fabrikam,DC=com"
dsadd succeeded:OU=Vancouver,DC=fabrikam,DC=com
dsadd succeeded:OU=Vancouver Users,OU=Vancouver,DC=fabrikam,DC=com
dsadd succeeded:OU=Vancouver Computers,OU=Vancouver,DC=fabrikam,DC=com
```

To move computer SEA-DESK144 from the Seattle Computers OU to the Vancouver Computers OU, use Dsmove like this:

```
C:\Users\tallen>dsmove "CN=SEA-DESK144,OU=Seattle Computers,
OU=Seattle,DC=fabrikam,DC=com" -newparent "OU=Vancouver Computers,
OU=Vancouver,DC=fabrikam,dc=com"
dsmove succeeded:CN=SEA-DESK144,
OU=Seattle Computers,OU=Seattle,DC=fabrikam,DC=com
```

Managing Active Directory Replication

To display all replication partners of domain controller SEA-SC1, use the Repadmin command from your administrator workstation running Windows Vista SP1 while logged on as a domain administrator, as follows:

```
C:\Users\tallen>repadmin /showrepl SEA-SC1.fabrikam.com
Default-First-Site-Name\SEA-SC1
DSA Options: IS_GC
Site Options: (none)
DSA object GUID: a412fd6d-d01d-4fe9-b147-f41b04fba688
DSA invocationID: a412fd6d-d01d-4fe9-b147-f41b04fba688

==== INBOUND NEIGHBORS ======================================
```

```
DC=fabrikam,DC=com
    Default-First-Site-Name\SEA-SC2 via RPC
        DSA object GUID: 734c1619-c811-466d-98b0-5ca578843797
        Last attempt @ 2008-05-21 13:35:48 was successful.

CN=Configuration,DC=fabrikam,DC=com
    Default-First-Site-Name\SEA-SC2 via RPC
        DSA object GUID: 734c1619-c811-466d-98b0-5ca578843797
        Last attempt @ 2008-05-21 12:50:18 was successful.

CN=Schema,CN=Configuration,DC=fabrikam,DC=com
    Default-First-Site-Name\SEA-SC2 via RPC
        DSA object GUID: 734c1619-c811-466d-98b0-5ca578843797
        Last attempt @ 2008-05-21 12:50:18 was successful.

DC=DomainDnsZones,DC=fabrikam,DC=com
    Default-First-Site-Name\SEA-SC2 via RPC
        DSA object GUID: 734c1619-c811-466d-98b0-5ca578843797
        Last attempt @ 2008-05-21 12:50:18 was successful.

DC=ForestDnsZones,DC=fabrikam,DC=com
    Default-First-Site-Name\SEA-SC2 via RPC
        DSA object GUID: 734c1619-c811-466d-98b0-5ca578843797
        Last attempt @ 2008-05-21 12:50:18 was successful.
```

To force a full replication of all objects contained in the DC=fabrikam,DC=com naming context from domain controller SEA-SC1 to domain controller SEA-SC2, use the Repadmin command like this:

```
C:\Users\tallen>repadmin /replicate SEA-SC2 SEA-SC1 DC=fabrikam,DC=com /full
Sync from SEA-SC2 to SEA-SC1 completed successfully.
```

To check the replication state of domain controllers in your forest, use the Repadmin command like this:

```
C:\Users\tallen>repadmin /replsummary
Replication Summary Start Time: 2008-05-21 13:45:07

Beginning data collection for replication summary, this may take awhile:
    .....


Source DSA          largest delta    fails/total %%   error
    SEA-SC1             46m:50s       0 /   5    0
    SEA-SC2             54m:49s       0 /   5    0


Destination DSA     largest delta    fails/total %%   error
    SEA-SC1             54m:49s       0 /   5    0
    SEA-SC2             46m:50s       0 /   5    0is:
```

To display a list of the GUIDs of all computers that have an open connection with domain controller SEA-SC1, use Repadmin like this:

```
C:\Users\tallen>repadmin /showctx SEA-SC1 /nocache
7 open context handles.

NTDSAPI client @ 0.0.0.0 (PID 1640) (Handle 0x2328cb8)
    bound, refs=1, last used 2008-05-21 08:27:25

NTDSAPI client @  (PID 1816) (Handle 0x231f9d0)
    bound, refs=1, last used 2008-05-21 08:28:48

NTDSAPI client @ 0.0.0.0 (PID 1504) (Handle 0x2373848)
    bound, refs=1, last used 2008-05-21 08:31:28

a412fd6d-d01d-4fe9-b147-
f41b04fba688 @ 0.0.0.0 (PID 496) (Handle 0x2379c08)
    bound, refs=1, last used 2008-05-21 13:35:18

734c1619-c811-466d-98b0-5ca578843797 @  (PID 492) (Handle 0x2362290)
    bound, refs=1, last used 2008-05-21 13:46:36

NTDSAPI client @ 0.0.0.0 (PID 1504) (Handle 0x4e82230)
    bound, refs=1, last used 2008-05-21 13:50:53

NTDSAPI client @ 0.0.0.0 (PID 1480) (Handle 0x22ee7d8)
    bound, refs=2, last used 2008-05-21 13:51:51
```

To determine which computer has the GUID of 734c1619-c811-466d-98b0-5ca578843797 in the above command output, use Repadmin like this:

```
C:\Users\tallen>repadmin /dsaguid SEA-SC1 734c1619-c811-466d-98b0-5ca578843797
Caching GUIDs.
..
"734c1619-c811-466d-98b0-5ca578843797" = Default-First-Site-Name\SEA-SC2.
```

This display shows that computer SEA-SC2 has the GUID of 734c1619-c811-466d-98b0-5ca578843797 and has an open connection with SEA-SC1.

Working with Server Core Read-Only Domain Controllers

Read-Only Domain Controllers (RODCs) are a new type of domain controller available for Active Directory on Windows Server 2008. RODCs host a read-only replica of the directory database, as compared to a full or replica domain controller on which the directory database is both readable and writable. RODCs typically would be deployed at remote sites where physical security may be less stringent, no Active Directory administrator resides, or both. RODCs perform inbound replication with writable domain controllers and contain the same objects and attributes in their directory database that writable domain controllers have, but RODCs do not store passwords for domain users and computers unless they are configured to do so explicitly using a password replication policy.

The password replication policy for an RODC must be set on a writable domain controller running Windows Server 2008 and determines whether a user or a computer account's credentials can be replicated to the RODC. The password replication policy specifies which user and computer accounts should be permitted to be cached on the RODC and any accounts that should be explicitly denied from being cached. By default, the only passwords that an RODC caches are the password for its own computer account and the KRBTGT account used when signing and encrypting Kerberos ticket-granting-ticker (TGT) requests. The KRBTGT account on an RODC is different from the one on writable domain controllers, which provides added security if the RODC is stolen or compromised. By limiting credential caching to only those users and computers permitted and not denied by the password replication policy, you can ensure that the damage should an RODC be stolen or compromised would be minimized.

> **Important**   If an RODC is stolen from a remote site, or if you suspect that the RODC has been compromised, you should immediately reset the passwords for all user and computer accounts whose passwords were configured to be cached on the RODC. This should be done on a writable domain controller at your hub site.

Additional Limitations of RODCs

RODCs have the following additional limitations compared with writable domain controllers:

- They cannot hold any FSMO role because of their read-only nature.
- They cannot function as a bridgehead server designed to replicate directory database changes from other sites because they support only inbound replication.

In addition, certain administrative tasks performed at the branch office where an RODC resides fail if the RODC loses its connection to a writable domain controller at the hub site. These tasks include the following:

- Changing passwords
- Renaming computers
- Joining computers to a domain
- Running the gpupdate /force command
- Attempting authentications for accounts whose credentials are not cached by the RODC

Table 7-4 summarizes the differences between writable domain controllers and RODCs.

Table 7-4   Differences Between Writable Domain Controllers and RODCs

Function	Writable DC	RODC
Kerberos/NTLM Authentication	All	Only secret cached accounts
Lightweight Directory Access Protocol (LDAP)	Read/Write	Read
Global Catalog	Yes	Yes
RO Partial Attribute Set (RO-PAS)	No	Yes
DNS	Query/Update Records	Query
FSMO Roles	All	None
Bridge Head	Yes	No
Replication (AD & FRS)	Inbound/outbound	Inbound
Admin Role Separation	No	Yes
NTDS Stop & Start Feature	Yes	Yes
Core Server	Yes	Yes
RODC Group Membership Caching	Yes	Yes

Preparing a Forest for RODCs

If you plan on having RODCs in your forest, then in addition to updating your forest schema using the Adprep /Forestprep command, you must run the Adprep /Rodcprep command to prepare your forest for RODCs by further extending your schema. This additional step is required to enable RODCs to replicate their DNS partitions. You must run the Adprep /Rodcprep command any time after you have run the Adprep /Forestprep command, and you must allow time for the RODC schema updates to replicate to all domain controllers in your forest before installing RODCs in your forest. Running the Adprep /Rodcprep command has the following effects:

- Updates or creates the CN=ActiveDirecvtoryRodcUpdate,CN=ForestUpdates, CN=Configuration naming context in Active Directory

- Modifies permissions on ForestDNSZones, DomainDNSZones, and the DNS object in the domain partition

In addition to running the Adprep /Rodcprep command, you must make the following preparations before you install RODCs in your forest:

- You must have at least one domain controller running Windows Server 2008 in a domain that is not an RODC and that is configured as a GC server so that any RODC in that domain can replicate with it.

■ If your RODC will be a GC server, you must run Adprep /Domainprep in all domains in your forest regardless of whether a domain has a Windows Server 2008 domain controller in it. Doing this allows the RODC to replicate GC data from all domains in the forest so the RODC can advertise itself as a GC server.

■ You must ensure that your forest functional level is running at Windows Server 2003 or higher so that linked-value replication is available.

Note The first Windows Server 2008 domain controller in either a new Windows Server 2008 domain or in an existing Windows 2000 Server or Windows Server 2003 domain cannot be an RODC.

For more information on updating your forest schema, see the section "Preparing an Existing Active Directory Forest," earlier in this chapter.

Installing an RODC on Server Core

You install an RODC on Server Core the same way you install the writable AD DS role on Server Core—that is, by running Dcpromo with an unattend file. You must install an RODC into a domain in which there is already a writable domain controller running Windows Server 2008 so that the RODC can replicate its directory database from the writable domain controller. You cannot create a new forest, domain tree, or domain when you install an RODC—the forest, domain tree, or domain must exist already and have at least one writable domain controller within it.

For example, to install an RODC named SEA-SC3 within the fabrikam.com domain and within the Default-First-Site-Name site, replicate the directory database for the RODC from writable domain controller SEA-SC1 in the same domain, and cache credentials of members of the Seattle-Users security group, perform the following steps:

1. Use Notepad to create an unattend file containing the lines of text shown here and name the file AddRODC.txt:

```
[DCINSTALL]
UserName=FABRIKAM\Administrator
UserDomain=fabrikam.com
Password=Pa$$w0rd
PasswordReplicationAllowed=FABRIKAM\Seattle-Users
ReplicaOrNewDomain=ReadOnlyReplica
ReplicationSourceDC=SEA-SC1.fabrikam.com
ReplicaDomainDNSName=fabrikam.com
SiteName=Default-First-Site-Name
InstallDNS=yes
ConfirmGC=no
SafeModeAdminPassword=Pa$$w0rd
RebootOnCompletion=yes
```

2. On SEA-SC3, make sure that the Primary DNS Server setting is configured with the IP address of a writable domain controller in the domain to which you want to add your new domain controller. For example, if SEA-SC1 is a writable domain controller in fabrikam.com and has an IP address of 172.16.11.30, type the following commands on SEA-SC3 installation to remove its existing DNS Server settings and assign the correct Primary DNS server setting:

   netsh interface ipv4 delete dnsserver "Local Area Connection" all

   netsh interface ipv4 add dnsserver "Local Area Connection" 172.16.11.30

3. Now type **dcpromo /unattend:<*path*>\AddRODC.txt**, where <*path*> is the path to your unattend file. If your path contains spaces, you must enclose <*path*>*AddRODC.txt* in quotes.

You can also perform a staged installation of an RODC in which the hub administrator creates a computer account for the RODC in Active Directory and the branch office administrator (who can have delegated authority) installs AD DS on the server that will become the RODC and attaches the new domain controller to the computer account previously created for it using the Dcpromo /UseExistingAccount command. For information on how to do this, see the "Step-by-Step Guide for Read-Only Domain Controllers" in the Windows Server 2008 Technical Library at *http://technet.microsoft.com/en-us/windowsserver/default.aspx*.

Configuring the Password Replication Policy for an RODC

You can configure the password replication policy for an RODC by using the Active Directory Users And Computers (ADUC) console. For example, to use ADUC to configure the password replication policy for RODC named SEA-SC3 on writable domain controller SEA-SC1, perform the following steps:

1. Open ADUC and connect to the writable domain controller SEA-SC1 by right-clicking the root node of the console tree and selecting Change Domain Controller.

2. Select the Domain Controllers container. SEA-SC3 should be displayed as an RODC, as shown here.

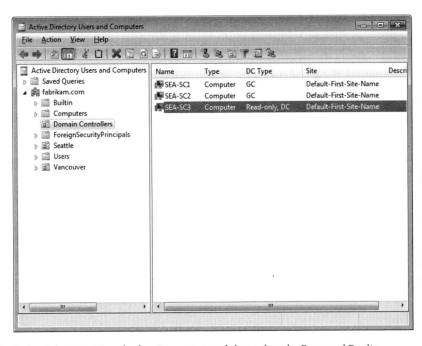

3. Right-click SEA-SC3 and select Properties, and then select the Password Replication tab. Note that the Seattle-Users security group has Allow displayed (as
   shown here), meaning that credentials for users belonging to this group will be
   cached on the RODC.

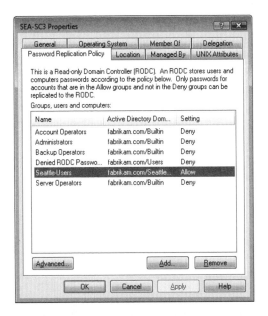

4. Click Add to allow or deny caching of credentials for specific users and groups as desired. You can also click Remove to remove any user or group you have added to the password replication policy list.

5. Click Advanced to display a list of accounts whose credentials are already cached on the RODC, as shown here.

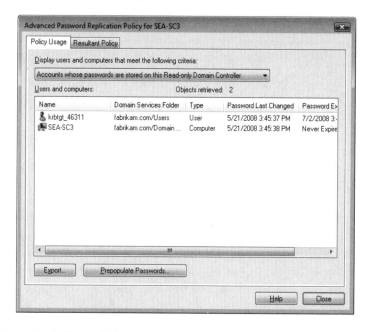

Important If your RODC is stolen, delete its computer account using the ADUC console. A dialog box appears when you do this, and you should select the Reset All Passwords For User Accounts That Were Cached On This Read-Only Domain Controller check box.

A discussion of further aspects of administering an RODC is beyond the scope of this book. See the "Step-by-Step Guide for Read-Only Domain Controllers" in the Windows Server 2008 Technical Library at http://technet.microsoft.com/en-us/windowsserver/ default.aspx *for detailed steps on administering an RODC in a Windows Server 2008 Active Directory environment.*

Chapter 8
DHCP Server Role

DHCP (Dynamic Host Configuration Protocol) lets you reduce the administration burden of configuring hosts on a Transmission Control Protocol/Internet Protocol (TCP/IP) network by dynamically leasing IP addresses and other configuration settings to clients so they can communicate on the network. DHCP servers are, therefore, the backbone of reliable network communications, and the Server Core installation of Windows Server 2008 supports running the DHCP Server role for this purpose. This chapter looks at how to install, manage, and troubleshoot DHCP servers running on Server Core.

Installing the DHCP Server Role on Server Core

Installing the DHCP Server role on Server Core is straightforward and can be done from the command prompt, either locally or via a Remote Desktop connection. You can also install the DHCP Server role using an answer file when performing an unattended install of Server Core.

Installing the DHCP Server Role from the Command Prompt

To install the DHCP Server role on Server Core from the command prompt, perform the following steps:

1. Type **start /w ocsetup DHCPServerCore** at a command prompt.

2. Verify the DHCP Server role is installed:

   ```
   C:\Users\administrator>oclist | find "  Installed"
       Installed:DHCPServerCore
   ```

Installing the DHCP Server Role Using an Answer File

To install the DHCP Server Role using an answer file, perform the following steps:

1. Begin by creating and configuring an answer file for an unattended installation of Server Core. For information on how to do this, see Chapter 2, "Deploying Server Core."

2. On your technician computer, open your answer file in Windows System Image Manager (Windows SIM).

3. In the Windows Image pane, expand the Packages node to display the nodes beneath it. Expand the Foundation node to display the Microsoft-Windows-ServerCore-Package node beneath that. Then right-click the

Microsoft-Windows-ServerCore-Package node and select Add To Answer File. The Microsoft-Windows-ServerCore-Package should now be selected in the Answer File pane.

4. In the Properties pane, scroll down until the DHCPServerCore setting is visible under Windows Feature. Click the value field to the right of the DHCPServer-Core setting to display a drop-down arrow. Click the arrow and select Enabled, as shown here.

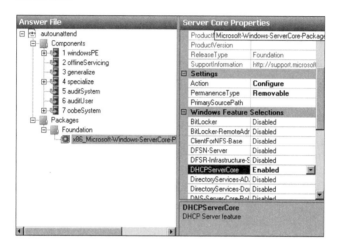

5. Validate your answer file and save it. Then deploy Server Core with your answer file using any of the methods outlined in Chapter 2. When installation is completed, log on, type **oclist | find "Installed"**, and verify that the DHCP Server role has been installed.

Starting the DHCP Server Service

Whatever way you install the DHCP Server role on Server Core, the DHCP Server services remain in a disabled state. To verify this fact after installing the DHPC Server role as described previously, use the Sc command as follows:

```
C:\Users\administrator>sc qc dhcpserver
[SC] QueryServiceConfig SUCCESS

SERVICE_NAME: dhcpserver
        TYPE               : 20  WIN32_SHARE_PROCESS
        START_TYPE         : 4   DISABLED
        ERROR_CONTROL      : 1   NORMAL
        BINARY_PATH_NAME   : C:\Windows\system32\svchost.exe -k DHCPServer
        LOAD_ORDER_GROUP   :
        TAG                : 0
```

```
DISPLAY_NAME        : DHCP Server
DEPENDENCIES        : RpcSs
                    : Tcpip
                    : SamSs
                    : EventLog
                    : EventSystem
SERVICE_START_NAME  : LocalSystem
```

To start the DHCP Server service, perform the following steps:

1. Use the Sc command to set the startup value for the DHCP Services to auto as follows:

```
C:\Users\administrator>sc config dhcpserver start= auto
[SC] ChangeServiceConfig SUCCESS
```

2. Start the DHCP Service using the Net command as follows:

```
C:\Users\administrator>net start dhcpserver
The DHCP Server service is starting....
The DHCP Server service was started successfully.
```

3. Verify the status of the DHCP server using the Netsh command as follows:

```
netsh dhcp server>show serverstatus

Server Status:
        Server Attrib - Rogue Authorization Succeeded :FALSE
        Server Attrib - Dynamic BootP Support Enabled :TRUE
        Server Attrib - DHCP Server Part Of DS        :TRUE
        Server Attrib - DHCP Server Bindings Aware     :TRUE
        Server Attrib - Administrative Rights          :TRUE
```

The DHCP server is running at this point, but it is not authorized. See the section "Authorizing a DHCP Server in Active Directory," later in this chapter, for more information concerning authorizing a DHCP Server.

> **Tip**   You can also test whether your Server Core DHCP Server is working properly by connecting to it using the DHCP console from a computer running Windows Vista SP1 or a Full installation of Windows Server 2008 that has the Remote Server Administration Tools (RSAT) installed. See the section "Managing DHCP Servers Using RSAT," later in this chapter, for more information.

Removing the DHCP Server Role

You can remove the DHCP Server role from Server Core by typing **start /w ocsetup DHCPServerCore /uninstall** at a command prompt. You do not have to stop the DHCP Server service before removing the DHCP Server role from your server.

Managing a Server Core DHCP Server

Once you've installed the DHCP Server role on Server Core, you need to configure the role and manage its configuration. This section covers basic DHCP Server administration tasks, focusing on command-line management of Server Core DHCP servers. For detailed information on managing DHCP Servers from the graphical user interface (GUI), see the *Windows Server 2008 Administrator's Pocket Consultant* by William Stanek (Microsoft Press, 2008).

Managing DHCP Servers

You can manage DHCP servers in three ways:

- Using the DHCP console that is included as part of RSAT
- From the command prompt interactively, using the Netsh command
- In scripted fashion, by creating a batch file that contains a series of Netsh commands

Managing DHCP Servers Using RSAT

You can manage a DHCP server running on a Server Core installation the same way you manage a DHCP Server running on a Full installation of Windows Server 2008– that is, by using the DHCP console. This console is available in two ways:

- On any Full installation of Windows Server 2008 on which you have added the DHCP Server role
- On any computer running Windows Vista SP1 or Full installation of Windows Server 2008 on which you have installed the RSAT

Note For instructions on how to install RSAT, see Chapter 6, "Remote Management."

For example, suppose you wanted to manage a Server Core DHCP server named SEA-SC1.fabrikam.com from a computer running Windows Vista SP1 belonging to the same domain and that has RSAT installed on it. You would perform the following steps:

1. On the computer running Windows Vista SP1, click Start, Administrative Tools, and finally DHCP to open the DHCP console.

2. Right-click the root node in the console tree and select Add Server.

3. Type the name of the server, as shown here, or search for it in Active Directory.

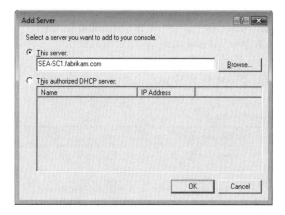

4. Click OK and expand the console tree to manage the DHCP server.

5. If needed, add more DHCP servers to the console by following steps 1-4 multiple times.

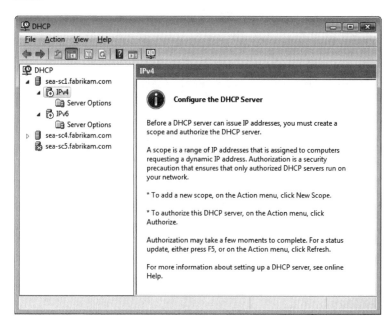

The DHCP Server node (indicated by the fully qualified domain name [FQDN]) has two subnodes as follows:

■ IPv4 contains configuration settings and status information for the DHCPv4 server

■ IPv6 contains configuration settings and status information for the DHCPv6 server

Support for DHCPv6 is new to Windows Server 2008, but that is beyond the scope of this book. For more information on DHCPv6 support in Windows Server 2008, see the Windows Server 2008 TechCenter on Microsoft TechNet at http://technet.microsoft.com/en-us/windowsserver/2008/default.aspx.

The symbols listed in Table 8-1 provide quick information concerning the status of a DHCP server.

Table 8-1   DHCP Server Status Symbols

Location	Symbol	Meaning
Server node	Red X	The console is unable to connect to the DHCP server.
	None	The console is connected to the DHCP server.
IPv4 or IPv6 node	Red down arrow	The DHCP server has not been authorized.
	Green up arrow	The DHCP server has been authorized.
	Blue warning icon	The state of the server has changed or a warning has been issued.
Scope node	None	The scope has been activated.
	Red down arrow	The scope has not been activated.
	Blue warning icon	The state of scope has changed or a warning has been issued.

Note   An example of when the blue warning icon is displayed would be when you create a new scope but do not configure a range of IP addresses for the scope. Because it has not been configured properly, the scope is deemed to be in an indeterminate state.

Managing DHCP Servers Interactively Using Netsh

To manage DHCP servers interactively using Netsh, open an admin-level command prompt and type **netsh** followed by **dhcp** to enter the DHCP context of the Netsh command as follows:

```
C:\Users\administrator>netsh
netsh>dhcp
netsh dhcp>
```

From this context, you can type commands or enter subcontexts where additional commands are available for managing DHCP servers. For a list of commands and subcontexts available for a given context, type **?** at the Netsh prompt.

Managing DHCP Servers in Batch Mode Using Netsh Scripts

You can also create a batch file of Netsh commands and run them as a script to automate the configuration of DHCP servers, scopes, and options, or to perform other types of DHCP management tasks. For an example of how to do this, see the section "Creating and Configuring a Scope Using a Batch File," later in this chapter.

Granting Users Privileges for Managing DHCP Servers

By default, members of the Domain Admins security group have full privileges for managing all aspects of DHCP servers in an Active Directory–based network. You can also grant DHCP administration privileges to specific users by making them members of either the DHCP Administrators group or the DHCP Users security group. These two domain local groups are found in the Users container in Active Directory Users And Computers, and the privileges granted to users as a result of membership in these groups are described in Table 8-2.

Table 8-2   Privileges Granted by Membership in the Default DHCP Security Groups

Group	Can Do	Can't Do
DHCP Users	Members of this group have read-only access to the DHCP console, which means they can view the DHCP server configuration, database, registry keys, and log files.	Members of this group cannot modify the DHCP server configuration, create or modify scopes, create or modify options, create or modify reservations and exclusion ranges, or perform any other DHCP server administration task, such as exporting or importing the DHCP server configuration and database.
DHCP Administrators	Members of this group can do everything members of the DHCP Users group can do, plus they can modify the DHCP server configuration, create or modify scopes, create or modify options, create or modify reservations and exclusion ranges, and perform any other DHCP server administration task, such as exporting or importing the DHCP server configuration and database.	Members of this group cannot authorize or unauthorize DHCP servers in Active Directory—only Domain Admins group members can do this.

You can use the Dsmod command to add a user to either the DHCP Users or DHCP Administrators group. For example, to add user Karen Berg to the DHCP Administrators domain local group, use the following command:

```
C:\Windows\system32>dsmod group "CN=DHCP Administrators,CN=Users,
DC=fabrikam,DC=com" -addmbr "CN=Karen Berg,OU=Seattle Users,OU=Seattle,
```

```
DC=fabrikam,DC=com"
dsmod succeeded:CN=DHCP Administrators,CN=Users,DC=fabrikam,DC=com
```

Authorizing a DHCP Server in Active Directory

In an Active Directory environment, a Windows Server DHCP server must be authorized before it can be used to lease out addresses to clients. DHCP server authorization is designed to protect against rogue DHCP servers running on your network. For example, if you have a domain controller or member server that is running as an authorized DHCP server and a stand-alone Windows Server DHCP server is introduced onto the network, the stand-alone DHCP server detects the presence of the authorized DHCP server. As a result, the stand-alone server automatically stops leasing addresses out to clients.

> **Note**   This feature works only when the rogue server is running some version of the Windows Server operating system—third-party rogue DHCP servers usually do not react this way.

You can authorize a DHCP server using the Netsh command. For example, to authorize a Server Core DHCP server that has the name SEA-SC1 and the IP address 172.16.11.30 and that belongs to the fabrikam.com domain, do the following:

```
C:\Users\administrator>netsh dhcp add server SEA-SC1.fabrikam.com 172.16.11.30

Adding server SEA-SC1.fabrikam.com, 172.16.11.30

Command completed successfully.
```

Note that you must specify both the FQDN and the IP address of the DHCP server in the previous command.

To verify the result, use Netsh again to display a list of authorized DHCP servers for the domain as follows:

```
C:\Users\administrator>netsh dhcp show server

1 Servers were found in the directory service:

        Server [SEA-SC1.fabrikam.com] Address [172.16.11.30]
Ds location: cn=SEA
-SC1.fabrikam.com

Command completed successfully.
```

You can unauthorize this DHCP server by typing **netsh dhcp delete server SEA-SC1.fabrikam.com 172.16.11.30** at a command prompt.

Selecting an Authorized DHCP Server to Manage

When the Netsh command is run at the command prompt (either locally or via Remote Desktop) of a Server Core DHCP server, it executes its commands against that particular DHCP server. If you need to configure or manage a different DHCP server on your network, you first must change the context of Netsh to the other server.

For example, if you are logged on locally to Server Core DHCP server SEA-SC1, any Netsh commands you execute interactively affect only the local DHCP server. Therefore, if you want to configure a different DHCP server that has the name SEA-SC4 and the IP address 172.16.11.33 from the local command prompt on SEA-SC1, you must do the following to run Netsh commands interactively against the other DHCP server:

```
C:\Users\administrator>netsh
netsh>dhcp
netsh dhcp>server \\SEA-SC4
netsh dhcp server>
```

Note that instead of typing **SEA-SC4**, you could type either **SEA-SC4.fabrikam.com** or **172.16.11.33** to achieve the same result.

To change the focus to a different DHCP server, type **server** *servername* at either the netsh dhcp or netsh dhcp server prompt. To change the focus back to the local DHCP server, type **server** at either prompt.

Viewing and Modifying DHCP Server Configuration

After you install the DHCP Server role, you may need to configure your DHCP server further before creating scopes on it for leasing out addresses. While the default configuration settings for the DHCP Server service may suffice in most cases, administrators who are responsible for specialized environments may want to modify some of these settings.

To view status and configuration information of the local DHCP server, use the Netsh command like this:

```
C:\Users\administrator>netsh dhcp server show all

MIBCounts:
        Discovers = 0.
        Offers = 0.
        Requests = 0.
        Acks = 0.
        Naks = 0.
        Declines = 0.
        Releases = 0.
        ServerStartTime = Friday, May 23, 2008 9:00:09 AM
        Scopes = 0.
```

```
Server Database Properties :

        DatabaseName              = dhcp.mdb
        DatabasePath              = C:\Windows\system32\dhcp
        DatabaseBackupPath        = C:\Windows\system32\dhcp\backup
        DatabaseBackupInterval    = 60 mins.
        DatabaseLoggingFlag       = 1
        DatabaseRestoreFlag       = 0
        DatabaseCleanupInterval   = 60 mins.


Server Status:
        Server Attrib - Rogue Authorization Succeeded  :TRUE
        Server Attrib - Dynamic BootP Support Enabled  :TRUE
        Server Attrib - DHCP Server Part Of DS          :TRUE
        Server Attrib - DHCP Server Bindings Aware      :TRUE
        Server Attrib - Administrative Rights           :TRUE
```

To view the status and configuration of a different DHCP server, such as SEA-SC4, type **netsh dhcp server \\SEA-SC4 show all** instead. You can also use *FQDN* or *ipaddress* to specify the DHCP server whose configuration you want to display.

To view the bindings of your DHCP server, use the following command:

```
C:\Users\administrator>netsh dhcp server show bindings

Binding information      : 0
=================================================================

Bound To Server                  : TRUE

Adapter Primary Address          : 172.16.11.30

Adapter Subnet Address           : 255.255.255.0

Interface Description            : Local Area Connection

Interface ID                       : E697519F36C60545BC7ED67D30DC5EAF
=================================================================

Binding information      : 1
=================================================================

Bound To Server                  : TRUE

Adapter Primary Address          : 172.16.12.25

Adapter Subnet Address           : 255.255.255.0

Interface Description            : Local Area Connection 2
```

```
Interface ID                    : 2938572F387928E749283CB982374FA2
============================================================================
```

```
Command completed successfully.
```

This command shows which local network connections your DHCP server can provide leases to, which is two local network connections in this case. By default, the DHCP server is bound to all available local network connections (that is, the server is multi-homed) that have static addresses assigned to them. To enable or disable the binding for a particular interface, such as Local Area Connection 2, use Netsh like this:

```
C:\Users\administrator>netsh dhcp server set bindings "Local Area
Connection 2" disable
```

Creating and Managing Scopes

Creating and managing scopes is the core of DHCP server management. A *scope* is a pool of IP addresses that the server can lease to clients that need them so they can communicate on the network. Administrative tasks involving scopes include:

- Creating new scopes
- Adding address ranges to scopes
- Adding exclusions to scopes
- Creating reservations for clients that need them
- Configuring scope options
- Activating and deactivating scopes

Creating a New Scope

You can use the Netsh command to create and configure a new scope. For example, the following command creates a new scope named "Main Office" that has a network ID of 172.16.11.0 and a subnet mask of 255.255.255.0:

```
C:\Users\administrator>netsh dhcp server add scope 172.16.11.0 255.255.255.0
"Main Office"
```

```
Command completed successfully.
```

Once you've created a new scope using Netsh, you can use additional Netsh commands to configure the scope as desired. This is illustrated in the following sections.

Adding an IP Address Range to a Scope

You can use Netsh to add a range of IP addresses to a scope. For example, to add the range 172.16.11.220 to 172.16.11.250 to the scope with network ID 172.16.11.0 that was created in the previous section, use the following command:

```
C:\Users\administrator>netsh dhcp server scope 172.16.11.0 add iprange
172.16.11.220 172.16.11.250
```

```
Changed the current scope context to 172.16.11.0 scope.
```

```
Command completed successfully.
```

> **Note** You must specify the network ID of the scope when you configure it because a DHCP server can have more than one scope created on it.

Adding Exclusions to a Scope

If certain addresses within the address range of a scope should not be leased out, you can create exclusions for the addresses. For example, you may already have servers with statically assigned IP addresses within the address range of the scope you created. If this is the case, you must configure exclusions for these servers so that your DHCP server won't try to lease addresses that are already used to clients.

You can add individual addresses, address ranges, or both as exclusions to a scope. For example, to exclude the address range 172.16.11.225 to 172.16.11.230 from the scope range you added in the previous section, do this:

```
C:\Users\administrator>netsh dhcp server scope 172.16.11.0 add excluderange
172.16.11.225 172.16.11.230
Changed the current scope context to 172.16.11.0 scope.
```

```
Command completed successfully.
```

To exclude the single address 172.16.11.244 from your scope, do this:

```
C:\Users\administrator>netsh dhcp server scope 172.16.11.0 add excluderange
172.16.11.244 172.16.11.244
Changed the current scope context to 172.16.11.0 scope.
```

```
Command completed successfully.
```

Creating Reservations

Servers generally require IP addresses that do not change so that clients can easily locate the network services these servers provide. You can assign a server an unchanging address in two ways:

- Configuring a static IP address for the server. If you do this and your server's IP address overlaps with a DHCP server's scope, you must exclude your server's address from the scope as described in the previous section.

- Configuring dynamic IP addressing for the server. If you do this, you must ensure that the server always leases the same address from your DHCP server by creating a reservation on your DHCP server.

A *reservation* is an IP address that is always leased to the same client (which in this context can be either a workstation or a server). To reserve an IP address for a client, you need to know the media access control (MAC) address (or physical address) of the client, which is assigned to the network interface card in your server by the manufacturer. There are several ways you can determine the MAC address:

- Locally, by typing **ipconfig /all**

- Remotely, by typing **nbtstat -A 172.16.11.133** where the address is that of the remote server

- Remotely, by typing **psexec \\172.16.11.133 -u Administrator -p Pa$$w0rd ipconfig /all** which uses Psexec, one of the Windows Sysinternals tools, to run the ipconfig /all command on the remote computer.

- Remotely, by using Windows Remote Shell (see Chapter 6 for more information)

Note   To obtain the Windows Sysinternals tools, see *http://technet.microsoft.com/ en-us/sysinternals/default.aspx*.

To create a reservation using Netsh, perform the following steps:

1. Determine the MAC address (for example, 00-03-FF-54-88-8C) of the computer for which you need to create a reservation using one of the methods described previously.

2. At the command prompt on your DHCP server, type the following command:

```
C:\Users\administrator>netsh dhcp server scope 172.16.11.0 add
reservedip 172.16.11.133 0003FF54888C
Changed the current scope context to 172.16.11.0 scope.

Command completed successfully.
```

   Note that the MAC address must be specified without dashes in the previous Netsh command.

3. On the computer for which you created a reservation, configure the local network connection for dynamic addressing. Then open a command prompt, type **ipconfig**, and confirm that the computer received the address 172.16.11.133 as planned.

Configuring DHCP Options

You can also configure DHCP options for your clients using the Netsh command. A DHCP option is additional information provided to the client when the client leases an address from the server. DHCP options that you typically want to configure include the following:

- Default gateway (router) address (option 003)
- DNS server addresses (option 006)
- DNS domain names (option 015)
- WINS server addresses (option 044)

DHCP options can be configured at different levels:

- **Server options**   These options apply globally to all DHCP clients but can be overridden by scope options.

- **Scope options**   These options apply on a per-scope basis.

- **Reservation options**   These options apply only to a particular reservation.

For example, to configure a scope option that assigns a default gateway address of 172.16.11.1 to all clients who lease addresses from the 172.16.11.0 scope, do this:

```
C:\Users\administrator>netsh dhcp server scope 172.16.11.0 set
optionvalue 003 IPADDRESS 172.16.11.1

Changed the current scope context to 172.16.11.0 scope.

Command completed successfully.
```

Verify the result as follows:

```
C:\Users\administrator>netsh dhcp server scope 172.16.11.0 show optionvalue

Changed the current scope context to 172.16.11.0 scope.

Options for Scope 172.16.11.0:

        DHCP Standard Options :
        General Option Values:
        OptionId : 51
        Option Value:
                Number of Option Elements = 1
                Option Element Type = DWORD
                Option Element Value = 691200
        OptionId : 3
        Option Value:
                Number of Option Elements = 1
                Option Element Type = IPADDRESS
                Option Element Value = 172.16.11.1
Command completed successfully.
```

Note   For an explanation of why option 051 is configured by default, see the section "Configuring Lease Duration," later in this chapter.

If you prefer, you can globally specify 172.16.11.1 as the default gateway for every scope on your DHCP server by configuring server option 003 instead of scope option 003 as follows:

```
C:\Users\administrator>netsh dhcp server 172.16.11.0 set optionvalue 003
IPADDRESS 172.16.11.1
```

```
Command completed successfully.
```

Creating and Configuring a Scope Using a Batch File

You can create and configure a scope interactively by typing the series of Netsh commands shown in the previous sections, or you can create a batch file that can execute a series of Netsh commands that create and configure a scope as a single operation. The following batch file creates the scope 172.16.11.0 on DHCP server 172.16.11.30 using the settings indicated in the previous sections:

```
REM -- Batch file to create a scope on a DHCP server
REM
REM -- Create scope 172.16.11.0 on DHCP server 172.16.11.30
netsh dhcp server 172.16.11.30 add scope 172.16.11.0 255.255.255.0
"Main Office"
REM
REM -- Assign address range 172.16.11.220 to 172.16.11.250 to new scope
netsh dhcp server 172.16.11.30 scope 172.16.11.0 add iprange 172.16.11.220
172.16.11.250
REM
REM -- Exclude address range 172.16.11.225 through 172.16.11 230
from new scope
netsh dhcp server 172.16.11.30 scope 172.16.11.0 add excluderange 172.16.1
1.225 172.16.11.230
REM
REM -- Exclude single address 172.16.11.244 from new scope
netsh dhcp server 172.16.11.30 scope 172.16.11.0 add excluderange 172.16.1
1.244 172.16.11.244
REM
REM -- Reserve address 172.16.11.133 for mail server
netsh dhcp server 172.16.11.30 scope 172.16.11.0 add reservedip 172.16.11.
133 0003FF54888C
REM
REM -- Configure scope option 003 to assign default gateway of
172.16.11.1 to clients
netsh dhcp server 172.16.11.30 scope 172.16.11.0 set optionvalue 003 IPADD
RESS 172.16.11.1
```

Type these lines into Notepad and save the file as C:\Scripts\MakeScope.bat. Then at the command prompt, type the following:

```
C:\Users\Administrator>C:\scripts\MakeScope.bat > Results.txt
```

Open Results.txt in Notepad to view the result of running the commands. Alternatively, use RSAT from another computer to connect to Server Core DHCP server 172.16.11.30 and view the results graphically as shown in Figure 8-1.

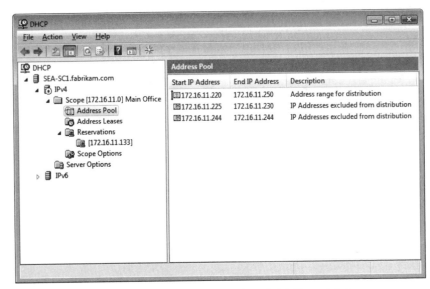

Figure 8-1 The results of creating a new scope using a batch file containing Netsh commands

Configuring Lease Duration

Some aspects of scopes are configured differently in the GUI than from the command line. For example, to configure the lease duration of a scope using the Netsh command, you can specify the value of DHCP option 051. In the section "Configuring DHCP Options," earlier in this chapter, you saw that by default the value of this scope option is 691,200 seconds (or 8 days). If your network changes infrequently, you could increase this lease duration to 1,296,000 seconds (15 days) or even longer by using the following Netsh command:

```
C:\Users\administrator>netsh dhcp server set optionvalue 051 DWORD 1296000

Changed the current scope context to 172.16.11.0 scope.

Command completed successfully.
```

If you are managing your DHCP server using the DHCP console, however, you'll see that there is no way to assign a value in the GUI to DHCP option 051 using the Scope Options dialog box (shown in Figure 8-2).

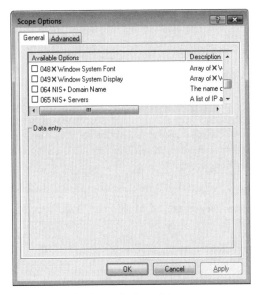

Figure 8-2   The Scope Options dialog box

Instead, you must configure lease duration from the General tab of the scope's properties sheet (shown in Figure 8-3).

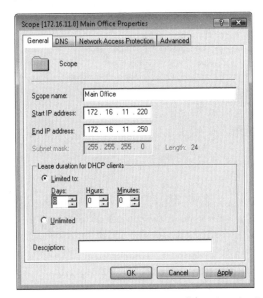

Figure 8-3   Lease duration being configured on the General tab of the scope's properties sheet

In general, you can configure any aspect of a scope either using the GUI or from the command line using Netsh. For more information about configuring a scope using Netsh, see the information concerning the netsh dhcp server scope context of Netsh in the Netsh.chm help file for Windows Server 2008, which can be obtained from the Microsoft Download Center at http://www.microsoft.com/downloads/.

Activating a Scope

You can activate or deactivate a scope using Netsh. A scope that is active leases out addresses to clients that request them. A scope that is inactive does not; however, any addresses that were previously leased out remain valid until they expire, even if you deactivate the scope from which they were leased.

To activate the scope 172.16.11.0 on DHCP server 172.16.11.30 using Netsh, do this:

```
C:\Users\Administrators>netsh dhcp server 172.16.11.30 scope 172.16.11.0
set state 1

Changed the current scope context to 172.16.11.0 scope.

Command completed successfully.
```

To deactivate a scope, use **set state 0** in this command.

Viewing Scopes

You can use the Netsh command to display a list of all scopes created on your DHCP server as follows:

```
C:\Users\administrator>netsh dhcp server show scope
========================================================================
Scope Address  - Subnet Mask   - State   - Scope Name     -  Comment
========================================================================

172.16.11.0   - 255.255.255.0  -Active      -Main Office       -


 Total No. of Scopes = 1
Command completed successfully.
```

Deleting a Scope

You can delete a scope using the Netsh command if the scope is no longer needed on the DHCP server. To delete a scope, you must specify the network ID of the scope. The following command deletes scope 172.16.11.0, provided that there are no active DHCP clients leasing addresses from the scope:

```
C:\Users\Administrators>netsh dhcp server delete scope 172.16.11.0
DhcpNoForce

Command completed successfully.
```

You can also forcibly delete a scope even if the scope has active clients. You do this as follows:

```
C:\Users\Administrators> netsh dhcp server delete scope 172.16.11.0
DhcpFullForce

Command completed successfully.
```

Maintaining DHCP Servers

You can maintain DHCP servers by either using the DHCP console from RSAT or using the Netsh command. DHCP server maintenance tasks include the following:

- Viewing DHCP server activity
- Viewing DHCP scope statistics
- Backing up and restoring the DHCP server database
- Exporting and importing the DHCP server configuration
- Reconciling DHCP scopes
- Dumping and loading the DHCP server configuration
- Monitoring and troubleshooting DHCP servers

Viewing DHCP Server Activity

You can use the Netsh command to display DHCP server activity by querying the management information base (MIB) using Simple Network Management Protocol (SNMP) as follows:

```
C:\>netsh dhcp server show mibinfo

MIBCounts:
        Discovers = 0.
        Offers = 0.
        Requests = 0.
        Acks = 1.
        Naks = 0.
        Declines = 0.
        Releases = 0.
        ServerStartTime = Sunday, May 25, 2008 12:38:06 PM
        Scopes = 1.
        Subnet = 172.16.11.0.
                No. of Addresses in use = 1.
                No. of free Addresses = 23.
                No. of pending offers = 0.
```

The previous command output indicates that scope 172.16.11.0 has 1 address in use and 23 addresses that are still available.

Viewing DHCP Scope Statistics

You can use the Netsh command to display a list of clients currently leasing addresses from a specified scope. For example, to list all clients currently leasing addresses from the scope with network ID 172.16.11.0, do the following:

```
C:\Users\administrator>netsh dhcp server scope 172.16.11.0 show clients

Changed the current scope context to 172.16.11.0 scope.

Type : N - NONE, D - DHCP B - BOOTP, U - UNSPECIFIED, R - RESERVATION IP
===========================================================================
========
IP Address      - Subnet Mask     - Unique ID         -
  Lease Expires       -Type
===========================================================================
========

172.16.11.133   - 255.255.255.0   -00-03-ff-54-88-8c    -
  NEVER EXPIRES         -U
172.16.11.220   - 255.255.255.0   - 00-03-ff-43-88-8c   -6/9/
2008 11:41:18 AM    -D

No of Clients(version 4): 2 in the Scope : 172.16.11.0.

Command completed successfully.
```

Typing **show clients 1** instead of **show clients** causes the FQDN of each client to be included in the listing.

To view more detailed scope statistics, use the DHCP console in RSAT.

Backing Up the DHCP Server Database

The DHCP database is the repository for all DHCP server information, including scopes, reservations, leases, options, configuration settings, and registry keys. The DHCP database is located under the %SystemRoot%\System32\DHCP folder and consists of database (.mdb and .edb) files, checkpoint (.chk) files, and transaction log (.log) files, among other types of files. By default, Windows Server 2008 automatically backs up the DHCP database files and DHCP registry configuration (DhcpCfg) every 60 minutes and saves these backups under the %SystemRoot%\System32\ DHCP\Backup folder.

You can back up the DHCP server database manually at any time by using the Netsh command. For example, to back up your DHCP server database to the local folder C:\DHCP Backups, do the following:

```
C:\Users\administrator>netsh dhcp server backup "C:\DHCP Backups"

Command completed successfully.
```

View the results using recursive dir as follows:

```
C:\Users\administrator>dir "C:\DHCP Backups" /s
 Volume in drive C has no label.
 Volume Serial Number is D073-E5CE

 Directory of C:\DHCP Backups

05/25/2008  12:02 PM    <DIR>          .
05/25/2008  12:02 PM    <DIR>          ..
05/25/2008  12:02 PM             8,192 DhcpCfg
05/25/2008  12:02 PM    <DIR>          new
               1 File(s)          8,192 bytes

 Directory of C:\DHCP Backups\new

05/25/2008  12:02 PM    <DIR>          .
05/25/2008  12:02 PM    <DIR>          ..
05/25/2008  12:02 PM         1,060,864 dhcp.mdb
05/25/2008  12:02 PM             8,192 dhcp.pat
05/25/2008  12:02 PM         1,048,576 j5000011.log
               3 File(s)      2,117,632 bytes

     Total Files Listed:
               4 File(s)      2,125,824 bytes
               5 Dir(s)  26,645,712,896 bytes free
```

Depending on the needs of your enterprise, you may also decide to copy the contents of the %SystemRoot%\System32\DHCP\Backup to a remote network share so that you can restore the latest version of the DHCP server database should your DHCP server fail. This could be done automatically as a scheduled task by running the Robocopy command. For more information on using this command, type **robocopy /?** at a command prompt.

You also typically back up your DHCP server database as part of the general (daily or weekly) backup for your servers. For more information about backing up a Server Core installation, see Chapter 13, "Maintaining Server Core."

Restoring the DHCP Server Database

If your DHCP server fails, you can restore the server from backup. Depending on your backup strategy, you may be able to perform this restore in several ways:

- By restoring the DHCP server database from the %SystemRoot%\System32\ DHCP\Backup folder (if this is available), or from the latest copy of this database that has been copied to a network share

- By restoring the DHCP server database from the most recent daily (incremental) backup of your server

- By restoring the DHCP server database from the most recent weekly (full) backup of your server

To restore your DHCP server database from a backup of the database (either a manually created backup or the most recent automatic backup under the %SystemRoot%\System32\DHCP\Backup folder) use the Netsh command like this:

```
C:\Users\administrator>netsh dhcp server restore "C:\DHCP Backups"

Need to stop and restart the DHCP server service in order for this change
to take effect.

Command completed successfully.
```

Note   The DHCP service temporarily stops during the restore operation. This means that clients cannot contact the DHCP server to renew their leases or obtain new addresses while the restore is being performed.

Exporting and Importing a DHCP Server Configuration

You can export all or portions of your DHCP server configuration by using the Netsh command. Afterwards, you can use the Netsh command to import your exported DHCP server configuration into a different DHCP server running Windows Server 2008. You can thus use the export and import operations to move the DHCP server database from one DHCP server to another.

For example, to export the full configuration of your DHCP server as a file named Dhcpconfig in a folder named C:\DHCP Configs that you have created, do the following:

```
C:\Users\administrator>netsh dhcp server export "C:\DHCP Configs\
dhcpconfig" all

Command completed successfully.
```

To export only the configuration information for the scope 172.16.11.0, do this instead:

```
C:\Users\administrator>netsh dhcp server export "C:\DHCP Configs\
dhcpconfig" 172.16.11.0
```

Once you have exported a DHCP server configuration, you can import this configuration into a different Windows Server 2008 computer by performing the following steps:

1. Install the DHCP Server role on your destination server.

2. Type **netsh dhcp server import** *<path_to_config_file>* **all** to move the entire DHCP server configuration from your original DHCP server to the destination server. Alternatively, type **netsh dhcp server import** *<path_to_config_file>* **scope** [**scope**...] to move the configuration for one or more scopes from your original DHCP server to the destination server.

Reconciling DHCP Scopes

You can use the Netsh command to verify and reconcile any database inconsistencies that the server is able to find. Reconciling a scope checks the client leases and reservations against the DHCP database and, optionally, fixes any inconsistencies that were found. To reconcile a scope, do the following:

```
C:\>netsh dhcp server scope 172.16.11.0 initiate reconcile

Changed the current scope context to 172.16.11.0 scope.

No database-registry inconsistencies detected for scope 172.16.11.0.

DHCP Initiate Reconcile request is successfully queued.
```

To fix any inconsistencies found in this scope, use **initiate reconcile fix** instead of **initiate reconcile** in the previous command.

Dumping and Loading a DHCP Server Configuration

You can dump the configuration (not the database) of a DHCP server using the Netsh command. Before you dump the configuration, you should reconcile all scopes on the server as described in the previous section.

To dump the configuration of your server as a text file named C:\DHCP Dumps\ dhcp.dmp, type **netsh dhcp server dump > "C:\DHCP Dumps\dhcp.dmp"** at the command prompt. The resulting text file consists of scriptable commands that you can use to recreate the DHCP server configuration by typing **netsh dhcp exec <path_to_dump_file>** at the command prompt.

The netsh dhcp server dump command is used only for advanced troubleshooting scenarios, such as problems resulting from a multilingual DHCP server environment. For an example of this issue, see http://support.microsoft.com/kb/885687.

Monitoring and Troubleshooting DHCP Servers

You can monitor and troubleshoot DHCP servers using a variety of tools including the following:

- Windows event logs
- Performance logs and alerts
- DHCP audit logs

Note   For information on viewing event logs and monitoring performance counters on a Server Core installation, see Chapter 13.

DHCP audit logs are comma-delimited text files found in the %SystemRoot%\ System32\DHCP folder on a DHCP server. DHCP audit logs are automatically created on a daily basis by the DHCP server and are named after the day of the week they were created. For example, DhcpSrvLog-Sun.Log would be the log file created on Sunday for DHCPv4 service activity, while DhcpV6SrvLog-Sun.Log would be the log file created on the same day for DHCPv6 service activity.

An excerpt from a DHCP audit log might look like this:

```
ID,Date,Time,Description,IP Address,Host Name,MAC Address,User Name,
TransactionID, QResult,Probationtime, CorrelationID.
00,05/25/08,10:32:14,Started,,,,,0,6,,,
50,05/25/08,10:32:43,Unreachable Domain,,fabrikam.com,,,0,6,,,
55,05/25/08,10:32:43,Authorized(servicing),,fabrikam.com,,,0,6,,,
24,05/25/08,11:32:16,Database Cleanup Begin,,,,,0,6,,,
25,05/25/08,11:32:16,0 leases expired and 0 leases deleted,,,,,0,6,,,
25,05/25/08,11:32:16,0 leases expired and 0 leases deleted,,,,,0,6,,,
30,05/25/08,11:36:42,DNS Update Request,172.16.11.133,SEA-SRV2,,,0,6,,,
11,05/25/08,11:36:42,Renew,172.16.11.133,SEA-SRV2,0003FF54888C,,2843712581,0,,,
31,05/25/08,11:36:42,DNS Update Failed,172.16.11.133,SEA-SRV2,,,0,6,,,
```

DHCP audit logs can be used to monitor DHCP service activity, troubleshoot address leasing, troubleshoot dynamic DNS updates (when enabled), and for other similar purposes. For more information on interpreting these log files, see the DHCP Operations Guide in the Windows Server 2008 Technical Library at http://technet.microsoft.com/en-us/ windowsserver/default.aspx.

Chapter 9
DNS Server Role

The Domain Name System (DNS) is central to the operation of both an Active Directory Domain Services (AD DS) environment and the Internet. DNS provides a unique, hierarchical way of naming computers and services on a network and a mechanism for resolving these names into Internet Protocol (IP) addresses so that network communications can take place. The DNS Server role is one of the roles that can be installed on a Server Core installation of Windows Server 2008, and this chapter examines how to install, configure, manage, and troubleshoot DNS servers running on Server Core.

Installing the DNS Server Role on Server Core

You can install the DNS Server role on Server Core in several ways:

- During the process of installing the AD DS role on a computer
- From the command prompt, using the Ocsetup.exe utility
- Using an answer file during an unattended installation of Server Core

Installing the DNS Server Role on a Domain Controller

When you use Dcpromo in unattend mode to install the AD DS role on a Server Core installation, you have the option of also installing the DNS Server role on your new domain controller. To ensure that the DNS Server role is installed on a Server Core installation that you are promoting to the role of a domain controller, you must include the following line in your Dcpromo unattend file:

```
InstallDNS=yes
```

You must include this line in your unattend file if you are using Dcpromo to create a new forest, domain tree, or child domain. You may include this line if you are installing a new replica domain controller in an existing domain. If you are installing a new replica domain controller and do not include this line, Dcpromo uses its own internal heuristics to determine whether to install the DNS Server role on the new domain controller. Specifically, if DNS dynamic updates are not currently available in the domain, or if Dcpromo determines that the domain has an insufficient number of DNS servers, then the DNS Server role is installed on the new domain controller even if you omit the previous line from the unattend file.

When the DNS Server role is installed on the first domain controller in a domain, two new zones are created on the server (as shown in Figure 9-1):

- A zone for the domain itself (such as fabrikam.com) that contains resource records for all the computers in your domain.

213

■ A zone for a special subdomain named _msdsc (such as _msdsc.fabrikam.com) that contains only SRV resource records dynamically registered by the Netlogon process on the domain controller. Clients can use these SRV records to locate domain controllers in the domain so the clients can access the Global Catalog, perform Lightweight Directory Access Protocol (LDAP) queries, use Kerberos authentication, and perform other actions relating to AD DS.

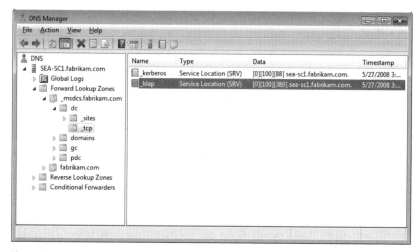

Figure 9-1   Two zones created on a DNS server on a domain controller, with the LDAP SRV record for the domain controller selected

By default, these two zones are automatically configured as AD DS–integrated zones. For more information on AD DS–integrated zones, see the section "Configuring a Primary DNS Server," later in this chapter.

Note   For more information on using Dcpromo in unattend mode to install the AD DS role, see Chapter 7, "Active Directory Domain Services Role."

Verifying the SRV Resource Records for a Domain Controller

You can use the Nslookup command to verify that the SRV resource records needed by AD DS were created properly during an unattended Dcpromo operation. To do this, type the following commands and verify that the command output displays the correct name of a domain controller in the domain, the correct name for the domain, and the correct IP address for the domain controller, as follows:

```
C:\Users\administrator>nslookup
Default Server:  UnKnown
Address:  ::1

> set type=all
```

```
> _ldap._tcp.dc._msdcs.fabrikam.com
Server:  UnKnown
Address:  ::1

_ldap._tcp.dc._msdcs.fabrikam.com        SRV service location:
        priority      = 0
        weight        = 100
        port          = 389
        svr hostname  = sea-sc1.fabrikam.com
sea-sc1.fabrikam.com    internet address = 172.16.11.30
> quit
C:\Users\administrator>
```

See Figure 9-1 for a graphical representation of this information. For more information on verifying the DNS Server configuration of a domain controller, see http://support.microsoft.com/kb/816587.

Configuring the Priority and Weight of SRV Resource Records

As shown in the previous command output, an SRV resource record has the attributes of priority and weight. *Priority* indicates the priority that DNS referrals made to the domain controller identified by the SRV record. This is because clients attempt to contact the domain controller with the lowest priority. *Weight* is a load-balancing mechanism used when selecting a domain controller from several DNS referrals that have the same priority. This is because clients randomly choose SRV records that specify domain controllers to be contacted, with the probability being proportional to the weight. The default values for priority and weight of SRV records created in AD DS are 0 and 100, respectively.

You can use the Scregedit.wsf script found in the %SystemRoot%\System32 folder on a Server Core installation to view or modify the priority and weight of SRV records on a Server Core domain controller by modifying registry keys that override the built-in defaults for these settings. For example, to change the priority to 200, do the following:

```
c:\Windows\System32>cscript scregedit.wsf /DP 200
Microsoft (R) Windows Script Host Version 5.7
Copyright (C) Microsoft Corporation. All rights reserved.

Registry has been updated.
```

Verify the result:

```
c:\Windows\System32>cscript scregedit.wsf /DP /v
Microsoft (R) Windows Script Host Version 5.7
Copyright (C) Microsoft Corporation. All rights reserved.

SYSTEM\CurrentControlSet\Services\Netlogon\Parameters LdapSrvPriority
View registry setting.
200
```

To change the weight to 50, do the following:

```
c:\Windows\System32>cscript scregedit.wsf /DW 50
Microsoft (R) Windows Script Host Version 5.7
Copyright (C) Microsoft Corporation. All rights reserved.

Registry has been updated.
```

Verify the result as follows:

```
c:\Windows\System32>cscript scregedit.wsf /DW /v
Microsoft (R) Windows Script Host Version 5.7
Copyright (C) Microsoft Corporation. All rights reserved.

SYSTEM\CurrentControlSet\Services\Netlogon\Parameters LdapSrvWeight
View registry setting.
50
```

You can also use Nslookup to verify these modifications as follows:

```
C:\Users\administrator>nslookup
Default Server:  UnKnown
Address:  ::1

> set type=all
> _ldap._tcp.dc._msdcs.fabrikam.com
Server:  UnKnown
Address:  ::1

_ldap._tcp.dc._msdcs.fabrikam.com        SRV service location:
          priority       = 200
          weight         = 50
          port           = 389
          svr hostname   = sea-sc1.fabrikam.com
sea-sc1.fabrikam.com   internet address = 172.16.11.30
```

By adjusting the priority and weight of SRV records, you can do things like reduce the workload on your PDC Emulator by reducing the number of clients that DNS refers to that domain controller. For more information, search for the terms "LdapSrvPriority" and "LdapSrvWeight" on Microsoft TechNet.

Installing the DNS Server Role from the Command Prompt

You can use the Ocsetup.exe utility to install the DNS Server role separately on a Server Core installation that does not have the AD DS role installed. To install the DNS Server role on a member server or stand-alone server running Server Core, use the Ocsetup command. For example, to install the DNS Server role on a member server named SEA-SC4 in the fabrikam.com domain, do this:

```
C:\Users\administrator>start /w ocsetup DNS-Server-Core-Role
```

Verify the result as follows:

```
C:\Users\administrator>oclist | find "   Installed"
    Installed:DNS-Server-Core-Role
```

When you use Ocsetup to install the DNS Server role on Server Core, your new DNS server has no forward or reverse lookup zones configured on it (as shown in Figure 9-2).

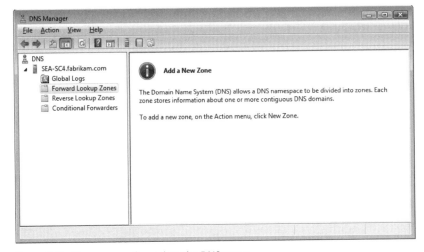

Figure 9-2   No zones configured on the DNS server

You cannot create AD DS–integrated zones on a DNS server running on a member server or stand-alone server; you can create only standard zones.

Installing the DNS Server Role Using an Answer File

To install the DNS Server Role using an answer file, perform the following steps:

1. Create and configure an answer file for an unattended installation of Server Core. For information on how to do this, see Chapter 2, "Deploying Server Core."

2. On your technician computer, open your answer file in Windows System Image Manager (Windows SIM).

3. In the Windows Image pane, expand the Packages node to display the nodes beneath it. Expand the Foundation node to display the Microsoft-Windows-ServerCore-Package node beneath that. Then right-click the address Microsoft-Windows-ServerCore-Package node and select Add To Answer File. The Microsoft-Windows-ServerCore-Package should be selected in the Answer File pane.

4. In the Properties pane, scroll down until the DNS-Server-Core-Role setting is visible under Windows Feature. Click the value field to the right of the DNS-Server-Core-Role setting to display a drop-down arrow. Click the arrow and select Enabled.

5. Validate your answer file and save it, then deploy Server Core using your answer file using any of the methods outlined in Chapter 2. When installation is completed, log on, type **oclist | find " Installed"**, and verify that the DNS Server role has been installed.

Removing the DNS Server Role

You can use Ocsetup to remove the DNS Server role from a DNS server running on a member server or stand-alone server. You should not remove the DNS Server role from a domain controller. To remove the DNS Server role, type **start /w ocsetup DNS-Server-Core-Role /uninstall** at the command prompt.

Managing a Server Core DNS Server

Once you've installed the DNS Server role on Server Core, you need to configure the role and manage its configuration. This section covers basic DNS Server administration tasks, mainly focusing on command-line management of Server Core DNS servers. For detailed information on managing DNS Servers from the GUI, see the companion title *Windows Server 2008 Administrator's Pocket Consultant* by William Stanek (Microsoft Press, 2008).

Managing DNS Servers

You can manage DNS servers in two ways:

- Using the DNS console, which is included as part of Remote Server Administration Tools (RSAT)

- Using the Dnscmd command interactively from the command prompt

Managing a Server Core DNS Server Using RSAT

You can manage a DNS server running on a Server Core installation the same way you manage a DNS Server running on a Full installation of Windows Server 2008—that is, by using the DNS console. This console is available in two ways:

- On any Full installation of Windows Server 2008 on which you have added the DNS Server role

- On any computer running Windows Vista SP1 or Full installation of Windows Server 2008 on which you have installed the RSAT

Note For instructions on how to install RSAT, see Chapter 6, "Remote Management."

For example, to manage a Server Core DNS server named SEA-SC1.fabrikam.com from a computer running Windows Vista SP1 belonging to the same domain and that has RSAT installed on it, perform the following steps:

1. On the computer running Windows Vista SP1, click Start, Administrative Tools, and finally DNS to open the DNS console.

2. Right-click the root node in the console tree and select Connect To DNS Server.

3. Type the name of the server or search for it in AD DS, as shown here.

4. Click OK and expand the console tree to manage the DNS server.

5. Add more DNS servers to the console by following steps 1-4 as many times as needed.

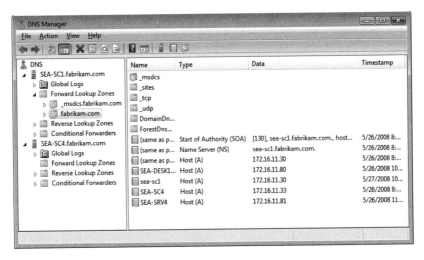

Managing a Server Core DNS Server from the Command Line

You can manage DNS servers from an elevated command prompt by using the Dnscmd command. Almost any task that you can perform from the graphical user interface (GUI) can also be performed from the command line using Dnscmd, including displaying and modifying properties for DNS servers, zones, and resource records, and forcing replication between DNS server physical memory, DNS databases, and data files. Dnscmd can be run either locally on the DNS server or remotely from a computer running either Windows Vista or Windows Server 2008 that belongs to the same domain or a trusted domain. To use Dnscmd, you must be a member of either the Domain Admins or the Server Operators group.

For a list of options for this command, type **dnscmd /?** at the command prompt. For help concerning a particular command option of Dnscmd, type **dnscmd <option> /?** instead. For example, to display help concerning the /config option, type **dnscmd /config /?** at the command prompt.

Configuring DNS Servers

You can use Dnscmd to configure your DNS server as a primary, secondary, or caching-only DNS server. A *primary DNS server* is the DNS server that is authoritative for a particular zone and which contains a writable copy of the DNS database for the zone. A *zone* is a portion of the domain tree that is administered by a single DNS server. You can think of a zone as a contiguous portion of the domain namespace (that is, a parent domain and one or more subdomains). A zone contains the *resource records* (entries in the DNS database for the zone that are used to process DNS queries from clients) for the parent domain, while for subdomains, the zone can contain either the resource records or the *delegations* (references to authoritative DNS servers) for the subdomains.

There can be two types of primary DNS servers: standard primary and AD DS–integrated. A *standard primary DNS server* must be either a member server or a stand-alone server, and the DNS database is stored in text files called *zone files*. An *AD DS–integrated primary DNS server* must be a domain controller, and the DNS database is stored within the AD DS directory database. AD DS–integrated primary DNS servers support a *secure dynamic update*, a process by which clients can use DNS with Dynamic Host Configuration Protocol (DHCP) to automatically register and dynamically update their resource records within the DNS server's database. Standard primary DNS servers do not support secure dynamic updates—resource records for clients must be created and updated manually.

A *secondary DNS server* is a DNS server that has a read-only copy of the DNS server database for a particular zone. Secondary DNS servers are not authoritative for their particular zone, and they replicate their copy of the zone database from the primary (authoritative) DNS server for that zone (which is also called the *master DNS server* for that zone) by using a process called *zone transfer*. Replication between standard primary and secondary DNS servers uses incremental zone transfers; replication between AD DS–integrated DNS servers uses the same mechanism used by AD DS replication. A zone can have only one primary DNS server, but it can have multiple secondary servers for load balancing and fault tolerance. A single DNS server can be the primary (authoritative) DNS server for one or more zones and a secondary DNS server for other zones at the same time.

A *caching-only DNS server* does not host any zones and is not authoritative for any domain. Caching-only DNS servers build a local server cache of DNS names learned while performing recursive queries on behalf of clients. This cached information is then available for responding to subsequent queries from clients. Caching-only DNS servers can be useful at sites where DNS functionality is needed, but it is not administratively desirable to create a separate domain or zone for that location.

Two other steps should usually be performed when configuring a DNS server: config-uring forwarders and configuring root hints. A *forwarder* is another DNS server to which your DNS server forwards any DNS queries that it cannot answer. The *root hints* file contains the names and IP addresses of the root DNS servers that form the foun-dation upon which the entire domain name system operates.

The simplest way of configuring a freshly installed DNS server is to use the DNS console in RSAT as follows:

1. Open the DNS console and connect to your freshly installed DNS server.

2. Right-click the server node beneath the root node in your console tree and select Configure A DNS Server.

3. Follow the steps of the Configure A DNS Server Wizard to create forward and reverse lookup zones, configure forwarders, and configure root hints as needed.

The remainder of this chapter focuses on configuring and maintaining DNS servers using the Dnscmd command at the Server Core command prompt. For more information on con-figuring DNS servers from the GUI, see the companion title Windows Server 2008 Administrator's Pocket Consultant *by William Stanek (Microsoft Press, 2008).*

For a detailed explanation of DNS server concepts, download the DNS Service Product Operations Guide from the Microsoft Download Center at http://www.microsoft.com/downloads/.

Configuring a Caching-Only DNS Server

To configure a caching-only DNS server on Server Core, simply install the DNS Server role on a stand-alone server (in a workgroup) or on a member server (in a domain). No other configuration is required. See the section "Installing the DNS Server Role from the Command Prompt," earlier in this chapter, for instructions.

Configuring a Primary DNS Server

You can configure a primary DNS server in two ways:

■ Perform an unattended Dcpromo that also installs the DNS Server role on Server Core. The Server Core installation then is both a domain controller and the authoritative DNS server for the domain. Zone information for the domain will be stored in AD DS. You may need to perform further configuration of your DNS server, such as configuring forwarders and root hints, after Dcpromo runs. For information on how to do this, see the section "Performing Other DNS Management Tasks," later in this chapter.

■ Install a caching-only DNS server and then create one or more primary forward and reverse lookup zones on the server, configuring forwarders and root hints as needed. For information on how to create primary forward and reverse lookup zones, see the section "Creating and Managing Zones," later in this chapter. For information on how to configure forwarders and root hints, see the section "Performing Other DNS Management Tasks," later in this chapter.

Configuring a Secondary DNS Server

You can configure a secondary DNS server in two ways:

■ Perform an unattended Dcpromo that also installs the DNS Server role on Server Core. The Server Core installation then is both a domain controller and the authoritative DNS server for the domain, but it can also be configured as a secondary DNS server for other domains by creating one or more secondary forward and reverse lookup zones on the server. For information on how to create secondary forward and reverse lookup zones, see the section "Creating and Managing Zones," later in this chapter.

■ Install a caching-only DNS server and then create one or more secondary forward and reverse lookup zones on the server, configuring forwarders and root hints as needed. For information on how to create secondary forward and reverse lookup zones, see the section "Creating and Managing Zones," later in this chapter. For information on how to configure forwarders and root hints, see the section "Performing Other DNS Management Tasks," later in this chapter.

Creating and Managing Zones

Creating and managing zones is one of the key DNS server management tasks. Zones can be classified in several ways. First, you can classify zones as either primary or secondary by specifying whether they are writable or read-only. A *primary zone* is a zone that contains a writable copy of the DNS database for a domain and that is authoritative for the domain. A *secondary zone* is a zone that contains a read-only copy of the DNS database for a domain and that is not authoritative for the domain.

Second, you can classify zones as either forward or reverse lookup by specifying whether they resolve DNS names into IP addresses or vice versa. A *forward lookup zone* is a zone that contains resource records that can be used to resolve DNS names into IP addresses. A *reverse lookup zone* is a zone that contains resource records that can be used to resolve IP addresses into fully qualified domain names (FQDNs).

Third, you can classify zones as either standard or AD DS–integrated by specifying whether the DNS database for the zone is a zone (.dns) file or is contained within AD DS. A *standard zone* is a zone whose DNS database is a zone (.dns) file on the DNS server. An *AD DS–integrated zone* is a zone whose DNS database is contained within AD DS.

Finally, a special type of zone called a *stub zone* contains only the Start of Authority (SOA) resource record for the zone, the Name Server (NS) records for the zone's authoritative DNS servers, and the Host (A) records for the zone's authoritative DNS servers. Stub zones can be used to reduce the number of DNS queries on a network and to reduce the load on the primary DNS servers for a domain.

When all this is put together, there are basically five types of forward (or reverse) lookup zones you can create on DNS servers running Windows Server:

- Forward lookup standard primary zone
- Forward (or reverse) lookup AD DS–integrated primary zone
- Forward (or reverse) lookup standard secondary zone
- Forward (or reverse) lookup standard stub zone
- Forward (or reverse) lookup AD DS–integrated stub zone

Each of these types of zones can be created on domain controllers, member servers, or stand-alone servers, with the exception of AD DS–integrated zones, which can be created only on domain controllers.

Later sections in this chapter show how to use Dnscmd to create each of these different types of zones.

Displaying a List of Zones on a DNS Server

You can use Dnscmd to display a list of all the zones on a DNS server. For example, to display a list of zones on the local server (a Server Core domain controller named SEA-SC1.fabrikam.com), do the following:

```
C:\Users\administrator>dnscmd /enumzones

Enumerated zone list:
       Zone count = 3

Zone name                     Type       Storage       Properties

.                             Cache      AD-Domain
_msdcs.fabrikam.com           Primary    AD-Forest     Secure
fabrikam.com                  Primary    AD-Domain     Secure
```

To display only the primary zones on SEA-SC1, do this:

```
C:\Users\administrator>dnscmd /enumzones /primary

Enumerated zone list:
       Zone count = 2

Zone name                     Type       Storage       Properties

_msdcs.fabrikam.com           Primary    AD-Forest     Secure
fabrikam.com                  Primary    AD-Domain     Secure
```

To display only the zones stored in the domain DNS partition on AD DS, do this:

```
C:\Users\administrator>dnscmd /enumzones /DomainDirectoryPartition

Enumerated zone list:
```

```
        Zone count = 2

Zone name                        Type       Storage         Properties

    .                            Cache      AD-Domain
fabrikam.com                     Primary    AD-Domain       Secure
```

To display all zones on the remote server SEA-SC4 (a Server Core member server with the DNS Server role installed), do this:

```
C:\Users\administrator>dnscmd SEA-SC4 /enumzones

Enumerated zone list:
        Zone count = 1

Zone name                        Type       Storage         Properties

    .                            Cache      File
```

You can see from the previous code that server SEA-SC4 is currently configured as a caching-only DNS server.

Creating a Forward Lookup Standard Primary Zone

You can use the command shown here to create a forward lookup standard primary zone named research.fabrikam.com on a DNS server named SEA-SC4 that has the DNS Server role installed on it. The command stores the database for this zone on the server in a file named research.dns, as follows:

```
C:\Users\administrator>dnscmd SEA-SC4 /zoneadd research.fabrikam.com
/primary /file research.dns
DNS Server SEA-SC4 created zone research.fabrikam.com:

Command completed successfully.
```

To display the resource records for the zone root (signified by "@") of the newly created zone, do this:

```
C:\Users\administrator>dnscmd SEA-SC4.fabrikam.com
/enumrecords research.fabrikam.com @
Returned records:
@ 3600 NS        sea-sc4.fabrikam.com.
                 3600 SOA        sea-sc4.fabrikam.com.
hostmaster.fabrikam.com. 1
 900 600 86400 3600

Command completed successfully.
```

The newly created zone has two resource records, an SOA record and an NS record, that are the same as for the parent domain fabrikam.com. For more information on creating and managing resource records, see the section "Creating and Managing Resource Records," later in this chapter.

Creating a Forward Lookup AD DS–Integrated Primary Zone

You can use the command shown here to create a forward lookup AD DS–integrated primary zone named marketing.fabrikam.com on a DNS server named SEA-SC1 that is also a domain controller. The command stores this zone information in the domain DNS partition within AD DS, as follows:

```
C:\Users\administrator>dnscmd SEA-SC1 /zoneadd marketing.fabrikam.com
/dsprimary

DNS server SEA-SC1 version is 6.0.6001

Creating zone in built-in domain directory partition...
DNS Server SEA-SC1 created zone marketing.fabrikam.com:

Command completed successfully.
```

Creating a Forward Lookup Standard Secondary Zone

You can use the command shown here to create a forward lookup standard secondary zone named research.fabrikam.com on a DNS server named SEA-SC1 that is also a domain controller. The command stores the database for this zone in the domain DNS partition within AD DS, and it assigns the zone the address 172.16.11.33 as the master DNS server for replication purposes, as follows:

```
C:\Users\administrator>dnscmd SEA-SC1 /zoneadd research.fabrikam.com
/secondary 172.16.11.33 /file research.dns
DNS Server SEA-SC1 created zone research.fabrikam.com:

Command completed successfully.
```

The secondary zone created here will not contain any resource records in its database until a zone transfer has been performed with its master DNS server. For more information about zone transfers and master DNS servers, see the section "Configuring Zone Transfers," later in this chapter.

Creating a Forward Lookup Standard Stub Zone

You can use the command here to create a forward lookup standard stub zone named marketing.fabrikam.com on a DNS server named SEA-SC4 that has the DNS Server role installed on it. The command stores the database for this zone on the server in a file named marketing.dns, and it assigns the zone the address 172.16.11.30 as the master DNS server for replication purposes, as follows:

```
C:\Users\administrator>dnscmd SEA-SC4 /zoneadd marketing.fabrikam.com
/stub 172.16.11.30 /file marketing.dns
DNS Server SEA-SC4 created zone marketing.fabrikam.com:

Command completed successfully.
```

Creating a Forward Lookup AD DS–Integrated Stub Zone

You can use the command shown here to create a forward lookup AD DS–integrated stub zone named finance.fabrikam.com on a DNS server named SEA-SC1 that is also a domain controller. The command stores the database for this zone in the domain DNS partition within AD DS, and it assigns the zone the address 172.16.11.33 as the master DNS server for replication purposes, as follows:

```
C:\Users\administrator>dnscmd SEA-SC1 /zoneadd finance.fabrikam.com
/stub 172.16.11.33
DNS Server SEA-SC1 created zone finance.fabrikam.com:

Command completed successfully.
```

Creating Reverse Lookup Zones

Each of the five zone types described in the previous sections can also be created as reverse lookup zones. While forward lookup zones are named using the FQDN of the domain to which the zone maps, reverse lookup zones are named using the following convention:

<octet address form of network ID in reverse order>.in-addr.arpa.

For example, if the network ID for clients in the forward lookup zone is 172.16.11/24 (that is, 172.16.11.0 with subnet mask 255.255.255.0), then the reverse lookup zone usually is named 11.16.172.in-addr.arpa.

You can use the following command to create a reverse lookup standard primary zone named 11.16.172.in-addr.arpa on a DNS server named SEA-SC4 that has the DNS Server role installed on it:

```
C:\Users\administrator>dnscmd SEA-SC4 /zoneadd 11.16.172.in-addr.arpa
/primary
DNS Server SEA-SC4 created zone 11.16.172.in-addr.arpa:

Command completed successfully.
```

Deleting a Zone

You can delete a zone using the Dnscmd command if the zone is no longer needed for name resolution on your network. For example, to delete a zone named research .fabrikam.com from a DNS server named SEA-SC1 that is also a domain controller, do the following:

```
C:\Users\administrator>dnscmd SEA-SC1 /zonedelete research.fabrikam.com
/dsdel
Are you sure you want to delete zone from DS? (y/n)y
```

```
DNS Server SEA-SC1 deleted zone research.fabrikam.com:
   Status = 0 (0x00000000)
Command completed successfully.
```

The /dsdel switch is required when deleting an AD DS–integrated zone. To force the zone to be deleted without being prompted Yes or No, add the /f switch to this command.

Creating and Managing Resource Records

After you create your zones, you can add resource records to the zones. Resource records are entries in the DNS database for a zone. Each resource record is a structured entity that specifies the following information:

- **Owner**   Identifies the DNS domain name that owns the record.

- **Time to Live (TTL)**   Indicates the length of time that other DNS servers should cache information for a record before expiring and discarding it. Optional for some types of records.

- **Class**   Always IN for Windows DNS servers; means the record belongs to the Internet class.

- **Type**   Identifies the type of resource record, which indicates what the record is used for (see Table 9-1 for more information).

- **Record-specific data**   A variable-length field that contains any other information needed to describe the resource.

Table 9-1 summarizes the most common types of resource records used in Windows DNS servers.

Table 9-1   Common Types of DNS Resource Records

Type	Description
A	Host name record, used to resolve an FQDN of a host into the IPv4 address of the host.
AAAA	IPv6 host name record, used to resolve an FQDN of a host into the IPv6 address of the host.
CNAME	Canonical name resource record, used to resolve an alias or alternate name for a host into the FQDN of the host.
MX	Mail exchanger resource record, used to provide message routing to a mail exchanger host (that is, a mail server).
NS	Name server resource record, used to identify a host as a DNS server for the domain.
PTR	Pointer resource record, used to resolve the IPv4 or IPv6 address of a host into the FQDN of the host. IPv4 hosts are reverse-mapped to the in-addr.arpa domain, while IPv6 hosts are reverse-mapped to the ip6.arpa domain.

Table 9-1   Common Types of DNS Resource Records

Type	Description
SOA	Start of Authority resource record, used to specify basic properties of the zone, including zone name, zone version, whether the zone can be aged and scavenged, and the refresh, retry, and expire time intervals for the zone.
SRV	Service locator resource record, used to locate domain controllers, global catalog servers, and Kerberos Key Distribution Center servers.

Display a List of All Resource Records in a Zone

You can use the Dnscmd command to display a list of all resource records in a zone. For example, to display a list of all resource records in the zone for the fabrikam.com domain on the authoritative DNS server SEA-SC1, do the following:

```
C:\Users\administrator>dnscmd SEA-SC1 /enumrecords fabrikam.com
fabrikam.com.
Returned records:
@ [Aging:3571189] 600 A 172.16.11.30
                [Aging:3571189] 3600 NS        sea-sc1.fabrikam.com.
                [Aging:3571189] 3600 SOA       sea-
sc1.fabrikam.com. hostmaster
.fabrikam.com. 134 900 600 86400 3600
SEA-DESK155 [Aging:3571191] 1200 A      172.16.11.80
sea-sc1 [Aging:3571238] 3600 A   172.16.11.30
SEA-SC4 [Aging:3571189] 1200 A   172.16.11.33
SEA-SRV4 [Aging:3571192] 1200 A 172.16.11.81
```

The first portion of this command output lists the SOA, NS, and A zone root resource records (signified by "@"). The remaining portion of the command output shows four host (A) records for the four computers in the fabrikam domain: two Server Core installations (SEA-SC1 and SEA-SC4), another server (SEA-SRV4), and a desktop computer (SEA-DESK155).

The general syntax for displaying a list of resource records is the following:

dnscmd <*DNS server name*> /**enumrecords** <*domain name*> <*node name with period appended*> /**type** <*record type*>

If /type <*record type*> is omitted, all records for the domain are displayed. The period appended to the node name is required because it represents the root of the DNS namespace. See the section "Displaying the Resource Records for a Node," later in this chapter, for an explanation of what "node" means in DNS terminology.

As a second example, use the following command to display a list of all host (A) records in the fabrikam.com by using DNS server SEA-SC1, which is authoritative for the domain:

```
C:\Users\administrator>dnscmd SEA-SC1 /enumrecords fabrikam.com
fabrikam.com. /type A
```

```
Returned records:
@ [Aging:3571189] 600 A 172.16.11.30
SEA-DESK155 [Aging:3571191] 1200 A      172.16.11.80
sea-sc1 [Aging:3571238] 3600 A  172.16.11.30
SEA-SC4 [Aging:3571189] 1200 A  172.16.11.33
SEA-SRV4 [Aging:3571192] 1200 A 172.16.11.81


Command completed successfully.
```

Exporting Detailed Information Concerning All Resource Records in a Zone

You can use the Dnscmd command to export detailed information concerning all resource records in a zone and the zone itself to a text file. For example, to export the information stored in the fabrikam.com zone on a DNS server named SEA-SC1 that is also a domain controller, do the following:

```
C:\Users\administrator>dnscmd SEA-SC1 /zoneexport fabrikam.com
fabrikam.txt


DNS Server SEA-SC1 exported zone
   fabrikam.com to file %windir%\system32\dns\fabrikam.txt on the DNS server
Command completed successfully.
```

Open the exported zone information in Notepad by typing this command:

```
C:\Users\administrator>notepad %windir%\system32\dns\fabrikam.txt
```

The result might look something like this:

```
;
;  Database file (null) for fabrikam.com zone.
;     Zone version:  134
;

@                      IN  SOA sea-sc1.fabrikam.com. hostmaster.fabrikam.com. (
                       134            ; serial number
                       900            ; refresh
                       600            ; retry
                       86400          ; expire
                       3600       ) ; default TTL


;
;  Zone NS records
;

@                      NSsea-sc1.fabrikam.com.


;
;  Zone records
;
```

```
@                              600 A 172.16.11.30


;
;   Delegated sub-zone:  _msdcs.fabrikam.com.
;
_msdcs                     NS sea-sc1.fabrikam.com.
;   End delegation

_gc._tcp.Default-First-Site-Name._sites 600SRV0 100
3268sea-sc1.fabrikam.com.
_kerberos._tcp.Default-First-Site-Name._sites 600SRV0 100
88sea-sc1.fabrikam.com.
_ldap._tcp.Default-First-Site-Name._sites 600SRV0 100 389sea-sc1.
fabrikam.com.
_gc._tcp                   600SRV0 100 3268sea-sc1.fabrikam.com.
_kerberos._tcp             600SRV0 100 88sea-sc1.fabrikam.com.
_kpasswd._tcp              600SRV0 100 464sea-sc1.fabrikam.com.
_ldap._tcp                 600SRV0 100 389sea-sc1.fabrikam.com.
_kerberos._udp             600SRV0 100 88sea-sc1.fabrikam.com.
_kpasswd._udp              600SRV0 100 464sea-sc1.fabrikam.com.
DomainDnsZones             600A172.16.11.30
_ldap._tcp.Default-First-Site-Name._sites.DomainDnsZones
600SRV0 100 389sea-sc1.fabrikam.com.
_ldap._tcp.DomainDnsZones 600SRV0 100 389sea-sc1.fabrikam.com.
ForestDnsZones             600A172.16.11.30
_ldap._tcp.Default-First-Site-
Name._sites.ForestDnsZones 600SRV0 100 389sea-sc1.fabrikam.com.
_ldap._tcp.ForestDnsZones 600SRV0 100 389sea-sc1.fabrikam.com.


;
;   Delegated sub-zone:  marketing.fabrikam.com.
;
marketing                  NSsea-sc1.fabrikam.com.
;   End delegation



;
;   Delegated sub-zone:  research.fabrikam.com.
;
research                   ONSsea-sc1.fabrikam.com.
;   End delegation

SEA-DESK155                1200A172.16.11.80
SEA-SC1                    A172.16.11.30
SEA-SC4                    1200A172.16.11.33
SEA-SRV4                   1200A172.16.11.81
```

The last portion of the previous export file shows four host (A) records for the four computers in the fabrikam.com domain. The first portion of the file lists the SOA, NS, and A zone root resource records. The remaining middle portion of the file lists SRV resource records for subzones and which define delegations. AD DS uses this information to help clients locate services running on domain controllers, global catalog servers, and Kerberos Key Distribution Center servers.

Displaying the Resource Records for a Node

You can use the Dnscmd command to display any resource records associated with a particular node in a zone. Each domain label used in an FQDN indicates a *node* in the domain tree. For example, SEA-SRV4.fabrikam.com is an FQDN that represents the node SEA-SRV4, which is under the node fabrikam, which is under the node com, which is under the DNS root node. The root node is usually identified by a trailing dot appended to the FQDN.

For example, to display the host (A) resource record associated with the node SEA-SRV4.fabrikam.com (server SEA-SRV4 in the fabrikam.com domain) do the following:

```
C:\Users\administrator>dnscmd SEA-SC1 /enumrecords fabrikam.com
SEA-SRV4.fabrikam.com. /type A
Returned records:
@ [Aging:3571192] 1200 A        172.16.11.81

Command completed successfully.
```

Note   The trailing period in the FQDN is required for the node.

As a second example, use the following command to display the SOA resource record for the zone:

```
C:\Users\administrator>dnscmd SEA-SC1 /enumrecords fabrikam.com
fabrikam.com. /type SOA
Returned records:
@ [Aging:3571189] 3600 SOA      sea-sc1.fabrikam.com.
hostmaster.fabrikam.com. 1
34 900 600 86400 3600

Command completed successfully.
```

This time, the node being specified is the domain itself (signified by fabrikam.com) and not a subnode of the domain (that is, the host in the domain).

Creating Resource Records

You can use Dnscmd to create new resource records contained in a writable zone database. For example, to create a host (A) record in the fabrikam.com on authoritative DNS server SEA-SC1 for a server named SEA-SRV8 that has IP address 172.16.11.75, do the following:

```
C:\Users\administrator>dnscmd SEA-SC1 /recordadd fabrikam.com
SEA-SRV8.fabrikam.com. /aging /openacl A 172.16.11.75
```

```
Add A Record for SEA-SRV8.fabrikam.com. at fabrikam.com
Command completed successfully.
```

Verify the result by listing all A records in the domain as follows:

```
C:\Users\administrator>dnscmd SEA-SC1 /enumrecords fabrikam.com
fabrikam.com. /type A
Returned records:
@ [Aging:3571189] 600 A 172.16.11.30
SEA-DESK155 [Aging:3571191] 1200 A      172.16.11.80
sea-sc1 [Aging:3571238] 3600 A  172.16.11.30
SEA-SC4 [Aging:3571189] 1200 A  172.16.11.33
SEA-SRV4 [Aging:3571192] 1200 A 172.16.11.81
SEA-SRV8 [Aging:3571246] 3600 A 172.16.11.75
```

The /aging switch in the previous command indicates that the new resource record can be aged and scavenged. If you omit this parameter, the resource record remains in the DNS database until it is updated or removed manually. The /openacl switch indicates that any user can modify this record. Without this parameter, only administrators can modify the record.

Modifying Resource Records

You can use Dnscmd to modify resource records contained in a writable zone database. For example, in the previous section, Dnscmd was used to create a new host (A) record that maps the FQDN SEA-SRV8.fabrikam.com to the IP address 172.16.11.75. If you want to change the IP address for this host record to 172.16.11.74, first delete the old record, and then create a new one like this:

```
C:\Users\administrator>dnscmd SEA-SC1 /recorddelete fabrikam.com
SEA-SRV8.fabrikam.com. A 172.16.11.75 /f
Deleted A record(s) at fabrikam.com
Command completed successfully.
```

```
C:\Users\administrator>dnscmd SEA-SC1 /recordadd fabrikam.com
SEA-SRV8.fabrikam.com. /aging /openacl A 172.16.11.76
```

```
Add A Record for SEA-SRV8.fabrikam.com. at fabrikam.com
Command completed successfully.
```

Verify the result as follows:

```
C:\Users\administrator>dnscmd SEA-SC1 /enumrecords fabrikam.com
SEA-SRV8.fabrikam.com. /type A
Returned records:
@ [Aging:3571246] 3600 A      172.16.11.76
```

Modifying the SOA Resource Record

The SOA resource record specifies the authoritative DNS server, the refresh and retry intervals, and other properties of the zone. Table 9-2 summarizes the data fields of an SOA record.

Table 9-2 Data Fields of an SOA Record

Field	Description
Source host	The host where the zone file was created.
Contact e-mail	The e-mail address zone administrator (uses a period instead of "@" in the e-mail address).
Serial number	The revision number of the zone file. This value must be incremented each time the zone file is changed so the changes will be transferred to secondary DNS servers.
Refresh Time	The time (in seconds) that a secondary DNS server waits before querying the primary DNS server's SOA record to check for changes. The default value is 900 seconds (15 minutes).
Retry time	The time (in seconds) that a secondary DNS server waits before retrying a failed zone transfer. The default value is 600 seconds (10 minutes).
Expire time	The time (in seconds) that a secondary DNS server keeps trying to complete a zone transfer. The default value is 86,400 seconds (1 day).
Minimum TTL	The minimum time-to-live (in seconds) for all resource records in the zone file. The default value is 3,600 seconds (1 hour).

While the default SOA properties are usually sufficient, you can use Dnscmd to modify these settings. For example, the following command displays the SOA record for the hr.fabrikam.com standard primary zone on DNS server SEA-SC4:

```
C:\Users\administrator>dnscmd SEA-SC4 /enumrecords hr.fabrikam.com @
/type SOA
Returned records:
@ 3600 SOA      sea-sc4.fabrikam.com. hostmaster.fabrikam.com.
1 900 600 86400 3 600
```

The output of this command lists the fields of the SOA record in the same order as in Table 9-2. To change the expire time from 86,400 seconds (1 day) to 604,800 seconds (7 days), do this:

```
C:\Users\administrator>dnscmd SEA-SC4 /recordadd hr.fabrikam.com
@ SOA sea-sc4.f abrikam.com hostmaster.fabrikam.com 1 900 600 604800 3600

Add SOA Record for hr.fabrikam.com at hr.fabrikam.com
Command completed successfully.
```

Verify the result as follows:

```
C:\Users\administrator>dnscmd SEA-SC4 /enumrecords hr.fabrikam.com @
/type SOA
Returned records:
@ 3600 SOA      sea-sc4.fabrikam.com. hostmaster.fabrikam.com.
2 900 600 604800 3600
```

> **Note** You don't have to delete an SOA record and recreate it—you can simply modify it as previously described.

Performing Other DNS Management Tasks

Besides configuring zones and resource records, there are other tasks involved in managing DNS servers. The following sections show how to perform some common DNS administration tasks on Server Core:

- Configuring forwarders
- Configuring conditional forwarders
- Configuring zone transfers
- Integrating DNS with DHCP
- Configuring aging and scavenging
- Integrating DNS with Windows Internet Name Service (WINS)
- Configuring the GlobalNames zone

Configuring Forwarders

A *forwarder* is a special DNS server that you designate for handling client requests that your regular DNS servers cannot or should not resolve, such as requests for offsite or external DNS domain names. DNS clients typically make *recursive queries*, which are queries to which the responding DNS server must return a valid (success or failure) response. When the DNS server receives a client request and if a forwarder is configured on the DNS server, the DNS server sends a recursive query to the forwarder asking for a valid response.

You can use the Dnscmd command to configure one or more forwarders on a Server Core DNS server. For example, to configure the external DNS server 192.0.2.25 as a forwarder for DNS server SEA-SC4, do the following:

```
C:\Users\administrator>dnscmd SEA-SC4 /ResetForwarders 192.0.2.25
/timeout 5 /slave
Forwarders reset successfully.

Command completed successfully.
```

Use the DNS console on a computer that has RSAT installed to verify the result by performing the following steps:

1. Select the DNS server node in the console tree.

2. Double-click the Forwarders node in the details pane.

The /timeout parameter in this command specifies the amount of time that your DNS server waits for the forwarder to respond. The /slave parameter indicates that the DNS server does not attempt to perform its own iterative queries if the forwarder fails to resolve the query. An *iterative query* is when the DNS server issues additional non-recursive queries to other DNS servers and uses referrals from these servers to try to resolve the original query. To allow your DNS server to perform its own iterative queries if the forward fails to resolve a query, use the /noslave switch instead. Using the /noslave switch means that your DNS server uses its root hints file if no forwarders are available to resolve the query. The root hints (or cache hints) file contains entries for the root DNS servers on the Internet. These root DNS servers form the starting point for iterative queries.

Configuring Conditional Forwarders

A *conditional forwarder* is a forwarder that handles queries only for a specified domain name. Conditional forwarding enables a DNS server to forward queries for different domain names to different DNS servers according to the specific domain names that are contained in the queries. This improves conventional forwarding by adding a second condition to the forwarding process. To configure a conditional forwarder, you specify a domain and one or more IP addresses of DNS servers that can resolve queries directed to that domain.

You can use Dnscmd to configure conditional forwarders for your DNS server. For example, to configure a conditional forwarder that forwards all queries for hosts in the microsoft.com domain to the external DNS server 207.68.160.190, do the following:

```
C:\Users\administrator>dnscmd SEA-SC4 /zoneadd microsoft.com
/forwarder 207.68.160.190
DNS Server SEA-SC4 created zone microsoft.com:

Command completed successfully.
```

Use the DNS console on a computer that has RSAT installed to verify the result by expanding the DNS server node in the console tree and selecting the Conditional Forwarders node under it (as shown in Figure 9-3).

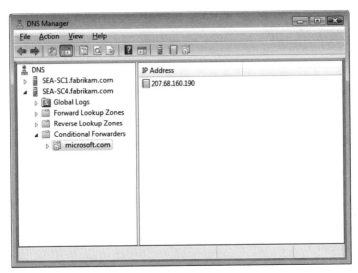

Figure 9-3   Configuring a conditional forwarder for the microsoft.com domain

If your DNS server is on a domain controller, use /dsforwarder instead of /forwarder in this command.

Configuring Zone Transfers

AD DS–integrated zones store their DNS information in AD DS and replicate this information between domain controllers by using AD DS directory replication. Standard zones store their information in zone files and replicate this information between DNS servers by a process called a *zone transfer*. When a zone transfer occurs, a primary DNS server for the zone provides the zone information for the secondary DNS server. In this situation, the primary DNS server is called the *master DNS server* for the zone.

As indicated in the section "Creating a Forward Lookup Standard Secondary Zone," earlier in this chapter, the master server is specified when you create a secondary zone. However, you can specify a different master server afterward by using Dnscmd. For example, if you are changing the master DNS server for the hr.fabrikam.com zone from SEA-SC2 (172.16.11.31) to SEA-SC4 (172.16.11.33), then you can use the following command to configure the new master on SEA-SC1 (the secondary DNS server for the zone):

```
C:\Users\administrator>dnscmd SEA-SC1 /zoneresetmasters
hr.fabrikam.com 172.16.11.33

Reset master servers for zone hr.fabrikam.com successfully.
Command completed successfully.
```

Before the secondary DNS server can load the zone information from the master DNS server for the zone, you must configure the master server to allow zone transfers with the secondary server. For example, to configure SEA-SC4 as the master server for the hr.fabrikam.com zone so that it allows zone transfers only to SEA-SC1 (the secondary server for the zone), do this:

```
C:\Users\administrator>dnscmd SEA-SC4 /zoneresetsecondaries
hr.fabrikam.com /securelist 172.16.11.30

Zone hr.fabrikam.com reset notify list successful

Command completed successfully.
```

Zone transfers take place automatically according to their default schedule, but you can also use Dnscmd to force a secondary server to initiate a zone transfer with its master server. For example, to force SEA-SC1 (the secondary server for the hr.fabrikam.com zone) to update its zone information from SEA-SC4 (the master server for the zone), do this:

```
C:\Users\administrator>dnscmd SEA-SC1 /zonerefresh hr.fabrikam.com

DNS Server SEA-SC1 forced refresh of zone hr.fabrikam.com:
    Status = 0 (0x00000000)
Command completed successfully.
```

Integrating DNS with DHCP

A feature called a *DNS dynamic update* enables client computers to register and dynamically update their resource records with a DNS server whenever changes occur. Dynamic updates are especially useful in an environment that uses DHCP to lease addresses to clients since it simplifies the management of both IP addresses and DNS resource records for your network.

You can enable or disable DNS dynamic update functionality on a per-zone basis for either standard primary or AD DS–integrated zones. In addition, AD DS–integrated zones also support secure updates, which uses access control lists (ACLs) to control which hosts can dynamically update their resource records on DNS servers.

By default, secure updates are enabled when you use unattended Dcpromo to install the AD DS role with the DNS role on Server Core. And by default, dynamic updates are disabled when you create a standard primary zone. You can use Dnscmd to modify the configuration of a standard primary zone to allow dynamic updates, but not secure updates. For example, to configure the standard primary zone hr.fabrikam.com on DNS server SEA-SC4 to allow dynamic updates, do this:

```
C:\Users\administrator>dnscmd SEA-SC4 /config hr.fabrikam.com
/allowupdate 1

Registry property allow update successfully reset.
Command completed successfully.
```

To disable dynamic updates, use /allowupdate 0 instead.

Configuring Aging and Scavenging

You can use aging and scavenging to remove stale resource records from primary zones on your DNS server. Aging and scavenging can be configured at two levels: at the server level and at the zone level.

By default, aging and scavenging of stale records are disabled on a DNS server, but you can use Dnscmd to enable them. For example, to enable automatic scavenging of stale records on DNS server SEA-SC4 using the standard settings, do this:

```
C:\Users\administrator>dnscmd SEA-SC4 /config /scavenginginterval 168
/defaultagingstate 1 /defaultnorefreshinterval 168

Registry property scavenging interval successfully reset.
Command completed successfully.
```

Once you have configured scavenging at the server level, you must configure aging at the zone level for it to work. For example, to enable aging on the hr.fabrikam.com primary zone on DNS server SEA-SC4 using the standard settings, do this:

```
C:\Users\administrator>dnscmd SEA-SC4 /config hr.fabrikam.com /aging 1
/refreshinterval 168 /norefreshinterval 3600

Registry property aging successfully reset.
Command completed successfully.
```

Integrating DNS with WINS

You can configure a DNS server to use WINS servers to look up names that are not found in the DNS namespace managed by the DNS server. This can be useful if you have WINS servers on your network and users frequently try to connect to internal servers by typing only their DNS label (such as **www**) instead of their full DNS name (such as **www.fabrikam.com**). DNS and WINS integration is also useful in certain heterogeneous networking environments. WINS integration is configured at the zone level on your DNS servers.

However, you cannot configure a WINS server on a DNS server by using Dnscmd; you must use the DNS console instead. To configure WINS lookups for your DNS server, do the following:

1. Open the DNS console on a computer that has RSAT installed and connect to your DNS server.

2. Right-click the zone that you want to integrate with WINS lookups and select Properties.

3. Select the WINS tab on the zone's properties sheet.

4. Select the Use WINS Forward Lookup check box to enable WINS lookups for the zone.

5. Select the Do Not Replicate This Record to prevent the special resource records created for WINS lookups from being propagated to other DNS servers on your network.

6. In the Properties dialog box, type the IP address for one or more WINS servers and click Add for each address you type:

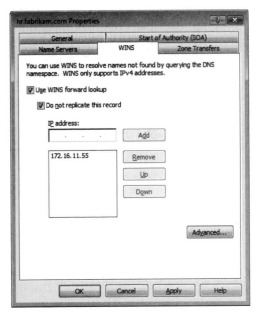

7. Click Advanced and modify the caching and lookup timeout values as desired.

Configuring the GlobalNames Zone

The GlobalNames zone (GNZ) is a new feature of Windows Server 2008 DNS servers that is intended to replace DNS integration with WINS by providing a way to register static, global records with single-label names. The typical replication scope for GNZ is the entire forest, which enables clients anywhere in the forest to resolve single-label names for key servers and other hosts quickly—without needing any WINS servers deployed on your network. Without GNZ, a DNS query for a single-label domain name such as www (for the Web server www.fabrikam.com) can take up to 12 seconds to time out before attempting a WINS lookup (assuming WINS servers are available and DNS is integrated with WINS). With GNZ configured, however, a DNS query for a single-label name like www is almost instantaneous.

You can use the Dnscmd command to enable and configure support for GNZ in your forest. For example, if you want to enable GNZ for the fabrikam.com domain, you must do the following on the forest root domain controller SEA-SC1. First, enable GNZ functionality by running the following command:

```
C:\Users\administrator>dnscmd SEA-SC1 /config /enableglobalnamessupport 1

Registry property enableglobalnamessupport successfully reset.
Command completed successfully.
```

Then create a new forward lookup zone named GlobalNames in the forest-wide DNS directory partition like this:

```
C:\Users\administrator>dnscmd SEA-SC1 /zoneadd GlobalNames /dsprimary
/dp /forest
DNS Server SEA-SC1 created zone GlobalNames:

Command completed successfully.
```

Wait for the new zone to replicate to all DNS servers in your forest. Now you can create CNAME records for each key server or host that you want users to be able to access using single-label names. For example, to create a CNAME record within the GNZ that enables users to access using the single-label name www16 instead of the FQDN SRV16.research,fabrikam.com, do this:

```
C:\Users\administrator>dnscmd SEA-SC1 /recordadd GlobalNames www16
CNAME SEA-SRV16.research.fabrikam.com.

Add CNAME Record for www16.GlobalNames at GlobalNames
Command completed successfully.
```

For more information on implementing GNZ, download the DNS Server GlobalNames-Zone Deployment guide from the Microsoft Download Center at http://www.microsoft.com/downloads/.

Maintaining DNS Servers

To maintain DNS servers, you must be able to start and stop the DNS Server service, pause and resume zones, initiate scavenging, and perform other actions. You must also be able to monitor and troubleshoot DNS in your environment.

Starting and Stopping the DNS Server Service

You can start and stop the DNS Server service by using the Net command. For example, to stop the DNS Server service on server SEA-SC4, type **net stop dns** at a command prompt on the server. To restart the service, type **net start dns** at the command prompt.

Pausing and Resuming Zones

You can pause a zone to temporarily prevent its resource records from being updated by clients. For example, to pause the hr.fabrikam.com zone on DNS server SEA-SC4, do this:

```
C:\Users\administrator>dnscmd SEA-SC4 /zonepause hr.fabrikam.com

DNS Server SEA-SC4 paused zone hr.fabrikam.com:
    Status = 0 (0x00000000)
Command completed successfully.
```

To resume operation of the zone, do this:

```
C:\Users\administrator>dnscmd SEA-SC4 /zoneresume hr.fabrikam.com

DNS Server SEA-SC4 resumed use of zone hr.fabrikam.com:
    Status = 0 (0x00000000)
Command completed successfully.
```

Initiating Scavenging

If aging and scavenging are configured as described in the section "Configuring Aging and Scavenging," earlier in this chapter, then you can use Dnscmd to force scavenging of stale records to occur at any time. For example, to begin immediate scavenging on DNS server SEA-SC1, do this:

```
C:\Users\administrator>dnscmd SEA-SC1 /startscavenging

SEA-SC1 completed successfully. Command completed successfully.
```

Monitoring and Troubleshooting DNS

You can monitor and troubleshoot DNS servers using a variety of tools including the following:

- Windows event logs
- Performance logs and alerts
- DNS debug logs
- The DNS console
- Nslookup

Note   For information on viewing event logs and monitoring performance counters on a Server Core installation, see Chapter 13, "Maintaining Server Core."

Configuring DNS Server Debug Logging

You can configure DNS server debug logging to log detailed information concerning the operation of your DNS server. The DNS server debug log is named Dns.log and is located in the %Windir%\System32\dns folder. By default, debug logging is not enabled because it can affect the performance of your server during its use.

To enable and configure debug logging, you must use the DNS console as follows:

1. Open the DNS console on a computer that has RSAT installed and connect to your DNS server.

2. Right-click the DNS server node and select Properties.

3. Select the Debug Logging tab on the DNS server's properties sheet.

4. Select the Log Packets For Debugging check box, as shown here.

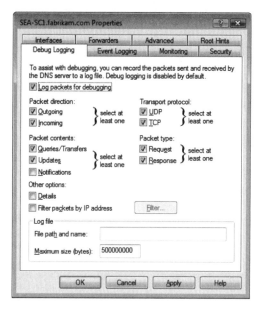

5. Configure other debug logging settings as desired.

Verifying DNS Server Configuration Using the DNS Console

You can use the DNS console to verify the configuration of your DNS server by performing test queries against it. To do this, perform the following steps:

1. Open the DNS console on a computer that has RSAT installed and connect to your DNS server.

2. Right-click the DNS server node and select Properties.

3. Select the Monitoring tab on the DNS server's properties sheet.

4. Select the check boxes for the types of queries you want to test, as shown here, and then click Test Now.

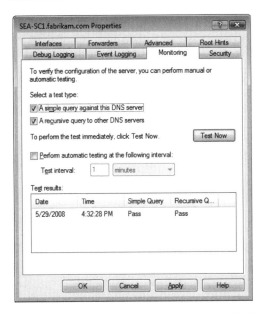

5. You can also configure automatic testing periodically as indicated.

Verifying DNS Server Configuration Using Nslookup

You can verify whether your DNS server is responding to queries by using the Nslookup command as follows:

1. Open a command prompt on your DNS server.

2. Type **nslookup** *<IP address of DNS server>* 127.0.0.1

3. If the server responds with localhost, your server is listening for queries. If it doesn't respond, make sure the DNS Server service is running on your server.

For more information about using Nslookup, type **nslookup** *followed by* **help** *at the command prompt.*

Chapter 10
File and Print Services Roles

File and print services have long been key elements of enterprise networks. Using Server Core, you can now implement these services on a reduced-footprint platform that can be more secure and requires fewer updates. This chapter examines how to install and manage the File and Print Services roles on Server Core.

Installing and Managing the File Services Role on Server Core

Unlike most other roles, the File Services role cannot be installed on Server Core using a single Ocsetup command. Instead, the Server service is enabled and started by default on Server Core to provide administrative share support for remote management tools. You can verify if the Server service is running on your Server Core installation by using the Sc command as follows:

```
C:\Users\Administrator>sc query lanmanserver

SERVICE_NAME: lanmanserver
        TYPE               : 20  WIN32_SHARE_PROCESS
        STATE              : 4   RUNNING
                               (STOPPABLE, PAUSABLE, ACCEPTS_SHUTDOWN)
        WIN32_EXIT_CODE    : 0   (0x0)
        SERVICE_EXIT_CODE  : 0   (0x0)
        CHECKPOINT         : 0x0
        WAIT_HINT          : 0x0
```

Installing File Services Role Services from the Command Line

As Table 10-1 indicates, four additional role services can be installed on Server Core to provide additional functionality for the File Services role.

Table 10-1   Additional File Services Role Services on Server Core

Role Service	Package Name	Description
DFS Namespaces	DFSN-Server	Lets you group shared folders on different servers in multiple sites as logically structured namespaces, with each namespace appearing to users as a single shared folder with a tree of subfolders.

Table 10-1   Additional File Services Role Services on Server Core

Role Service	Package Name	Description
DFS Replication	DFSR-Infrastructure-ServerEdition	Lets you synchronize folders on multiple servers across local or wide area network (WAN) network connections using multimaster replication. DFS Replication can be used by itself or in conjunction with DFS Namespaces.
Services for Network File System	ServerForNFS-Base	Lets you transfer files between computers running Windows Server 2008 and various UNIX operating systems using the Network File System (NFS) protocol.
File Replication Service	FRS-Infrastructure	Lets you synchronize folders with file servers that use File Replication Service (FRS) instead of the newer DFS Replication service. For example, you can use it to provide backward compatibility with the Windows Server 2003 and Microsoft Windows 2000 implementations of Distributed File System (DFS).

You can use the Oscetup command to install these role services on Server Core. For example, to install the DFS Namespaces and DFS Replication role services in a single step, type **start /w ocsetup DFSN-Server && start /w ocsetup DFSR-Infrastructure-ServerEdition** at the command prompt. Then verify the installation as follows:

```
C:\Users\Administrator>oclist | find "   Installed"
    Installed:DFSN-Server
    Installed:DFSR-Infrastructure-ServerEdition
```

For the NFS role service, you can install either or both of the NFS client and server components as follows:

- To install the NFS server component, type **start /w ocsetup ServerForNFS-Base**

- To install the NFS client component, type **start /w ocsetup ClientForNFS-Base**

To uninstall any File Services role service, use Ocsetup as described previously, but with the /uninstall parameter.

Installing File Services Role Services Using an Answer File

You can also install File Services role services using an answer file during an unattended installation of Server Core. For example, to install the DFS Namespaces role service using an answer file, perform the following steps:

1. Begin by creating and configuring an answer file for an unattended installation of Server Core. For information on how to do this, see Chapter 2, "Deploying Server Core."

2. On your technician computer, open your answer file in Windows System Image Manager (Windows SIM).

3. In the Windows Image pane, expand the Packages node to display the nodes beneath it. Expand the Foundation node to display the Microsoft-Windows-ServerCore-Package node beneath that. Then right-click the Microsoft-Windows-ServerCore-Package node and select Add To Answer File. The Microsoft-Windows-ServerCore-Package should now be selected in the Answer File pane.

4. In the Properties pane, scroll down until DFSN-Server setting is visible under Windows Feature Selections. Click the value field to the right of the DFSN-Server setting to display a drop-down arrow, then click the arrow and select Enabled.

5. Validate your answer file and save it, and then deploy Server Core using your answer file using any of the methods outlined in Chapter 2. When installation is completed, log on, type **oclist | find "   Installed"**, and verify that the DFS Namespaces role service has been installed.

Managing Disks and File Systems

Server Core includes a number of command-line tools that you can use for managing the underlying disk storage needed to support the File Services role. Table 10-2 lists some of the more important command-line tools available for managing disks and file systems on Server Core. For detailed syntax of any of these commands, type the command followed by /? at a command prompt.

Table 10-2   Command-Line Tools for Managing Disks and File Systems on Server Core

Tool	Use
Chkdsk	Checks for and repairs logical and physical errors in the file system on a volume
Defrag	Consolidates fragmented files on local volumes to improve performance
Diskpart	Manages disks, partitions, and volumes from the command line
Diskraid	Configures and manages redundant array of independent disks (RAID) storage subsystems
Fltmc	Displays, loads, and unloads file system mini-filters
Format	Formats a storage device using a file system
Fsutil	Performs file system tasks such as mounting and dismounting volumes, managing reparse points, managing sparse files, and performing many other tasks
Icacls	Displays and modifies discretionary access control lists (DACLs) on files (deprecates Cacls)
Mklink	Creates symbolic links, hard links, and directory junctions
Robocopy	Copies file system data (deprecates Xcopy)

In addition to the command-line tools listed in the table, you can use Windows Explorer and the Disk Management snap-in from a different computer to manage disks and file systems remotely on Server Core. For information on how to do this, see Chapter 6, "Remote Management."

Note   Disk Management has been enhanced in Windows Server 2008 so that it automatically and implicitly converts a basic volume to dynamic when you try to create a new spanned, striped, mirrored, or RAID-5 volume, when you extend a volume, and when you add a mirror.

The following sections describe some common administration tasks (plus some advanced and useful tasks) involving managing disks and file systems on Server Core. The focus of these sections is on performing administrative tasks from the Server Core command prompt. For information on how to manage disks and file systems using graphic user interface (GUI) tools, see the Windows Server 2008 Administrator's Pocket Consultant *by William Stanek (Microsoft Press, 2008).*

Managing Disks and Volumes Using Diskpart

Diskpart is a powerful command that you can use to create, format, extend, shrink, and perform many other actions on partitions and volumes. The following are examples of some common tasks you can perform using Diskpart.

Begin by starting Diskpart as follows:

```
C:\Users\Administrator>diskpart

Microsoft DiskPart version 6.0.6001
Copyright (C) 1999-2007 Microsoft Corporation.
On computer: SEA-SC1

DISKPART>
```

The DISKPART> prompt indicates that Diskpart is running, and you can now type various commands to manage disks, volumes, and partitions on the computer.

Note   Diskpart takes a few moments to start on a default Server Core installation because the Virtual Disk Service (VDS) is started manually when you start Diskpart. The service is also stopped when you type **exit** to end a Diskpart command session.

List all disks (including removable USB drives and flash media ports) on the computer as follows:

```
DISKPART> list disk

  Disk ###  Status      Size     Free     Dyn  Gpt
  --------  ----------  -------  -------   ---  ---
  Disk 0    Online      149 GB   129 GB
  Disk 1    No Media      0 B      0 B
```

Select disk zero as the one you wish to manage as follows:

```
DISKPART> select disk 0
```

```
Disk 0 is now the selected disk.
```

View details concerning the selected disk as follows:

```
DISKPART> detail disk
```

```
ST3160021A ATA Device
Disk ID: 37BFBFEC
Type    : ATA
Bus     : 0
Target  : 0
LUN ID  : 0
Read-only  : No
Boot Disk  : Yes
Pagefile Disk  : Yes
Hibernation File Disk  : No
Crashdump Disk  : Yes

  Volume ###  Ltr  Label      Fs     Type       Size    Status    Info
  ----------  ---  ---------- -----  ---------- -------  --------- --------
* Volume 2    C               NTFS   Partition  25 GB   Healthy   System
```

You can also display only the attributes of the selected disk by using the following command:

```
DISKPART> attributes disk
Read-only  : No
Boot Disk  : Yes
Pagefile Disk  : Yes
Hibernation File Disk  : No
Crashdump Disk  : Yes
```

To list all partitions on the selected disk, do the following:

```
DISKPART> list partition
```

```
  Partition ###  Type             Size     Offset
  -------------  ---------------- -------  -------
  Partition 1    Primary          20 GB    1024 KB
```

Listing partitions doesn't display all the information available. You can get more information by listing the volumes on the disk as follows:

```
DISKPART> list volume
```

```
  Volume ###  Ltr  Label      Fs     Type       Size    Status    Info
  ----------  ---  ---------- -----  ---------- -------  --------- --------
  Volume 0    D                      DVD-ROM            0 B  No Media
  Volume 1    E                      CD-ROM             0 B  No Media
```

```
Volume 2     C                      NTFS   Partition    20 GB  Healthy    System
Volume 4     F                             Removable     0 B   No Media
```

Select partition 1 (or volume 2), which is the C: drive (the system partition), as the partition (volume) you want to manage as follows:

```
DISKPART> select partition 1
```

```
Partition 1 is now the selected partition.
```

List the partitions again on the selected disk as follows:

```
DISKPART> list partition
```

```
  Partition ###  Type              Size     Offset
  -------------  ----------------  -------  -------
* Partition 1    Primary           20 GB    1024 KB
```

Note the asterisk beside Partition 1, which indicates that the partition is selected.

Extend the C: drive by 10240 megabytes (MB), or 10 gigabytes (GB), as follows:

```
DISKPART> extend size=10240
```

```
DiskPart successfully extended the volume.
```

Verify the result as follows:

```
DISKPART> list partition
```

```
  Partition ###  Type              Size     Offset
  -------------  ----------------  -------  -------
* Partition 1    Primary           30 GB    1024 KB
```

Determine how much you can shrink the C: drive as follows:

```
DISKPART> shrink querymax
```

```
The maximum number of reclaimable bytes is:    10 GB
```

Shrink the C: drive by 5120 MB (5 GB), which is half the possible amount, as follows:

```
DISKPART> shrink desired=5120
```

```
DiskPart successfully shrunk the volume by: 5120 MB
```

Verify the result as follows:

```
DISKPART> list partition
```

```
  Partition ###  Type              Size     Offset
  -------------  ----------------  -------  -------
* Partition 1    Primary           25 GB    1024 KB
```

Create a new primary partition that is 40,960 MB (40 GB) in size as follows:

```
DISKPART> create partition primary size=40960

DiskPart succeeded in creating the specified partition.
```

Verify the result as follows:

```
DISKPART> list volume
```

Volume ###	Ltr	Label	Fs	Type	Size	Status	Info
Volume 0	D			DVD-ROM	0 B	No Media	
Volume 1	E			CD-ROM	0 B	No Media	
Volume 2	C		NTFS	Partition	25 GB	Healthy	System
Volume 3	F			Removable	0 B	No Media	
* Volume 4			RAW	Partition	40 GB	Healthy	

Note that the new volume is now selected and is unformatted (indicated by "RAW").

Format the new partition using NTFS and assign it the label "DataVol" as follows:

```
DISKPART> format fs=ntfs label=DataVol

  100 percent completed

DiskPart successfully formatted the volume.
```

Assign the drive letter R to the newly formatted volume as follows:

```
DISKPART> assign letter=R

DiskPart successfully assigned the drive letter or mount point.
```

Verify the result as follows:

```
DISKPART> list volume
```

Volume ###	Ltr	Label	Fs	Type	Size	Status	Info
Volume 0	D			DVD-ROM	0 B	No Media	
Volume 1	E			CD-ROM	0 B	No Media	
Volume 2	C		NTFS	Partition	25 GB	Healthy	System
Volume 3	F			Removable	0 B	No Media	
* Volume 4	R	DataVol	NTFS	Partition	40 GB	Healthy	

Display detailed information concerning the selected volume as follows:

```
DISKPART> detail volume
```

Disk ###	Status	Size	Free	Dyn	Gpt
* Disk 0	Online	149 GB	84 GB		

```
Read-only            : No
Hidden               : No
No Default Drive Letter: No
Shadow Copy          : No
Dismounted           : No
BitLocker Encrypted  : No


Volume Capacity      :    40 GB
Volume Free Space    :    40 GB
```

Display the volume's current file system and determine what file systems the volume can support as follows:

```
DISKPART> filesystems

Current File System

  Type                : NTFS
  Allocation Unit Size : 4096

File Systems Supported for Formatting

  Type                : NTFS (Default)
  Allocation Unit Sizes: 512, 1024, 2048, 4096 (Default), 8192, 16K, 32K, 64K
```

Some other useful Diskpart commands include the following:

- **Active** Marks the selected partition as the active partition

- **Delete** Deletes the selected disk, partition, or volume

- **Remove** Removes the drive letter or mount point from the selected volume

- **Repair** Repairs a RAID-5 volume by replacing the failed RAID-5 member with the specified dynamic disk

- **Rescan** Finds any new disks that may have been added to the computer

Finally, here are three Diskpart commands that are new in Windows Server 2008:

- **Offline** Transitions the selected disk from the online to the offline state

- **Online** Transitions the selected disk or volume from offline to online state

- **Recover** Refreshes the state of all disks in a disk pack, attempts recovery on disks in an invalid pack, or resynchronizes mirrored and RAID-5 volumes that have stale parity information

For more information about a Diskpart command such as Recover, type **help recover** at the DISKPART> prompt.

Scripting Diskpart Commands

You can also script Diskpart commands to perform a series of commands in Batch mode. And you can comment your Diskpart command scripts using the Rem command. For example, the following Diskpart command script creates an extended partition and then creates two logical drives within this partition:

```
ren Diskpart command script to create an extended partition with
two logical drives
create partition extended size=102400
create partition logical size=51200
assign e:
create partition logical size=51200
assign f:
```

Save your command script as Command.txt and then run it by typing **diskpart /s command.txt** at the command prompt.

Displaying Detailed File System Information

You can use the Fsutil Fsinfo command to display detailed file system about a volume. For example, the following command returns detailed information concerning the C: drive:

```
C:\Users\Administrator>fsutil fsinfo ntfsinfo C:
NTFS Volume Serial Number :        0x9e9832ba983290af
Version :                          3.1
Number Sectors :                   0x000000000270ffff
Total Clusters :                   0x00000000004e1fff
Free Clusters  :                   0x00000000003e6e11
Total Reserved :                   0x0000000000000040
Bytes Per Sector  :                512
Bytes Per Cluster :                4096
Bytes Per FileRecord Segment     : 1024
Clusters Per FileRecord Segment  : 0
Mft Valid Data Length :            0x0000000001060000
Mft Start Lcn  :                   0x00000000000c0000
Mft2 Start Lcn :                   0x0000000000270fff
Mft Zone Start :                   0x00000000000c1060
Mft Zone End   :                   0x00000000000cd7c0
RM Identifier:        4A852C61-3717-11DD-91ED-D02E31493742
```

Displaying Free Space on a Volume

To display the free space on a volume, use the Fsutil Volume command. For example, do the following to display the free space on the C: drive:

```
C:\Users\Administrator>fsutil volume diskfree C:
Total # of free bytes        : 16753954816
Total # of bytes             : 20971515904
Total # of avail free bytes  : 16753954816
```

Search for Files or Folders on a Volume

Neither the Windows Search Service role service nor the older Indexing Service can be installed on Server Core. This means that if you need to search for files or folders on disk volumes on Server Core, you must do it using one of the following two ways: by using the Dir command with the /s switch to search all subdirectories on a volume, or by using grep search in Windows Explorer running on a remote computer.

For example, to use the Dir command to search the entire C: drive for files named Test.txt, do the following:

```
C:\Users\Administrator>dir C:\Test.txt /s
 Volume in drive C has no label.
 Volume Serial Number is 9832-90AF

 Directory of C:\Data

06/12/2008  11:38 AM                   16 Test.txt
              1 File(s)             16 bytes

 Directory of C:\Data2

06/12/2008  11:56 AM                   14 Test.txt
              1 File(s)             14 bytes

 Directory of C:\Data3

06/12/2008  12:05 PM                   14 Test.txt
              1 File(s)             14 bytes

     Total Files Listed:
              3 File(s)             44 bytes
              0 Dir(s)  22,167,846,912 bytes free
```

To use Windows Explorer to accomplish the same task, do this:

1. Log on to a remote computer running Windows Vista using credentials that have administrative privileges on your Server Core installation.

2. Press the Windows key+R to open the Run box.

3. Type **\\SEA-SC1\C$**, where SEA-SC1 is the name of your Server Core installation.

4. Click OK to connect to the C$ administrative share on your Server Core installation using Windows Explorer.

5. Type **Test.txt** in the Start Search box at the top right of the Explorer window to display all instances of the file Test.txt on your Server Core installation, as shown here.

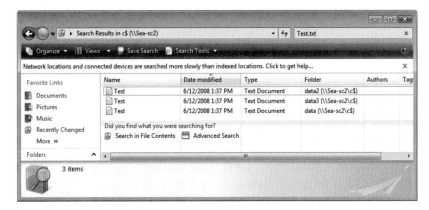

6. You can also search for text within files by clicking the Search In File Contents link in the Explorer window. Note that searching for text within files can take a long time because it uses the slower grep search method and not the indexed search method.

Displaying File System Filters

Filter Manager (Fltmc.exe) is a file system filter driver that simplifies the development of third-party filter drivers. Using Filter Manager, you can display file system filters, including mini-filters (filter drivers developed to the Filter Manager model) and legacy filters; control the load order of filters by using an assigned altitude; attach or remove filters to and from volumes; enumerate volumes and redirectors; and perform other file system filter–related tasks.

For example, to list all file system filters currently registered on a new Server Core installation that has no roles installed on it, do the following:

```
C:\Users\administrator>fltmc filters
```

```
No filters loaded
```

If the DFS role services for the File Services role are installed, the result is as follows:

```
C:\Users\Administrator>fltmc filters
```

Filter Name	Num Instances	Altitude	Frame
DfsDriver	0	405000	0

To display volumes and redirectors on your system, do this:

```
C:\Users\Administrator>fltmc volumes
Dos Name                      Volume Name
 FileSystem    Status
----------------------------  --------------------------------------  --
```

```
---------   --------
                              \Device\Mup
Remote

C:                            \Device\HarddiskVolume1
NTFS

                              \Device\RdpDr
TermSrv
```

File-system filters may be installed automatically by antivirus software, file-replication software, quota management software, backup software, and other types of applications. For more information concerning managing filter drivers, see http://www.microsoft.com/whdc/driver/filterdrv/default.mspx *on Windows Hardware Developer Central.*

Setting the Dirty Bit on a Volume

The *dirty bit* is a bit on a disk volume that is automatically set when Windows detects file system corruption on the volume. Windows checks during the boot process whether the dirty bit is set on each volume, and if it is set, then Autochk runs to try to repair the volume.

You can use the Fsutil Dirty command to query the state of the dirty bit on a volume. For example, to determine whether the dirty bit is set on the C: drive, do this:

```
C:\Users\Administrator>fsutil dirty query C:
Volume - C: is NOT Dirty
```

You can set the dirty bit on a volume manually to force Autochk to run when the system reboots. For example, do the following to set the dirty bit on the C: drive:

```
C:\Users\Administrator>fsutil dirty set C:
Volume - C: is now marked dirty
```

Running Chkdsk

Chkdsk is a command-line tool that checks volumes for corruption and optionally can be configured to repair any problems it finds. Chkdsk can repair a wide range of disk problems, including bad sectors, lost clusters, cross-linked files, and directory errors. However, Chkdsk cannot repair a volume if Windows is unable to mount the volume.

Chkdsk has been improved in Windows Server 2008 to provide better information when events with source Chkdsk are logged to the Application Event log. Specifically, Chkdsk now distinguishes between read-only and read-write runs, and between running on a live volume as opposed to on a snapshot. The Details tab in event messages has also been enhanced to display the output of running Chkdsk (as shown in Figure 10-1).

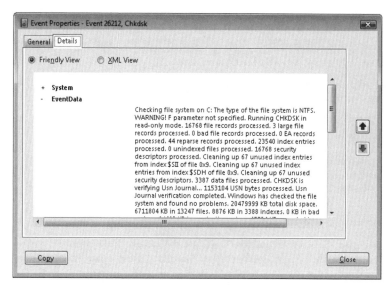

Figure 10-1   The Details tab of an Application log event with source Chkdsk and event ID 26212

Note   Chkdsk output may be truncated when displayed in the Details tab of a Chkdsk event if the output from running the command is too long.

An additional enhancement to Chkdsk in Windows Server 2008 is the ability to cancel operation of the command by pressing Ctrl+C. In previous versions of Windows, the only way to stop a Chkdsk operation was by using Task Manager. Finally, Chkdsk operating has been enhanced in Windows Server 2008, providing up to 30 percent faster performance over previous Windows Server operating systems.

To view the command options for running Chkdsk, type **chkdsk /?** at the command prompt. These options have not changed in Windows Server 2008.

Configuring Self-Healing NTFS

Self-Healing NTFS is a new feature of NTFS (introduced in Windows Vista) that allows Windows to attempt to correct corruption found on NTFS volumes without needing to run the Chkdsk command. This helps provide continuous availability for NTFS volumes, reduce failed file system remount requests, and preserve data.

Self-Healing NTFS is enabled by default on Windows Server 2008 and should generally remain enabled. If you need to disable Self-Healing NTFS on a volume for testing or troubleshooting purposes, you can use the Fsutil command. For example, to view the current state of this feature on volume C: use the following command:

```
C:\Users\Administrator>fsutil repair query C:
Self healing is enabled for volume C: with flags 0x1.
```

```
flags: 0x01 - enable general repair
       0x08 - warn about potential data loss
       0x10 - disable general repair and bugcheck once on first corruption
```

To disable Self-Healing NTFS on the C: drive, do this:

```
C:\Users\Administrator>fsutil repair set C: 0
Self healing is now disabled for volume C:.
```

To re-enable this feature and view other options for this feature, replace 0 with 1 in the previous command.

> **Tip** If an event with source NTFS and event ID 131 is logged in the System Event log, Self-Healing NTFS cannot repair a problem that it has encountered. If this happens, run Chkdsk on the volume identified by the event.

Enabling BugcheckOnCorrupt

Self-Healing NTFS has been enhanced in Windows Vista SP1 and Windows Server 2008 with a new BugcheckOnCorrupt option that allows the system to check for bugs with a 0x00000024 stop error when the system encounters corruption on an NTFS volume. Enabling this feature allows administrators to prevent NTFS from silently deleting data without their knowledge so they can back up data on volumes before enabling Self-Healing NTFS or running Chkdsk to try to repair the volume.

BugcheckOnCorrupt is disabled by default on all NTFS volumes. To enable this feature (such as on the C: drive), do the following:

1. Use the Fsutil Behavior command to set BugcheckOnCorrupt to 1 as follows:

   fsutil behavior set BugcheckOnCorrupt 1

2. Reboot the computer.

3. Use the Fsutil Repair command to set Self-Healing NTFS to 0x10 on any disk volumes on which you want to have BugcheckOnCorrupt enabled. For example, to enable BugcheckOnCorrupt for the C: drive, do this:

   fsutil repair set C: 0x10

To disable BugcheckOnCorrupt on an individual volume, use 0x01 instead of 0x10 in the previous command. To disable this feature for all volumes, type **fsutil behavior set BugcheckOnCorrupt 0** at the command prompt.

Defragment a Volume

Windows Vista has disk defragmentation automatically scheduled to improve the user experience, but on Windows Server 2008, automatic scheduling of disk defragmentation is disabled by default. On a Server Core installation, you can defragment a volume manually by using the Defrag command. For example, to perform a fragmentation analysis of the C: drive only, do the following:

```
C:\Users\Administrator>defrag C: -a
Windows Disk Defragmenter
Copyright (c) 2006 Microsoft Corp.

Analysis report for volume C:

        Volume size                     = 19.53 GB
        Free space                      = 15.61 GB
        Largest free space extent       = 9.76 GB
        Percent file fragmentation      = 2 %

    Note: On NTFS volumes, file fragments larger than 64MB are not
included in t
he fragmentation statistics

    You do not need to defragment this volume.
```

More verbose output can be provided by adding the −v parameter to this command.

To defragment the C: drive, simply type **defrag C:** at the command prompt. This command reports fragmentation statistics before and after the defragmentation operation. Once again, you can add the −v parameter to provide more verbose statistics. To defrag all volumes on the computer, use the −c parameter and omit the drive letter; for example, type **defrag −c** at the command prompt.

If you attempt to defragment a volume that has the dirty bit set, you see the following:

```
C:\Users\Administrator>defrag C:
Windows Disk Defragmenter
Copyright (c) 2006 Microsoft Corp.

The volume is marked as dirty. you must run chkdsk on the volume to
correct any problems before you attempt to defragment it again.
```

> **Tip**   You should defragment volumes regularly to ensure optimal disk subsystem performance. You can also use the Schtasks command on Server Core to schedule automatic defragmentation to occur on a periodic basis. For more information, type **schtasks /?** at the command prompt.

Viewing and Modifying the ACLs for Files and Folders

To view or modify the access control list (ACL) for a file or folder, use the Icacls command. You can also save ACLs and restore them later, as the following example

illustrates. To begin, use the following command to view the ACLs on the folder
C:\Data and the file Test.txt within this folder:

```
C:\Users\Administrator>icacls C:\Data /t
C:\Data NT AUTHORITY\SYSTEM:(I)(OI)(CI)(F)
        BUILTIN\Administrators:(I)(OI)(CI)(F)
        BUILTIN\Users:(I)(OI)(CI)(RX)
        BUILTIN\Users:(I)(CI)(AD)
        BUILTIN\Users:(I)(CI)(WD)
        CREATOR OWNER:(I)(OI)(CI)(IO)(F)

C:\Data\Test.txt NT AUTHORITY\SYSTEM:(I)(F)
                 BUILTIN\Administrators:(I)(F)
                 BUILTIN\Users:(I)(RX)

Successfully processed 2 files; Failed processing 0 files
```

You can use Tables 10-3 through 10-5 (which appear later in this section) to interpret
this ACL information.

To save these ACLs in a file named Acls.txt, do this:

```
C:\Users\Administrator>icacls C:\Data /save acls.txt /t
processed file: C:\Data
processed file: C:\Data\Test.txt
Successfully processed 2 files; Failed processing 0 files
```

You can display the saved ACLs using Notepad as follows:

```
C:\Users\Administrator>notepad acls.txt
```

Notepad displays the following ACL information (which you can again interpret using
Tables 10-2 through 10-4):

```
Data
D:AI(A;OICIID;FA;;;SY)(A;OICIID;FA;;;BA)(A;OICIID;0x1200a9;;;BU)(A;CIID;LC;;;BU)
(A;CIID;DC;;;BU)(A;OICIIOID;GA;;;CO)
Data\Test.txt
D:AI(A;ID;FA;;;SY)(A;ID;FA;;;BA)(A;ID;0x1200a9;;;BU)
```

> **Caution**   Be careful not to save the file opened in Notepad because then Notepad
> modifies the file and you won't be able to use it to restore the ACLs on the files
> and folders it was generated from.

Modify the ACL for the C:\Data folder to grant Read And Execute permission for the
Guests group as follows:

```
C:\Users\Administrator>icacls C:\Data /grant Guests:(OI)(CI)(RX)
processed file: C:\Data
Successfully processed 1 files; Failed processing 0 files
```

Display the modified ACLs as follows:

```
C:\Users\Administrator>icacls C:\Data /t
C:\Data BUILTIN\Guests:(OI)(CI)(RX)
        BUILTIN\Users:(OI)(CI)(RX)
        NT AUTHORITY\SYSTEM:(I)(OI)(CI)(F)
        BUILTIN\Administrators:(I)(OI)(CI)(F)
        BUILTIN\Users:(I)(OI)(CI)(RX)
        BUILTIN\Users:(I)(CI)(AD)
        BUILTIN\Users:(I)(CI)(WD)
        CREATOR OWNER:(I)(OI)(CI)(IO)(F)

C:\Data\Test.txt BUILTIN\Guests:(I)(RX)
                 BUILTIN\Users:(I)(RX)
                 NT AUTHORITY\SYSTEM:(I)(F)
                 BUILTIN\Administrators:(I)(F)

Successfully processed 2 files; Failed processing 0 files
```

Note from this command output that Test.txt has inherited Read And Execute permission from its parent folder C:\Data.

Now restore the previously saved ACL for the C:\Data folder as follows:

```
C:\Users\Administrator>icacls C:\Data\.. /restore acls_Data.txt
processed file: C:\Data\..\Data processed file: C:\Data\..\Data\Test.txt
Successfully processed 2 files; Failed processing 0 files
```

Verify that the ACLs for the folder and file have been restored as follows:

```
C:\Users\Administrator>icacls C:\Data /t
C:\Data NT AUTHORITY\SYSTEM:(I)(OI)(CI)(F)
        BUILTIN\Administrators:(I)(OI)(CI)(F)
        BUILTIN\Users:(I)(OI)(CI)(RX)
        BUILTIN\Users:(I)(CI)(AD)
        BUILTIN\Users:(I)(CI)(WD)

        CREATOR OWNER:(I)(OI)(CI)(IO)(F)

C:\Data\Test.txt NT AUTHORITY\SYSTEM:(I)(F)
                 BUILTIN\Administrators:(I)(F)
                 BUILTIN\Users:(I)(RX)

Successfully processed 2 files; Failed processing 0 files
```

Tip   Using **icacls C:\Data /save** means that you want to save all the ACLs in C:\ that pattern match the "Data" string. The /t parameter means that the operation is performed on all specified files in the current directory and its subdirectories. If you want lcacls to work only on the files in C:\Data, use C:\Data* instead.

Table 10-3 Icacls Letter Codes That Define Simple Rights

Code	Simple Rights
F	Full Access
M	Modify Access
RX	Read And Execute Access
R	Read-Only Access
W	Write-Only Access

Table 10-4 Icacls Letter Codes That Define Specific Rights

Code	Specific Rights
RC	Read Control
WDAC	Write DAC
WO	Write Owner
S	Synchronize
AS	Access System Security
MA	Maximum Allowed
GR	Generic Read
GW	Generic Write
GE	Generic Exclude
GA	Generic All
RD	Read Data/List Directory
WD	Write Data/Add File
AD	Append Data/Add Subdirectory
REA	Read Extended Attributes
WEA	Write Extended Attributes
X	Execute/Traverse
D	Delete
DC	Delete Child
RA	Read Attributes
WA	Write Attributes

Table 10-5   Icacls Letter Codes That Define Inheritance

Code	Inheritance Behavior
OI	Object Inheritance
IO	Inherit Only
CI	Container Inheritance
NP	Non-Propagate Inheritance

Creating Symbolic Links

A *symbolic link* is a file system object that points to another file system object. The object being pointed to by the link is called the *target,* which can be either a file or a directory on the same local drive, on a different local drive, or on a remote UNC share. Symbolic links are features of NTFS file systems that can be created on Windows Vista SP1 and Windows Server 2008, and they are designed to help in migration and application compatibility with UNIX operating systems. Symbolic links can also provide command-line functionality similar to what shortcuts provide for the Windows desktop shell.

You can use the Mklink command on Server Core to create symbolic links and other types of file system links. For example, use Notepad to create a file named Test.txt that contains the text "This is a test" and save it in the Documents folder. Then create a symbolic link *t* that points to Test.txt as its target as follows:

```
C:\Users\Administrator>mklink t Documents\test.txt
symbolic link created for t <<===>> Documents\test.txt
```

Verify the link's creation using the Dir command as follows:

```
C:\Users\Administrator>dir t
 Volume in drive C has no label.
 Volume Serial Number is 9832-90AF

 Directory of C:\Users\Administrator

06/11/2008  12:12 PM    <SYMLINK>       t [Documents\test.txt]
               1 File(s)              0 bytes
               0 Dir(s)  16,752,721,920 bytes free
```

Use the link as a shortcut for the Type command as follows:

```
C:\Users\Administrator>type t
This is a test
```

You can also type **notepad t** to open Test.txt in Notepad.

Formatting USB Flash Drives Using exFAT

Extended FAT (exFAT) file system is a new file system supported by Windows Vista and Windows Server 2008. The exFAT file system is intended mainly for removable flash media such as USB flash drives. Such media typically use either FAT or FAT32 as their file system, but these file systems have several limitations. For example, FAT32 has a maximum file size of 4 GB, and the Windows format restricts the maximum FAT32 volume size to 32 GB. FAT is even more restrictive on file and volume size. To overcome these limitations, Microsoft created exFAT, which can support files up to 2^{64} bytes in size and can handle more than 1,000 files in a single directory.

You can use the Format command on Server Core to format removable flash media using exFAT. For example, if K: is a USB flash device plugged into Server Core, you can type **format k: /fs:exfat** to format the device using exFAT.

Managing Hardware RAID Using Diskraid

You can use the Diskraid command on Windows Server 2008 to configure hardware RAID subsystems that use a VDS hardware provider. VDS hardware providers are supplied by the manufacturers of hardware RAID devices and are not included in Windows Server 2008. At least one registered VDS hardware provider must be installed on your server before you can run Diskraid on the server.

Like the Diskpart command described in the section "Managing Disks and Volumes Using Diskpart," earlier in this chapter, Diskraid can be run in two ways: by typing **Diskraid** to enter the DISKRAID> prompt, from which you can type additional commands, and by creating a batch file of Diskraid commands and running this file using the /s parameter. See the section "Scripting Diskpart Commands," earlier in this chapter, for more information.

Using Diskraid, you can manage hardware RAID configurations of levels 0 (striping), 1 (mirroring), and 5 (striping with parity). Diskpart can also be used to manage both Fibre Channel and iSCSI hardware RAID systems. The examples here show how Diskraid can be used to manage a Hewlett-Packard Enterprise Virtual Array (EVA) storage system that uses Fibre Channel.

Start Diskraid on the server:

```
C:\Users\Administrator>diskraid
Microsoft DiskRAID version 6.0.6001
Copyright (C) 2003-2007 Microsoft Corporation.
On computer: SEA-SC1
```

Display available VDS hardware providers as follows:

```
DISKRAID> list provider
 Prov ### Name              Version   Type
-------- ---------------------------------------------- ---------- -----
 Prov 0 HP EVA VDS Hardware Provider   4.02.03.2 FC
```

Select the available provider as follows:

```
DISKRAID> select prov 0

Provider 0 is now the selected provider.
```

List the subsystems managed by the provider as follows:

```
DISKRAID> list subsystem

Subsys ### Name            Status   Health
---------- ----------------------------- ---------- ----------
Subsys 0 HP EVA-MDEVA3000 (HSV100)  Online   Healthy
```

From this command output, the storage system is online and ready to use, and the type of Fibre Channel controller being used is HSV100.

Select the available subsystem as follows:

```
DISKRAID> select subsys 0

Subsystem 0 is now the selected subsystem.
```

List the controllers for the subsystem as follows:

```
DISKRAID> list controller

Ctlr ### Name        Status   Health   Ports LUNs
-------- -------------------- ---------- ------------ ----- ----
Ctlr 0 \Hardware\Rack 1\Con Online   Healthy   2   2
Ctlr 1 \Hardware\Rack 1\Con Online   Healthy   2   2
```

Select controller 0 as follows:

```
DISKRAID> select controller 0

Controller 0 is now the selected controller.
```

List details for the controller, including its two ports and connected logical unit numbers (LUNs), as follows:

```
DISKRAID> detail con

Name      : \Hardware\Rack 1\Controller Enclosure 1\Controller A
Identifier  : P64EC152LX5G45
Status    : Online
Health    : Healthy

2 Port(s):

Port ### Name      Identifier    Status
-------- -------------------- -------------------- ----------
Port 0 hostport1    50001fe15003432d  Online
Port 1 hostport2    50001fe15003432c  Online

2 Associated LUN(s):

LUN ### Status  Health  Type  Size  Device
```

```
------- ---------- ------------ -------- -------- ------
LUN 0 Online  Healthy  Mirror  500 GB
LUN 1 Online  Healthy  Mirror  500 GB
```

Select LUN 0 as follows:

```
DISKRAID> select LUN 0

LUN 0 is now the selected LUN.
```

Once you've selected a LUN, you can manage it using other Diskraid commands. Each LUN has at least one or more plex (mirror of the data), and you can do things like add or remove plexes from a LUN, break a plex, create new LUNs or delete existing ones, take a LUN offline or bring it online, perform maintenance actions, and other actions. For more information, type **diskraid /?** at the command prompt.

> **Note** The equivalent Microsoft Management Console (MMC) console for the Diskraid command is Storage Manager for storage area networks (SANs), which can be run on a remote computer running Windows Server 2008 to manage a Fibre Channel or iSCSI storage system.

Managing Shared Folders

You can create, delete, view, and manage shared folders on a Server Core installation, even if no File Services role services have been installed on your server. You can perform administrative tasks relating to shared folders either locally from the command prompt or remotely using MMC snap-ins.

Creating Shared Folders

You can create and configure a shared folder using the Net Share command. For example, to create a share named UserData that shares the contents of the C:\Data folder, do the following:

```
C:\Users\administrator>net share UserData=C:\data /remark:"General share
for user data"
UserData was shared successfully.
```

The /remark parameter is optional and provides users with a description of the share when they browse the server over the network.

The previous command assigns the default shared folder permissions (Everyone has Read access) to the UserData share. You can also explicitly assign share permissions if desired. For example, to share the folder C:\Data2 as Invoices and grant Allow Read share permission to Domain Users and Allow Full Control share permission to Domain Admins, do this:

```
C:\Users\administrator>net share Invoices=C:\data2
/grant:"FABRIKAM\Domain Users",Read /grant:"FABRIKAM\Domain Admins",Full
Invoices was shared successfully.
```

To verify that you've assigned the desired shared folder permissions for your share, use the Net Share command again to display the properties of the share as follows:

```
C:\Users\administrator>net share Invoices
Share name          Invoices
Path                C:\data2
Remark Maximum users      No limit
Users
Caching             Manual caching of documents
Permission          FABRIKAM\Domain Admins, FULL
                    FABRIKAM\Domain Users, READ

The command completed successfully.
```

> **Caution**   Be sure to configure NTFS permissions properly on the underlying folder being shared. Do not rely on shared folder permissions alone for securing shares. To configure NTFS permissions on a folder, use either the Icacls command locally or use Windows Explorer running remotely.

Viewing Shared Folders

You can use Net Share to view a list of shared folders (including hidden administrative shares that begin with "$") as follows:

```
C:\Users\administrator>net share

Share name   Resource                          Remark

-------------------------------------------------------------------------
-----
C$           C:\                               Default share
IPC$                                           Remote IPC
ADMIN$       C:\Windows                        Remote Admin
Invoices     C:\data2
UserData     C:\data                           General share for user data
The command completed successfully.
```

You can also view all shares on your Server Core installation by using the Shared Folders snap-in from a remote computer (as shown in Figure 10-2).

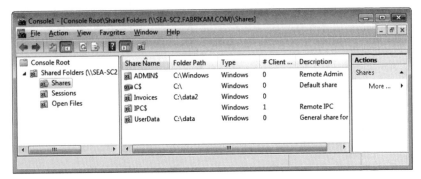

Figure 10-2 Using the Shared Folders snap-in to manage shares on a remote Server Core installation

> **Note** You may need to allow exceptions in Windows Firewall on your Server Core installation to remotely manage shares on it using Shared Folders. In addition, in a workgroup scenario, you may need to use Cmdkey to save credentials for your Server Core installation on your remote management workstation. For more information about managing Server Core remotely using MMC snap-ins, see Chapter 6.

Configuring Shared Folder Permissions

As described in the section "Creating Shared Folders," earlier in this chapter, you can configure shared folder permissions for a share when you create the share using the Net Share command. However, you cannot use Net Share to modify shared folder permissions after the share has been created. You can do this remotely only by using a MMC snap-in such as Shared Folders.

For example, to view the current shared folder permissions on the Invoices share on SEA-SC1, do the following:

1. Connect to this computer using the Shared Folders snap-in running on a remote computer (see Figure 10-2).

2. Double-click the Invoices share and select the Share Permissions tab to display the current shared folder permissions for the share.

3. Select the user or group (such as Domain Users) whose share permissions you want to modify, as shown here.

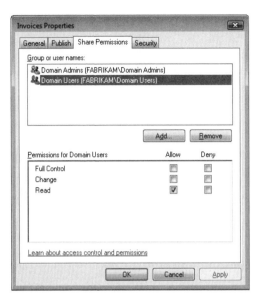

4. Change the permissions as desired. For example, select the Allow check box beside Change to assign Allow Change shared permissions to Domain Users.

5. Click Add or Remove to add or remove access control entries (ACEs) for various users and groups as desired.

Deleting a Share

You can delete a share either by typing **net share sharename /delete** at the command prompt or by right-clicking the share in the Shared Folders snap-in and selecting Stop Sharing.

Using the Share And Storage Management Snap-in

You can use the Share And Storage Management snap-in from a remote computer to create and manage shared folders and volumes on a Server Core installation. The remote management can be a computer running Windows Server 2008 that has the File Services role installed, or it can be either a computer running Windows Vista SP or running Windows Server 2008 with the Remote Server Administration Tools (RSAT) installed. If you are using a computer running Windows Vista SP1 with RSAT installed, the Share And Storage Management console is provided by enabling Share And Storage Management Tools under File Services Tools, which is found under Role Administration Tools.

Before you can use the Share and Storage Management snap-in from a remote computer, you must do the following on your Server Core installation:

- Enable the Remote Administration rule group by typing **netsh advfirewall firewall set rule group="Remote Administration" new enable=yes** from the command prompt.

- Enable the File and Printer Sharing rule group by typing **netsh advfirewall firewall set rule group="File and Printer Sharing" new enable=yes** from the command prompt.

- Enable the Remote Volume Management rule group by typing **netsh advfirewall firewall set rule group="Remote Volume Management" new enable=yes** from the command prompt.

In addition, you must also enable the Remote Volume Management rule group on the computer on which you will be running the Share And Storage Management snap-in (that is, on your remote management computer).

To use the Share And Storage Management snap-in to manage shared folders and volumes on a Server Core installation, do the following:

1. Start Share And Storage Management by either selecting Share And Storage Management Console from Administrative Tools on the Start menu or by opening a new (blank) MMC console and adding the Share And Storage Management snap-in to the console.

2. Right-click the Share And Storage Management node in the console tree and select Connect To Another Computer to open the Connect To Another Computer dialog box.

3. Type the name of the Server Core installation that you want to manage, or click Browse to find the computer on your network, as shown here.

4. When the Share And Storage Management console appears, select the Shares tab to manage shared folders on your Server Core installation, as shown here.

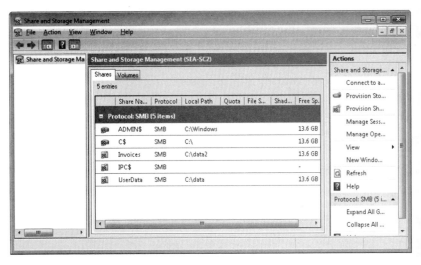

5. Use the Share And Storage Management console to perform various tasks on shared folders and volumes on your Server Core installation. Examples of tasks that you can perform include the following:

   ❑ Click Provision Share in the right-hand action pane to start the Provision A Shared Folder Wizard. This wizard lets you share an existing folder or create a new folder you want to share, assign both share and NTFS permissions to the folder, enable Server Message Block (SMB) sharing, Network File System (NFS) sharing, or both for the folder, and optionally publish SMB shares to a DFS namespace if you have created one.

   ❑ Click Provision Storage in the right-hand action pane to start the Provision Storage Wizard. This wizard lets you create and format new volumes on locally attached disks or create and format new LUNs on Fibre Channel or iSCSI SANs.

   ❑ Select a shared folder on the Shares tab and Manage Sessions to view and, if desired, disconnect any users connected to the share.

   ❑ Select a shared folder on the Shares tab and Manage Open Files to view and, if desired, close any open files in the share.

   ❑ Select a volume or LUN on the Volumes tab and view properties, format, and perform other management tasks.

Implementing DFS

DFS enables administrators to transparently group shared folders found on different servers into one or more hierarchical folder trees called *DFS namespaces*. A DFS namespace is thus a virtual view of the shared folders found on different file servers, and when a user views the namespace, the folders look like they reside on a single server. This allows users to navigate the namespace without needing to know the actual server names hosting the data.

DFS is implemented in Windows Server 2008 using two role services:

- **DFS Namespaces (DFSN)**   Enables creation and management of logically structured DFS namespaces that appear to users as a single shared folder with a series of subfolders. DFSN increases the availability of shared resources, and in an Active Directory Domain Services (AD DS) environment, DFSN causes users to be connected to shared folders in the same site automatically when available instead of routing their requests over slow WAN links.

- **DFS Replication (DFSR)**   Enables the contents of folders found on different servers to be kept synchronized even on limited bandwidth connections. DFSR is an enfficient, multimaster replication engine that replaces the FRS used by previous Windows Server operating systems. DFSR can be used both for synchronizing folders in a DFS namespace and for replicating the SYSVOL content on domain controllers.

See the section "Installing File Services Role Services from the Command Line," earlier in this chapter, for instructions on how to install the DFSN and DFSR role services. Note that after installing the DFSN role service, you must reboot your computer to start the DFS Namespace service on the computer.

Understanding DFS Management Tools

The following command-line tools can be used to manage DFS namespaces and replication on a Server Core installation, either locally or over a Remote Desktop connection:

- **Dfsutil**   Manages DFS namespaces, servers, and clients
- **Dfscmd**   Configures a DFS namespace tree
- **Dfsdiag**   Diagnoses namespace issues

In addition to these command-line tools, you can manage DFS namespaces and replication using the DFS Management snap-in running on a remote computer running Windows Vista SP1 or Windows Server 2008 that has RSAT installed on it.

The following tasks focus on using command-line tools to create and manage DFS namespaces and replication on Server Core computers. For more detailed information, see the section on File Services in the Windows Server 2008 Technical Library on Microsoft TechNet at http://technet.microsoft.com/en-us/windowsserver/default.aspx.

Creating a Domain-Based Namespace

You can use the Dfsutil command to create a new namespace on Server Core. A stand-alone namespace is one that does not use AD DS. A *stand-alone namespace* can ensure namespace availability by implementing failover clustering on the server on which the namespace is created. A *domain-based namespace* is one that uses AD DS. Domain-based namespaces can ensure namespace availability by using multiple servers as *namespace roots* (that is, multiple targets for the root folder in the namespace).

Note   To create a domain-based namespace that takes full advantage of DFSN and DFSR features in Windows Server 2008, your domain functional level must be Windows Server 2008 mode.

For example, to create a domain-based namespace named Corp for the fabrikam.com domain that uses the Server Core computer SEA-SC1 as its namespace server, perform the following steps:

1. On SEA-SC1, create a folder named DFSRoots on the root of the system volume as follows:

   ```
   C:\Users\Administrator>mkdir C:\DFSRoots
   ```

2. Create a subfolder named Corp that will be the root folder of your namespace as follows:

   ```
   C:\Users\Administrator>mkdir C:\DFSRoots\Corp
   ```

3. Share the Corp folder as sharename Corp and assign Allow Read share permissions for the Everyone group as follows:

   ```
   C:\Users\Administrator>net share Corp=C:\DFSRoots\Corp
   Corp was shared successfully.
   ```

4. Verify the share permissions as follows:

   ```
   C:\Users\Administrator>net share Corp
   Share name        Corp
   Path              C:\DFSRoots\Corp
   Remark
   Maximum users     No limit
   Users
   Caching           Manual caching of documents
   Permission        Everyone, READ
   ```

5. Use Dsutil to create the namespace as follows:

   ```
   C:\Users\Administrator>dfsutil root addDom \\SEA-SC1\Corp
   "Namespace for internal Corp network"

   DfsUtil command completed successfully.
   ```

6. Verify the creation of the namespace using Dfsutil as follows:

```
C:\Users\Administrator>dfsutil domain fabrikam.com

Roots on Domain fabrikam.com

        corp

Done with Roots on Domain fabrikam.com

Done processing this command.
```

7. You can also verify the creation of the namespace by opening the DFS Management console on a remote computer that has RSAT installed. Right-click the Namespaces node and select Add Namespaces To Display.

8. In the Add Namespaces To Display dialog box, select Domain under Scope and select fabrikam.com as the domain. Click Show Namespaces and then select the \\fabrikam.com\Corp namespace, as shown here.

9. Click OK to return to the DFS Management console and expand the Namespaces node to display the \\fabrikam.com\Corp domain-based namespace as shown here.

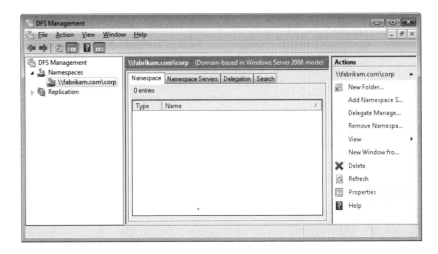

Adding an Additional Namespace Server

You can add more namespace servers to a domain-based namespace to increase the availability of the namespace. For example, to add Server Core computer SEA-SC2 as a second namespace server for the Corp namespace created in the previous procedure, do the following:

1. Perform steps 1 through 4 of the previous procedure on SEA-SC2 to create a C:\DFSRoots\Corp folder and Corp share on SEA-SC2 just as you did on SEA-SC1.

2. On SEA-SC1, add \\SEA-SC2\Corp as a folder target for the \\fabrikam.com\Corp namespace as follows:

```
C:\Users\Administrator>dfsutil target add \\SEA-SC2\Corp

DfsUtil command completed successfully.
```

3. Use Dfsutil to verify the creation of the folder target (that is, the addition of the second namespace server) as follows:

```
C:\Users\Administrator>dfsutil server SEA-SC2

Roots on machine sea-sc2

        \FABRIKAM\corp

Done with Roots on machine sea-sc2

Done processing this command.
```

You can also use Dfscmd to verify the addition of the second namespace server as follows:

```
C:\Users\Administrator>dfscmd /view \\fabrikam.com\Corp /full
\\FABRIKAM\corp                                             Namespace
 for internal Corp network
        \\sea-sc1\corp
        \\sea-sc2\corp
The command completed successfully.
```

You can also use the DFS Management console from a remote computer to verify the addition of the second namespace server by selecting the Namespace Servers tab in the center pane and clicking Refresh in the right-hand Actions pane, as shown here.

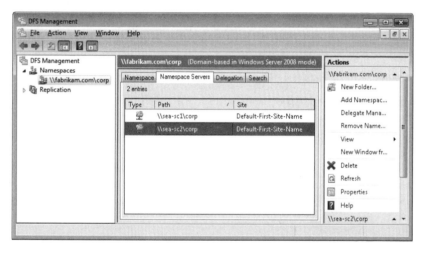

Creating Folders

Folders help organize the way a DFS namespace is presented to users. Folders may or may not have *folder targets* (that is, they may or may not be mapped to shared folders on file servers on your network). You can use the Dfsutil command to create folders that have folder targets, but you cannot use Dfsutil (or any other DFS command-line tool) to create folders that do not have folder targets. To create folders that do not have folder targets, you must use the DFS Management console. For example, to create a folder named Sales directly beneath the namespace root of the \\fabrikam.com\Corp namespace, perform the following steps:

1. Select the \\fabrikam.com\Corp namespace in the console tree and click New Folder in the Actions pane.

2. Type **Sales** in the New Folder dialog box, but do not click Add to add a target to your folder.

3. Click OK to return to the DFS Management console and you will see your new Sales folder, as shown here.

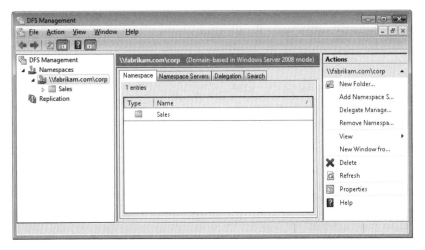

4. If you now select the new folder in the console tree, you can configure the properties of the folder by clicking Properties in the Action pane. If desired, you can also add a target to the folder by clicking Add Folder Target.

    Tip Another option for creating folders that do not have folder targets is to create a dummy shared folder and then use Dfsutil to create folders that have this dummy share as their target.

You can use Dfsutil to create a folder that has a folder target. For example, to create a subfolder named Invoices beneath the Sales folder and map this subfolder to the \\SEA-SC1\UserData share, do this:

```
c:\DFSRoots\Corp\Sales>dfsutil link add \\fabrikam.com\Corp\Sales\Invoices
\\SEA-SC1\UserData
```

```
Done processing this command.
```

Verify using Dfsutil as follows:

```
c:\DFSRoots\Corp\Sales>dfsutil link \\fabrikam.com\Corp\Sales\Invoices
```

```
Link Name="sales\invoices" State="OK" Timeout="300"
        Target="\\SEA-SC1\UserData" State="ONLINE"  [Site: Default-First-
Site-Name]
```

```
Done processing this command.
```

Adding a Folder Target

You can use Dfsutil to add more folder targets to folders. For example, to add the
\\SEA-SC2\UserData share as a second folder target for the Invoices folder created in
the previous procedure, do this:

```
c:\DFSRoots\Corp\Sales>dfsutil target add \\fabrikam.com\Corp\Sales\Invoic
es \\SEA-SC2\UserData
```

```
Done processing this command
```

Verify using Dfsutil as follows:

```
c:\DFSRoots\Corp\Sales>dfsutil link \\fabrikam.com\Corp\Sales\Invoices
```

```
Link Name="sales\invoices" State="OK" Timeout="300"
        Target="\\SEA-SC1\UserData" State="ONLINE"  [Site: Default-First-
Site-Name]
        Target="\\SEA-SC2\UserData" State="ONLINE"  [Site: Default-First-
Site-Name]
```

```
Done processing this command.
```

As Figure 10-3 illustrates, you can use the DFS Management console to verify
the previous procedure and also to display the current structure of the
\\fabrikam.com\Corp namespace.

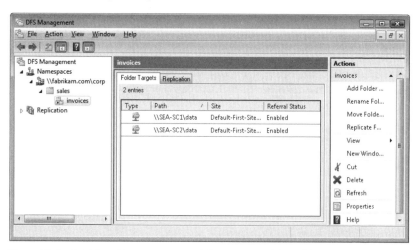

Figure 10-3 A folder with two targets and the structure of the \\fabrikam.com\Corp
namespace

Replicating a Folder

The previous two procedures created a DFS folder named Invoices that has two targets: \\SEA-SC1\UserData and \\SEA-SC2\UserData. If both of these servers are in the same site and a user tries to access the Invoices folder, the user might access the underlying target folder on either server. Therefore, when you add multiple targets to a folder like this, it is important to keep the contents of the underlying shared folders in sync. The DFS Replication service can accomplish this if configured appropriately on the servers.

To replicate a folder in a DFS namespace using the DFS Replication service, you must use the DFS Management console from a remote workstation. You cannot use the Dfsradmin command because it is not supported on Server Core.

The following procedure shows how to configure replication between the two target folders for the Invoices folder created previously. Before you perform this procedure, make sure you have some files in the \\SEA-SC1\UserData but none in the \\SEA-SC2\UserData share.

1. Select the Invoices folder in the DFS Management console and click Replicate Folder in the Actions pane to start the Replicate Folder Wizard, as shown here.

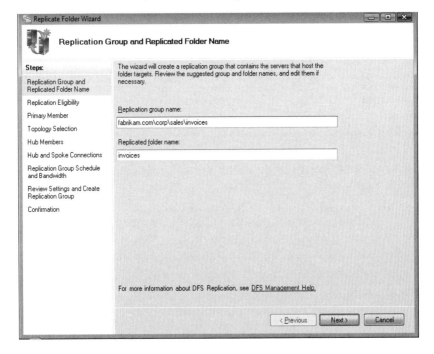

2. Click Next and verify that both \\SEA-SC1\UserData and \\SEA-SC2\UserData are eligible to be DFS replication members.

3. Click Next and select SEA-SC1 as the primary replication partner. This means that any files found in this share will be replicated to the other partner (that is, to the UserData share on SEA-SC2), as shown here.

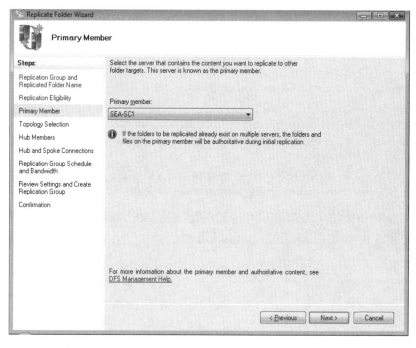

4. Click Next and select a replication topology. Because there are only two partners in this replication group, the topology doesn't matter, so leave Full Mesh selected.

5. Click Next and choose whether to replicate continuously (preferred for servers on a local area network) or using a schedule (use if replication will be over a WAN).

6. Click Next and then Create. When you have verified that no errors occurred, click Close to return to the DFS Management console.

7. Expand the Replication node in the console tree and select the replication group named \\fabrikam.com\Corp\Sales\Invoices, as shown here.

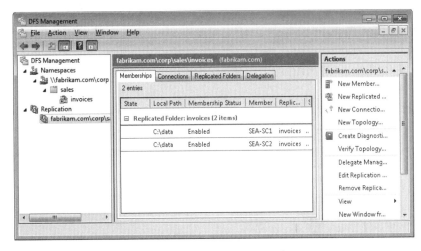

8. Select the various tabs in the center pane to view more information concerning the selected replication group.

Testing a DFS Namespace

You can use the Dfsdiag command to test the configuration of your namespace. For example, to test the integrity of the domain-based namespace created in the previous sections of this chapter, do the following:

```
C:\Users\Administrator>dfsdiag /testdfsintegrity
/dfsroot:\\fabrikam.com\Corp /full

Starting TestDfsIntegrity ....

Validating DFS Metadata Integrity of \\FABRIKAM\Corp ....
Checking for DFS Metadata consistency between DCs and PDC in the domain
....
DFSDIAG_INFO - APPL - DFS metadata is consistent across all accessible
set of DC
s and PDC.

Checking registry of the DFS root servers ....
DFSDIAG_INFO - APPL - Registry information on DFS root servers is
consistent wit
h the metadata in AD.

Validating reparse points of all links in all Root targets of namespace
\\FABRIKAM\Corp ....
Validating Access,ACL,Target state,Link overlaps and Duplicates of
namespace \\FABRIKAM\Corp ....
Finished TestDfsIntegrity.
```

For more information on using Dfsdiag, type **dfsdiag /?** at the command prompt.

Installing and Managing the Print Services Role on Server Core

The Print Services role enables you to manage printers and print queues on a Server Core installation. You can install the Print Services role using Ocsetup by doing the following:

```
C:\Users\administrator>start /w ocsetup Printing-ServerCore-Role
```

You must reboot your server for installation of the Print Services role to complete. To verify installation of the service, use the Oclist command as follows:

```
C:\Users\administrator>oclist | find "   Installed"
    Installed:Printing-ServerCore-Role
```

After you have installed the Print Services role on Server Core, you can install the additional Line Printer Daemon (LPD) service which enables UNIX-based computers using the Line Printer Remote (LPR) service to print to shared printers on your server. To install this additional role service, do the following:

```
C:\Users\administrator>start /w ocsetup Printing-LPDPrintService
```

Verify the result:

```
C:\Users\administrator>oclist | find "   Installed"
    Installed:Printing-ServerCore-Role
    |---      Installed:Printing-LPDPrintService
```

The output of this command shows that the Printing-LPDPrintService component depends upon the Printing-ServerCore-Role component for its operation.

> **Important** If you try installing the Printing-LPDPrintService component without previously installing the Printing-ServerCore-Role component, the installation appears to succeed with errors but the LPD Service does not function properly afterwards. This is because Ocsetup does not handle package dependencies in the way that Server Manager and ServerManagerCmd.exe do on a Full installation of Windows Server 2008.

To uninstall either of these components, append the /uninstall parameter to the previous commands.

Managing Server Core Print Servers Using Print Management

You can manage the Print Services role on Server Core computers by using the Print Management console running on a remote computer. This remote computer can be either a computer running Windows Vista SP1 that has the Print Management console installed by default, or a computer running Windows Server 2008 that either has the Print Services role installed or has RSAT installed.

For example, to use Print Management to manage the Print Services role remotely on a Server Core installation named SEA-SC1 from a Windows Vista workstation named SEA-DESK155, do the following:

1. Open the Print Management console on your management workstation.

2. Right-click the root node in the console tree and select Add/Remove Servers to open the Add/Remove Servers dialog box, as shown here.

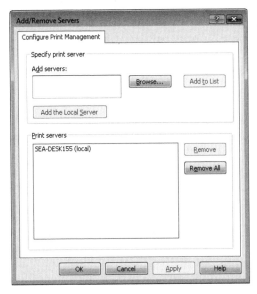

3. Select SEA-DESK155 in the Print Servers box and click Remove to remove the local workstation from the list of print servers being managed.

4. Type **SEA-SC1** in the Add Servers box and click Add To List to add the remote Server Core server to the list of print servers being managed.

5. Click OK to return to the Print Management console.

6. Expand the Print Servers node in the console tree and select SEA-SC1 to manage the Server Core print server, as shown here.

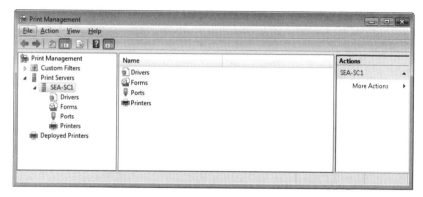

7. Add more print servers to the console, if desired.

Using the Print Management console, you can perform tasks such as the following:

- Installing and configuring different kinds of printers, including locally attached, network, TCP/IP, and Web Services printers

- Creating and managing different types of printer ports, including local ports and standard TCP/IP ports

- Installing and managing printer drivers on your print servers

- Managing printer forms

- Managing print jobs and printer queues

- Deploying printer connections using Group Policy

For more information on using the Print Management console to perform such tasks, see the Windows Server 2008 Administrator's Pocket Consultant *by William Stanek (Microsoft Press, 2008).*

Managing Server Core Print Servers from the Command Line

You can manage many aspects of Print Services running on Server Core from the command line. Table 10-6 lists the various commands and scripts available for managing printers, printer drivers, and print queues from the command line.

Table 10-6   Commands and Scripts Available on Server Core for Managing Print Services

Command	Description
Net Print	Displays information about a specified printer queue, displays information about a specified print job, or controls a specified print job
Print	Sends a text file to a printer
Prncnfg.vbs	Configures or displays configuration information about a printer
Prndrvr.vbs	Adds, deletes, and lists printer drivers
Prnjobs.vbs	Pauses, resumes, cancels, and lists print jobs
Prnmngr.vbs	Adds, deletes, and lists printers or printer connections, in addition to setting and displaying the default printer
Prnport.vbs	Creates, deletes, and lists standard TCP/IP printer ports, in addition to displaying and changing port configuration
Prnqctl.vbs	Prints a test page, pauses or resumes a printer, and clears a printer queue
Pubprn.vbs	Publishes a printer to AD DS
Lpq	Displays the status of a print queue on a computer running LPD
Lpr	Sends a file to a computer or printer sharing device running LPD in preparation for printing

Note   The Printer Migration command-line tool PrintBrm.exe is not available on Server Core. If you need to consolidate or replace print servers, back up or restore a printer configuration, import or export printer settings and print queues, or perform other printer migration tasks, you must perform these actions using the available tools on a Full installation of Windows Server 2008.

Using the Printer Admin Scripts

The scripts Prncnfg.vbs, Prndrvr.vbs, Prnjobs.vbs, Prnmngr.vbs, Prnport.vbs, Prnqctl.vbs, and Pubprn.vbs are located in the %SystemRoot%\System32\ Printing_Admin_Scripts\En-us folder. You need to use these scripts with Cscript.exe, and the easiest way to do this on a Server Core installation is to perform the following steps:

1. Type **cd %SystemRoot%\System32\Printing_Admin_Scripts\en-us** to make the script directory your current directory.

2. Once you've done this, you can run a particular script (such as prncnfg.vbs) by typing **cscript prncnfg.vbs [options]** at the command prompt.

For information about the available options you can use with these scripts, type the script's name (with the .vbs extension) followed by /? at the command prompt.

Using PrintUI.dll with Rundll32.exe

You can also use the PrintUI.dll with Rundll32.exe to expose various aspects of Print Services for management purposes on Server Core. The general syntax for using the PrintUI.dll is as follows:

```
rundll32 PrintUI.dll,PrintUIEntry [options] @[commandfile]
```

Possible options for this command are listed in Table 10-7. Note that not all these options are fully functional on Server Core.

Table 10-7   Available Options for the Rundll32 PrintUI.dll,PrintUIEntry Command

Option	Description
/a[file]	Binary file name
/b[name]	Base printer name
/c[name]	UNC machine name, if the action is on a remote machine
/dl	Deletes local printer
/dn	Deletes network printer connection
/dd	Deletes printer driver
/e	Displays printing preferences
/f[file]	Either an .inf file or an output file
/F[file]	Location of an .inf file that the .inf file specified with /f
/ga	Adds per machine printer connections (the connection will be propagated to the user upon user logon)
/ge	Enumerates per machine printer connections
/gd	Deletes per machine printer connections (the connection will deleted upon user logon)
/h[arch]	Driver architecture (x86, x64, or Itanium)
/ia	Installs printer driver using .inf file
/id	Installs printer driver using the Add Printer Driver Wizard
/if	Installs printer using the .inf file
/ii	Installs printer using Add Printer Wizard with an .inf file
/il	Installs printer using the Add Printer wizard
/in	Adds network printer connection
/ip	Installs printer using the Network Printer Installation wizard
/j[provider]	Prints provider name
/k	Prints test page to specified printer, cannot be combined with any command that installs a printer

Table 10-7   Available Options for the Rundll32 PrintUI.dll,PrintUIEntry Command

Option	Description
/I[path]	Printer driver source path
/m[model]	Printer driver model name
/n[name]	Printer name
/o	Displays printer queue view
/p	Displays printer properties
/q	Quiet mode (does not display error messages)
/r[port]	Port name
/s	Displays server properties
/Ss	Stores printer settings into a file (requires additional option flags)
/Sr	Restores printer settings from a file (requires additional option flags)
/u	Uses the existing printer driver if it's already installed
/t[#]	Zero-based index page to start on
/v[version]	Driver version (one of the following: Type 2—Kernel Mode or Type 3—User Mode)
/w	Prompts the user for a driver if specified driver is not found in the .inf file
/y	Sets printer as the default
/Xg	Gets printer settings
/Xs	Sets printer settings
/z	Does not auto share this printer
/Y	Does not auto generate a printer name
/K	Changes the meaning of /h to accept 2,3,4 for x86 or x64 or Itanium and /v to accept 3 for Type 3—User Mode
/Z	Shares this printer (can be used only with the /if option)
/?	Help
@[file]	Command-line argument file
/Mw[message]	Shows a warning message before committing the command
/Mq[message]	Shows a confirmation message before committing the command
/W[flags]	Specifies flags and switches for the wizards r = make the wizards to be restartable from the last page
/G[flags]	Specifies global flags and switches w = suppress setup driver warnings UI (super quiet mode)

The following sections illustrate some common Print Services management tasks that you can perform from the command line on Server Core.

Configuring Print Server Properties

You can configure the properties of a Server Core print server by typing the command **rundll32 PrintUI.dll,PrintUIEntry /s** to display the properties sheet shown in Figure 10-4.

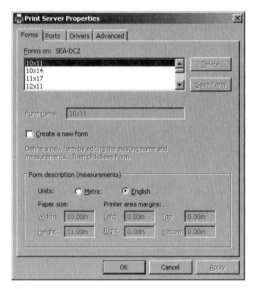

Figure 10-4 Properties of a print server

Install a Printer

You can install a printer on a Server Core print server by typing the command **rundll32 PrintUI.dll,PrintUIEntry /il** to display the Add Printer wizard, as shown in Figure 10-5.

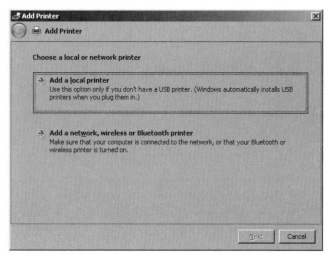

Figure 10-5   The Add Printer wizard

You can use this wizard to add locally attached printers or network printers, including wireless printers. (Note, however, that Bluetooth is not supported by Windows Server 2008.) For example, to add a local printer using this wizard, do the following:

1. Click Add A Local Printer.

2. Select an existing printer port, such as LPT1, or create a new port.

3. Provide a driver for your printer using removable media or use Windows Update to search for the latest drivers because Server Core does not come with any printer drivers in its driver store.

4. Type a name for your printer and click Next to finish the wizard and install the printer.

Your new printer should appear in the Print Management console running on a remote computer—look under the Printers node beneath your print server's node and press F5 to refresh the view if necessary.

> **Tip**   If you delete a printer that you previously created using Print Management, the printer driver for that printer remains available on your server for future installations of printers of the same make and model. However, you can remove printer drivers from the driver store by selecting the Drivers node beneath the node for your printer server in Print Management, right-clicking a driver, and selecting Remove Driver Package.

You can also perform .inf-based installations of printers by using the Rundll32 command. For more information on how to do this, see *http://support.microsoft.com/kb/189105* in the Microsoft Knowledge Base on TechNet. And you can add, delete, and list printers or printer connections using the Prnmngr.vbs script. For example, the following command lists all printers installed on the print server SEA-SC1:

```
C:\Windows\System32\Printing_Admin_Scripts\en-US>cscript prnmngr.vbs -l
-s SEA-SC1
Microsoft (R) Windows Script Host Version 5.7
Copyright (C) Microsoft Corporation. All rights reserved.


Server name SEA-SC1
Printer name SamsungCLX
Share name
Driver name Samsung CLX-8380 Series PCL 6
Port name LPT2:
Comment
Location
Print processor CL83PPC
Data type RAW
Parameters
Attributes 2624
Priority 1
Default priority 0
Average pages per minute 0
Printer status Idle
Extended printer status Unknown
Detected error state Unknown
Extended detected error state Unknown

Server name SEA-SC1
Printer name SamsungML
Share name
Driver name Samsung ML-4050 Series PCL 6
Port name LPT1:
Comment
Location
Print processor ML405PPC
Data type RAW
Parameters
Attributes 2628
Priority 1
Default priority 0
Average pages per minute 0
Printer status Other
```

```
Extended printer status Error
Detected error state Other
Extended detected error state Other

Number of local printers and connections enumerated 2
```

Viewing and Configuring Printer Properties

You can view or configure the properties of a particular printer managed by a
Server Core print server by typing **rundll32 PrintUI.dll,PrintUIEntry /p /n
\\<*servername*>\<*printername*>** at the command prompt. For example, if your printer
is named SamsungML and your print server is named SEA-SC1, type **rundll32
PrintUI.dll,PrintUIEntry /p /n\\SEA-SC1\SamsungML** to display the Properties
sheet for the printer.

You can also view or configure printer properties using the Prncnfg.vbs script. For
example, to view the properties of the previously cited printer, do this:

```
C:\Windows\System32\Printing_Admin_Scripts\en-US>cscript prncnfg.vbs -g
-s SEA-SC1 -p SamsungML
Microsoft (R) Windows Script Host Version 5.7
Copyright (C) Microsoft Corporation. All rights reserved.

Server name SEA-SC1
Printer name SamsungML
Share name
Driver name Samsung ML-4050 Series PCL 6
Port name LPT1:
Comment
Location
Separator file
Print processor ML405PPC
Data type RAW
Parameters
Priority 1
Default priority 0
Printer always available
Attributes local default enable_bidi do_complete_first

Printer status Idle
Extended printer status Unknown
Detected error state Unknown
Extended detected error state Unknown
```

Displaying Printer Settings

You can specify a printer as the default printer on a Server Core print server by typing
rundll32 PrintUI.dll,PrintUIEntry /Xg /n"<*printername*>". For example, if your

printer is named SamsungML, type **rundll32 PrintUI.dll,PrintUIEntry /Xg /n"SamsungML"** to display the printer settings as shown in Figure 10-6.

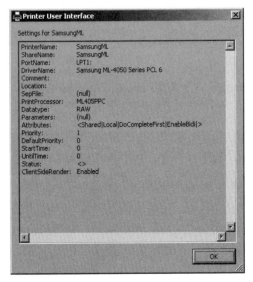

Figure 10-6   Printer settings

Specifying the Default Printer

You can specify a printer as the default printer on a Server Core print server by typing **rundll32 PrintUI.dll,PrintUIEntry /y /n"*<printername>*"**.

Adding Printer Drivers

You can add a printer driver to a Server Core print server by typing **rundll32 PrintUI.dll,PrintUIEntry /id**, which starts the Add Printer Driver wizard (shown in Figure 10-7). This wizard allows you to add printer drivers of different hardware architectures to your print server.

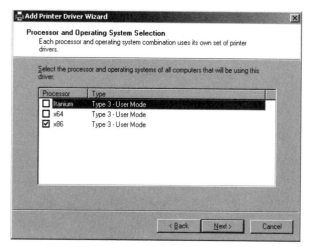

Figure 10-7   The Add Printer Driver wizard

You can also add, delete, and list printer drivers using the Prndrvr.vbs script. For example, the following command lists all available printer drivers on server SEA-SC1 (the command output has been truncated due to its length):

```
C:\Windows\System32\Printing_Admin_Scripts\en-US>cscript prndrvr.vbs -l
-s SEA-SC1
Microsoft (R) Windows Script Host Version 5.7
Copyright (C) Microsoft Corporation. All rights reserved.


Server name SEA-SC1
Driver name Samsung CLX-8380 Series PCL 6,3,Windows NT x86
Version 3
Environment Windows NT x86
Monitor name CL83P Langmon
Driver path C:\Windows\system32\spool\DRIVERS\W32X86\3\cl83P.dll
Data file C:\Windows\system32\spool\DRIVERS\W32X86\3\cl83Ppp.dll
Config file C:\Windows\system32\spool\DRIVERS\W32X86\3\cl83Pdu.dll
Help file
Dependent files
 C:\Windows\system32\spool\DRIVERS\W32X86\3\cl83Pu.dll
 C:\Windows\system32\spool\DRIVERS\W32X86\3\cl83Pu2.dll
 C:\Windows\system32\spool\DRIVERS\W32X86\3\cl83Po.dll
...
Number of printer drivers enumerated 5
```

Managing Print Queues and Print Jobs

You can use the Net Print command to display information about a print queue or job
as follows:

```
C:\Users\administrator>net print \\SEA-SC1\SamsungML

Printers at \\SEA-SC1


Name                          Job #      Size          Status

-------------------------------------------------------------------------
-----
SamsungML Queue               1 jobs                   *Printer error*
    administrator                 2          0         Error
The command completed successfully.
```

To view the number of print jobs pending on your server's print queues, use the
Prnjobs.vbs script like this:

```
C:\Windows\System32\Printing_Admin_Scripts\en-US>cscript prnjobs.vbs
-s SEA-SC1 -l
Microsoft (R) Windows Script Host Version 5.7
Copyright (C) Microsoft Corporation. All rights reserved.


Printer

Number of print jobs enumerated 1
```

To cancel all print jobs in the SamsungML print queue on the server, use the Prn-
qctl.vbs script like this:

```
C:\Windows\System32\Printing_Admin_Scripts\en-US>cscript prnqctl.vbs
-s SEA-SC1 -p SamsungML -x
Microsoft (R) Windows Script Host Version 5.7
Copyright (C) Microsoft Corporation. All rights reserved.


Success Purge Printer SamsungML
```

Chapter 11
Web Server Role

Also known as Internet Information Services 7.0 (IIS 7.0), the Web Server role has been completely redesigned in Windows Server 2008 to provide simplified configuration and deployment, enhanced security, delegated administration, and improved diagnostic and troubleshooting features. Using the Web Server role, you can share information with users on a corporate intranet or extranet, or over the Internet.

Understanding the Web Server Role

Before you install the various role services and features that comprise the Web Server role, you need to understand two points. First, the Web Server role is made up of a combination of role services and features, and you must understand the functionality that these roles and services provide and also the dependencies between them. Second, you must understand the limitations imposed because the .NET Framework is not supported on Server Core.

Understanding IIS 7.0 Components and Their Dependencies

The Web Server role is comprised of both role services and features. The packages for these role services and features (which we'll collectively call *IIS 7.0 components*) are organized hierarchically with parent/child dependencies between packages. This means that if you install a particular child package without installing its parent package, the child package may appear to install correctly, but it may not function.

The easiest way to view the dependencies between different IIS packages is to examine the output of the Oclist command when it is run on a Server Core installation that has no roles installed (the command output here has been excerpted to remove everything except IIS packages:

```
C:\Users\Administrator>oclist
...
Not Installed:IIS-WebServerRole
    |--- Not Installed:IIS-FTPPublishingService
    |        |--- Not Installed:IIS-FTPServer
    |--- Not Installed:IIS-WebServer
    |        |--- Not Installed:IIS-ApplicationDevelopment
    |        |        |--- Not Installed:IIS-ASP
    |        |        |--- Not Installed:IIS-CGI
    |        |        |--- Not Installed:IIS-ISAPIExtensions
    |        |        |        |--- Not Installed:IIS-ASP
    |        |        |--- Not Installed:IIS-ISAPIFilter
    |        |        |--- Not Installed:IIS-ServerSideIncludes
```

```
|        |--- Not Installed:IIS-CommonHttpFeatures
|        |        |--- Not Installed:IIS-DefaultDocument
|        |        |--- Not Installed:IIS-DirectoryBrowsing
|        |        |--- Not Installed:IIS-HttpErrors
|        |        |--- Not Installed:IIS-HttpRedirect
|        |        |--- Not Installed:IIS-StaticContent
|        |--- Not Installed:IIS-HealthAndDiagnostics
|        |        |--- Not Installed:IIS-CustomLogging
|        |        |--- Not Installed:IIS-HttpLogging
|        |        |--- Not Installed:IIS-HttpTracing
|        |        |--- Not Installed:IIS-LoggingLibraries
|        |        |--- Not Installed:IIS-ODBCLogging
|        |        |--- Not Installed:IIS-RequestMonitor
|        |--- Not Installed:IIS-Performance
|        |        |--- Not Installed:IIS-HttpCompressionDynamic
|        |        |--- Not Installed:IIS-HttpCompressionStatic
|        |--- Not Installed:IIS-Security
|        |        |--- Not Installed:IIS-BasicAuthentication
|        |        |--- Not Installed:IIS-
ClientCertificateMappingAuthentication
|        |        |--- Not Installed:IIS-DigestAuthentication
|        |        |--- Not Installed:IIS-
IISCertificateMappingAuthentication
|        |        |--- Not Installed:IIS-IPSecurity
|        |        |--- Not Installed:IIS-RequestFiltering
|        |        |        |--- Not Installed:IIS-ASP
|        |        |--- Not Installed:IIS-URLAuthorization
|        |        |--- Not Installed:IIS-WindowsAuthentication
|--- Not Installed:IIS-WebServerManagementTools
|        |--- Not Installed:IIS-IIS6ManagementCompatibility
|        |        |--- Not Installed:IIS-LegacyScripts
|        |        |--- Not Installed:IIS-Metabase
|        |        |        |--- Not Installed:IIS-FTPServer
|        |        |        |--- Not Installed:IIS-LegacyScripts
|        |        |--- Not Installed:IIS-WMICompatibility
|        |        |        |--- Not Installed:IIS-LegacyScripts
|        |--- Not Installed:IIS-ManagementScriptingTools
...
Not Installed:WAS-WindowsActivationService
|--- Not Installed:WAS-ProcessModel
|        |--- Not Installed:IIS-ASP
|        |--- Not Installed:IIS-BasicAuthentication
|        |--- Not Installed:IIS-CGI
|        |--- Not Installed:IIS-ClientCertificateMappingAuthentication
|        |--- Not Installed:IIS-CustomLogging
|        |--- Not Installed:IIS-DefaultDocument
|        |--- Not Installed:IIS-DigestAuthentication
|        |--- Not Installed:IIS-DirectoryBrowsing
|        |--- Not Installed:IIS-HttpCompressionDynamic
```

```
    |           |--- Not Installed:IIS-HttpCompressionStatic
    |           |--- Not Installed:IIS-HttpErrors
    |           |--- Not Installed:IIS-HttpLogging
    |           |--- Not Installed:IIS-HttpRedirect
    |           |--- Not Installed:IIS-HttpTracing
    |           |--- Not Installed:IIS-IISCertificateMappingAuthentication
    |           |--- Not Installed:IIS-IPSecurity
    |           |--- Not Installed:IIS-ISAPIExtensions
    |           |            |--- Not Installed:IIS-ASP
    |           |--- Not Installed:IIS-ISAPIFilter
    |           |--- Not Installed:IIS-LoggingLibraries
    |           |--- Not Installed:IIS-ODBCLogging
    |           |--- Not Installed:IIS-RequestFiltering
    |           |            |--- Not Installed:IIS-ASP
    |           |--- Not Installed:IIS-RequestMonitor
    |           |--- Not Installed:IIS-ServerSideIncludes
    |           |--- Not Installed:IIS-StaticContent
    |           |--- Not Installed:IIS-URLAuthorization
    |           |--- Not Installed:IIS-WindowsAuthentication
...
```

Note that some role services and features are listed twice in this command output. For example, the package named IIS-ASP, the component that provides Active Service Pages (ASP) server-side scripting functionality, appears twice in the hierarchy. First it appears here:

```
Not Installed:IIS-WebServerRole
    |--- Not Installed:IIS-WebServer
    |           |--- Not Installed:IIS-ApplicationDevelopment
    |           |            |--- Not Installed:IIS-ASP
```

And then it appears here:

```
Not Installed:WAS-WindowsActivationService
    |--- Not Installed:WAS-ProcessModel
    |           |--- Not Installed:IIS-ASP
```

What this indicates is that the IIS-ASP package has dependencies upon both the IIS-ApplicationDevelopment package (which depends upon the IIS-WebServer package, which itself depends upon the IIS-WebServerRole package) and the WAS-ProcessModel package (which depends upon the WAS-WindowsActivationService package). Therefore, if you want to install the IIS-ASP package on your server, you must also install the IIS-ApplicationDevelopment and WAS-ProcessModel packages (and their parent packages).

Categories of IIS 7.0 Components

From the standpoint of the modular architecture of IIS 7.0, the role services for the Web Server role are grouped into seven main categories (parent packages) organized under a top-level package named IIS-WebServerRole, with five of them grouped under the subcategory IIS-WebServer. In addition, there is an eighth main category of IIS components consisting of a feature, the Windows Process Activation Service (WAS). Table 11-1 describes these eight categories of IIS components with their package names, which are needed for installing these categories.

Note Component categories marked with an asterisk (*) are only partially supported on Server Core, as indicated in Table 11-2.

Table 11-1 Main Categories of IIS Components and Their Package Names

Category	Description	Package Name
Common HTTP Features	Provides support for standard Web server features	IIS-CommonHttpFeatures
Application Development*	Provides infrastructure support for applications	IIS-ApplicationDevelopment
Health and Diag-nostics	Allows IIS to capture information you can use to manage, monitor, and troubleshoot the Web server	IIS-HealthAndDiagnostics
Security	Allows administrators to restrict access to the Web server	IIS-Security
Performance	Allows administrators to manage network bandwidth	IIS-Performance
Management Tools*	Provides various tools administer-ing Web servers	IIS-WebServerManagementTools
FTP Publishing Service	Allows you to create and config-ure FTP sites for uploading and downloading files	IIS-FTPPublishingService
Windows Pro-cess Activation Service*	Enables Web applications to start and stop dynamically in response to incoming requests from clients	WAS-WindowsActivationService

Individual IIS 7.0 Components

Beneath the eight categories of components (role services and features) listed in Table 11-1 are additional subcomponents (which are also role services or features) having the parent/child dependencies shown previously by the output of the Oclist command. Table 11-2 describes these various subcomponents and identifies their package names, which are needed for installing these subcomponents.

Note Components marked with an asterisk (*) are not available on Server Core.

Table 11-2   IIS 7.0 Components and Their Corresponding Package Names

Component	Description	Package Name
Common HTTP Features		
Static Content	Enables publishing of Web sites that consist only of HTML and image files	IIS-StaticContent
Default Document	Specifies the name of the file that client browsers will load by default	IIS-DefaultDocument
Directory Browsing	Allows clients to view a listing of files in a directory	IIS-DirectoryBrowsing
HTTP Errors	Allows the administrator to create customized messages for specific HTTP errors	IIS-HttpErrors
HTTP Redirection	Allows the Web server to forward incoming requests for a specific URL to a different URL	IIS-HttpRedirect
Application Development		
ASP.NET*	Implements a server-side, object-oriented programming environment based on the .NET Framework	IIS-ASPNET
.NET Extensibility*	Allows developers to modify the functionality of the Web server using the ASP.NET extensibility model and .NET APIs	IIS-NetFxExtensibility
ASP	Provides a server-side scripting environment for development of Web applications that support VBScript and Jscript	IIS-ASP
CGI	Provides a scripting interface that allows a Web server to pass incoming requests to another program	IIS-CGI

Table 11-2   IIS 7.0 Components and Their Corresponding Package Names

Component	Description	Package Name
ISAPI Extensions	Allows the Web server to execute compiled ISAPI applications	IIS-ISAPIExtensions
ISAPI Filters	Supports applications that use ISAPI filters to modify the functionality of the Web server	IIS-ISAPIFilter
Server Side Includes (SSI)	Supports a scripting language that allows the Web server to dynamically generate HTML pages	IIS-ServerSideIncludes
Health and Diagnostics		
HTTP Logging	Allows the Web server to maintain logs of Web site activity	IIS-HTTPLogging
Logging Tools	Provides tools for managing logs	IIS-LoggingLibraries
Request Monitor	Captures information about HTTP requests for monitoring and troubleshooting performance issues	IIS-RequestMonitor
Tracing	Saves information about failed application requests for troubleshooting purposes	IIS-HttpTracing
Custom Logging	Enables logging of Web server activity using a customized log file format	IIS-CustomLogging
ODBC Logging	Enables logging to an ODBC-compliant database	IIS-ODBCLogging
Security		
Basic Authentication	Allows simple authentication using user names and passwords	IIS-BasicAuthentication
Windows Authentication	Enables secure NTLM- or Kerberos-based authentication for domain users	IIS-WindowsAuthentication

Table 11-2 IIS 7.0 Components and Their Corresponding Package Names

Component	Description	Package Name
Digest Authentication	Allows authentication using a password hash	IIS-DigestAuthentication
Client Certificate Mapping Authentication	Allows certificate-based authentication using Active Directory Domain Services for one-to-one certificate mapping	IIS-ClientCertificateMapping-Authentication
IIS Client Certificate Mapping Authentication	Allows certificate-based authentication using IIS for one-to-one or many-to-one certificate mapping	IIS-IISCertificateMapping-Authentication
URL Authorization	Allows administrators to restrict access to specific URLs by authorizing only specific users or groups	IIS-URLAuthorization
Request Filtering	Allows blocking of malicious traffic by filtering incoming requests based on rules	IIS-RequestFiltering
IP and Domain Restrictions	Allows access to the Web server to be restricted to computers with certain IP addresses or domain names	IIS-IPSecurity
Performance		
Static Content Compression	Enables compression of static Web site content before sending it to the client	IIS-HttpCompressionStatic
Dynamic Content Compression	Enables compression of dynamic Web site content before sending it to the client	IIS-HttpCompressionDynamic
Management Tools		
IIS Management Console*	MMC snap-in used to manage IIS 7.0 Web servers	IIS-ManagementConsole

Table 11-2 IIS 7.0 Components and Their Corresponding Package Names

Component	Description	Package Name
IIS Management Scripts and Tools	Allows administrators to automate IIS 7.0 management tasks using command-line tools and scripts	IIS-ManagementScriptingTools
Management Service*	Allows the Web server to be managed remotely using the IIS Management Console	IIS-ManagementService
IIS 6 Management Compatibility	Enables administrators to manage an IIS 7.0 Web server using IIS 6.0 tools and scripts	IIS-IIS6ManagementCompatibility
IIS 6 Metabase Compatibility	Translates interfaces and scripts designed for the IIS 6.0 metabase into the new IIS 7.0 format	IIS-Metabase
IIS 6 WMI Compatibility	Provides support for IIS 6.0 WMI scripts	IIS-WMICompatibility
IIS 6 Scripting Tools	Enables administrators to use IIS 6.0 scripting tools to manage IIS 7.0 Web servers	IIS-LegacyScripts
IIS 6 Management Console*	MMC snap-in used to manage IIS 6.0 Web servers	IIS-LegacySnapIn
FTP Publishing Service		
FTP Server	Enables hosting of FTP sites	IIS-FTPServer
FTP Management Console*	MMC snap-in for managing IIS 7.0 FTP sites	IIS-FTPManagement
Windows Process Activation Service		
Process Model	Hosts Web and WCF services and removes the dependency upon HTTP	WAS-ProcessModel
.NET Environment*	Supports managed code activation	WAS-NetFxEnvironment
Configuration APIs*	Enables .NET applications to configure the process activation model programmatically	WAS-ConfigurationAPI

Understanding the Limitations of IIS 7.0 on Server Core

As you can see from Table 11-2, the following eight IIS 7.0 components are not supported on Server Core (the corresponding package names for these components are listed in parentheses after each component):

- ASP.NET (IIS-ASPNET)

- .NET Extensibility (IIS-NetFxExtensibility)

- IIS Management Console (IIS-ManagementConsole)

- Management Service (IIS-ManagementService)

- IIS 6 Management Console (IIS-LegacySnapIn)

- FTP Management Console (IIS-FTPManagement)

- .NET Environment (WAS-NetFxEnvironment)

- Configuration APIs (WAS-ConfigurationAPI)

These components are not supported on Server Core for two reasons. First, because Server Core has no desktop shell, any components that have dependencies upon the desktop shell cannot be installed. This prevents the IIS Management Console, IIS 6 Management Console, and FTP Management Console components from installing on Server Core.

Second, because Server Core does not support running the .NET Framework, any components that have dependencies upon .NET cannot be installed. This prevents the ASP.NET, .NET Extensibility, .Net Environment, and Configuration APIs components from installing on Server Core. In addition, the Management Services component, which allows remote administration of IIS 7.0 using the IIS Management Console, relies on the .NET framework, so this component cannot be installed on Server Core, either.

> **Note**   Because you cannot install the Management Services component of IIS 7.0 on Server Core, you can administer a Server Core Web server only from the command line, by directly editing .config files, or by using Windows Management Instrumentation (WMI) or PowerShell cmdlets that use WMI. You cannot use the IIS 7.0 Management Console on a remote computer to connect to and administer a Server Core Web server.

Installing the Web Server Role

Because IIS 7.0 was designed with a modular architecture in mind, you can customize its installation in various ways. The following sections describe several different IIS 7.0 installation scenarios and how to perform them on Server Core.

Note The recommended way of installing IIS 7.0 components on Server Core is to use Package Manager (Pkgmgr.exe), not the Ocsetup.exe used to install most other server roles.

Installing a Default Web Server

The default installation of IIS 7.0 is the most basic configuration and provides support for serving static Hypertext Markup Language (HTML) files, documents, and images. The default installation also provides support for default documents, directory browsing, logging, and Anonymous authentication for a static Web content server.

To install IIS 7.0 on Server Core as a default Web server, type the following command:

```
C:\Users\administrator>start /w pkgmgr /iu:IIS-WebServerRole;
WAS-WindowsActivationService;WAS-ProcessModel
```

You can view the result of this command by using Oclist as follows:

```
C:\Users\administrator>oclist | find "   Installed"
    Installed:IIS-WebServerRole
  |---     Installed:IIS-WebServer
  |        |---     Installed:IIS-ApplicationDevelopment
  |        |---     Installed:IIS-CommonHttpFeatures
  |        |        |---     Installed:IIS-DefaultDocument
  |        |        |---     Installed:IIS-DirectoryBrowsing
  |        |        |---     Installed:IIS-HttpErrors
  |        |        |---     Installed:IIS-StaticContent
  |        |---     Installed:IIS-HealthAndDiagnostics
  |        |        |---     Installed:IIS-HttpLogging
  |        |        |---     Installed:IIS-RequestMonitor
  |        |---     Installed:IIS-Performance
  |        |        |---     Installed:IIS-HttpCompressionStatic
  |        |---     Installed:IIS-Security
  |        |        |---     Installed:IIS-RequestFiltering
  |---     Installed:IIS-WebServerManagementTools
    Installed:WAS-WindowsActivationService
  |---     Installed:WAS-ProcessModel
  |        |---     Installed:IIS-DefaultDocument
  |        |---     Installed:IIS-DirectoryBrowsing
  |        |---     Installed:IIS-HttpCompressionStatic
  |        |---     Installed:IIS-HttpErrors
  |        |---     Installed:IIS-HttpLogging
  |        |---     Installed:IIS-RequestFiltering
  |        |---     Installed:IIS-RequestMonitor
  |        |---     Installed:IIS-StaticContent
```

You can also display a list of installed IIS 7.0 components by using the Reg Query command as follows:

```
C:\Users\administrator>reg query HKLM\Software\Microsoft\InetStp\Components

HKEY_LOCAL_MACHINE\Software\Microsoft\InetStp\Components
    SharedLibraries    REG_DWORD    0x1
    ProcessModelLibraries    REG_DWORD    0x1
    ProcessModel    REG_DWORD    0x1
    CoreWebEngine    REG_DWORD    0x1
    W3SVC    REG_DWORD    0x1
    CachingBase    REG_DWORD    0x1
    Caching    REG_DWORD    0x1
    HttpCache    REG_DWORD    0x1
    CompressionBinaries    REG_DWORD    0x1
    HttpCompressionStatic    REG_DWORD    0x1
    DefaultDocument    REG_DWORD    0x1
    DirectoryBrowse    REG_DWORD    0x1
    HttpProtocol    REG_DWORD    0x1
    StaticContent    REG_DWORD    0x1
    AnonymousAuthenticationBinaries    REG_DWORD    0x1
    AnonymousAuthentication    REG_DWORD    0x1
    RequestFilteringBinaries    REG_DWORD    0x1
    RequestFiltering    REG_DWORD    0x1
    HttpErrors    REG_DWORD    0x1
    HttpLoggingBinaries    REG_DWORD    0x1
    HttpLogging    REG_DWORD    0x1
    RequestMonitor    REG_DWORD    0x1
```

To uninstall these IIS 7.0 components, change /iu to /uu in the installation command. For example, to uninstall the default configuration, you would use this command:

```
C:\Users\administrator>start /w pkgmgr /uu:IIS-WebServerRole;
WAS-WindowsActivationService;WAS-ProcessModel
```

Installing a Classic ASP Web Server

The classic ASP Web server is the common IIS 7.0 configuration for serving server-side scripted ASP pages. The Classic ASP Web server configuration adds the following additional functionality to the default Web server:

- ASP
- Request Filtering
- ISAPI extensions

To install IIS 7.0 on Server Core as a classic ASP Web server, type the following command:

```
C:\Users\administrator>Start /w pkgmgr /iu:IIS-WebServerRole;
IIS-WebServer;IIS-CommonHttpFeatures;IIS-StaticContent;
IIS-DefaultDocument;IIS-DirectoryBrowsing;IIS-HttpErrors;
IIS-ApplicationDevelopment;IIS-ASP;IIS-ISAPIExtensions;
```

```
IIS-HealthAndDiagnostics;IIS-HttpLogging;IIS-LoggingLibraries;
IIS-RequestMonitor;IIS-Security;IIS-RequestFiltering;
IIS-HttpCompressionStatic;IIS-WebServerManagementTools;
WAS-WindowsActivationService;WAS-ProcessModel
```

> **Tip** You can also save this command as a single-line batch file named Classic-ASP.bat and run this batch file on Server Core instead of typing the command.

Installing All IIS 7.0 Components

The full installation option installs all available IIS 7.0 components on Server Core. The command to implement this option is as follows:

```
C:\Users\administrator>start /w pkgmgr /iu:IIS-WebServerRole;
IIS-WebServer;IIS-CommonHttpFeatures;IIS-StaticContent;
IIS-DefaultDocument;IIS-DirectoryBrowsing;IIS-HttpErrors;
IIS-HttpRedirect;IIS-ApplicationDevelopment;IIS-ASP;IIS-CGI;
IIS-ISAPIExtensions;IIS-ISAPIFilter;IIS-ServerSideIncludes;
IIS-HealthAndDiagnostics;IIS-HttpLogging;IIS-LoggingLibraries;
IIS-RequestMonitor;IIS-HttpTracing;IIS-CustomLogging;IIS-ODBCLogging;
IIS-Security;IIS-BasicAuthentication;IIS-WindowsAuthentication;
IIS-DigestAuthentication;IIS-ClientCertificateMappingAuthentication;
IIS-IISCertificateMappingAuthentication;IIS-URLAuthorization;
IIS-RequestFiltering;IIS-IPSecurity;IIS-Performance;
IIS-HttpCompressionStatic;IIS-HttpCompressionDynamic;
IIS-WebServerManagementTools;IIS-ManagementScriptingTools;
IIS-IIS6ManagementCompatibility;IIS-Metabase;IIS-WMICompatibility;
IIS-LegacyScripts;IIS-FTPPublishingService;IIS-FTPServer;
WAS-WindowsActivationService;WAS-ProcessModel
```

Installing PHP on Server Core

PHP: Hypertext Preprocessor (PHP) is a free and widely used server-side scripting language for creating dynamic Web pages. You can install PHP version 5 on Server Core by performing these steps:

1. Download the latest release of PHP version 5 from *http://www.php.net/downloads.php*.

2. Create a folder named %SystemDrive%\PHP on your Server Core computer.

3. Unzip the contents of the download and copy the files to the %SystemDrive%\PHP folder on your Server Core computer.

4. Copy the %SystemDrive%\PHP\PHP.INI-Recommended file as %SystemDrive%\PHP\PHP.INI.

5. Install the default Web server configuration on Server Core with FastCGI support by running the following command:

start /w pkgmgr /iu:IIS-WebServerRole;IIS-WebServer;IIS-CommonHttp-
Features;IIS-StaticContent;IIS-DefaultDocument;IIS-DirectoryBrowsing;
IIS-HttpErrors;IIS-ApplicationDevelopment;IIS-CGI;IIS-HealthAndDiagnostics;
IIS-HttpLogging;IIS-LoggingLibraries;IIS-RequestMonitor;IIS-Security;
IIS-RequestFiltering;IIS-HttpCompressionStatic;IIS-WebServerManagement-
Tools;WAS-WindowsActivationService;WAS-ProcessModel

6. Create the PHP/FastCGI handler mapping by typing the following two
   commands:

   %windir%\System32\Inetsrv\appcmd set config /section:system.webServer/
   fastCGI /+[fullPath='C:\php\php-cgi.exe']

   %windir%\System32\Inetsrv\appcmd set config /section:system.webServer/
   handlers /+[name='PHP-FastCGI',path='*.php',verb='*',modules='FastCgi-
   Module',scriptProcessor='C:\php\php-cgi.exe',resourceType='Either']

Installing the Web Server Role Using an Answer File

You can also install the Web Server role in various configurations using an answer file
during an unattended installation of Server Core. To do this, perform the following
steps:

1. Begin by creating and configuring an answer file for unattended installation of
   Server Core. For information on how to do this, see Chapter 2, "Deploying Server
   Core."

2. On your technician computer, open your answer file in Windows System Image
   Manager (Windows SIM).

3. In the Windows Image pane, expand the Packages node to display the nodes
   beneath it. Expand the Foundation node to display the Microsoft-Windows-
   ServerCore-Package node beneath that. Then right-click on the address
   Microsoft-Windows-ServerCore-Package node and select Add To Answer File.
   The Microsoft-Windows-ServerCore-Package should now be selected in the
   Answer File pane.

4. In the Properties pane, scroll down until the IIS-WebServerRole setting is
   visible under Windows Feature Selections. Click this setting to display other IIS
   settings beneath it, and click the value field to the right of each setting to display
   a drop-down arrow. Click the arrow and select Enabled for each setting you want
   to install.

5. Validate your answer file and save it, then deploy Server Core using your answer
   file using any of the methods outlined in Chapter 2. When installation is
   completed, log on and type **oclist | find** " **Installed**" and verify that the desired
   Web Server role components have been installed.

Managing the Web Server Role

Because of the .NET dependencies of the IIS 7.0 Management Console snap-in, you cannot use this console from another computer to manage a Web server running on Server Core. The only ways you can manage a Server Core Web server are as follows:

- From the command line using Appcmd.exe, a new command in Windows Server 2008 for administering IIS 7.0. Appcmd.exe is the standard tool for administering individual Web servers, sites, directories, and content hosted on Server Core, and you can group such commands into a batch file to automate IIS 7.0 configuration and administration tasks. The common administrative tasks described in the sections that follow use Appcmd.exe.

- By modifying the Web sever configuration (.config) files, which you can either edit directly on the server using Notepad or by copying them from a different computer to your Web server. Administration by modification of .config files is typically used in hosting scenarios where service providers need to create and configure hundreds or thousands of sites. For information on how to administer IIS 7.0 by modifying .config files, see the IIS 7.0 Operations Guide in the Windows Server 2008 Technical Library on Microsoft Technet at *http://technet.microsoft.com/en-us/windowsserver/*.

- By accessing the IIS 7.0 Windows Management Interface (WMI) provider on your Server Core Web server using scripts written in VBScript or using Power-Shell commands that use only WMI. For more information, see the IIS 7.0 WMI Provider Reference at *http://msdn.microsoft.com/en-us/library/aa347459.aspx* on MSDN.

- By using managed code running on another computer that calls the Microsoft.Web.Administration application programming interfaces (APIs) on a Server Core Web server that has been configured to allow remote administration using this method. For more information, see the post titled "Connecting to IIS 7.0 configuration remotely with Microsoft.Web.Administration" on the blog of Mike Volodarsky, Program Manager on the IIS team at Microsoft, which can be found at *http://mvolo.com/blogs/serverside/*.

Note The PowerShell Provider for IIS 7.0 (available from *http://www.iis.net/downloads/*) cannot be installed on Server Core.

Using Appcmd.exe

Appcmd.exe is a command-line tool that enables you to configure and query objects on a Windows Server 2008 Web server and return output in either text or Extensible Markup Language (XML). Using Appcmd.exe, you can create and configure sites, applications, application pools, and virtual directories; start and stop sites; start, stop, and recycle application pools; and display information about worker processes and requests running on a Web server.

Appcmd.exe is found in the %WinDir%\System32\Inetsrv, which is not in the system path. This means to use this command, you need to either change your current directory to %WinDir%\System32\Inetsrv or add the \Inetsrv directory to your system path by typing **setx path "%path%;C:\Windows\System32\inetsrv" /m** and rebooting your computer.

Appcmd.exe can be used to configure settings at the server, site, application, or virtual directory level. You can use Appcmd.exe commands to view or change configuration settings for an Appcmd.exe object by typing **appcmd <object> /?** at the command prompt. For example, to view a list of commands for the site object, do the following:

```
C:\Users\administrator>appcmd site /?
Administration of virtual sites

APPCMD (command) SITE <identifier> <-parameter1:value1 ...>

Supported commands:

  list      List virtual sites
  set       Configure virtual site
  add       Add new virtual site
  delete    Delete virtual site
  start     Start virtual site
  stop      Stop virtual site

(To get help for each command use /?, e.g. 'appcmd.exe add site /?'.)
```

Table 11-3 summarizes the supported object types that can be managed using Appcmd.exe.

Table 11-3   Appcmd.exe Supported Object Types

App	Administration of Applications
AppPool	Administration of application pools
Backup	Administration of server configuration backups
Config	Administration of general configuration sections
Module	Administration of server modules
Request	Administration of HTTP requests
Site	Administration of virtual sites
Trace	Working with failed request trace logs
Vdir	Administration of virtual directories
Wp	Administration of worker processes

Note For additional help on using Appcmd.exe, type **appcmd /?** at the command prompt. Another useful resource on using Appcmd.exe is the IIS 7.0 Operations Guide in the Windows Server 2008 Technical Library on Microsoft TechNet at *http://technet.microsoft.com/en-us/windowsserver/*.

Common Management Tasks

The following sections describe a few common administration tasks that you can perform on Server Core Web servers. These tasks all use the Appcmd.exe command-line tool and can be performed either locally, at the Server Core command prompt, or remotely, using either Remote Desktop or the Windows Remote Shell. The tasks described here are predicated on the fact that you have installed all IIS 7.0 components available on Server Core—see the section "Installing All IIS 7.0 Components," earlier in this chapter, for information on how to do this.

Note For information on how to configure and use Remote Desktop and the Windows Remote Shell for remotely managing Server Core, see Chapter 6, "Remote Management." For detailed information about administering the Web Server role on Windows Server 2008, see the IIS 7.0 Operations Guide in the Windows Server 2008 Technical Library on Microsoft TechNet at *http://technet.microsoft.com/en-us/ windowsserver/*.

Verifying the Default Web Site

When you install the Web Server role, a default Web site is created in the \Inetpub\ Wwwroot directory. This default Web site and default directory can be used to publish Web content immediately if desired.

You can verify the installation of the default Web site from a remote computer by opening Windows Internet Explorer on that computer and opening a Uniform Resource Locator (URL) that specifies the Internet Protocol (IP) address or name of your Web server. For example, if you install the Web Server role on a Server Core installation which is named SEA-SC2 and which belongs to the fabrikam.com domain, and if the IP address of the Web server is 172.16.11.21, then you can use Internet Explorer on a remote computer to view the default document of the default Web site by typing any of the following URLs into the address bar (as shown in Figure 11-1):

- *http://SEA-SC2* (use this only on an intranet)
- *http://SEA-SC2.fabrikam.com*
- *http://172.16.11.21*

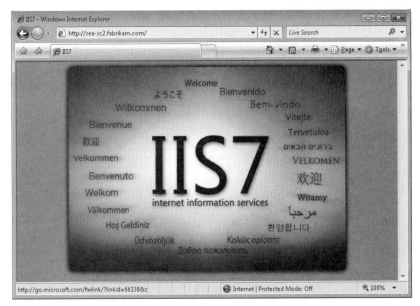

Figure 11-1   Verifying the existence of the default Web site

You can also use the Telnet client running on your Server Core Web server to verify whether the default Web site exists and is working properly. To do this, you must install the Telnet Client feature on your Server Core Web server by typing **start /w ocsetup TelnetClient** at the command prompt. Then perform the following steps:

1. Type **telnet** to display the Telnet command prompt, which looks like this:

```
Welcome to Microsoft Telnet Client

Escape Character is 'CTRL+]'

Microsoft Telnet>
```

2. Type **set localecho** to display any text you type at the Telnet prompt, as follows:

```
Microsoft Telnet> set localecho
Local echo on
```

3. Type **open SEA-SC2.fabrikam.com 80** to open a connection to the Server Core Web server on port 80, as follows:

```
Microsoft Telnet> open sea-sc2.fabrikam.com 80
Connecting To sea-sc2.fabrikam.com...
```

At this point, the cursor moves to the top left corner of your command prompt window, and any text that you enter types over the existing text in the window.

4. Type the following two lines of text, pressing Enter after each line to send an HTTP GET request to the default Web site on your server, requesting that the server return the default document (iisstart.htm) for the site:

```
GET /iisstart.htm HTTP/1.1
host: SEA-SC2.fabrikam.com
```

5. Press Enter again after the second line. The server should return the HTML stream for the default document as follows:

```
HTTP/1.1 200 OK
Content-Type: text/html
Last-Modified: Wed, 18 Jun 2008 17:00:34 GMT
Accept-Ranges: bytes
ETag: "55af5d264d1c81:0"
Server: Microsoft-IIS/7.0
Date: Thu, 19 Jun 2008 16:05:31 GMT
Content-Length: 689

<!DOCTYPE html PUBLIC "-//W3C//DTD XHTML 1.0 Strict//EN"
"http://www.w3.org/TR/x
html1/DTD/xhtml1-strict.dtd">
<html xmlns="http://www.w3.org/1999/xhtml">
<head>
<meta http-equiv="Content-Type" content="text/html; charset=iso-8859-1" />
<title>IIS7</title>
<style type="text/css">
<!--
body {
        color:#000000;
        background-color:#B3B3B3;
        margin:0;
...
```

The return of this HTML stream verifies that the default Web site is present and working properly.

Creating a Web Site

You can create a new Web site on a Server Core Web server in order to publish content for access by users on a corporate intranet or over the Internet. To create a new Web site, you need to specify a name for the site, a site ID number, a physical directory where the site's content will be located, and bindings for the site. The *bindings* for a Web site specify how the site listens for and responds to incoming HTTP requests from clients. Bindings consist of three pieces of information:

- **IP address**   Specify either a single IP address on which the site will listen or use an asterisk (*) to indicate that the site will listen on all IP addresses bound to the Web server's network adapter.

■ **Port number**   Specify the port number on which the site will listen or omit to have the site listen on the default port number, which is TCP port 80.

■ **Host header**   Specify a fully qualified domain name (FQDN) on which the site will listen. Any HTTP requests received that have this FQDN in the second line of their request header invoke a response from the site that has this FQDN configured as the site's host header.

Tip   The number 1 is automatically assigned as the site ID for the default Web site. Site IDs do not need to be created in numerical order.

To create a new Web site named New Site on Server Core Web server SEA-SC2, follow these steps:

1. Create a home directory for the site, such as the following:

    ```
    C:\Windows\System32\Inetsrv>mkdir C:\newsite
    ```

2. Create a default document in the home directory, such as by typing the following Copy command and then pressing Ctrl+Z as shown here:

    ```
    C:\Windows\System32\inetsrv>copy con C:\newsite\default.htm
    <html><head><title>Test Page</title></head><body><h1>This is a test
    </h1></body></
    html>
    ^Z
            1 file(s) copied.
    ```

3. Create the new site, assigning it a site ID of 2 and bindings of *:80:www. fabrikam.com, which indicates that the new site will listen on all IP addresses bound to the server's network adapter, and on the default port 80, but only listens for HTTP requests that specify www.fabrikam.com as the host being requested, as follows:

    ```
    C:\Windows\System32\inetsrv>appcmd add site /name:"New Site" /id:2
    /physicalPath:C:\newsite /bindings:http//*:80:www.fabrikam.com
    SITE object "New Site" added
    APP object "New Site/" added
    VDIR object "New Site/" added
    ```

4. Before your new site can respond to HTTP requests issued for www.fabrikam.com, you must create a new CNAME (alias) record in the fabrikam.com zone on your Domain Name System (DNS) server so that name queries issued for www.fabrikam.com will return the IP address assigned to SEA-SC2.fabrikam.com. To do this, either use the DNS console on your DNS server or type **dnscmd SEA-DC2 /recordadd fabrikam.com www CNAME SEA-SC2.fabrikam.com** at the command prompt on your DNS server.

5. Verify the new site by typing **http://www.fabrikam.com** into the address bar of Internet Explorer on another computer, as shown here.

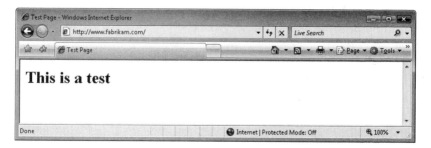

6. You can also verify the new site locally on your Server Core computer by opening a Telnet connection to www.fabrikam.com on port 80 and typing the following two lines, pressing Enter after each line to send an HTTP request to the site:

```
GET /default.htm HTTP/1.1
Host: www.fabrikam.com
```

Press Enter again after the second line and the following response should be returned from the site:

```
HTTP/1.1 200 OK
Content-Type: text/html
Last-Modified: Thu, 19 Jun 2008 16:33:36 GMT
Accept-Ranges: bytes
ETag: "7fb1f5382ad2c81:0"
Server: Microsoft-IIS/7.0
Date: Thu, 19 Jun 2008 16:53:57 GMT
Content-Length: 87

<html><head><title>Test Page</title><head><body><h1>This is a test
</h1></body></html>
```

7. Another way to verify your new site is to list all sites on the Web server like this:

```
C:\Windows\System32\inetsrv>appcmd list site
SITE "Default Web Site" (id:1,bindings:http/*:80:,state:Started)
SITE "New Site" (id:2,bindings:http/*:80:www.fabrikam.com,state:Started)
```

Stopping and Starting a Web Site

When you create a new Web site, the state of the site is set to Running, which allows the site to respond to HTTP requests from clients. You may want to change the state to Stopped to perform maintenance on your site. For example, to stop the site named New Site that was created in the previous section, do this:

```
C:\Windows\System32\inetsrv>appcmd stop site /site.name:"New Site"
"New Site" successfully stopped
```

List the site to verify that it has stopped as follows:

```
C:\Windows\System32\inetsrv>appcmd list site /site.name:"New Site"
SITE "New Site" (id:2,bindings:http/*:80:www.fabrikam.com,state:Stopped)
```

To restart the site, do this:

```
C:\Windows\System32\inetsrv>appcmd start site /site.name:"New Site"
"New Site" successfully started.
```

Creating a Virtual Directory

A *virtual directory* is a directory name used in a URL or Web address that maps to a physical directory located either on the local server or on a network share. Virtual directories can be thought of as subsections of a Web site.

For example, to create a virtual directory named /Addy that maps to the physical folder C:\Code and which belongs to a site named New Site created in the previous sections, use these commands:

```
C:\Windows\System32\inetsrv>mkdir C:\code
C:\Windows\System32\inetsrv>appcmd add vdir /app.name:"New Site"/
/path:/addy /physicalPath:C:\code
VDIR object "New Site/addy" added
```

Verify that this occurred by listing all virtual directories for the site named New Site as follows:

```
C:\Windows\System32\inetsrv>appcmd list vdir /app.name:"New Site"/
VDIR "New Site/" (physicalPath:C:\newsite)
VDIR "New Site/addy" (physicalPath:C:\code)
```

You can also verify this by creating a default document in the physical directory that the virtual directory maps to and then opening the URL *http://www.fabrikam.com/addy/* using Internet Explorer running on a remote computer. For example, do the following to create default.htm in the C:\code directory:

```
C:\Windows\System32\inetsrv>copy con C:\code\default.htm
<body>It works!</body>
^Z
        1 file(s) copied.
```

Figure 11-2 shows what happens when you successfully browse to the virtual directory from a remote computer.

Figure 11-2 Verifying a virtual directory

Creating an Application

A *Web application* (also called simply an *application*) is a grouping of content at either the root level of a Web site or in a virtual directory under the root of a Web site. Creating an application designates a particular virtual directory as the application root or starting point for the application. By default, when you create a new Web site, a new application is created at the root of the Web site. To see this, use the following command to display a list of all applications associated with a site:

```
C:\Windows\System32\inetsrv>appcmd list app /site.name:"New Site"
APP "New Site/" (applicationPool:DefaultAppPool)
```

For example, to create a new application (and also a new virtual directory) named Userinfo beneath the root of the site named New Site, and to map this application (and virtual directory) to the physical directory C:\Apps, do the following:

```
C:\Windows\System32\inetsrv>mkdir C:\apps
C:\Windows\System32\inetsrv>appcmd add app /site.name:"New Site"
/path:/userinfo /physicalPath:C\apps
APP object "New Site/userinfo" added
VDIR object "New Site/userinfo" added
```

Verify the creation of the new application as follows:

```
C:\Windows\System32\inetsrv>appcmd list app /site.name:"New Site"
APP "New Site/" (applicationPool:DefaultAppPool)
APP "New Site/userinfo" (applicationPool:DefaultAppPool)
```

Verify also the creation of the new virtual directory as follows:

```
C:\Windows\System32\inetsrv>appcmd list vdir
VDIR "Default Web Site/" (physicalPath:%SystemDrive%\inetpub\wwwroot)
VDIR "New Site/" (physicalPath:C:\newsite)
VDIR "New Site/addy" (physicalPath:C:\code)
VDIR "New Site/userinfo/" (physicalPath:C\apps)
```

To test your new application, enter the following text into Notepad and save it as a file named Default.asp:

```
<html>
<head>
<title>Your IP address</title>
</head>

<body>

<%
ipAddress=Request.ServerVariables("REMOTE_ADDR")
Response.Write("Your IP address is: ")
Response.Write(ipAddress)
```

```
%>
```

```
</body>
</html>
```

The dynamic Web page Default.asp uses RequestObject, a built-in ASP object in IIS, to obtain and display the IP address of any client computer that opens the page. Copy the Default.asp file to the C:\Apps folder of your Web server and then, on another computer, open the URL *http://www.fabrikam.com/userinfo/* using Internet Explorer. The result should look like Figure 11-3.

Figure 11-3   Opening the default document of an ASP application

Creating an Application Pool

Application pools can be used to isolate Web sites and applications to enhance the reliability, availability, and security of sites and applications hosted on a Web server. For example, you might create a new application pool and then group all sites and applications that have the same configuration settings or use the same custom identity into this new pool. You can also use application pools to prevent resources in one application from accessing resources in another application, or to improve performance by isolating poorly behaved applications (for example, applications that are prone to crashing) from those that are well-behaved.

To view a list of application pools on the Web server, use this command:

```
C:\Windows\System32\inetsrv>appcmd list apppool
APPPOOL "DefaultAppPool" (MgdVersion:,MgdMode:Integrated,state:Started)
```

The default application pool (DefaultAppPool) displayed in this command output is created when the Web Server role is installed, and any new applications you create automatically are assigned to that pool.

To create a new application pool named Test, do this:

```
C:\Windows\System32\inetsrv>appcmd add apppool /name:Test
APPPOOL object "Test" added
```

Verify the new pool exists as follows:

```
C:\Windows\System32\inetsrv>appcmd list apppool
APPPOOL "DefaultAppPool" (MgdVersion:,MgdMode:Integrated,state:Started)
APPPOOL "Test" (MgdVersion:,MgdMode:Integrated,state:Started)
```

Isolating an Application in a Separate Pool

As explained in the previous section, it's sometimes useful for reliability, performance, or troubleshooting reasons to isolate an application in a separate application pool. For example, use the following command to display all the applications that are currently assigned to the default application pool:

```
C:\Windows\System32\inetsrv>appcmd list app /apppool.name:DefaultAppPool
APP "Default Web Site/" (applicationPool:DefaultAppPool)
APP "New Site/" (applicationPool:DefaultAppPool)
APP "New Site/userinfo" (applicationPool:DefaultAppPool)
```

Now move the New Site/Userinfo application from the DefaultAppPool into the Test pool as follows:

```
C:\Windows\System32\inetsrv>appcmd set app /app.name:"New Site/userinfo"
/applicationPool:Test
APP object "New Site/userinfo" changed
```

Verify the result as follows:

```
C:\Windows\System32\inetsrv>appcmd list app /apppool.name:Test
APP "New Site/userinfo" (applicationPool:Test)
C:\Windows\System32\inetsrv>appcmd list app /apppool.name:DefaultAppPool
APP "Default Web Site/" (applicationPool:DefaultAppPool)
APP "New Site/" (applicationPool:DefaultAppPool)
```

The Userinfo application in the site named New Site is now isolated in a separate pool named Test.

Managing an Application Pool

You can configure and manage various aspects of application pools, including stopping and starting pools, configuring idle time-outs, configuring worker process identities, and recycling worker processes. What follows here are a few examples of what you can do. For more information, see the IIS 7.0 Operations Guide in the Windows Server 2008 Technical Library on Microsoft Technet at *http://technet.microsoft.com/en-us/windowsserver/*.

To stop the application pool named Test, use the following command:

```
C:\Windows\System32\inetsrv>appcmd stop apppool /apppool.name:Test
"Test" successfully stopped
```

Stopping an application pool causes the WAS to shut down all running worker processes that are serving that application pool, and any clients trying to open applications in the pool receive an HTTP 503 error, as shown in Figure 11-4.

Figure 11-4   An unsuccessful attempt to open the default document of an ASP application

To restart the stopped pool, do this:

```
C:\Windows\System32\inetsrv>appcmd start apppool /apppool.name:Test
"Test" successfully started.
```

Worker processes that serve a pool automatically shut down after a specified period of inactivity (that is, no requests from clients) called the *idle timeout,* which by default has a value of 20 minutes. If your application is under a heavy load, you may want to shorten this timeout to 5 minutes like this:

```
c:\Windows\System32\inetsrv>appcmd set config /section:applicationPools
/[name='Test'].processModel.idleTimeout:0.00:05:00
Applied configuration changes to section "system.applicationHost/
applicationPools" for "MACHINE/WEBROOT/APPHOST" at configuration commit
path "MACHINE/WEBROOT/APPHOST"
```

By default, application pools use the built-in identity Network Service as their security context. This identity is used because it has low-level user rights. If desired, you can configure application pools to run under a different built-in identity, such as Local System, that has higher-level user rights than Network Service. However, be aware that running an application pool under an identity that has high-level user rights can be a serious security risk. You can also configure application pools to use a custom user account as its identity, and any custom user account you use for this purpose should have only the minimum rights your application needs. Using a custom user account as a pool's identity can be useful if you are hosting Web sites for multiple customers on a single Web server or if you need to trace security events for each application running on the Web server.

For example, to create a local user account named App1 on Web server SEA-SC2 that belongs to the Users group and has the password Pa$$w0rd, and then assign this account to the Test application pool as the identity for the pool, do this:

```
C:\Windows\System32\inetsrv>net user app1 Pa$$w0rd /add
The command completed successfully.
c:\Windows\System32\inetsrv>appcmd set config /section:applicationPools
```

```
/[name='Test'].processModel.identityType:SpecificUser
/[name='Test'].processModel.userName:SEA-SC2\app1
/[name='Test'].processModel.password:Pa$$W0rd
Applied configuration changes to section "system.applicationHost/
applicationPools" for "MACHINE/WEBROOT/APPHOST" at configuration commit
path "MACHINE/WEBROOT/APPHOST"
```

If your Web server has a problematic application and you are not able to correct the code that causes the problem, you can limit the impact of the problems by periodically recycling the worker process that services the application. In addition, you can configure an application pool to recycle a worker process at a particular time or after an elapsed period of time, after a specified number of requests have been handled, or when virtual or used memory reaches a certain threshold.

From time to time, you may also have to recycle an unhealthy worker process immediately instead of waiting for the next configured recycle event to occur. Instead of manually stopping the worker process, which can cause service interruptions, you can use on-demand recycling, which marks an unhealthy worker process for recycling and prevents the worker process from accepting any new requests but continues handling any requests that this unhealthy process has already received. When all pending requests have been handled, the unhealthy worker process then shuts down.

To recycle the application pool named Test on demand, use the following command:

```
C:\Windows\System32\inetsrv>appcmd recycle apppool /apppool.name:Test
"Test" successfully recycled
```

Chapter 12
Hyper-V and Other Roles

In addition to the roles described in the previous chapters of this book, Server Core supports running the Microsoft Hyper-V (Virtualization), Active Directory Lightweight Directory Services (AD LDS), and Streaming Media Services roles. This chapter examines how to install and manage these different roles on Server Core.

Installing and Managing the Hyper-V Role on Server Core

Hyper-V is a hypervisor-based virtualization platform built into Windows Server 2008 that provides the ability to create and manage virtual machines. Hyper-V provides a robust and scalable platform for managing and consolidating workloads in enterprise environments and for optimizing the use of physical hardware resources. The term *virtualization* refers to any technology that can abstract the physical characteristics of computing resources and present them as logical resources to operating systems that interact with these resources. A *virtual machine* is a computing environment in which a computer's hardware resources have been virtualized (abstracted) so that multiple operating systems can run simultaneously on a single physical computer.

The following three Windows Server 2008 product SKUs support running Hyper-V:

- Windows Server 2008 Standard Edition x64
- Windows Server 2008 Enterprise Edition x64
- Windows Server 2008 Datacenter Edition x64

> **Note** The Standard, Enterprise, and Datacenter editions of Windows Server 2008 are available in both Hyper-V–capable and non-Hyper-V–capable versions, with the non-Hyper-V–capable versions identified by having the phrase "without Hyper-V" in their product name. For example, the Windows Server 2008 Standard Edition x64 SKU supports Hyper-V, while the Windows Server 2008 Standard Edition without Hyper-V x64 SKU does not. Also, Hyper-V is not supported by any x86 SKU of Windows Server 2008.

Hyper-V Terminology

You should familiarize yourself with basic Hyper-V terminology before implementing Hyper-V on Server Core. The following is a brief summary of some important Hyper-V concepts and terms. Additional concepts and terms will be introduced later in this chapter as needed.

Hypervisor

The *hypervisor* is a layer of software that allows multiple operating systems to execute on a single physical computer. The primary purpose of the hypervisor is to provide isolated execution environments within which virtual machines can run. The hypervisor also controls access to the underlying hardware resources of the physical computer, manages partitions on the physical computer, and manages virtual processor and virtual memory resources.

In the Microsoft Hyper-V implementation, the hypervisor uses a 64-bit microkernel architecture in which hypervisor-aware device drivers are not required. This is because the operating system running in the parent partition provides the execution environment for the drivers needed to access hardware on the physical computer. Device drivers need be installed only in the parent partition; guest operating systems running in child partitions then communicate with the parent partition for device-specific operations. An additional advantage of the microkernel approach is that no foreign code (that is, no third-party driver) needs to run in the hypervisor, making the hypervisor more secure. Other features of Hyper-V include support for up to four virtual processors per virtual machine, the ability to migrate a running virtual machine from one physical computer to another, support for network load balancing of virtual machines on different physical computers, support for virtual machine snapshots, the ability to mange virtualized environments using Windows Management Instrumentation (WMI) and application programming interfaces (APIs), and support for a broad range of 32-bit and 64-bit guest operating systems, including versions of Windows, Linux, and others.

Partition

A *partition* is a unit of isolation within the hypervisor that is allocated physical memory address space and virtual processors. Partitions are also commonly referred to as *virtual machines*. The initial release of Hyper-V uses two types of partitions:

■ The *parent partition* (or *root partition*) is the controlling partition that owns hardware devices and within which the virtualization stack runs. It is the only partition that has direct access to memory and devices on the physical computer. The parent partition creates and manages all child partitions, manages and assigns hardware devices, and handles all power management, Plug and Play, and hardware failure events. The parent partition must be running a version of Windows Server 2008 that supports Hyper-V, and this can be either a Full or Server Core installation.

■ A *child partition* is a partition in which a guest operating system can be installed and on which applications can run. Child partitions don't have access to the physical processor and don't handle processor interrupts. Instead, the hypervisor handles processor interrupts and redirects them to the respective partition. Each child partition has its own virtual view of the processors on the system, and each child partition runs in a virtual memory address region that is private to the partition.

Snapshot

A *snapshot* is a point-in-time saved state of a virtual machine that provides the ability to restore a virtual machine to the state when the snapshot was created. Previous Microsoft virtualization platforms, such as Microsoft Virtual Server and Microsoft Virtual PC, had similar functionality known as *undo disks,* but snapshots allow multiple restore points to be created. In addition, if the system is rolled back, it can also be rolled forward again to a later snapshot.

Enlightenments

Enlightenments are modifications made to operating system code to make the operating system hypervisor-aware. As a result, the system runs more efficiently when it detects that it is running as a guest within a hypervisor environment. Hyper-V supports enlightenment of the following resources: storage, networking, graphics, and input subsystems. An *enlightened guest* is an operating system whose kernel can detect whether it is running in a virtualized environment. Windows Server 2008 is built from the ground up as an enlightened guest and is therefore a fully enlightened operating system. Windows Vista SP1 is an operating system that can reach a degree of enlightenment by installing Integration Services onto it.

Integration Services

Integration Services consists of user-mode processes that are run on a child partition to provide a level of integration between the parent and child partitions and to improve the performance and usability of unenlightened operating systems running in child partitions. Integration Services also provides the components needed to enable child partitions to communicate with the parent partition and the hypervisor. Integration Services includes the following services: Hyper-V Heartbeat Service, Hyper-V Guest Shutdown Service, Hyper-V Data Exchange Service, Hyper-V Volume Shadow Copy Requestor, and Hyper-V Time Synchronization Service. In previous Microsoft virtualization platforms, such as Virtual Server and Virtual PC, the Integration Services feature was referred to as Virtual Machine Additions.

Synthetic Devices

Synthetic devices are virtual device stacks that do not correspond to a physical device. Synthetic devices use logical communications channels to enable communications between guest operating systems in child partitions and physical devices in the parent partition. An example of a synthetic device would be a synthetic network adapter or synthetic video adapter. Other examples of synthetic devices include synthetic video controllers, synthetic Human Interface Device (HID) controllers, synthetic storage devices, synthetic interrupt controllers, and memory service routines. Synthetic devices communicate over the VMBus, a channel-based logical communication mechanism used for inter-partition communication and device enumeration on systems with multiple active virtualized partitions.

Emulated Devices

Virtual device stacks that emulate a real piece of hardware traditionally emulate legacy devices for their guests. In virtualization platforms, emulated devices typically include motherboard chipsets with integrated development environment (IDE) controllers, legacy network cards, and a video chipset; processors, in contrast, are typically reported as the ones actually present on the physical computer.

Emulation works by simulating the presence of devices by providing the ports and input/output (I/O) memory for these devices. This enables the original driver in the guest to find the device and load the appropriate driver. The drawback of using emulated devices rather than synthetic ones is that frequent transitions to the hypervisor are needed, in addition to further transitions to the parent partition where the device emulation is handled by a worker process. The emulated device in the worker process then must translate the device request for the physical device and call the physical device driver in the parent partition, which sends its response back to the guest again through the hypervisor. Previous Microsoft virtualization platforms, such as Virtual Server and Virtual PC, used emulated devices only to virtualize hardware resources for guests; they did not support synthetic devices.

Note   The term *virtual machine* is often used to refer to a child partition combined with a guest operating system installed and running within the partition.

Installing the Hyper-V Role

Before you install the Hyper-V role on a Server Core installation, you must ensure the following:

- Your computer must be running an x64 version of Windows Server 2008 that supports Hyper-V. You cannot be running any edition of Windows Server 2008 that has the phrase "without Hyper-V" in its name, such as Windows Server 2008 Enterprise Edition without Hyper-V.

- Your computer must have processors that include extensions to provide hardware-assisted virtualization, a technology that provides the ability to load a hypervisor layer between the physical computer's hardware and the partitions. Examples of processors that support hardware-assisted virtualization include the AMD-V and Intel VT families of processors. In addition, you must have hardware-assisted virtualization enabled in the system BIOS on your computer.

- Your computer must also have processors that support hardware-based Data Execution Protection (DEP), a technology that prevents processes from executing code from non-executable memory regions.

- Your computer should have sufficient physical memory to support the virtualization workloads you plan to use.

To find computer systems that are capable of running the Hyper-V role, use the Windows Server Catalog at http://www.windowsservercatalog.com.

Verifying Operating System Support for Hyper-V

Before installing the Hyper-V update package on a Server Core installation, you should verify that the edition of Windows Server 2008 that you used for your installation supports Hyper-V. You can do this by running the following command:

```
C:\Users\Administrators>wmic os get OperatingSystemSKU /value
```

```
OperatingSystemSKU=14
```

By comparing the value for OperatingSystemSKU returned by this command with the values shown in Table 12-1, we see that our Server Core installation uses Windows Server 2008 Enterprise Edition, which supports running the Hyper-V role.

Table 12-1   Server Core SKU Support for Hyper-V

OperatingSystemSKU	Server Core Installation	Support for Hyper-V
12	Datacenter Edition	✓
13	Standard Edition	✓
14	Enterprise Edition	✓
39	Datacenter Edition without Hyper-V	
40	Standard Edition without Hyper-V	
41	Enterprise Edition without Hyper-V	

Installing the Hyper-V Update Package

The release version of Windows Server 2008 does not include the final Hyper-V bits. This means that before you can install the Hyper-V role on x64 versions of Windows Server 2008, you must download and install the Hyper-V Update Package (.msu file) on your computer. The release version of the Hyper-V technology for Windows Server 2008 is described in Microsoft Knowledge Base (KB) article KB 950050 at *http://support.microsoft.com/kb/950050.*

To install the Hyper-V bits on an x64 version of Server Core, download the Hyper-V update for Windows Server 2008 x64 Edition from the link in the previously cited KB article. Then copy the update package, which is named Windows6.0-KB950050-x64.msu, to a folder such as C:\Updates on your Server Core installation. Then open a command prompt at this folder and type **Windows6.0-KB950050-x64.msu** to install the update. You will need to reboot your computer for the update to be applied.

> **Tip** Alternatively, you can apply this update package silently (without prompts) by typing **start /w wusa /quiet Windows6.0-KB950050-x64.msu** at a command prompt.

Installing the Hyper-V RC1 update on an x64 version of Server Core also installs the following:

- Updated versions of the Hyper-V Manager console and Virtual Machine Connection remote connection tool for x64-based versions of Windows Server 2008.

- Updated versions of Integration Services for Windows Server 2008, Windows Vista SP1, Windows Server 2003 SP2, and Windows XP SP 3.

> **Tip** The KB article referred to previously also includes a link for you to download an additional update named Windows6.0-KB950050-x86.msu. This update provides updated versions of the Hyper-V Manager console and Virtual Machine Connection remote connection tool for x86-based versions of Windows Server 2008.

Installing the Hyper-V Role

Once the Hyper-V update has been applied on your Server Core installation, you can use Ocsetup.exe to add the Hyper-V role to your computer. To do this, type **start /w ocsetup Microsoft-Hyper-V** at the command prompt. Reboot your computer again to finish the installation of the role.

> **Tip** You can avoid having to perform the second reboot by typing **bcdedit /set hypervisorlaunchtype auto** at a command prompt before you run the Ocsetup command. This configures the Boot Configuration Data (BCD) store on the computer so that the hypervisor is automatically started during the boot process.

Verifying Role Installation

To verify installation of the Hyper-V role, use Oclist like this:

```
C:\Users\Administrators>oclist | find "   Installed"
    Installed:Microsoft-Hyper-V
```

Troubleshooting Role Installation

If you discover that Hyper-V did not start properly after performing the previously described procedures, try shutting down your computer completely and performing a cold boot of the system. If Hyper-V still fails to start, do the following to troubleshoot the problem:

- Verify with the manufacturer that the processors in your system support both hardware-assisted virtualization and hardware Data Execution Prevention (DEP).

- Make sure that hardware-assisted virtualization is enabled in the BIOS. If it isn't, enable it and then shut down your computer before rebooting it so the BIOS change can take effect.

- Check the manufacturer's Web site to see whether an updated version of the BIOS is available for your computer; install the update if one is available.

- Verify that the BCD store is configured properly by typing **bcdedit /enum** and verifying that HypervisorLaunchType is set to AUTO.

Managing the Hyper-V Role

To manage a Server Core installation running the Hyper-V role, you must use the Hyper-V Management console running on a remote computer because Server Core does not support running Microsoft Management Console (MMC) consoles locally. This remote computer can be any of the following:

- A Full installation of Windows Server 2008 x64 Edition that has the Hyper-V role installed on it

- A Full installation of Windows Server 2008 (x86 or x64) that has the Remote Server Administration Tools (RSAT) feature installed on it and the appropriate Hyper-V update package (RC1 or RTM) applied

- A computer running Windows Vista SP1 (x86 or x64) on which you have downloaded and installed the RSAT and on which you have applied the appropriate Hyper-V update package (RC1 or RTM)

For information about how to download and install RSAT on Windows Vista SP1, see the section "Installing RSAT on Windows Vista SP1," in Chapter 6, "Remote Management."

The following sections describe how to perform some common Hyper-V management tasks. These sections assume the presence of an x64 Server Core installation named SEA-SCV that has the Hyper-V role installed and that belongs to the fabrikam.com domain, and an administrator workstation running Windows Vista SP1 that has RSAT installed, has the Hyper-V update package applied, and belongs to the fabrikam.com domain.

Managing the Hyper-V role on a Server Core installation joined to a domain from a domain member computer that has RSAT installed on it requires no special configuration. In contrast, when one or both of the computers (the Server Core computer running Hyper-V and the management workstation) belong to a workgroup, considerable extra configuration is required before you can use Hyper-V Manager on the workstation to manage the Hyper-V server. For detailed steps on how to perform such a configuration, see the series of posts from April and May 2008 on the blog of John Howard, Senior Program Manager for the Hyper-V team in the Windows Core Operating System Division. The blog can be found at http://blogs.technet.com/jhoward/.

Using the Hyper-V Management Console

To use the Hyper-V Management console from a computer running Windows Vista SP1 to manage the Hyper-V role remotely on a Server Core installation named SEA-SCV, perform the following steps:

1. On your Windows Vista SP1 workstation that has RSAT installed, click Start, Administrative Tools, and finally Hyper-V Manager to open the Hyper-V Manager console.

2. Right-click the root node and select Connect To Server to open the Select Computer dialog box.

3. Select Another Computer and type **SEA-SCV**, or browse to select your Server Core installation in Active Directory Domain Services (AD DS), as shown here.

4. Hyper-V Manager opens and displays the parent partition (your Server Core installation with the Hyper-V role installed on it) beneath the root node, as shown here.

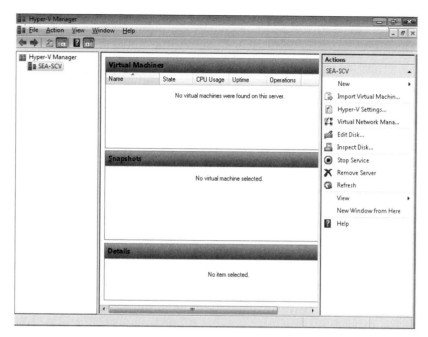

5. Add more Hyper-V servers to the console as desired by repeating steps 2 and 3. Then manage each Hyper-V server by selecting the server's node in the console tree.

Once you have opened the Hyper-V Management console from your management workstation and have connected to the parent partition on your Server Core installation, you can manage the Hyper-V role on your Server Core installation by performing tasks such as the following:

- Configuring Hyper-V settings
- Configuring virtual networks
- Creating new virtual machines
- Configuring virtual machine settings
- Installing guest operating systems
- Managing virtual machines
- Installing Integration Services
- Creating snapshots

Configuring Hyper-V Settings

You can use the Hyper-V Management console to manage settings for the Hyper-V role on your Server Core installation. For example, to manage settings for the Hyper-V role on SEA-SCV, right-click the node for this server and select Hyper-V Settings to open the Hyper-V Settings dialog box (shown in Figure 12-1).

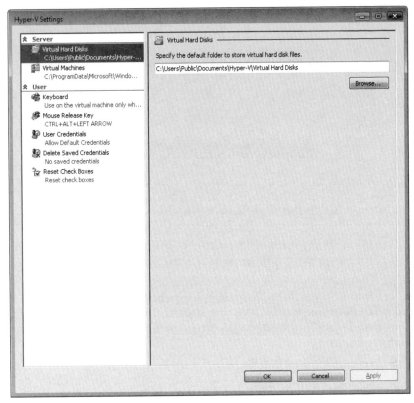

Figure 12-1 Configuring the settings for a Hyper-V server

Server settings for Hyper-V include the following:

- Configuring the default location where virtual hard drives are stored. The default location is the %Public%\Documents\Hyper-V\Virtual Hard Disks folder.

- Configuring the default location where virtual machine configuration files are stored. The default location is the %ProgramData%\Microsoft\Windows\Hyper-V folder.

User settings for Hyper-V include the following:

- Specifying keyboard shortcuts for running Virtual Machine Connection.

- Specifying the keystroke sequence for releasing the mouse from inside a virtual machine (the default is Ctrl+Alt+Left arrow) for unenlightened guests.

- Specifying the user credential to use when connecting to a virtual machine. The default credentials are those of the currently logged on user.

- Deleting saved credentials on your Hyper-V management workstation.

- Resetting all Hyper-V settings to their defaults.

For more information concerning Hyper-V settings available for configuration, select Help Topics from the Help menu of the Hyper-V Management console.

Configuring Virtual Networks

Before you create any child partitions on your Hyper-V server, you must create at least one virtual network on your server. Hyper-V supports the creation of three types of virtual networks:

- **External network**   A virtual network that binds to a specific physical network adapter on the Hyper-V server. External networks allow virtual machines to have access to a physical network to which the physical computer (the Hyper-V server) is connected.

- **Internal network**   A virtual network internal to the Hyper-V server that allows virtual machines running on the server to communicate with each other and with the parent partition, but not with other computers on the physical network on which the Hyper-V server resides.

- **Private network**   A virtual network internal to the Hyper-V server and which allows virtual machines running on the server to communicate only with each other and not with the parent partition or with computers on the physical network on which the Hyper-V server resides.

You can use Virtual Network Manager to create and manage virtual networks on a Hyper-V server. For example, to create a new external network that binds to the physical network adapter on your server, perform the following steps:

1. Open Virtual Network Manager by right-clicking your server node in Hyper-V Manager and selecting Virtual Network Manager.

2. Select External and click Add.

3. Specify a name and, optionally, a description for your new network.

4. Under Connection Type, select External and choose a physical network adapter from the drop-down list of adapters on the physical computer as shown here.

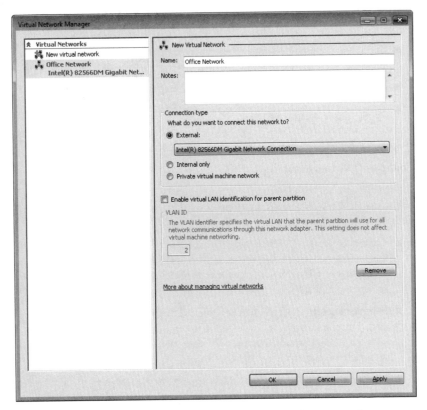

5. Configure other settings as desired, and then click Apply to create the new network.

Best Practices If you are deploying your Hyper-V in a production environment—especially if it is on a perimeter network—you should always have at least two physical network adapters on your Hyper-V server: one for system management that is connected to your internal network, and the other that is connected to the external network for the virtual machines.

Creating New Virtual Machines

You can create and manage new virtual machines on a Server Core installation by using the Hyper-V Management console. Creating a new virtual machine involves creating a child partition in which you can install a guest operating system. You can create virtual machines using two kinds of disk storage:

■ **Virtual hard disk** A file-based disk format (.vhd) similar in format to that used by previous Microsoft virtualization technologies such as Virtual Server and

Virtual PC. Virtual hard disks can be dynamic, fixed, or differencing disks, and they can be stored locally on the Hyper-V server, on Direct Attached Storage (DAS), or on a Storage Area Network (SAN).

■ **Pass-through disk**   Bypasses the Hyper-V server operating system and allows the virtual machine to access a physical disk directly on the Hyper-V server. Pass-through disks can be locally attached, or they can be SAN logical unit numbers (LUNs).

Note   Pass-through disks must appear marked as Offline in the parent partition.

For example, to create a new virtual machine on a Server Core installation named SEA-SRV, perform the following steps:

1. Using the Hyper-V Management console running on your management workstation, right-click the server node SEA-SVC, select New, and then select Virtual Machine. This opens the New Virtual Machine Wizard.

2. Click Next and type a name such as SEA-SRV1-V for your new virtual machine, as shown here.

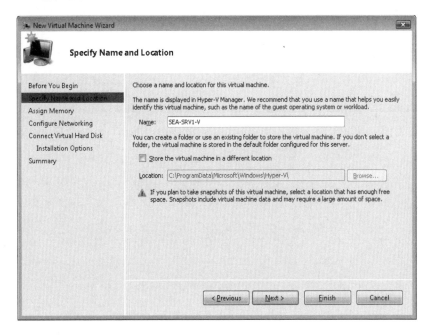

3. Proceed through the wizard, assigning memory to the virtual machine, selecting a configured virtual network, creating a virtual hard disk, and performing the rest of the tasks.

4. Verify the options you have chosen on the final page of the wizard as shown here.

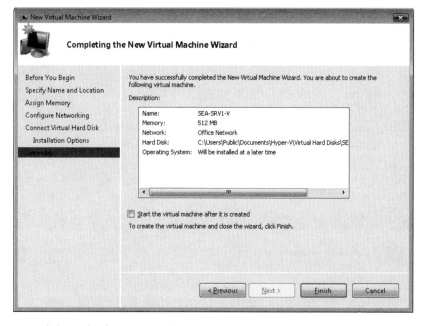

5. Click Finish. The new virtual machine is displayed in the center pane of Hyper-V Manager, as shown here.

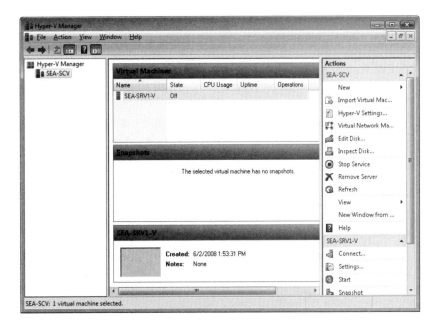

Note   You should specify a virtual network in the previous procedure only if you are planning on installing an enlightened guest operating system in your new child partition. If you plan on installing an unenlightened guest, you need to either install Integration Services first or configure a legacy network adapter for connectivity. For more information, see the section "Installing Integration Services," later in this chapter.

Configuring Virtual Machine Settings

Once you have created a new virtual machine, you can configure settings for it using Hyper-V Manager. For example, to configure settings for a virtual machine named SEA-SRV1-V, perform the following steps:

1. Using the Hyper-V Management console running on your management workstation, right-click the virtual machine named SEA-SRV1-V in the Virtual Machines pane and select Settings. This opens the Settings For SEA-SRV1-V dialog box.

2. Configure hardware and management settings for your virtual machine as desired. For example, if your Hyper-V has a quad-core processor, you can configure your virtual machine to use four virtual processors instead of one by selecting Processor in the left column and selecting 4 from the Number Of Logical Processors drop-down list control, as shown here.

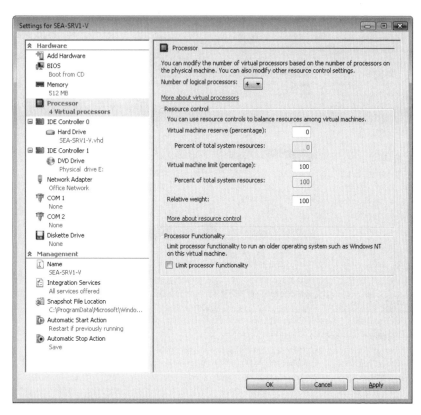

Hardware settings for virtual machines include the following:

- Adding hardware such as Small Computer System Interface (SCSI) adapters or legacy network adapters to your virtual machines

- Modifying the BIOS settings for your virtual machines

- Changing the amount of physical memory allocated to guest operating systems running in your virtual machines

- Changing the number of logical processors allocated to guest operating systems running in your virtual machines

- Adding hard drives and DVD drives to your virtual machines using the IDE controllers available on your virtual machines

- Adding up to four SCSI controllers to your virtual machines, which allows you to control up to 63 additional disks for a total of 252 drives

- Configuring the virtual network adapter to which the guest operating system will connect

- Configuring COM ports for debugging guest operating system issues

- Connecting to a 1.4 MB virtual floppy disk (.vfd file)

Management settings for virtual machines include the following:

- Changing the display name of your virtual machines and adding a descriptive note.

- Viewing which Integration Services are currently installed on your virtual machines.

- Displaying the location where snapshots of your virtual machines are stored.

- Configuring what happens to virtual machines when the parent partition starts, and configuring a start delay to prevent contention from multiple virtual machines for parent partition resources.

- Configuring what happens to virtual machines when the parent partition stops. The default is Save The Virtual Machine State.

For more information concerning the different virtual machine settings that are available for configuration, select Help Topics from the Help menu of the Hyper-V Management console.

Installing Guest Operating Systems

Once you have created and configured a new virtual machine, you can install a guest operating system on it. Installation of guest operating systems can be performed manually (from the product DVD or over the network), or automatically (using unattend files, Windows Deployment Services, Microsoft Deployment Toolkit, or System Center Configuration Manager as desired and depending on your business needs). As an example, to install Windows Server 2008 Standard Edition x64 manually on a new virtual machine named SEA-SRV1-V, perform the following steps:

1. Insert your Windows Server 2008 product DVD into the DVD-ROM drive of your Hyper-V server.

2. Using the Hyper-V Management console running on your management work-station, right-click the virtual machine named SEA-SRV1-V in the Virtual Machines pane, select Connect, and click the Start icon to start the virtual machine using the Virtual Machine Connection interface. Alternatively, you can double-click the thumbnail in the SEA-SRV1-V pane. Each virtual machine is opened using a separate Virtual Connection Manager interface, and the name of the virtual machine is displayed in the top bar of the interface so that you can distinguish between different virtual machines.

3. When each virtual machine starts, Windows Setup starts, and you are given a choice of operating systems to install, as shown here. This list varies depending on the product media you are using.

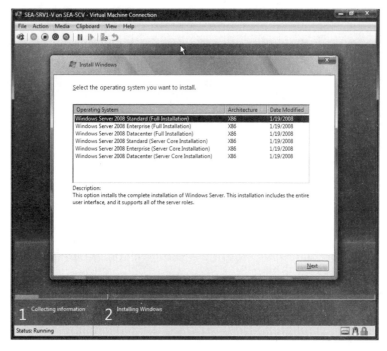

4. Select the operating system that you wish to install on your virtual machine and proceed with your installation in the usual way. As the install is running, you can close Virtual Machine Connection and view the installation progress from the Hyper-V Management console, which shows the virtual machine as running and displays a thumbnail version of the running virtual machine in the bottom pane of the console, as shown here.

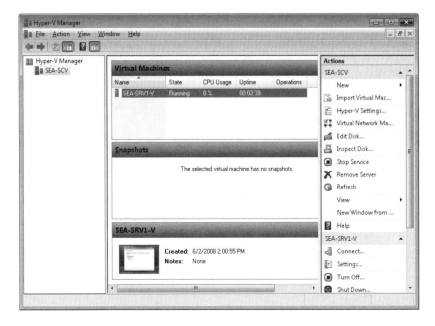

Managing Virtual Machines

You can manage virtual machines using several different tools and methods as follows. For instance, using the Hyper-V Management console, you can connect to virtual machines and open them using Virtual Connection Manager. In addition to connecting to them, you can use the Hyper-V Management console to do any or all of the following:

- Turn off, shut down, save, pause, or reset a virtual machine

- Take a snapshot of a virtual machine

- Modify the settings for a virtual machine

Once you've opened a virtual machine in Virtual Connection Manager, you can use the toolbar at the top of the interface to turn off, shut down, save, pause, or reset the virtual machine (as shown in Figure 12-2). You can also use the menu bar at the top of the interface to capture a CD/DVD or mount an .iso file, capture the screen or copy text to the clipboard, switch between Window and Full Screen mode, and view the Help information concerning using Virtual Connection Manager.

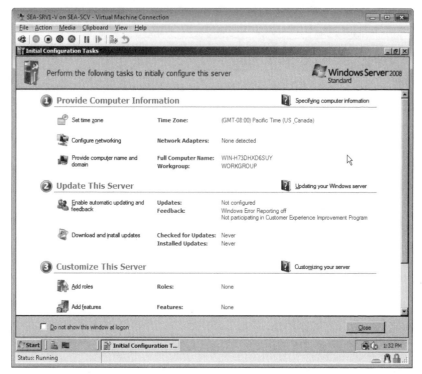

Figure 12-2 Using Virtual Machine Connection to manage a virtual machine that has Windows Server 2008 installed in it

Another tool that you can use for managing virtual machines running on Hyper-V servers is System Center Virtual Machine Manager (SCVMM) 2008. The benefits of using SCVMM 2008 for managing virtual machines running on Hyper-V include the following:

- Support for consolidating multiple physical servers within a virtualized infrastructure, as well as intelligent placement of virtual workloads on the best-suited physical servers

- Rapid provisioning of virtual machines by using virtual machine templates that include sysprepped guest operating system configurations and a self-service portal for delegated provisioning scenarios

- The ability to manage Hyper-V, Virtual Server 2005 R2, and VMWare (VI3) virtual machines

- Physical-to-virtual (P2V) machine conversions in which the P2V process handles reconfiguration of the machine so it works correctly in a virtualized environment

- Virtual-to-virtual (V2V) machine conversions when working with offline VMware virtual machines

- Host cluster awareness to support the creation of highly available virtual machines running in a cluster

- Offline patching of virtual machines when used in conjunction with System Center Configuration Manager (SCCM)

Note   SCVMM 2008 is still in beta; you can download the beta version from *http://www.microsoft.com/systemcenter/scvmm/default.mspx* and use it for evaluation purposes. However, you cannot use SCVMM 2007 to manage virtual machines running on Hyper-V servers.

You can also use WMI to manage virtual machines running on Hyper-V servers. For examples of how to do this, see the section "Managing Virtual Machines Using WMI," later in this chapter.

Finally, you can also use Windows PowerShell to manage virtual machines running on Server Core installations that have the Hyper-V role installed on them—with two limitations: you must run your PowerShell scripts remotely from a different computer that has PowerShell installed on it, and your PowerShell scripts can use only WMI. Both of these limitations are in effect because PowerShell cannot be installed on Server Core. For examples of managing virtual machines using PowerShell, see the section "Managing Virtual Machines Using PowerShell," later in this chapter.

Installing Integration Services

Hyper-V Integration Services provide similar functionality to what Virtual Machine Additions provided for earlier Microsoft virtualization platforms such as Virtual Server and Virtual PC. In particular, installing Integration Services in a child partition provides for better interoperability with the parent partition. Integration Services is also designed to improve the performance of guest operating systems and the overall experience of using virtual machines. In addition, Integration Services is needed to address various problems that arise due to the high level of isolation provided to virtual machines.

In the initial release of Hyper-V, Integration Services is available for both x86 and x64 versions of the following operating systems:

- Windows Server 2008
- Windows Vista SP1
- Windows Server 2003 SP2
- Windows XP SP3

Integration Services is not provided for Microsoft Windows operating systems earlier than Windows XP. This does not mean that you cannot run such operating systems as guests in Hyper-V; it means simply that the usability and performance of such operating systems running in Hyper-V will not be at the same level as they are for operating systems that have Integration Services you can install. If you do need to run versions of older Windows operating systems within a virtualized environment, you can consider using Virtual Server or Virtual PC, each of which has Virtual Machine Additions available for older Windows operating systems.

Note Integration Services is also expected to be made available in the future for certain Linux distributions, including Suse Linux Enterprise Server and Red Hat Enterprise Linux.

To install Integration Services on a virtual machine, you must have an enlightened (fully or partially) guest operating system installed in your virtual machine. If you have an unenlightened guest operating system installed in your virtual machine, you won't be able to install Integration Services in your virtual machine. The procedure for installing Integration Services is as follows:

1. Open the virtual machine using the Virtual Machine Connection interface.

2. From the Action menu, select Insert Integration Services Setup Disk. This causes the Vmguest.iso file to be loaded into the DVD drive for your virtual machine and begins the process of installing Integration Services into the machine.

3. Once the installation of Integration Services is finished, restart the virtual machine. To verify the installation, open the settings for the virtual machine and select Integration Services.

Tip To install Integration Services in a virtual machine running Server Core, mount the Vmguest.iso file as a DVD drive for your virtual machine and run the command **<DVD_drive>\support\<*architecture*>\setup.exe**, where <*architecture*> is either x86 or x64. This extra step is needed because Server Core does not provide autorun functionality.

Creating Snapshots

You can create point-in-time snapshots of virtual machines running on your Hyper-V server. When a snapshot is taken, memory is saved if the machine is in a running or saved state, the current virtual disk becomes read-only, and the changes are stored in an .avhd file. The current state of the virtual machine disk is the sum of the original disk and one or more .avhd files, and rolling back to an earlier state means discarding one or more .avhd files. Because the .avhd files are retained, it is possible to apply snapshots that are not direct ancestors of the current machine state. Because .avhd files contain changes, they reduce the overall efficiency of running virtual machines, so they are primarily intended for use during the test and development stages of product development cycles; they should generally not be used in production environments and are not intended as a replacement for a backup strategy.

Snapshots are displayed in the middle section of the center pane of Hyper-V Manager, and a green arrow followed by the word Now indicates the current running configuration of the virtual machine (as shown in Figure 12-3).

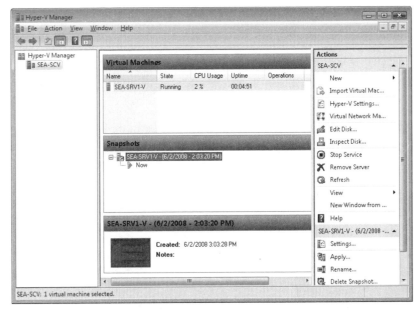

Figure 12-3   Selecting a snapshot of a virtual machine

To create a snapshot of a virtual machine, perform one of the following actions:

- In the Hyper-V Management console, right-click the virtual machine and select Snapshot (or select the virtual machine and click Snapshot in the Actions pane on the right side). (The snapshot created in Figure 12-3 was taken this way.) By default, the snapshot is named using a combination of the virtual machine name and the time and date of creation of the snapshot.

- In the Virtual Machine Connection interface when running in Window mode, click the Snapshot icon in the toolbar (or select Snapshot from the Action menu). In the Snapshot Name dialog box that appears, type a descriptive name for your snapshot and click Yes.

If you select a particular snapshot like the one selected in Figure 12-3, you have four options:

- **Apply**   Copies the complete virtual machine state from the selected snapshot to the currently active virtual machine. Any unsaved data in the currently active virtual machine will be lost unless you create another snapshot of your current active virtual machine before applying the selected snapshot (as shown in Figure 12-4).

■ **Rename** Lets you give a snapshot a more descriptive name than the default name.

■ **Delete Snapshot** Removes the snapshot's associated files from the server so that you no longer can restore your currently active virtual machine to the point in time when the snapshot was taken.

■ **Delete Snapshot Subtree** Removes the selected snapshot and any snapshots hierarchically beneath it.

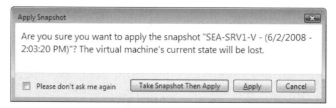

Figure 12-4 Presenting an option to create a snapshot

Once one or more snapshots have been created, you can use the Revert option, which takes your currently active virtual machine back to the last snapshot that was taken or applied and removes any changes that have been made since that snapshot.

Managing Virtual Machines Using WMI

You can use WMI to manage many aspects of virtual machines on Server Core installations. On a Server Core installation that has the Hyper-V role installed, you can run .vbs scripts locally to manage virtual machines using WMI. In addition, provided you have appropriate credentials, you can run .vbs scripts remotely to manage virtual machines using WMI.

The following are a few examples of how you can use WMI to manage virtual machines running on a Server Core installation. These scripts are presented as samples only and may need to be customized to work in your environment.

CreateVM.vbs—WMI Script That Creates a New Virtual Machine

```
Dim wmiService
Dim vmMgmtService
Dim outputParams
Dim objVirtualSystemSettingData
Dim objDefineVirtualSystemIPParams

' Get an instance of the Virtualization WMI Service on the local computer
Set wmiService = GetObject("winmgmts:\\.\root\virtualization")
```

```
' Get the VM Management Service object
Set vmMgmtService = wmiService.ExecQuery("select * from Msvm_VirtualSystem
ManagementService").ItemIndex(0)

' Set the properties for the Virtual System Setting data instance
Set objVirtualSystemSettingData = wmiService.Get("Msvm_VirtualSystemSetting
Data").SpawnInstance_
objVirtualSystemSettingData.ElementName = "Virtual Machine Name"
objVirtualSystemSettingData.BiosNumLock = false ' This value can be true
or false
objVirtualSystemSettingData.BootOrder = Array("0","1","2","3") ' 0=Floppy
1=CD 2=IDE 3=Legacy Network Adapter
objVirtualSystemSettingData.Notes = "Some Notes for the Virtual Machine"

' Create an instance for the input parameters
Set objDefineVirtualSystemIPParams = vmMgmtService.Methods_("DefineVirtual
System").INParameters.SpawnInstance_

' Set the input parameters
objDefineVirtualSystemIPParams.SystemSettingData = objVirtualSystemSetting
Data.GetText_(1)
objDefineVirtualSystemIPParams.ResourceSettingData = NULL

' Execute Method to create the virtual machine
Set outputParams = vmMgmtService.ExecMethod_("DefineVirtualSystem",
objDefineVirtualSystemIPParams)
If outputParams.ReturnValue <> 0 Then
WScript.Echo "ERROR - Unable to create Hyper-V virtual machine. Return
Code: " & outputParams.ReturnValue
Else
WScript.Echo "SUCCESS - Hyper-V virtual machine created successfully."
End If
```

ListVMs.vbs—WMI Script That Lists All VMs and Displays Their States

```
strComputer = "."
Set objWMIService = GetObject("winmgmts:\\" & strComputer & "\root\
virtualization")
Set vmcollecion = objWMIService.ExecQuery("SELECT * FROM Msvm_ComputerSystem
",,48)

Wscript.Echo VbCrLF
Wscript.Echo "Name                                        Description
              State "
Wscript.Echo "------------------------------------ --------------------
-------------- -------------"

For Each vm in vmcollecion

VMStateCode = vm.EnabledState
```

```
Select Case VMStateCode
        Case2VMState = "Running"
         Case3      VMState= "PowerOff"
         Case4      VMState = "ShuttingDown"
        Case10    VMState = "Reset"
        Case32768VMState= "Paused"
        Case32770VMState = "Starting"
Case32771VMState = "SnapshotInProgress"
        Case32772VMState = "Migrating"
        Case32773VMState= "Saving"
        Case32774VMState= "Stopping"
        Case32776VMState= "Pausing"
        Case32777VMState= "Resuming"
        Case32769VMState = "Saved"
Case Else VMState = "Unclassified (so far)"
End Select


    Wscript.Echo vm.ElementName & Space(40 - Len(vm.ElementName)) & _
  vm.Description & Space(35 - Len(vm.Description)) & _
  VMState & " (" &VMStateCode & ")"

Next
```

SaveStateAll.vbs—WMI Script That Saves the State of All VMs

```
strComputer = "."
Set objWMIService = GetObject("winmgmts:\\" & strComputer & "\root\virtual
ization")
Set vmcollecion = objWMIService.ExecQuery("SELECT * FROM Msvm_ComputerSyst
em",,48)


Wscript.Echo VbCrLF
Wscript.Echo "Name                                    Description
             State "
Wscript.Echo "--------------------------------------- --------------------
-------------- -------------"

' loop through all instances in collection
For each vm in vmcollecion
' decode system state, based on codes identified via trial and error
VMStateCode = vm.EnabledState
Select Case VMStateCode
        Case2VMState = "Running"
         Case3      VMState= "PowerOff"
         Case4      VMState = "ShuttingDown"
        Case10    VMState = "Reset"
        Case32768VMState= "Paused"
        Case32770VMState = "Starting"
Case32771VMState = "SnapshotInProgress"
```

```
        Case32772VMState = "Migrating"
        Case32773VMState= "Saving"
        Case32774VMState= "Stopping"
        Case32776VMState= "Pausing"
        Case32777VMState= "Resuming"
        Case32769VMState = "Saved"
Case Else VMState = "Unclassified (so far)"
End Select


' print out VM info state
Wscript.Echo VbCrLF
Wscript.Echo vm.ElementName & Space(40 - Len(vm.ElementName)) & _
 vm.Description & Space(35 - Len(vm.Description)) & _
VMState & " (" & VMStateCode & ")"


' request state change if appropriate - the host should never be eligible
if (VMState = "Running" or VMState = "Paused") and vm.Description <>
"Microsoft Hosting Computer System" Then
Wscript.Echo Space(40) & "Saving " & vm.ElementName

RequestReturn = vm.RequestStateChange(32769)


if RequestReturn = 4096 Then
Wscript.Echo Space(40) & "Save request submitted"
Else
Wscript.Echo Space(40) & "Something goofy happened (" & RequestReturn & ")"
End If
End If
Next
Wscript.Echo VbCrLF
```

For more information about the Virtualization WMI Provider and the 13 WMI classes that it provides, see http://msdn.microsoft.com/en-us/library/cc136992(VS.85).aspx.

Managing Virtual Machines Using PowerShell

You can use PowerShell to manage virtual machines running on Hyper-V servers running Server Core, but you must run your scripts remotely from a computer that has PowerShell installed on it. In addition, your PowerShell scripts can be used only to access the WMI interface on the targeted Server Core installation. This means that the primary PowerShell cmdlet you will use to manage virtual machines running on Server Core is the Get-WmiObject cmdlet, which also has the associated gwmi alias in PowerShell.

The following are a few examples of how you can use PowerShell scripts to manage virtual machines running on a Server Core installation. These scripts are presented as samples only and may need to be customized to work in your environment.

ListVMs.ps1—PowerShell Script That Displays the State of All VMs

```
$VMState=@{2="Running" ; 3="Stopped" ; 32768="Paused" ; 32769="Suspended";
 32270="Starting" ; 32771="Snapshotting" ; 32773="Saving" ; 32774="Stopping" }
get-wmiobject -computername localhost -Namespace root\Virtualization
-query "Select * from MSVM_Computersystem where Description like
'%Virtual%' " | format-table -autosize @{Label="VM Name";
expression={$_.elementName}}, Description, @{Label ="VM State";
expression={$VmState[$_.EnabledState]}}
```

CreateSnapshotAll.ps1—PowerShell Script That Creates a Snapshot of All VMs

```
$VSMgtSvc=Get-WmiObject -ComputerName localhost
-NameSpace "root\virtualization"
-Class "MsVM_virtualSystemManagementService"
get-wmiobject -computername localhost -Namespace root\Virtualization
-query "Select * from MSVM_Computersystem where Description like
'%Virtual%' " | foreach-object {$VSMgtSvc.psbase.invokeMethod
("CreateVirtualSystemSnapshot",@($_,$Null,$null)) }
```

SaveStateAll.ps1—PowerShell Script That Saves the State of All Running VMs

```
$VSMgtSvc=Get-WmiObject -ComputerName localhost -NameSpace "root\
virtualization" -Class "MsVM_virtualSystemManagementService"
Get-WmiObject -computername Localhost -NameSpace "root\virtualization"
-Query "Select * From MsVM_ComputerSystem Where Caption Like 'Virtual%'
and EnabledState = 2" | foreach-Object {$_.RequestStateChange(32769) }
```

Installing and Managing the AD LDS Role on Server Core

The Active Directory Lightweight Directory Services (AD LDS) server role is a Lightweight Directory Access Protocol (LDAP) directory service that can be used to provide directory services for directory-enabled applications without the need to implement an AD DS forest. The AD LDS role can be used to store private directory data that is relevant only to the application using a local directory service that can be hosted on the same server as the application or a different server. For more complex scenarios, AD LDS servers can also replicate directory data with one another.

A typical scenario for deploying the AD LDS role might be a Web portal application that provides extranet access to corporate business applications and services outside your corporate forest. Another scenario might be a hosting environment where a provider offers domain and storage services to clients using dedicated Web servers. The AD LDS role is a good choice for these kinds of scenarios because its authentication store can host user objects that are not Windows security principals but can be authenticated using simple LDAP.

Note   AD LDS was known as Active Directory Application Mode (ADAM) on the Windows Server 2003 platform.

Installing the AD LDS Role

The AD LDS server role can be installed on a stand-alone server, a member server, or a domain controller running Windows Server 2008. To install the AD LDS role on a Server Core installation, use the following command:

```
C:\Users\Administrator>start /w ocsetup DirectoryServices-ADAM-ServerCore
```

Verify the installation using Oclist as follows:

```
C:\Users\Administrator>oclist | find "    Installed"
    Installed:DirectoryServices-ADAM-ServerCore
```

If desired, you can also uninstall the AD LDS role by adding /**uninstall** to the first command.

Managing the AD LDS Role

To manage a Server Core installation running the AD LDS role, you must use one of the following:

- A Full installation of Windows Server 2008 that has the AD LDS role installed on it

- A Full installation of Windows Server 2008 that has RSAT installed on it

- A computer running Windows Vista SP1 on which you have downloaded and installed RSAT

Creating a New AD LDS Instance

Before you can manage the AD DLS role, you must create a new instance of the AD LDS. An *AD LDS instance* is a single running copy of the AD LDS. Multiple instances of AD LDS can run simultaneously on the same server, with each instance having its own unique directory data store, service name, and service description.

You must use the AdamInstall.exe command with an unattend file to create a new instance on a Server Core installation that has the AD LDS role installed. For example, the following unattend file can be used to create a unique AD LDS instance named CrmApplication on Server Core:

```
[ADAMInstall]
InstallType=Unique
InstanceName=CrmApplication
LocalLDAPPortToListenOn=389
NewApplicationPartitionToCreate="CN=crm,DC=fabrikam,DC=com"
DataFilesPath=C:\Program Files\Microsoft ADAM\CRM\data
```

```
LogFilesPath=C:\Program Files\Microsoft ADAM\CRM\data
ImportLDIFFiles="ms-inetorgperson.ldf" "ms-user.ldf"
```

The AD LDS instance created by this unattend file creates a new application partition called crm.fabrikam.com which listens for LDAP binds on TCP port 389. The directory database and log file paths are located in the C:\Program Files\Microsoft ADAM\CRM folder, and two Lightweight Directory Interchange Format (LDIF) files (ms-inetorgperson.ldf and ms-user.ldf) are imported into the schema for the new AD LDS instance.

To create an AD LDS instance using the unattend file described previously, open a command prompt on your Server Core installation, browse to the %SystemRoot%\ADAM directory, and do the following:

```
C:\Windows\ADAM>adaminstall /answer:J:\unattend.txt
Configure AD LDS
Copying...
Copying file adamntds.dit...
Copied files
Configuring...
Starting Active Directory Lightweight Directory Services installation
Validating user supplied options
Determining a site in which to install
Examining an existing configuration set...
Configuring the local computer to host Active Directory Lightweight
Directory Services
Creating directory partition: CN=Schema,CN=Configuration,CN={8FB717F8-
0930-4037-
811D-C81677849C7A}; 299 objects remaining
Creating directory partition: CN=Configuration,CN={8FB717F8-0930-4037-
811D-C8167
7849C7A}; 51 objects remaining
Creating directory partition: CN=Configuration,CN={8FB717F8-0930-4037-
811D-C8167
7849C7A}; 50 objects remaining
Creating directory partition: CN=Configuration,CN={8FB717F8-0930-4037-
811D-C8167
7849C7A}; 49 objects remaining
Creating directory partition: CN=Configuration,CN={8FB717F8-0930-4037-
811D-C8167
...
Creating directory partition: CN=Configuration,CN={8FB717F8-0930-4037-
811D-C8167
7849C7A}; 0 objects remaining
Creating directory partition: CN=Configuration,CN={8FB717F8-0930-4037-
811D-C8167
7849C7A}; 0 objects remaining
Creating directory partition: CN=Configuration,CN={8FB717F8-0930-4037-
811D-C8167
```

```
7849C7A}; 0 objects remaining
Creating directory partition: CN=Configuration,CN={8FB717F8-0930-4037-
811D-C8167
7849C7A}; 0 objects remaining
Creating Active Directory Lightweight Directory Services objects on the
local Active Directory Lightweight Directory Services instance
Creating directory partition: CN=crm,DC=fabrikam,DC=com; 8 objects remaining
Creating directory partition: CN=crm,DC=fabrikam,DC=com; 0 objects remaining
Completing Active Directory Lightweight Directory Services installation
Starting the AD LDS service...
Importing LDIF file ms-inetorgperson.ldf...
Importing LDIF file ms-user.ldf...
AD LDS Installed
You have successfully completed the Active Directory Lightweight Directory
 Services Setup Wizard.
```

To verify the successful creation of the new instance, open Registry Editor and browse to HKLM\Software\Microsoft\Windows\CurrentVersion. If a key named ADAM_Installer_Results is there, errors, warnings, or both were generated during the creation of the instance, and the values under this key will provide more information.

Managing the New Instance

To manage the new instance, you can use any of the following RSAT tools:

- Active Directory Sites and Services
- ADSI Edit
- Schema Manager

These tools are installed on your administrative workstation when you install the RSAT tools for AD LDS. For example, to connect to the crm.fabrikam.com application partition on a Server Core installation named SEA-SC1, perform the following steps:

1. Open the ADSI Edit console from Administrative Tools on an administrative workstation or server that has RSAT installed.

2. Right-click the root node in the console tree and select Connect To to open the Connection Settings dialog box.

3. Select the first option under Computer and type the instance name and LDAP listening port number with a colon between them. For example, type **SEA-SC1:389** to bind to TCP port 389 on server SEA-SC1.

4. Select the first option under Connection Point and type the distinguished name of the connection point you want to bind to in the directory. For example, type CN=crm,DC=fabrikam,DC=com to bind to the crm.fabrikam.com application partition, as shown here.

5. Configure additional connection settings as desired and click OK. The connection point is displayed under the root node of the console tree; expand this to display directory nodes beneath it, as shown here.

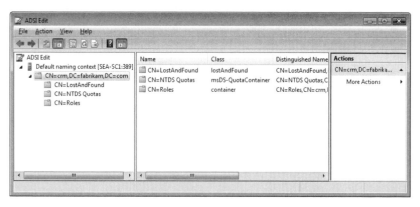

6. Repeat steps 2 through 5 to bind to other connection points in your partition or to bind to other AD LDS instances.

For more information about managing the AD LDS role, see the Step-by-Step guides for AD LDS in the Windows Server 2008 Technical Library on Microsoft TechNet at http://technet.microsoft.com/en-us/windowsserver/2008/default.aspx.

Installing and Managing the Streaming Media Services Role on Server Core

The Streaming Media Services role enables you to deploy Windows Server 2008 as a Windows Media server that can provide live streaming, on-demand digital Windows Media Audio (WMA) and Windows Media Video (WMV) content, or both over the network to computers and other media devices.

Installing the Streaming Media Services Role

The Streaming Media Services role is not available in-box on the release version of Windows Server 2008. Instead, you must download and apply a Microsoft Update stand-alone Package (.msu file) before you can install this role on your server. After applying this update package, you can add the Streaming Media Services role to your server in the usual way.

Downloading and Applying the Windows Media Services 2008 Update Package

To download and apply the update package for Windows Media Services 2008 on Server Core, perform the following steps:

1. On your administrative workstation, browse to *http://support.microsoft.com/kb/ 934518,* click the link provided, and download the appropriate .msu file from the Microsoft Download Center as follows:

   ❑ Download the file Windows6.0-KB934518-x86-Core.msu for 32-bit versions of Server Core.

   ❑ Download the file Windows6.0-KB934518-x64-Core.msu for 64-bit versions of Server Core.

2. Save the downloaded file onto removable storage such as a USB flash drive and use this device to copy the update to a folder such as C:\Temp on your Server Core installation.

3. Run the update on your Server Core installation to install the bits for Windows Media Services 2008 on your server. For example, do the following to install the bits on a 32-bit Server Core installation, type **Windows6.0-KB934518-x86-Core.msu** at the command prompt, click OK, read and accept the licensing terms, and click Close when the update is finished being applied.

   Alternatively, you can apply this update package silently (without prompts) by running the following command:

   start /w wusa /quiet Windows6.0-KB934518-x86-ServerCore.msu

Installing the Streaming Media Services Role on Server Core

Once you have applied the appropriate update package for Windows Media Services 2008, you can use Ocsetup to install the Streaming Media Services Role on Server Core like this:

```
C:\Users\Administrator>start /w ocsetup MediaServer
```

Verify the installation as follows:

```
C:\Users\Administrator>oclist | find "   Installed"
   Installed:MediaServer
```

Starting the Windows Media Services Service

After you install the Streaming Media Services role, you need to start the Windows Media Services service on the server. Use the Net Start command to do this as follows:

```
C:\Users\Administrator>net start wmserver
The Windows Media Services service is starting.
The Windows Media Services service was started successfully.
```

Managing the Streaming Media Services Role

To manage a Server Core installation running the Streaming Media Services role, you must use one of the following:

- A Full installation of Windows Server 2008 that has the Streaming Media Services role installed on it

- A Full installation of Windows Server 2008 that has RSAT installed on it, including the update package for the Windows Media Services Remote Server Administration Tools snap-in

- A computer running Windows Vista SP1 on which you have downloaded and installed RSAT, including the update package for the Windows Media Services Remote Server Administration Tools snap-in

Downloading and Applying the Windows Media Services Remote Server Administration Tools Update Package

To download and apply the update package (.msu file) for the Windows Media Services Remote Server Administration Tools snap-in onto an administrative workstation running Windows Vista SP1, perform the following steps:

1. On your administrative workstation, browse to *http://support.microsoft.com/kb/ 934518,* click the link provided, and download the appropriate .msu file from the Microsoft Download Center as follows:

❑ Download the file Windows6.0-KB934518-x86-Admin.msu for 32-bit versions of Windows Vista SP1.

❑ Download the file Windows6.0-KB934518-x64-Admin.msu for 64-bit versions of Windows Vista SP1.

2. Save the downloaded file into a folder such as C:\Temp on your administrative workstation.

3. Run the update on your administrative workstation. For example, to apply the update on a Windows Vista SP1 x32 workstation, type **start /w wusa /quiet Windows6.0-KB934518-x86-Admin.msu** at the command prompt.

Using the Windows Media Services Remote Server Administration Tools Snap-in

After applying the update package for the Windows Media Services Remote Server Administration Tools snap-in, you can use this snap-in on your administrative work-station to manage the Streaming Media Services role on a Server Core installation. For example, to connect to a Server Core installation that has the Streaming Media Services role installed, perform the following steps:

1. On your administrative workstation that has RSAT installed and the Windows Media Services 2008 update applied, click Start, Administrative Tools, and finally Windows Media Services to open the Windows Media Services console.

2. Right-click the root node in your console tree and select Add Server.

3. In the Add Server dialog box, type the name or Internet Protocol (IP) address of your Server Core installation, as shown here.

4. Click OK to connect to the Streaming Media Services role on your Server Core installation, as shown here.

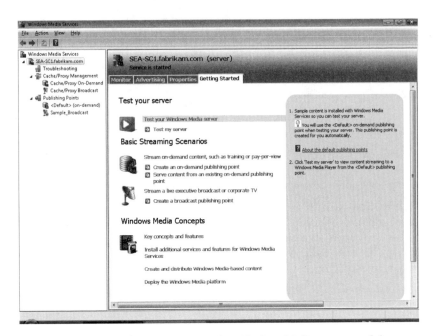

5. Repeat steps 3 and 4 to connect to other Windows Media servers, and then configure your media servers as desired.

For more information about managing the Streaming Media Services role, see the Windows Media Services Deployment Guide in the Windows Server 2008 Technical Library on Microsoft TechNet at http://technet.microsoft.com/en-us/windowsserver/ 2008/default.aspx.

Chapter 13
Maintaining Server Core

Once you've deployed and configured Server Core and installed the roles and features you need on it, you need to maintain the platform. This chapter deals with a number of different server maintenance issues, including managing services, devices and device drivers, processes, and scheduled tasks on Server Core. Also covered in this chapter are event logging, performance monitoring, backup and restore, installing software updates, and installing applications on Server Core.

The sections in this chapter assume that you are managing Server Core computers that belong to an Active Directory Domain Services (AD DS) domain. Additional configuration, such as opening Windows Firewall ports, may be required when trying to manage remotely Server Core computers that belong to a workgroup. For more information on managing stand-alone Server Core computers, see Chapter 6, "Remote Management."

This chapter focuses mainly on maintaining Server Core from the command line. For more information about performing many of these tasks using Microsoft Management Console (MMC) consoles and other graphical user interface (GUI) tools, see the companion title Windows Server 2008 Administrator's Pocket Consultant *by William Stanek (Microsoft Press, 2008).*

Managing Services

As described earlier in Chapter 1, "Examining Server Core," a Server Core installation of Windows Server 2008 has a reduced service footprint compared with a Full installation of the same platform. Having fewer running services means that Server Core has a smaller attack surface than the Full installation version. It also means simplified update management and fewer critical software updates to apply.

Managing Services from the Command Line

You can manage services locally on Server Core using two command-line tools:

- Net.exe commands like Net Start and Net Stop.

- Sc.exe commands like Sc Config, Sc Qc, Sc Query, Sc Start, Sc Stop, and others for interacting with the Service Control Manager (SCM).

Determining What Services Are Running

Table 1-1, shown in Chapter 1, lists the services installed by default on Server Core, the start mode for each service, and the security context under which each service runs. Installing roles and features on Server Core may install additional services on the platform. Depending on the role or feature being installed, these additional services may have their start mode configured as Automatic, Manual, or Disabled, and they may have their state configured as either Running or Stopped. In addition, installing roles and features may change the configuration (start mode, state, or both) of existing services on the computer.

To determine what services are currently running on a Server Core installation, type **net start** at the command prompt. You can also use this with the Fc command to determine what additional services are running after a particular role or feature has been installed. For example, to determine what additional services are running after you install the Print Services role on Server Core, do the following:

1. Type **net start > before.txt** to save the initial list of running services as a text file named Before.txt in the current directory.

2. Type **start /w ocsetup Printing-ServerCore-Role** to install the Print Services role.

3. Reboot the server to complete installation of the role, and then log on again as Administrator and type **net start > after.txt** to save the new list of running services as after.txt.

4. Use the Fc command to compare the two text files as follows:

```
C:\Users\administrator>fc before.txt after.txt
Comparing files before.txt and AFTER.TXT
***** before.txt
   Application Experience
   Background Intelligent Transfer Service
   Base Filtering Engine
***** AFTER.TXT
   Application Experience
   Base Filtering Engine
*****

***** before.txt
   Diagnostic Policy Service
   Diagnostic System Host
   Distributed Transaction Coordinator
   DNS Client
***** AFTER.TXT
   Diagnostic Policy Service
   DNS Client
*****

***** before.txt
   IPsec Policy Agent
   KtmRm for Distributed Transaction Coordinator
   Netlogon
***** AFTER.TXT
```

```
    IPsec Policy Agent
    Netlogon
*****

***** before.txt
    Plug and Play
    Remote Procedure Call (RPC)
***** AFTER.TXT
    Plug and Play
    Print Spooler
    Remote Procedure Call (RPC)
*****

***** before.txt
    Windows Management Instrumentation
    Windows Remote Management (WS-Management)
    Windows Time
    Windows Update
    Workstation
***** AFTER.TXT
    Windows Management Instrumentation
    Windows Modules Installer
    Windows Time
    Workstation
```

The results of running the Fc command indicate that installing the Print Services role results in two new services (Print Spooler and Windows Modules Installer) running on the computer and five existing services (Background Intelligent Transfer Service, Diagnostic System Host, Distributed Transaction Coordinator, KtmRm for Distributed Transaction Coordinator, and Windows Remote Management) that no longer run on the computer.

Note   Uninstalling a role or feature may not return Server Core to the identical service configuration that it had before that role or feature was installed. To see this in the case of the Print Services role cited previously, type **start /w ocsetup Printing-ServerCore-Role /uninstall** to remove the role, then reboot the computer, log on and type **net start > before2.txt**, and then type **fc before.txt before2.txt** and view the result.

Stopping and Starting Services

You can start or stop services on a Server Core computer using the Net Start and Net Stop commands. You can also use Net Start to determine whether a service is currently running. For example, to verify that the Background Intelligent Transfer Service (BITS) is currently running, use Net Start with Find like this:

```
C:\Users\administrator>net start | find "Background"
    Background Intelligent Transfer Service
```

To stop the service, use Net stop like this:

```
C:\Users\administrator>net stop BITS
The Background Intelligent Transfer Service service is stopping.
The Background Intelligent Transfer Service service was stopped
successfully.
```

Note that you must use the short name for the service (BITS) and not the display name (Background Intelligent Transfer Service) when stopping or starting services using Net Start. If you don't know the short name for a service and only know its display name (the service names displayed when you type **net start**), you can use the Sc Getkeyname command to find it like this:

```
C:\Users\administrator>sc getkeyname "Background Intelligent Transfer
Service"
[SC] GetServiceKeyName SUCCESS
Name = BITS
```

To restart the service after stopping it, do this:

```
C:\Users\administrator>net start BITS
The Background Intelligent Transfer Service service is starting.
The Background Intelligent Transfer Service service was started
successfully.
```

Displaying Service Configuration Information

You can display a list of active (running) services using either Net Start (as shown previously) or by using the Sc Query command. For example, to display a list of active services one screen at a time, type **sc query | more** at the command prompt. The output looks similar to this:

```
SERVICE_NAME: AppMgmt
SERVICE_NAME: AeLookupSvc
DISPLAY_NAME: Application Experience
        TYPE               : 20  WIN32_SHARE_PROCESS
        STATE              : 4   RUNNING
                                 (STOPPABLE, NOT_PAUSABLE, IGNORES_SHUT
        WIN32_EXIT_CODE    : 0   (0x0)
        SERVICE_EXIT_CODE  : 0   (0x0)
        CHECKPOINT         : 0x0
        WAIT_HINT          : 0x0

SERVICE_NAME: BFE
DISPLAY_NAME: Base Filtering Engine
        TYPE               : 20  WIN32_SHARE_PROCESS
        STATE              : 4   RUNNING
                                 (STOPPABLE, NOT_PAUSABLE, IGNORES_SHUT
        WIN32_EXIT_CODE    : 0   (0x0)
        SERVICE_EXIT_CODE  : 0   (0x0)
```

```
        CHECKPOINT         : 0x0
        WAIT_HINT          : 0x0

SERVICE_NAME: BITS
DISPLAY_NAME: Background Intelligent Transfer Service
        TYPE               : 20  WIN32_SHARE_PROCESS
-- More  --
```

Press Enter to display further output from the command one line at a time, or press the spacebar to display output one screenful at a time. Press Q to quit displaying output and return to the command prompt. For more information on using the More command, type **more /?** at the command prompt.

To display a list of inactive (stopped or paused) services installed on the computer, type **sc query state= inactive | more** at the command prompt. The output looks similar to this:

```
DISPLAY_NAME: Application Management
        TYPE               : 20  WIN32_SHARE_PROCESS
        STATE              : 1  STOPPED
        WIN32_EXIT_CODE    : 1077  (0x435)
        SERVICE_EXIT_CODE  : 0  (0x0)
        CHECKPOINT         : 0x0
        WAIT_HINT          : 0x0

SERVICE_NAME: Browser
DISPLAY_NAME: Computer Browser
        TYPE               : 20  WIN32_SHARE_PROCESS
        STATE              : 1  STOPPED
        WIN32_EXIT_CODE    : 1077  (0x435)
        SERVICE_EXIT_CODE  : 0  (0x0)
        CHECKPOINT         : 0x0
        WAIT_HINT          : 0x0

SERVICE_NAME: CertPropSvc
DISPLAY_NAME: Certificate Propagation
        TYPE               : 20  WIN32_SHARE_PROCESS
        STATE              : 1  STOPPED
        WIN32_EXIT_CODE    : 1077  (0x435)
-- More  --
```

To display detailed configuration information for a service such as the Application Management service (inactive in the previous command output), use the Sc Qc command like this:

```
C:\Users\administrator>sc qc AppMgmt
[SC] QueryServiceConfig SUCCESS

SERVICE_NAME: AppMgmt
        TYPE               : 20  WIN32_SHARE_PROCESS
```

```
START_TYPE              : 3    DEMAND_START
ERROR_CONTROL           : 1    NORMAL
BINARY_PATH_NAME        : C:\Windows\system32\svchost.exe -k netsvcs
LOAD_ORDER_GROUP        :
TAG                     : 0
DISPLAY_NAME            : Application Management
DEPENDENCIES            :
SERVICE_START_NAME : LocalSystem
```

From the previous command output, we can see that the Application Management service on this particular Server Core computer has its start mode configured as Manual (DEMAND START), is using the LocalSystem account as its security context, and has no dependencies upon other services. This is the same type of service information that you can display using the Services snap-in—see the section "Managing Services Using the Services Snap-in," later in this chapter.

Configuring the Start Mode for a Service

You can modify the start mode for a service using the Sc Config command. For example, to change the start mode for the Application Management service from Manual to Disabled, do this:

```
C:\Users\administrator>sc config AppMgmt start= disabled
[SC] ChangeServiceConfig SUCCESS
```

Verify the result:

```
C:\Users\administrator>sc qc AppMgmt | find "START_TYPE"
        START_TYPE              : 4    DISABLED
```

Change the start mode to Automatic as follows:

```
C:\Users\administrator>sc config AppMgmt start= auto
[SC] ChangeServiceConfig SUCCESS
```

Start the service using Sc start:

```
C:\Users\administrator>sc start AppMgmt

SERVICE_NAME: AppMgmt
        TYPE                    : 20   WIN32_SHARE_PROCESS
        STATE                   : 2    START_PENDING
                                       (NOT_STOPPABLE, NOT_PAUSABLE, IGNORES_SHUTDOWN)
        WIN32_EXIT_CODE         : 0    (0x0)
        SERVICE_EXIT_CODE       : 0    (0x0)
        CHECKPOINT              : 0x0
        WAIT_HINT               : 0x7d0
        PID                     : 868
        FLAGS                   :
```

Verify the service is running using Sc Query like this:

```
C:\Users\administrator>sc query AppMgmt | find "STATE"
        STATE         : 4  RUNNING
```

For more information about configuring the start mode for services and drivers, see the section "Displaying a List of Drivers," later in this chapter. For more information on using Sc to manage services, type **sc /?** at the command prompt.

Managing Services Using the Services Snap-in

You can also manage services on Server Core by using the Services MMC snap-in from a remote computer running either Windows Vista or Windows Server 2008. To do this, follow these steps:

1. On your Server Core computer, open the Remote Service Management rule group in Windows Firewall by typing **netsh advfirewall firewall set rule group="Remote Service Management" new enable=yes** at the command prompt.

2. On your management station, open Services from Administrative Tools, right-click the Services (Local) node, and select Connect To Another Computer.

3. Type the name of your Server Core computer or browse to find it in AD DS, then click OK, as shown here.

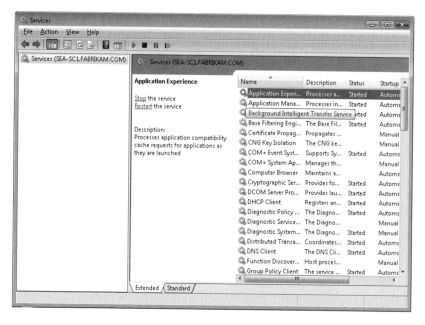

4. Now you can right-click services and view or modify their properties as desired in the usual way.

Managing Devices and Device Drivers

As described in Chapter 1, a Server Core installation of Windows Server 2008 includes only a minimal number of device drivers. The in-box device drivers that are included in Server Core are identical to those found on a Full installation of Windows Server 2008, but in Server Core, the only types of drivers included are those for storage devices, network adapters, and the standard Video Graphics Array (VGA) video driver. No print drivers or any other kinds of drivers are available in-box in Server Core. If you need drivers for any other types of devices, you must install them manually on your Server Core computer.

If you need to install printer drivers on Server Core, the easiest way to do this is to use the Print Management Console from a remote computer running Windows Vista SP 1 or Windows Server 2008. For more information, see the Print Management Step-by-Step Guide in the Windows Server 2008 Technical Library at http://technet.microsoft.com/ en-us/windowsserver/2008/default.aspx.

Server Core does include the Plug and Play (PnP) subsystem, however, and this means that if you want to install a device for which a driver already exists in-box in the driver store, all you need to do is plug the device into your system and the PnP subsystem automatically installs the driver. Because Server Core does not support balloon notifications, the only indication you may see that a driver is being installed is that the cursor changes to an hourglass.

You can manage devices and device drivers on Server Core in two ways:

■ You can add, remove, and enumerate drivers from the command prompt using tools like Driverquery, Sc, and Pnputil. This is the primary method for managing device drivers on Server Core.

■ You can use the Device Manager snap-in from a remote computer running Windows Vista or a Full installation of Windows Server 2008 to view information concerning devices and device drivers on a Server Core computer. Note that Device Manager is always read-only when used remotely.

Managing Devices from the Command Line

The available commands for managing device drivers from the command line on Server Core are as follows:

■ **Driverquery**   Displays a list of installed device drivers and their settings

■ **Pnputil**   Adds driver packages to the driver store or removes them from the store

■ **Sc**   View and manage system properties of services and drivers

Displaying a List of Drivers

You can enumerate and display a list of all installed device drivers by using the Driver-query command. For example, to view a complete list of device drivers on your Server Core computer, do this (the command output has been truncated here and in the other examples in this chapter):

```
C:\Users\administrator>driverquery
```

```
Module Name  Display Name            Driver Type   Link Date
============ ======================= ============= ======================
ACPI         Microsoft ACPI Driver   Kernel        1/18/2008 11:32:48 PM
adp94xx      adp94xx                 Kernel        4/24/2007 4:00:29 PM
adpahci      adpahci                 Kernel        5/1/2007 12:29:26 PM
adpu160m     adpu160m                Kernel        2/21/2007 12:04:35 PM
adpu320      adpu320                 Kernel        2/27/2007 6:03:08 PM
AFD          Ancilliary Function Dr  Kernel        1/18/2008 11:57:00 PM
...
Wdf01000     Kernel Mode Driver Fra  Kernel        1/18/2008 11:52:21 PM
WmiAcpi      Microsoft Windows Mana  Kernel        1/18/2008 11:32:47 PM
ws2ifsl      Winsock IFS driver      Kernel        1/18/2008 11:56:49 PM
```

Tip   You can also type **sc query type= driver** to display a list of drivers on your computer.

To display the output from Driverquery in list format, use the /fo parameter like this:

```
C:\Users\administrator>driverquery /fo:list
```

```
Module Name:     ACPI
Display Name:    Microsoft ACPI Driver
Driver Type:     Kernel
Link Date:       1/18/2008 11:32:48 PM

Module Name:     adp94xx
Display Name:    adp94xx
Driver Type:     Kernel
Link Date:       4/24/2007 4:00:29 PM
...
```

Tip   You can also display the output in comma-separated format and redirect the result to a text file by typing **driverquery /fo:csv > drivers.csv**, so that you can open the text file using Microsoft Office Excel running on another computer.

To display a list of signed drivers along with their .inf files, use the /si parameter like this:

```
C:\Users\administrator>driverquery /si /fo:list
```

```
DeviceName:      UMBus Enumerator
InfName:         umbus.inf
```

```
IsSigned:      TRUE
Manufacturer: Microsoft

DeviceName:    UMBus Root Bus Enumerator
InfName:       umbus.inf
IsSigned:      TRUE
Manufacturer: Microsoft

DeviceName:    Generic volume
InfName:       volume.inf
IsSigned:      TRUE
Manufacturer: Microsoft
...
```

To display detailed (verbose) information concerning drivers, including the driver filename and path, use the /v parameter like this:

```
C:\Users\administrator>driverquery /v /fo:list
```

```
Module Name:        ACPI
Display Name:       Microsoft ACPI Driver
Description:        Microsoft ACPI Driver
Driver Type:        Kernel
Start Mode:         Boot
State:              Running
Status:             OK
Accept Stop:        TRUE
Accept Pause:       FALSE
Paged Pool(bytes):  69,632
Code(bytes):        147,456
BSS(bytes):         0
Link Date:          1/18/2008 11:32:48 PM
Path:               C:\Windows\system32\drivers\acpi.sys
Init(bytes):        8,192
...
```

To configure the system properties of a driver, such as by modifying the start mode of a driver, use the Sc command in the same way that you used it earlier in this chapter to configure services—see the section "Configuring the Start Mode for a Service," earlier in this chapter, for more information. The possible start modes of drivers (and also of services) are listed in Table 13-1.

Table 1-1   Possible Start Modes of Drivers and Services

Value	Description
Boot	The device driver is loaded by the boot loader.
System	The device driver is started during kernel initialization.
Auto	The device driver or service automatically starts each time the computer is restarted and runs even when no one is logged on to the computer.

Table 1-1   Possible Start Modes of Drivers and Services

Value	Description
Demand	The device driver or service must be started manually.
Disabled	The device driver or service is installed but cannot be started.
Delayed-auto	The service starts automatically a short time after other auto services are started.

Installing Drivers Manually Using Pnputil

You can use Pnputil to install device drivers manually on Server Core. If the device you need to install did not come with driver media, you need to obtain a driver first—see the section "Obtaining Drivers for Devices," later in this chapter, for information on how to do this.

For example, to install the Dell SAS 5-E Storage Adapter from LSI Corporation (driver files lsi_sas.inf and lsi_sas.sys), follow these steps:

1. Begin by copying the driver files to a folder such as C:\Driver on your Server Core computer.

2. You now have a choice of either adding the package to the driver store and then connecting the device and letting the PnP subsystem install the driver, or, if the device is already connected, you can add the driver to the store and install it in one step.

   ❑ If you choose the first approach, type the following command:

   ```
   C:\Users\administrator>pnputil -a C:\driver\lsi_sas.inf
   Microsoft PnP Utility

   Processing inf : lsi_sas.inf
   Driver package added successfully.
   Published name : oem0.inf
   ```

   Then connect the device and the driver should install automatically.

   ❑ If you choose the second approach, type the following command:

   ```
   C:\Users\administrator>pnputil -i -a C:\driver\lsi_sas.inf
   Microsoft PnP Utility

   Processing inf : lsi_sas.inf
   Successfully installed the driver on a device on the system.
   Driver package added successfully.
   Published name : oem0.inf
   ```

   Once this command runs, the PnP service automatically rescans the system and binds the driver to the connected hardware. If the driver is signed, this is a silent process. If the driver is unsigned, a warning message will be displayed.

3. Verify the previous commands by enumerating all third-party drivers in the store like this:

```
C:\Users\administrator>pnputil -e
Microsoft PnP Utility

Published name : oem0.inf
Driver package provider : LSI Corporation
Class : Storage controllers
Driver version and date : 04/08/2008 1.27.03.00
Signer name : microsoft windows hardware compatibility publisher

Published name : oem1.inf
Driver package provider : LSI Corporation
Class : System devices
Driver version and date : 03/26/2008 0.0.5.0
Signer name : microsoft windows hardware compatibility publisher
```

4. If you need to delete the drivers from the store later, do this:

```
C:\Users\administrator>pnputil -d oem0.inf && pnputil -d oem1.inf
Microsoft PnP Utility

Driver package deleted successfully.
Microsoft PnP Utility

Driver package deleted successfully.
```

For more information on using Pnputil to manage drivers, type **pnputil /?** at the command prompt.

Obtaining Drivers for Devices

If your device manufacturer did not supply a driver for your device, try the manufacturer's Web site. If this doesn't work, check the Microsoft Update Catalog to see if a driver is available for that device. To find drivers for devices using the Microsoft Update Catalog, follow these steps:

1. From a management workstation, browse to the URL *http://catalog.update. microsoft.com/v7/site/Home.aspx* using Internet Explorer.

2. In the Start Your Search box, enter a description of the type of device for which you are searching for drivers. For example, you could type **Windows Server 2008 storage drivers**.

3. Scroll to find the driver you need (if available) and click the Add button beside it.

4. Repeat the previous steps for as many drivers as you need.

5. Click the View Basket link under the search box and verify that you have found all the drivers you need.

6. Click Download, and then browse to and select the folder on your hard drive where you want to download the drivers.

7. Click Continue, and when the progress indicator indicates the download is completed, click Close.

8. Extract the driver files from the cabinet file that you downloaded. These typically are one or more text files with the .inf file extension, and one or more binary .sys files. If there is a Readme.txt file, read it so you can determine which driver files are needed for installation on your server's architecture (x86, x64, or IA64) or for the particular version of the device that you want to install.

9. Save the driver files you need in a folder and copy the folder onto removable storage.

10. Copy this folder onto your Server Core computer and install the driver using Pnputil as described in the previous section of this chapter.

For more information on using the Microsoft Update Catalog, see http://catalog.update. microsoft.com/v7/site/Faq.aspx.

Managing Devices Using the Device Manager Snap-in

You can use the Device Manager snap-in to manage devices remotely on a Server Core installation from a computer running Windows Vista SP1 or a Full installation of Windows Server 2008. However, you can only view device settings; you cannot change them because Device Manager runs in read-only mode when operating remotely like this. If you need to modify device settings, such as by installing or removing device drivers, you must do this using the methods using command-line tools outlined in the previous section.

The steps you need to perform to allow the Device Manager snap-in to administer Server Core remotely are as follows:

1. On your Server Core computer, enable the Remote Administration rule group in Windows Firewall by typing **netsh advfirewall firewall set rule group="Remote Administration" new enable=yes** at the command prompt.

2. On a management station running either Windows Vista SP1 or the Full installation of Windows Server 2008, open a new MMC console by pressing the Windows key + R, typing **mmc**, and clicking OK.

3. Click File, and then click Add/Remove Snap-in to open the Add Or Remove Snap-ins dialog box, and then double-click Group Policy Object Editor to display the Group Policy Wizard.

4. Click Browse, select Another Computer, and type or browse to the name of your Server Core computer. Click Finish and then click OK.

5. Using the Group Policy Object Editor connected to your Server Core computer, browse the console tree to find and enable the following policy setting:

   Computer Configuration\Policies\Administrative Templates\System\Device Installation\Allow Remote Access To The PnP Interface.

6. Close the Group Policy Object Editor. Then, on your Server Core computer, type **shutdown –r –t 0** at the command prompt to restart the computer.

7. Once your Server Core computer has finished restarting, return to your management station and open a new MMC console by pressing the Windows key + R, typing **mmc**, and clicking OK. Alternatively, you can use the MMC console that you opened previously in step 2.

8. Click File, and then click Add/Remove Snap-in to open the Add Or Remove Snap-ins dialog box, and then double-click Device Manager to display the Device Manager dialog box.

9. Select Another Computer and type or browse to the name of your Server Core computer. Click Finish and then click OK.

10. Click the Device Manager On *<name of Server Core computer>* node, and then click OK when the dialog box appears saying Device Manager is running in read-only mode.

11. Expand the console tree to display the different device types on your Server Core computer, as shown here.

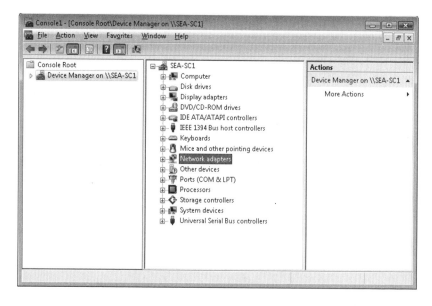

12. Expand a device type to display the installed devices, then right-click a device and select Properties to view the device settings in read-only mode, as shown here.

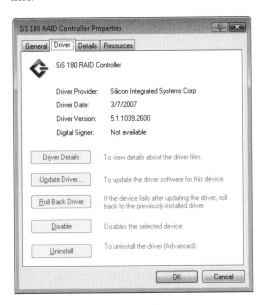

13. Click the View menu to display devices by type or connection, resources by type or connection, or to show hidden devices as desired.

Managing Processes

You can manage processes running on a Server Core computer. For example, you can display a list of running processes, start a new process, change the priority of a running process, and stop a process forcibly if needed. While the GUI tool Task Manager can be used on Server Core to perform many of these tasks, this section focuses on managing processes from the command line using commands like Tasklist, Taskkill, and Start.

The Windows Sysinternals tools also include Process Explorer, Process Monitor, and other tools for managing processes. You can find out more about and download the Windows Sysinternals tools from Microsoft TechNet at http://technet.microsoft.com/en-us/sysinternals/default.aspx.

Displaying Processes and Process Details

You can display a list of running processes on a Server Core computer by using the Tasklist command as follows:

```
C:\Users\administrator>tasklist
```

Image Name	PID	Session Name	Session#	Mem Usage
System Idle Process	0	Services	0	24 K
System	4	Services	0	996 K
smss.exe	320	Services	0	688 K
csrss.exe	388	Services	0	4,580 K
csrss.exe	432	Console	1	9,572 K
wininit.exe	440	Services	0	3,816 K
winlogon.exe	468	Console	1	4,108 K
services.exe	516	Services	0	6,044 K
lsass.exe	528	Services	0	8,824 K
lsm.exe	536	Services	0	3,636 K
svchost.exe	692	Services	0	5,084 K
svchost.exe	748	Services	0	5,252 K
svchost.exe	840	Services	0	6,712 K
svchost.exe	864	Services	0	6,900 K
svchost.exe	876	Services	0	20,392 K
SLsvc.exe	892	Services	0	8,792 K
svchost.exe	948	Services	0	6,996 K
svchost.exe	1008	Services	0	18,516 K
svchost.exe	1152	Services	0	8,924 K
spoolsv.exe	1352	Services	0	8,208 K
svchost.exe	1396	Services	0	4,856 K
svchost.exe	1408	Services	0	3,324 K
taskeng.exe	1712	Services	0	6,228 K
svchost.exe	1860	Services	0	3,068 K
taskeng.exe	2020	Console	1	6,116 K
cmd.exe	368	Console	1	2,332 K
msdtc.exe	828	Services	0	6,720 K
WmiPrvSE.exe	2008	Services	0	7,056 K
cmd.exe	724	Console	1	1,936 K
tasklist.exe	820	Console	1	4,560 K

In this command output, the process with process ID (PID) number 692 is an Svchost.exe process—that is, a generic host process name for services that run from dynamic-link libraries (DLLs). You can display a list of the services running within this host process by doing the following:

```
C:\Users\administrator>tasklist /svc /fi "PID eq 692"
```

Image Name	PID	Services
svchost.exe	692	DcomLaunch, PlugPlay

This command output indicates that two services, the DCOM Server Process Launcher and the Plug and Play services, are running within this host process. To display a list of all the modules (that is, DLLs) being used by these services (and hence by the host process itself), do the following:

```
C:\Users\administrator>tasklist /m /fi "PID eq 692"
```

```
Image Name                       PID Modules
========================= ======== =================================================
svchost.exe                      692 ntdll.dll, kernel32.dll, msvcrt.dll,
                                     ADVAPI32.dll, RPCRT4.dll, umpnpmgr.dll,
                                     USER32.dll, GDI32.dll, USERENV.dll,
                                     Secur32.dll, IMM32.DLL, MSCTF.dll, LPK.DLL,
                                     USP10.dll, POWRPROF.dll, GPAPI.dll,
                                     slc.dll, rpcss.dll, WS2_32.dll, NSI.dll,
                                     FirewallAPI.dll, OLEAUT32.dll, ole32.dll,
                                     VERSION.dll, credssp.dll, CRYPT32.dll,
                                     MSASN1.dll, schannel.dll, NETAPI32.dll,
                                     PSAPI.DLL, CLBCatQ.DLL, SETUPAPI.dll,
                                     apphelp.dll, NTMARTA.DLL, WLDAP32.dll,
                                     SAMLIB.dll, WINSTA.dll, Cabinet.dll
```

This command output indicates that one of the DLLs being used by this process is Slc.dll. To view a list of all processes currently using this DLL, do the following:

```
C:\Users\administrator>tasklist /fi "MODULES eq slc.dll"
```

```
Image Name                       PID Session Name        Session#    Mem Usage
========================= ======== ================ =========== ============
winlogon.exe                     468 Console                   1      4,108 K
lsass.exe                        528 Services                  0      8,824 K
svchost.exe                      692 Services                  0      5,124 K
svchost.exe                      840 Services                  0      6,736 K
svchost.exe                      864 Services                  0      6,900 K
svchost.exe                      876 Services                  0     20,448 K
SLsvc.exe                        892 Services                  0      8,792 K
svchost.exe                      948 Services                  0      6,984 K
svchost.exe                     1008 Services                  0     18,520 K
svchost.exe                     1152 Services                  0      8,924 K
spoolsv.exe                     1352 Services                  0      8,208 K
taskeng.exe                     1712 Services                  0      6,228 K
taskeng.exe                     2020 Console                   1      6,116 K
```

To display all processes running within session 1 and format the output in list style instead of the default table style, use the following command:

```
C:\Users\administrator>tasklist /fi "SESSION eq 1" /fo LIST
```

```
Image Name:   csrss.exe
PID:          432
```

```
Session Name: Console
Session#:      1
Mem Usage:     9,640 K

Image Name:    winlogon.exe
PID:           468
Session Name: Console
Session#:      1
Mem Usage:     4,108 K

Image Name:    taskeng.exe
PID:           2020
Session Name: Console
Session#:      1
Mem Usage:     6,116 K

Image Name:    cmd.exe
PID:           368
Session Name: Console
Session#:      1
Mem Usage:     2,332 K

Image Name:    cmd.exe
PID:           724
Session Name: Console
Session#:      1
Mem Usage:     1,936 K

Image Name:    notepad.exe
PID:           1992
Session Name: Console
Session#:      1
Mem Usage:     3,820 K

Image Name:    tasklist.exe
PID:           1648
Session Name: Console
Session#:      1
Mem Usage:     4,600 K
```

Stopping a Process

To list all processes that are currently in the Running state, do this:

```
C:\Users\administrator>tasklist /fi "STATUS eq RUNNING"
```

Image Name	PID	Session Name	Session#	Mem Usage
taskeng.exe	2020	Console	1	6,116 K

```
cmd.exe                             368 Console                  1      2,332 K
cmd.exe                             724 Console                  1      1,936 K
notepad.exe                        1992 Console                  1      3,832 K
```

To stop the process with PID number 368, do this:

```
C:\Users\administrator>taskkill /pid 368
```

Verify the result as follows:

```
C:\Users\administrator>tasklist /fi "STATUS eq RUNNING"

Image Name                         PID Session Name        Session#    Mem Usage
========================= ======== ================ =========== =============
taskeng.exe                       2020 Console                  1      6,128 K
cmd.exe                            724 Console                  1      1,944 K
notepad.exe                       1992 Console                  1      5,652 K
```

Now try to stop the System process that has PID number 4 by doing this:

```
C:\Users\administrator>taskkill /pid 4
ERROR: The process with PID 4 could not be terminated.
Reason: This process can only be terminated forcefully (with /F option).
```

This command output indicates that some processes can be terminated forcefully only by including the /f parameter in the command. Doing this gives this result:

```
C:\Users\administrator>taskkill /pid 4 /f
ERROR: The process with PID 4 could not be terminated.
Reason: Access is denied.
```

The System process cannot be killed.

Attempt to stop another operating system process, the Software Licensing Service (Slsvc.exe), as follows:

```
C:\Users\administrator>taskkill /pid 892 /f
SUCCESS: The process with PID 892 has been terminated.
```

Verify the result as follows:

```
C:\Users\administrator>tasklist | find "slsvc"

C:\Users\administrator>
```

Caution   While some operating system processes can be terminated, it's not a good idea to do so because it usually leads to system instability.

Starting a Process

To start a new process, use the Start command. For example, to start a new instance of Notepad, type **start notepad** at the command prompt. To start a new instance of the command prompt, type **start cmd** at the command prompt.

> **Tip** You can also simply type **start** to open a new instance of the command prompt process.

Managing Scheduled Tasks

Scheduled tasks are commands or programs that run at a predetermined time or under predefined conditions. The event or condition that causes a task to run is known as the task's *trigger*, while the command or program that executes when the conditions of the trigger are met is known as the task's *action*. You can create and manage scheduled tasks on a Server Core computer in two ways:

- From the command line, using the Schtasks command

- Using the Task Scheduler snap-in running on a remote computer that has Windows Vista SP 1 or Windows Server 2008 installed

> **Note** The At command is an older command-line tool for scheduling tasks that has been superseded by the newer Schtasks command. Microsoft recommends that you use Schtasks instead of At when managing scheduled tasks from the command line.

Managing Scheduled Tasks from the Command Line

You can use the Schtasks command to create, configure, modify, run, or delete scheduled tasks on Server Core. When creating and configuring scheduled tasks, remember the following:

- You must have the appropriate permissions to run the command. You must be a member of the local Administrators group on the computer to manage all tasks on the local computer. You can also manage tasks remotely using the /u parameter if you are a member of the local Administrators group on the computer on which you are scheduling the task.

- The task itself must have the appropriate permissions to run on the computer. The needed permissions vary depending on the task. By default, tasks run with the permissions of either the current user of the computer on which you are configuring the task, or with the permissions of the user specified using the /u parameter if one is included. To run a task with permissions of a different user or with system permissions, use the /ru parameter.

Viewing Scheduled Tasks

To view a list of scheduled tasks on the computer, use the Schtasks /query command as follows:

```
C:\Users\administrator>schtasks /query

Folder: \
TaskName                                    Next Run Time          Status
================================= ==================== ==============
INFO: There are no scheduled tasks presently available at your access level.

Folder: \Microsoft
TaskName                                    Next Run Time          Status
================================= ==================== ==============
INFO: There are no scheduled tasks presently available at your access level.

Folder: \Microsoft\Windows
TaskName                                    Next Run Time          Status
================================= ==================== ==============
INFO: There are no scheduled tasks presently available at your access level.

Folder: \Microsoft\Windows\CertificateServicesClient
TaskName                                    Next Run Time          Status
================================= ==================== ==============
SystemTask                                  N/A                    Running
UserTask                                    N/A                    Running
UserTask-Roam                               N/A                    Ready

Folder: \Microsoft\Windows\Customer Experience Improvement Program
TaskName                                    Next Run Time          Status
================================= ==================== ==============
Consolidator                                6/27/2008 6:00:00 PM   Could not start

Folder: \Microsoft\Windows\Customer Experience Improvement Program\Server
TaskName                                    Next Run Time          Status
================================= ==================== ==============
ServerCeipAssistant                         6/29/2008 2:59:53 AM   Ready
ServerRoleCollector                         6/29/2008 1:14:03 AM   Ready
...
```

The tasks displayed in the command output shown here are default tasks that are created by Microsoft Windows. For more information about these default scheduled tasks, see *http://support.microsoft.com/kb/939039* in the Microsoft Knowledge Base.

> **Tip** You can also simply type **schtasks** to display all scheduled tasks using the default table view.

To display verbose (detailed) information concerning all scheduled tasks, use the /v parameter as follows:

```
C:\Users\administrator>schtasks /query /v /fo LIST > mytasks.txt
```

You should use /v with either /fo LIST or /fo CSV and redirect the output to a text file so you can examine it later. The detailed information for a task looks something like this:

```
Folder: \Microsoft\Windows\Customer Experience Improvement Program
HostName:                               SEA-SC1
TaskName:                               \Microsoft\Windows\Customer Experien
ce Improvement Program\Consolidator
Next Run Time:                          6/27/2008 6:00:00 PM
Status:                                 Could not start
Logon Mode:                             Interactive/Background
Last Run Time:                          6/27/2008 8:20:49 AM
Last Result:                            -2147479295
Author:                                 Microsoft Corporation
Task To Run:                            %SystemRoot%\System32\wsqmcons.exe
Start In:                               N/A
Comment:                                If the user has consented to partici
pate in the Windows Customer Experience Improvement Program, this job coll
ects and sends usage data to Microsoft.
Scheduled Task State:                   Enabled
Idle Time:                              Disabled
Power Management:
Run As User:                            SYSTEM
Delete Task If Not Rescheduled:         Enabled
Stop Task If Runs X Hours and X Mins:   72:00:00
Schedule:                               Scheduling data is not available in
this format.
Schedule Type:                          One Time Only, Hourly
Start Time:                             12:00:00 AM
Start Date:                             1/2/2004
End Date:                               N/A
Days:                                   N/A
Months:                                 N/A
Repeat: Every:                          19 Hour(s), 0 Minute(s)
Repeat: Until: Time:                    None
Repeat: Until: Duration:                Disabled
Repeat: Stop If Still Running:          Disabled
```

Tip   Instead of redirecting output to a text file, you can pipe it to the More command instead.

Creating a New Task

You can use the Schtasks /create command to create a new task from the command prompt. The syntax for creating a new task is as follows:

```
schtasks /create /sc <ScheduleType> /tn <TaskName> /tr <TaskRun>
[/s <Computer> [/u [<Domain>\]<User> [/p <Password>]]]
[/ru {[<Domain>\]<User> | System}] [/rp <Password>] [/mo <Modifier>]
[/d <Day>[,<Day>...] | *] [/m <Month>[,<Month>...]] [/i <IdleTime>]
[/st <StartTime>] [/ri <Interval>] [{/et <EndTime> | /du <Duration>}
[/k]] [/sd <StartDate>] [/ed <EndDate>] [/it] [/z] [/f]
```

The Schtasks /create command provides a lot of flexibility for specifying the condition under which a task runs. For example, using this command, you can create tasks that run:

- Immediately

- Only once, at the date and time specified

- Periodically, every *N* minutes, hours, days, weeks, or months

- Periodically, on a specific day of the week or month, on a specific date each month, on the last day of each month, and so on

- Every time the system starts, a user logs on, or the system is idle

For example, to create a scheduled task that runs a program to perform a database inspection every second Friday at midnight local time, do the following:

```
C:\Users\administrator>schtasks /create /tn Inspection /tr
C:\DatabaseTools\Inspect.exe /sc weekly /mo 2 /d FRI /st 00:00
SUCCESS: The scheduled task "Inspection" has successfully been created.
```

Verify the result as follows:

```
C:\Users\administrator>schtasks /query /fo LIST | more

Folder: \
HostName:      SEA-SC1
TaskName:      \Inspection
Next Run Time: 7/11/2008 00:00:00 AM
Status:        Ready
Logon Mode:    Interactive only
...
```

For more information concerning the syntax for creating tasks, type **schtasks /create** /? at the command prompt.

Tip   If you need a scheduled task to run multiple commands, add the commands to a batch file and create a scheduled task to run the batch file.

Modifying an Existing Task

To change the credentials under which the task created in the previous section runs to the LocalSystem account, use Schtasks /change like this:

```
C:\Users\administrator>schtasks /change /tn Inspection /ru System
SUCCESS: The parameters of scheduled task "Inspection" have been changed.
```

To change the credentials under which this task runs to the built-in Administrator account in the fabrikam.com domain, do this:

```
C:\Users\administrator>schtasks /change /tn Inspection /ru
FABRIKAM\Administrator /rp Pa$$w0ord
SUCCESS: The parameters of scheduled task "Inspection" have been changed.
```

For more information on modifying existing tasks, type **schtasks /change /?** at the command prompt.

Running Tasks and Ending Running Tasks

To run a task immediately, use Schtasks /run like this:

```
C:\Users\administrator>schtasks /run /tn Inspection
SUCCESS: Attempted to run the scheduled task "Inspection".
```

To end the running task, use Schtasks /end like this:

```
C:\Users\administrator>schtasks /end /tn Inspection
SUCCESS: The scheduled task "Inspection" has been terminated successfully.
```

Deleting a Task

To delete the task from the Task Scheduler database, use Schtasks /delete like this:

```
C:\Users\administrator>schtasks /delete /tn Inspection
WARNING: Are you sure you want to remove the task "Inspection" (Y/N)? Y
SUCCESS: The scheduled task "Inspection" has been terminated successfully.
```

For more information about using the Schtasks command, type **schtasks /?** at the command prompt.

Managing Scheduled Tasks Using the Task Scheduler Snap-in

You can use the Task Scheduler snap-in from a remote computer to create, modify, run, and delete scheduled tasks on a Server Core computer. The remote computer must be running either Windows Vista SP1 or a Full installation of Windows Server 2008.

To use the Task Scheduler snap-in to manage scheduled tasks on a Server Core computer, perform these steps:

1. On your Server Core computer, enable the Remote Administration, Remote Scheduled Tasks Management, and Remote Event Log Management rule groups in Windows Firewall by typing the following commands at the command prompt:

netsh advfirewall firewall set rule group="Remote Administration" new enable=yes

netsh advfirewall firewall set rule group="Remote Scheduled Tasks Management" new enable=yes

netsh advfirewall firewall set rule group="Remote Event Log Management" new enable=yes

> **Note**   The Remote Event Log Management rule group must be enabled to collect and display information in the History tab of tasks.

2. On a management station running either Windows Vista SP1 or the Full installation of Windows Server 2008, open a new MMC console by pressing the Windows key + R, typing **mmc**, and clicking OK.

3. Click File, and then click Add/Remove Snap-in to open the Add Or Remove Snap-ins dialog box, and then double-click Task Scheduler to display the Select Computer dialog box.

4. Select Another Computer and type or browse to the name of your Server Core computer. Click Finish and then click OK.

5. Expand the console tree to view scheduled tasks on your Server Core computer, as shown here.

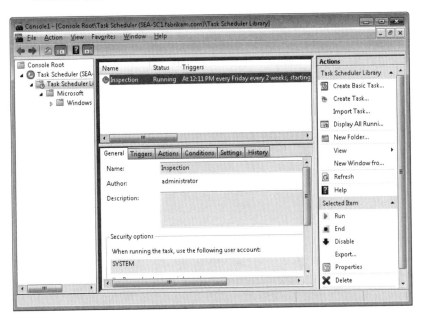

6. Manage existing scheduled tasks or create new ones as desired. For example:

   ❑ Select a task in the upper portion of the middle pane and then click the tabs for the task in the lower portion of the middle pane to view the properties for the task.

   ❑ Right-click the task and select Properties to open the properties for the task, then modify task properties as desired.

   ❑ Right-click the task and select Run to run the task immediately, End to stop a running task, Disable to prevent the task from running, or Delete to remove the task permanently.

   ❑ Right-click the task and select Export to export the task configuration as an Extensible Markup Language (XML) file that can later be imported into the Task Scheduler console running on a different computer.

   ❑ Expand the folders in the console tree to view or modify the properties of the default scheduled tasks. You can also right-click a node in the console tree and select New Folder to create your own folders for organizing any scheduled tasks you create.

   ❑ Right-click a folder in the console tree and select Create Basic Task to start a wizard that lets you create a scheduled task, or select Create Task to open a properties sheet for a new, unconfigured task you may create.

   ❑ Click any link in the Actions pane to create new tasks and perform other actions.

Event Logging

The Windows Event logs are a useful tool for monitoring and troubleshooting servers running Windows. The event log files (.evtx files) are located in the %SystemRoot%\System32\Winevt\Logs folder, and these files store event information as a stream of binary XML records. You can view and examine events in these logs on Server Core computers in two ways:

■ From the command line, using the Wevtutil command

■ Using Event Viewer running on a remote computer that has Windows Vista SP1 or Windows Server 2008 installed

You can also configure event subscriptions to forward events from a Server Core computer and store them on a central server for analysis and archiving purposes.

You also can use System Center Operations Manager (SCOM) 2007 to centralize event logging and analysis for Server Core computers. For more information about monitoring computers running Windows Server 2008 using SCOM 2007, search the Microsoft Download Center at http://www.microsoft.com/downloads/ *for the datasheet titled "Monitoring Your Windows Server 2008 Infrastructure."*

Viewing Events from the Command Line

You can use the Windows Events command-line utility Wevtutil to view and examine events locally from the command prompt on a Server Core computer. Using the Wevtutil command, you can perform common administrative tasks such as the following:

- Enumerating names of event logs
- Displaying the status of event logs
- Viewing and modifying the configuration of event logs
- Querying for specific events in an event log
- Exporting, archiving, and clearing event logs

Enumerating the Names of All Event Logs

To list the names of all event logs on a system, use the el (enum-logs) with Wevtutil as follows:

```
C:\Users\administrator>wevtutil el
Application
DNS Server
HardwareEvents
Internet Explorer
Key Management Service
Security
System
EndpointMapper
ForwardedEvents
Microsoft-Windows-ADSI/Debug
Microsoft-Windows-Bits-Client/Analytic
Microsoft-Windows-Bits-Client/Operational
...
Microsoft-Windows-WMI-Activity/Trace
Microsoft-Windows-WUSA/Debug
Setup
```

In addition to the standard Windows event logs (Application, Security, and System), you should see the following:

- **Setup log**   Used to store events related to application setup
- **Forwarded Events log**   Used to store events collected from remote computers using event subscriptions
- **Applications And Services logs**   Used to store events from a single application or component installed on the computer

Applications And Services logs in the previous command output include the DNS Server, HardwareEvents, Internet Explorer, and Key Management Service logs; and the various Admin, Analytic, Debug, Operational, and Trace logs found in component subfolders under the \Microsoft\Windows folder. For example, the Microsoft-Windows-TaskScheduler\Operational log can be used for analyzing and diagnosing problems or occurrences having to do with Scheduled Tasks on the computer.

Displaying the Status of an Event Log

You can display status information of an event log, such as the number of events in the log, by using the gli (get-loginfo) parameter. For example, to view status information for the System log, do this:

```
C:\Users\administrator>wevtutil gli System
creationTime: 2008-06-24T23:06:57.718Z
lastAccessTime: 2008-06-24T23:06:57.718Z
lastWriteTime: 2008-06-30T13:19:35.859Z
fileSize: 1118208
attributes: 32
numberOfLogRecords: 716
oldestRecordNumber: 1
```

Viewing and Modifying the Configuration of an Event Log

You can view the configuration of an event log, such as the maximum size of the log file, by using the gl (get-log) parameter. For example, to display the configuration of the Application log, do this:

```
C:\Users\administrator>wevtutil gl Application
name: Application
enabled: true
type: Admin
owningPublisher:
isolation: Application
channelAccess: O:BAG:SYD:(A;;0xf0007;;;SY)(A;;0x7;;;BA)(A;;0x7;;;SO)
(A;;0x3;;;IU)(A;;0x3;;;SU)(A;;0x3;;;S-1-5-3)(A;;0x3;;;S-1-5-33)
(A;;0x1;;;S-1-5-32-573)
logging:
  logFileName: %SystemRoot%\System32\Winevt\Logs\Application.evtx
  retention: false
  autoBackup: false
  maxSize: 20971520
publishing:
```

You can modify the configuration of a log file. For example, to increase the maximum size of the Application log to 100 megabytes (MB), enable retention so that the oldest events are dropped to make room for new events when the log becomes full, and automatically back up the log when it becomes full, type **wevtutil sl Application /ms:104857600 /rt:true /ab:true** at the command prompt. Then use Wevtutil gl again to verify the result as follows:

```
C:\Users\administrator>wevtutil gl Application
name: Application
```

```
enabled: true
type: Admin
owningPublisher:
isolation: Application
channelAccess: O:BAG:SYD:(A;;0xf0007;;;SY)(A;;0x7;;;BA)(A;;0x7;;;SO)
(A;;0x3;;;IU)(A;;0x3;;;SU)(A;;0x3;;;S-1-5-3)(A;;0x3;;;S-1-5-33)
(A;;0x1;;;S-1-5-32-573)
logging:
  logFileName: %SystemRoot%\System32\Winevt\Logs\Application.evtx
  retention: true
  autoBackup: true
  maxSize: 104857600
publishing:
```

Querying for Specific Events in an Event Log

You can query an event log for a specific event or type of event by using the qe (query-events) parameter. For example, to display the most recent two events in the System log in plain text format, use the /rd switch to set the read direction to True (meaning most recent events are returned first) as follows:

```
C:\Users\administrator>wevtutil qe System /c:2 /rd:true /f:text
Event[0]:
  Log Name: System
  Source: Microsoft-Windows-DistributedCOM
  Date: 2008-06-30T10:06:08.000
  Event ID: 10029
  Task: N/A
  Level: Information
  Opcode: N/A
  Keyword: Classic
  User: N/A
  User Name: N/A
  Computer: SEA-SC1.fabrikam.com
  Description:
DCOM  started the service TrustedInstaller with arguments ""
in order to run the server:
{752073A1-23F2-4396-85F0-8FDB879ED0ED}

Event[1]:
  Log Name: System
  Source: Microsoft-Windows-TBS
  Date: 2008-06-30T08:21:49.810
  Event ID: 537
  Task: N/A
  Level: Information
  Opcode: Info
  Keyword: N/A
  User: S-1-5-19
```

```
User Name: NT AUTHORITY\LOCAL SERVICE
Computer: SEA-SC1.fabrikam.com
Description:
A compatible Trusted Platform Module (TPM) Security Device cannot be
found on this computer.  TBS could not be started.
```

Tip You can display event output in XML format by using the /f:XML switch instead of /f:text.

To display the most recent critical (level=1) or error (level=2) event in the Operational log for Task Scheduler, use the /q switch to specify an XPath query for these types of events as follows:

```
C:\Users\administrator>wevtutil qe Microsoft-Windows-TaskScheduler/
Operational "/q:*[System[(Level=1 or Level=2)]]" /c:1 /rd:true
/f:text
Event[0]:
  Log Name: Microsoft-Windows-TaskScheduler/Operational
  Source: Microsoft-Windows-TaskScheduler
  Date: 2008-06-30T08:19:47.921
  Event ID: 101
  Task: Task Start Failed
  Level: Error
  Opcode: Launch Failure
  Keyword: N/A
  User: S-1-5-18
  User Name: NT AUTHORITY\SYSTEM
  Computer: SEA-SC1.fabrikam.com
  Description:
Task Scheduler failed to start "\Microsoft\Windows\
CertificateServicesClient\SystemTask" task for user "NT AUTHORITY\System".
Additional Data:
Error Value: 2147 750692.
```

Note The quotes are needed in the previous command because of the spaces in the XPath query statement.

To display the most recent event in the System log that has the Windows Time Service as its source, use this command:

```
C:\Users\administrator>wevtutil qe System /q:*[System[Provider[@Name=
'Microsoft- Windows-Time-Service']]] /c:1 /rd:true /f:text
```

```
Event[0]:
  Log Name: System
  Source: Microsoft-Windows-Time-Service
  Date: 2008-06-30T08:20:04.000
  Event ID: 35
  Task: N/A
  Level: Information
  Opcode: N/A
  Keyword: Classic
  User: N/A
  User Name: N/A
  Computer: SEA-SC1.fabrikam.com
  Description:
The time service is now synchronizing the system time with the
time source SEA-DC2.fabrikam.com (ntp.d|0.0.0.0:123->172.16.11.161:123).
```

To display the most recent instance of an event in the System log whose event ID is 1704, do the following:

```
C:\Users\administrator>wevtutil qe Application /q:*[System[(EventID=
1704)]] /c:1  /rd:true /f:text
Event[0]:
  Log Name: Application
  Source: SceCli
  Date: 2008-06-30T08:19:54.000
  Event ID: 1704
  Task: N/A
  Level: Information
  Opcode: N/A
  Keyword: Classic
  User: N/A
  User Name: N/A
  Computer: SEA-SC1.fabrikam.com
  Description:
Security policy in the Group policy objects has been applied successfully.
```

You can use Event Viewer to construct XPath query statements that you can then incorporate into Wevtutil qe commands using the /q switch. To do this, perform these steps:

1. Open Event Viewer on a Full installation of Windows Server 2008 that has the same roles and features installed as your Server Core computer. For querying events relating to specific roles and features, you must use a Full installation that has the same roles and features as your Server Core computer so that the necessary event types and sources are all available for constructing your XPath query statements.

2. Click Create Custom View in the Actions pane to open the Create Custom View dialog box.

3. Configure custom view properties as desired. For example, the following custom view displays all critical and error events in the System log:

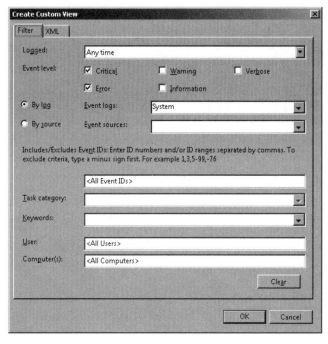

4. Switch to the XML tab and select the XPath query statement starting with the asterisk up to the </Select> tag, as shown here.

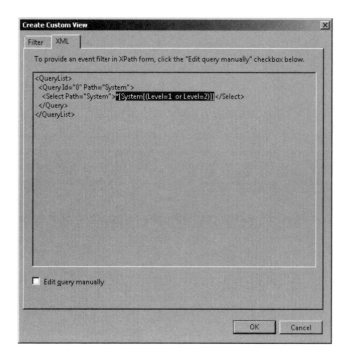

5. Press Ctrl+C to copy the query statement to the clipboard, and then copy it to the command line for use in your Wevtutil command as desired.

Exporting, Archiving, and Clearing an Event Log

You can export all events from an event log by using the epl (export-log) parameter. For example, to export the System log to the C:\EventLogBackups folder as a file named SystemEventLogBackup.evtx and overwrite any existing file with that name, type **wevtutil epl System C:\EventLogBackups\SystemEventLogBackup.evtx /ow:true** at the command prompt. You can also include an XPath query statement using the /q switch to export only events of a certain type. For example, to export all error events from the System event log to this directory and file, type **wevtutil epl System C:\EventLogBackups\SystemEventLogBackup.evtx /q:*[System[(Level=2)]] /ow:true** at the command prompt.

Once you've exported events as an .evtx file as described previously, you can archive the file using the al (archive-log) parameter. Archiving an exported log file saves it in a self-contained format that can be read whether the publisher is installed or not. The archived file is saved in a subdirectory with the name of the locale and having the .mta file extension. For example, to archive the exported file SystemEventLogBackup.evtx created previously, type **wevtutil al C:\EventLogBackups\SystemEventLogBackup .evtx** at the command prompt. On a U.S. English version of Windows, this creates a subdirectory named C:\EventLogBackups\LocalMetaData that contains a file named SystemEventLogBackup_1033.mta (1033 is the locale number for en-us). To clear the System log after exporting all events to a file, type **wevtutil cl System** at the command prompt. For more information on using Wevtutil, type **wevtutil /?** at the command prompt.

Viewing Events Using Event Viewer

You can use the Event Viewer snap-in from a remote computer to view and manage event logs on a Server Core computer. The remote computer must be running either Windows Vista SP1 or a Full installation of Windows Server 2008. If your remote computer is running an earlier version of Windows, some event information is not displayed.

To use Event Viewer to manage scheduled tasks on a Server Core computer, perform these steps:

1. On your Server Core computer, enable the Remote Administration, Remote Event Log Management, and Remote Scheduled Tasks Management rule groups in Windows Firewall by typing the following commands at the command prompt:

   netsh advfirewall firewall set rule group="Remote Administration" new enable=yes

   netsh advfirewall firewall set rule group="Remote Event Log Management" new enable=yes

   netsh advfirewall firewall set rule group="Remote Scheduled Tasks Management" new enable=yes

2. On a management station running either Windows Vista SP1 or the Full installation of Windows Server 2008, open Event Viewer from Administrative Tools, right-click the root node in the console tree, and select Connect To Another Computer.

3. In the Select Computer dialog box, type or browse to the name of your Server Core computer and then click OK.

4. Expand the console tree and manage events on the Server Core computer as desired, as shown here.

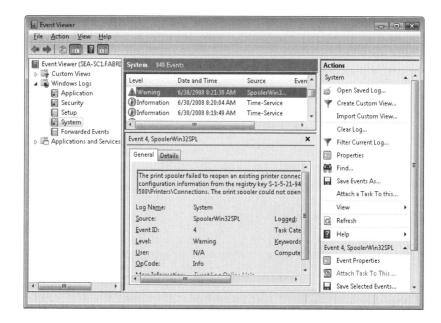

Configuring Event Subscriptions

Event subscriptions provide the ability to collect copies of events from multiple remote computers (called *source* computers) and forward them to another computer (called the *collector*) for storage and analysis. To specify which events you wish to collect, you must create a *subscription* to your source computers' event channels to enable the collector to access events from the remote channels without the need to connect to the source computers using Event Viewer first. The subscription specifies which events are collected and in which log they are stored on the collector. Once a subscription is active and events are being collected, you can view and manipulate these forwarded events as you would any other locally stored events.

Configuring the Source Computer

Event subscriptions use WS-Management to forward events from source computers to the collector. To configure a source computer running Server Core to accept WS-Management requests from the collector, use the Winrm Quickconfig command like this:

```
C:\Users\administrator>winrm quickconfig
WinRM is not set up to allow remote access to this machine for management.
The following changes must be made:

Create a WinRM listener on HTTP://* to accept
WS-Man requests to any IP on this machine.
```

```
Make these changes [y/n]? y

WinRM has been updated for remote management.

Created a WinRM listener on HTTP://* to accept
WS-Man requests to any IP on this  machine.
```

After you have configured WS-Management on your source computer, you must add the computer account of your collector computer to the local Administrators group on your source computer. For example, if the collector computer is a computer running Windows Vista named SEA-DESK155 in the fabrikam.com domain, type the following command on your source computer running Server Core:

```
C:\Users\administrator>net localgroup Administrators /add FABRIKAM\
SEA-DESK155$
The command completed successfully.
```

> **Note** Be sure to include the dollar sign ($) at the end of your collector computer's name, as shown in this example, because this indicates that the account being added to the group is a computer account, not a user account.

Configuring the Collector

The collector computer can be running either Windows Vista SP1 or a Full installation of Windows Server 2008. To configure the collector to pull the events from a source computer running Server Core, perform the following steps:

1. Open Event Viewer from Administrative Tools and click Subscriptions in the console tree.

2. If a dialog box appears saying that the Windows Event Collector Service must be configured, click Yes.

3. Click Create Subscription in the Actions pane to open the Subscription Properties dialog box.

4. Type a name and optional description for your subscription.

5. Leave the Destination Log setting set to Forwarded Events, or optionally specify a new destination for the collected events.

6. Click Select Computers, then click Add Domain Computers and type or browse to the Server Core source computer you wish to collect events from, as shown here.

7. Click Test to verify connectivity with the source computer selected, then click OK.

8. Click Select Events to open the Query Filter dialog box and use the controls to specify the criteria that events must meet to be collected, as shown here.

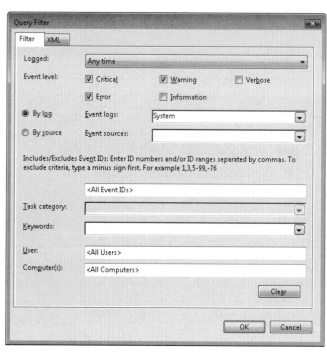

9. Click OK to return to the Subscription Properties dialog box, as shown here.

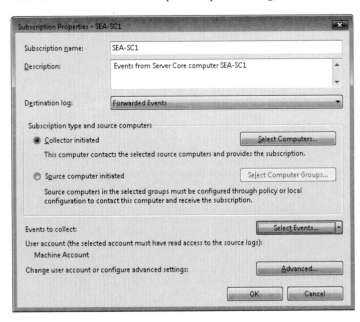

10. Click OK and verify that the status of the subscription is Active, as shown here.

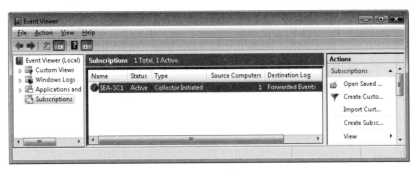

11. Right-click the subscription, select Runtime Status, and verify that no errors are displayed at the bottom of the Subscription Runtime Status dialog box, as shown here.

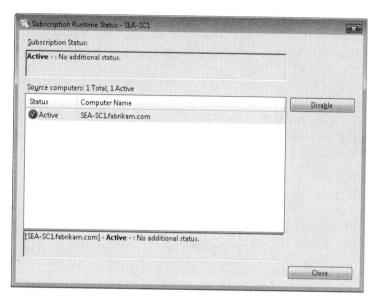

12. To view events collected from your source computer, select Forwarded Events under Windows Logs in Event Viewer (Local) on your collector computer:

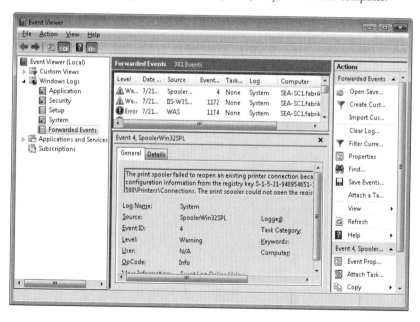

Note   Within a short period of time, events collected from the source computer should be displayed under Forwarded Events. If this doesn't happen, try restarting the Windows Event Collector service on the collector computer and the WinRM service on the source computer.

Managing Subscriptions Using Wecutil

You can manage subscriptions on your collector computer using the Wecutil command. For example, to enumerate existing subscriptions, use the es (enum-subscription) parameter like this:

```
C:\Users\Administrator>wecutil es
SEA-SC1
```

To display the properties of a subscription named SEA-SC1, use the gs (get-subscription) parameter as follows:

```
C:\Users\Administrator>wecutil gs SEA-SC1
Subscription Id: SEA-SC1
SubscriptionType: CollectorInitiated
Description: Events from Server Core computer SEA-SC1
Enabled: true
Uri: http://schemas.microsoft.com/wbem/wsman/1/windows/EventLog
ConfigurationMode: Normal
DeliveryMode: Pull
DeliveryMaxLatencyTime: 900000
HeartbeatInterval: 900000
Query: <QueryList><Query Id="0"><Select Path="System">*[System[(Level=1
or Level=2 or Level=3)]]</Select></Query></QueryList>
ReadExistingEvents: false
TransportName: HTTP
TransportPort: 80
ContentFormat: RenderedText
Locale: en-US
LogFile: ForwardedEvents
PublisherName: microsoft-windows-eventcollector
CredentialsType: Default

EventSource[0]:
        Address: SEA-SC1.fabrikam.com
        Enabled: true
```

To view the current runtime status of subscription SEA-SC1, use the gr (get-subscriptionruntimestatus) parameter like this:

```
C:\Users\Administrator>wecutil gr SEA-SC1

Subscription: SEA-SC1
        RunTimeStatus: Active
        LastError: 0
```

```
EventSources:
        SEA-SC1.fabrikam.com
                RunTimeStatus: Active
                LastError: 0
```

And to retry the subscription, use the rs (retry-subscription) parameter like this:

```
C:\Users\Administrator>wecutil rs SEA-SC1
 C:\Users\Administrator>
```

For more information on using Wecutil, type **wecutil /?** at the command prompt.

Performance Monitoring

You can monitor system performance and gauge the effect on the performance of Server Core of making configuration changes by using the standard Windows Server 2008 performance monitoring tools. You can also collect and analyze performance data either from the command line, or by using the Reliability And Performance Monitor console from another computer. While Reliability And Performance Monitor console is not available on Server Core, the Performance Logs and Alerts service and underlying performance subsystem is the same as on a Full installation of Windows Server 2008.

Collecting and Analyzing Performance Data Using the Reliability and Performance Monitor

You can use the Reliability and Performance Monitor console running on either a Full installation of Windows Server 2008 or on a computer running Windows Vista SP1 to collect and analyze performance data for a Server Core computer.

To connect to a Server Core computer using Reliability and Performance Monitor, perform these steps:

1. On your Server Core computer, open the Performance Logs And Alerts and File And Print Sharing rule groups in Windows Firewall by typing the following two commands:

   netsh advfirewall firewall set rule group="Performance Logs and Alerts" new enable=yes

   netsh advfirewall firewall set rule group="File and Printer Sharing" new enable=yes

2. On your management station, open Reliability And Performance Monitor from Administrative Tools, right-click the root node in the console tree, and select Connect To Another Computer.

3. Type the name of your Server Core computer or browse to find it in the Browse For Computer dialog box, and then click OK twice.

4. Expand the console tree to collect and analyze performance data as desired.

Note You cannot use the Reliability Monitor portion of the Reliability And Performance Monitor console to view reliability info from a Server Core computer. In addition, the Reports node is not present when Reliability And Performance Monitor is connected to a Server Core computer.

A full discussion of how to collect and analyze performance data using the Reliability And Performance Monitor console is beyond the scope of this book. A good source of information on this topic is the "Step-by-Step Guide for Performance and Reliability Monitoring in Windows Server 2008" white paper in the Windows Server 2008 Technical Library on Microsoft TechNet at http://technet.microsoft.com/en-us/windowsserver/2008/default.aspx.

Collecting and Analyzing Performance Data from the Command Line

You can use the following command-line tools on Server Core to collect and analyze performance data:

- **Logman** Used to manage performance counter and event trace log collections, to configure data collector sets, and to query currently running logs and event traces

- **Relog** Used to create new performance logs from data in existing performance logs by changing the sampling rate, converting the file format, or both

- **Tracerpt** Used to parse performance logs, event trace logs, and real-time event trace providers, and to generate dump files, report files, and report schemas

- **Typeperf** Used to write performance data to the command window or to a supported log file format, and to display all currently available counters on the computer

For more information concerning any of these commands, type the command followed by /? at the command prompt.

The recommended method for collecting performance data on a Server Core computer is to create a data collector set using the Reliability And Performance Monitor on a Full installation of Windows Server 2008 or on a computer running Windows Vista SP1, export the data collector set configuration as an XML template, and then use Logman on your Server Core computer to import and start the data collector set. Afterward, you can use the Reliability And Performance Monitor running on another computer to analyze the logs you've collected on your Server Core computer. The steps for doing this are as follows:

1. On your management station, open Reliability And Performance Monitor from Administrative Tools and expand the Data Collector Sets node.

2. Right-click User Defined and select New, Data Collector Set to open the Create New Data Collector Set wizard.

3. Type a descriptive name and select one of the following two options:

   ❑ Select the Create From A Template (Recommended) option and click Next to create your new data collector set using a built-in template data collector set such as Basic, System Diagnostics, or System Performance. Choose a template from which to create your new data collector set and click Next. Additional types of built-in template data collector sets may be available to choose from if your management station is running Windows Server 2008 instead of Windows Vista and if you have roles or features installed on your server. For example, a Windows Server 2008 domain controller has an Active Directory Diagnostics template data collector set.

   ❑ Select the Create Manually (Advanced) option and click Next to create your data collector set manually by adding counters, alerts, trace logs, and system configuration information queries. The example that continues here assumes that this second option has been selected.

4. Select the Performance Counter check box to use your data collector set to collect performance data, as shown here, and click Next.

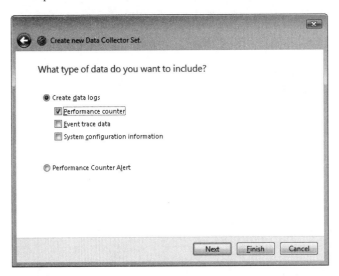

5. Click Add, click Browse, and select the Server Core computer whose performance you want to monitor from AD DS. Then select the counters you want to monitor and add them to the list of added counters, as shown here.

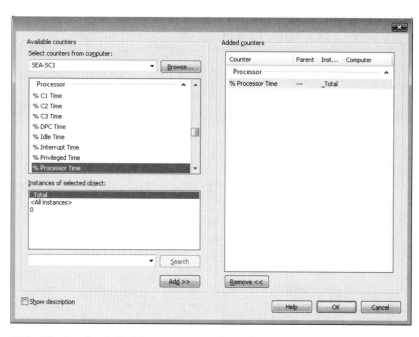

6. Click OK when finished adding counters and specify a collection interval, as shown here.

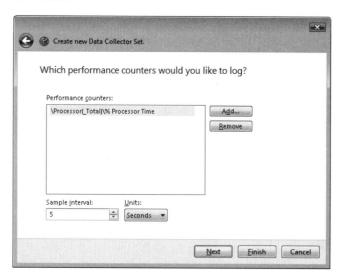

7. Click Next twice and then click Finish to create the new data collector set.

8. Expand the User Defined node in the console tree, right-click your new data collector set, and select Save Template to save the configuration of your data collector set as an XML configuration file.

9. Specify a name for your data collector set XML configuration file and save the file onto removable media or onto a network share accessible from your Server Core computer, and then copy the data collector set to a directory on your Server Core computer.

10. On your Server Core computer, use Logman Import to import the XML configuration file for the data collector. For example, to import the configuration file "C:\DCS\DCS for SEA-SC1.xml" and name the data collection set created from this file "DCS for SEA-SC1" do this:

```
C:\Users\administrator>logman import -n "DCS for SEA-SC1"
-xml "C:\DCS\DCS for SEA-SC1.xml"
The command completed successfully.
```

11. Use Logman Start to start collecting data with your data collector set as follows:

```
C:\Users\administrator>logman start -n "DCS for SEA-SC1"
The command completed successfully.
```

12. Use Logman query to verify your data collection set is running as follows:

```
C:\Users\administrator>logman query
Data Collector Set                    Type              Status
------------------------------------------------------------------------
DCS for SEA-SC1                       Counter           Running
```

13. When desired, stop collecting data by typing the following:

```
C:\Users\administrator>logman stop -n "DCS for SEA-SC1"
The command completed successfully.
```

14. The running data collection set will have created a binary performance log (.blg) file and saved it in a numbered subdirectory similar to the following:

```
C:\Users\administrator>dir "C:\PerfLogs\Admin\DCS for SEA-SC1\000001"
 Volume in drive C has no label.
 Volume Serial Number is E8B3-3EBE

 Directory of C:\PerfLogs\Admin\DCS for SEA-SC1\000001

07/01/2008  01:30 PM    <DIR>          .
07/01/2008  01:30 PM    <DIR>          ..
07/01/2008  01:32 PM           131,072 DataCollector01.blg
               1 File(s)        131,072 bytes
               2 Dir(s)  16,732,491,776 bytes free
```

15. Copy the .blg file onto removable media or to a network share that is accessible from your management station.

16. On your management station, open Reliability And Performance Monitor, expand the console tree, and select Performance Monitor under Monitoring Tools.

17. Click the View Log Data button on the toolbar to open the Performance Data Properties sheet.

18. Under Data Source, select Log Files. Then click Add and browse to the .blg file you copied over from your Server Core computer, as shown here.

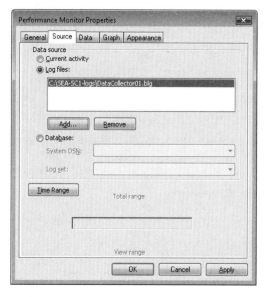

19. Click OK, and then click the Add Counter button on the toolbar and add the counters from your data collector set.

20. Click OK to display the collected performance data from your Server Core computer, as shown here.

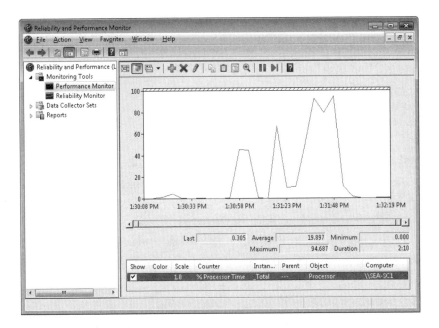

Tip   You can create data collector sets manually on Server Core using the Logman Create command. For example, to create a data collector set that collects up to 10 MB of performance data using the \Processor(_Total)\% Processor Time counter for a time interval of 5 minutes, type **logman create counter CPU-5min -c "\Processor(_Total)\% Processor Time" -max 10 -rf 05:00** at the command prompt. You can also view all performance counters and their instances on Server Core by typing **typeperf /qx** at the command prompt. For example, if you aren't sure of the correct syntax for the counter used in the previous Logman Create command, type **typeperf /qx | find "\Processor"** at the command prompt to display all instances of the Processor counter. For more information on using Logman Create, type **logman create /?** at the command prompt.

Backup and Recovery

You can use the Windows Server Backup feature to perform a single backup or to schedule backups for Server Core computers. You can perform backups either from the command line, using the Wbadmin tool, or remotely, using the Windows Server Backup snap-in running on a Full installation of Windows Server 2008. You can use Windows Server Backup to back up all volumes on your computer, selected volumes, or the system state on the computer. You can then recover volumes, folders, files, applications, or the system state from your backups. You can also perform a complete recovery of a failed system by using a full server backup with the Windows Recovery Environment (WinRE).

You can use Windows Server Backup to perform backups to external or internal hard disks, optical media drives, or removable media drives such as USB drives. You cannot use Windows Server Backup to perform backups to tape drives. For a more robust and scalable backup solution, use System Center Data Protection Manager instead.

Note The Windows Server Backup snap-in is not available on Windows Vista, and it is not included in the Remote Server Administration Tools (RSAT) package that you can install on Windows Vista.

Installing the Windows Server Backup Feature

Before you can back up a Server Core computer, you must install the Windows Server Backup feature. This can be done in two ways:

- From the command line, using the Ocsetup command
- By using an answer file during an unattended installation of Server Core

Installing the Windows Server Backup Feature from the Command Line

You can install the Windows Server Backup feature from the command line by using the following command:

```
C:\Users\Administrator.FABRIKAM>start /w ocsetup WindowsServerBackup
```

Verify the result:

```
C:\Users\Administrator.FABRIKAM>oclist | find "   Installed"
    Installed:WindowsServerBackup
```

Installing the Windows Server Backup Feature Using an Answer File

To install the Windows Server Backup feature using an answer file, perform the following steps:

1. Begin by creating and configuring an answer file for unattended installation of Server Core. For information on how to do this, see Chapter 2, "Deploying Server Core."

2. On your technician computer, open your answer file in Windows System Image Manager (Windows SIM).

3. In the Windows Image pane, expand the Packages node to display the nodes beneath it. Expand the Foundation node to display the Microsoft-Windows-ServerCore-Package node beneath that. Then right-click the address Microsoft-Windows-ServerCore-Package node and select Add To Answer File. The Microsoft-Windows-ServerCore-Package should now be selected in the Answer File pane.

4. In the Properties pane, scroll down until the WindowsServerBackup setting is visible under Windows Feature. Click the value field to the right of the WindowsServerBackup setting to display a drop-down arrow. Click the arrow and select Enabled.

5. Validate your answer file and save it, and then deploy Server Core using your answer file using any of the methods outlined in Chapter 2. When installation is completed, log on, type **oclist | find " Installed"**, and verify that the Windows Server Backup feature has been installed.

Performing Backup and Recovery Using the Windows Server Backup Snap-in

You can perform a backup of a Server Core computer using the Windows Server Backup snap-in from a remote computer running a Full installation of Windows Server 2008. To do this, follow these steps:

1. On your Server Core computer, enable the Remote Administration rule group in Windows Firewall on your Server Core computer. You can do this by typing **netsh advfirewall firewall set rule group="Remote Administration" new enable=yes** at the command prompt.

2. On a Full installation of Windows Server 2008, open the Windows Server Backup console from Administrative Tools and click Connect To Another Computer in the Actions pane.

3. In the ComputerChooser dialog box, select Another Computer, type or browse to the name of the Server Core computer you wish to back up, and then click Finish to return to the Windows Server Backup console, as shown here.

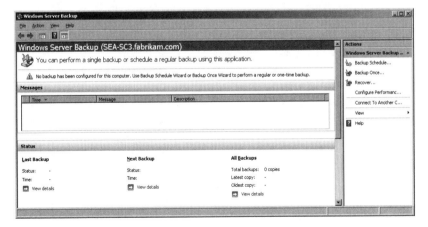

4. Perform backup tasks as desired. For example, using Windows Server Backup you can do any of the following:

   ❑ Perform a full backup of your computer manually

   ❑ Schedule periodic backups

   ❑ Configure the type of backup to be performed

   ❑ Recover files, applications, or volumes from a previous backup

You can also perform a complete system recovery, including the system/boot volume, by using the Windows Recovery Environment with a full system backup created using Windows Server Backup.

Performing a Manual Backup

To do an initial full backup of every fixed volume on your Server Core computer using the Windows Server Backup console, connect to the computer as described in the previous section and click Backup Once in the Actions pane. This starts the Backup Once Wizard, which leads you through the steps of performing your backup. Be sure to select the Full Server (Recommended) option in the wizard if this is the first time you are backing up your Server Core computer, and for the destination type setting, select either a remote shared folder specified using a Universal Naming Convention (UNC) path (preferred) or an available volume on a separate fixed disk or removable USB drive.

If you choose to perform your initial full backup to a remote shared folder, you must decide whether the backup will be accessible to anyone who has access to that shared folder or only to a user whose credentials you specify (the user must have write access to the remote shared folder). If you back up your server to a remote shared folder, your backup will be overwritten if you use the same folder to back up the same computer again. Furthermore, if the backup operation fails, you may end up with no valid backup because the older backup would be overwritten even if the newer backup is not usable. To avoid this problem, create subfolders in the remote shared folder to organize your backups. Be aware that if you do this, these subfolders require twice the space of the parent folder.

To back up system state data—the registry, system files, boot files, certificate database, and other files, including the NTDS.dit database and the Sysvol folder if you are backing up a domain controller—perform a full backup of your boot/system volumes. You cannot back up system state data separately from your boot/system volumes.

Windows Server Backup begins the initial backup process by creating a shadow copy of each fixed disk volume on your computer, after which it backs up the full contents of each volume to the destination you have specified.

To verify the backup, view the contents of the following directory:

<destination_path>\WindowsImageBackup\<server_name>\Backup yyyy-mm-dd hhmmss

where <destination_path> is the drive letter of your removable storage backup media or the UNC path to a network share and <server_name> is the NetBIOS name of your Server Core computer. The date and time the backup was made are also included in the name of the backup folder. Backup files consist of .vhd files that use the same virtual hard disk format used by Microsoft virtualization products, plus a series of XML files containing configuration information concerning the backup, as follows:

```
C:\Users\Administrator.FABRIKAM>dir "e:\WindowsImageBackup\SEA-SC3\
Backup 2008-07-01 210910"
 Volume in drive E is New Volume
 Volume Serial Number is F07A-FE15

 Directory of e:\WindowsImageBackup\SEA-SC3\Backup 2008-07-01 210910

07/01/2008  04:14 PM    <DIR>          .
07/01/2008  04:14 PM    <DIR>          ..
07/01/2008  04:14 PM     1,695,015,424 6d5ab0d1-46c9-11dd-97b1-
806e6f6e6963.vhd
07/01/2008  04:14 PM             3,188 b90684da-8492-4ce7-a4ea-
4c109208b59d_Addi
tionalFilesc3b9f3c7-5e52-4d5e-8b20-19adc95a34c7.xml
07/01/2008  04:14 PM            10,114 b90684da-8492-4ce7-a4ea-
4c109208b59d_Components.xml
07/01/2008  04:14 PM             3,614 b90684da-8492-4ce7-a4ea-
4c109208b59d_Regi
stryExcludes.xml
...
```

Scheduling Backups

To schedule regular backups of a Server Core computer using the Windows Server Backup console, connect to the computer and click Backup Schedule in the Actions pane. This starts the Backup Schedule Wizard, which leads you through the steps of scheduling your backups. You can schedule backups to occur once a day or multiple times per day at times you specify. When scheduling backups, the destination can be only a volume on a fixed local disk or on a removable storage device—you cannot schedule backups to shared folders on the network. The volume that you choose as your destination will be formatted and used by Windows exclusively as a dedicated volume for storing backups of your system. This destination volume is formatted each time a scheduled backup occurs, and the scheduled backup is displayed in the bottom portion of the Windows Server Backup console. Windows Server Backup also automatically manages disk space on the destination volume so that you don't need to worry about running out of disk space after multiple backups are performed.

Once you have scheduled regular backups using Windows Server Backup, you can prevent such backups from occurring or modify your backup schedule if desired. To change your backup schedule, click Schedule Backup in the Actions Pane and then follow the steps of the Backup Schedule Wizard to reschedule your backups. To stop scheduled backups from occurring, click Schedule Backup in the Actions Pane and select Stop Backup followed by Next and then Finish. Stopping scheduled backups does not delete any existing backups on your destination volume, and it releases the destination volume for other uses.

> **Tip** You can use the Wbadmin command if you need to schedule backups less frequently than once per day or if you want to schedule backups to a shared folder on your network.

Configuring Backup Type

To configure the type of backup to be performed, perform these steps:

1. On your Full installation of Windows Server 2008, open Windows Server Backup from Administrative Tools and click Configure Performance Settings in the Actions pane.

2. In the Optimize Backup Performance dialog box, select Always Perform Full Backup or Always Perform Incremental Backup option as desired, as shown here.

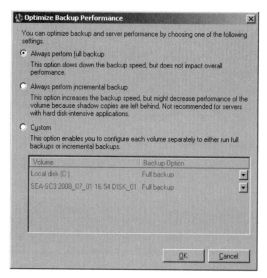

3. If you want, you can select the Custom option to configure the backup type individually for each volume being backed up.

Performing a Recovery

To recover a file, application, or volume that has become corrupted or has been deleted from your Server Core computer, use the Windows Server Backup console to connect to the computer as described in the previous section and click Recover in the Actions pane. This starts the Recovery Wizard, which leads you through the steps of performing your recovery. Using this wizard, select the backup that you want to restore by selecting the calendar date and the time the backup was made. If the selected backup resides on a remote network share, you must supply credentials for accessing the backup. Then choose whether to recover an entire volume or only the files and folders you specify (you can select multiple items by holding down the Ctrl key while you click each item).

If you choose to recover files or folders, you can indicate whether to restore the selected items to their original location or to a different location that you specify, whether to restore the security settings (permissions) along with the item, and what to do when a conflict occurs, such as when you try to restore an item to a location where a copy of the item already exists.

If you choose to recover a volume, you must specify a destination volume whose size is greater than or equal to the size of the source volume. Note that you cannot restore the boot/system volume (C: drive) or perform a full server recovery using this wizard—you must use WinRE to do this. See the section "Performing a Full Server Recovery," immediately following this section, for details.

Finally, at the conclusion of the wizard, click Recover to begin the recovery process.

> **Note**   You cannot use Windows Server Backup to recover backups that you created using Ntbackup on an earlier version of Windows Server; however, you can download a version of Ntbackup that you can use on Windows Server 2008 to recover data from backups created using Ntbackup. To obtain this utility, go to the Microsoft Download Center at *http://www.microsoft.com/downloads/* and search for "Windows NT Backup — Restore Utility."

Performing a Full Server Recovery

To perform a full server recovery of all volumes, including the boot/system volume on your Server Core computer, or optionally to recover only the boot/system volume, follow these steps:

1. Start your Server Core computer, insert your Windows Server 2008 product DVD in the DVD drive, and press a key to boot from the DVD when prompted to do so.

2. Click Next when regional and language options are displayed.

3. Click Repair Your Computer (do *not* click Install Now).

4. The System Recovery Options dialog box should be empty because you are restoring onto a system that has no operating system, so click Next when this box appears.

5. When the Choose A Recover Tool dialog box appears, click Windows Complete PC Restore.

6. Supply your backup media by either inserting your backup DVD, attaching your removable storage backup device, or specifying the network share where your backup is stored and credentials for accessing the share.

7. Select the backup that you want to restore.

8. When the Choose How To Restore The Backup dialog box appears, install any mass storage device drivers you need and then choose one of these options:

9. Select Format And Repartition to perform a full recovery of your server onto new hardware.

10. Select Restore Only System Volumes to restore only the boot/system volume(s) on your existing hardware.

Performing Backup and Recovery from the Command Line

You can use the Wbadmin tool to back up and recover a Server Core computer from the command line. The following sections illustrate some common uses for this tool.

Managing Scheduled Backups Using Wbadmin

You can use Wbadmin to schedule regular daily backups of your Server Core computer from the command line. To do this, follow these steps:

1. Begin by using the Wbadmin Get Disks command to obtain the DiskIdentifier of the volume you want to back up to. For example, do this:

```
C:\Users\Administrator.FABRIKAM>wbadmin get disks
wbadmin 1.0 - Backup command-line tool
(C) Copyright 2004 Microsoft Corp.


Disk name        : WDC WD20 00JS 60NCB1 SCSI Disk Device
Disk number      : 0
Disk identifier  : {c48d23bb-0000-0000-0000-000000000000}
Total space      : 186.82 GB
Used space       : 2.56 GB
Volumes          : C:[(no volume label)]


Disk name        : HDS72808 0PLAT20 USB Device
Disk number      : 1
Disk identifier  : {f015ce01-0000-0000-0000-000000000000}
```

```
Total space      : 78.66 GB
Used space       : 92.06 MB
Volumes          : E:[SEA-SC3 2008_07_01 16:54 DISK_01]
```

2. The second portion of this command output identifies the removable USB drive (disk 1 or the E: drive) that will be your destination volume for storing backups. Next, use the Wbadmin Enable Backup command to schedule and enable a daily backup of your computer. For example, to schedule backup of all critical volumes (volumes that contain the system state) to occur at 3:00 A.M. every day, do this:

```
C:\Users\Administrator.FABRIKAM>wbadmin enable backup -addtarget:
{f015ce01-0000-0000-0000-000000000000} -schedule:03:00 -allcritical
wbadmin 1.0 - Backup command-line tool
(C) Copyright 2004 Microsoft Corp.

Retrieving volume information...

The scheduled backup settings:

Volumes in backup: Local Disk(C:)
Location to store backup: HDS72808 OPLAT20 USB Device
Times of day to run backup: 03:00

Do you want to enable backups with the above settings?
[Y] Yes [N] No y

Do you want to format and use HDS72808 OPLAT20 USB Device
(having volumes E:) as the l
ocation to store
scheduled backups?
[Y] Yes [N] No y

Label the backup disk as SEA-SC3 2008_07_02 04:57 DISK_01.
This information will be used to identify this backup disk in a recovery.


The scheduled backup is enabled.
```

3. Once the scheduled backup has been enabled, be sure to attach a label to your removable drive that says "SEA-SC3 2008_07_02 04:57 DISK_01," as indicated by this command output.

> **Tip**   You can add the −quiet switch to suppress user prompts when running the Wbadmin command. To suppress progress information, append **> nul** to your command to redirect the command output to the NULL device.

If your computer has an additional fixed disk with volumes G: and X: on it, you can include these volumes in your scheduled backups by typing **wbadmin enable backup -addtarget:{f015ce01-0000-0000-0000-000000000000} -schedule:03:00 −include:G:,X: -allcritical** instead of the previous command.

To reschedule your daily backups to occur at 2:00 A.M. instead, type **wbadmin enable backup -schedule:02:00** at the command prompt. To view details concerning scheduled backups (if any) on your computer, type **wbadmin enable backup** with no parameters as follows:

```
C:\Users\Administrator.FABRIKAM>wbadmin enable backup
wbadmin 1.0 - Backup command-line tool
(C) Copyright 2004 Microsoft Corp.

The scheduled backup settings:

Volumes in backup: Local Disk(C:)
Location to store backup: HDS72808 OPLAT20 USB Device
Times of day to run backup: 02:00
```

Tip   You can force a scheduled backup to run immediately by typing **wbadmin start backup** with no additional parameters at the command prompt.

Performing a Manual Backup Using Wbadmin

You can use Wbadmin to perform a manual backup of your Server Core computer from the command line. You can perform a manual backup either to an available disk volume (fixed or removable) or to a shared folder on the network. To perform a manual backup of all critical volumes on your server and copy the backups to the remote share \\SEA-DC2\Backups on a network file server using domain administrator credentials, do the following:

```
C:\Users\Administrator.FABRIKAM>wbadmin start backup -backuptarget:
\\SEA-DC2\Backups -user:FABRIKAM\Administrator -password:Pa$$w0rd -allcritical
wbadmin 1.0 - Backup command-line tool
(C) Copyright 2004 Microsoft Corp.

Retrieving volume information...

This would backup volume Local Disk(C:) to \\SEA-DC2\Backups.

Do you want to start the backup operation?
[Y] Yes [N] No y

Backup to \\SEA-DC2\Backups is starting.

Creating the shadow copy of volumes requested for backup.
Creating the shadow copy of volumes requested for backup.
Creating the shadow copy of volumes requested for backup.
Running backup of volume Local Disk(C:), copied (1%).
Running backup of volume Local Disk(C:), copied (2%).
Running backup of volume Local Disk(C:), copied (4%).
...
Running backup of volume Local Disk(C:), copied (97%).
```

```
Running backup of volume Local Disk(C:), copied (99%).
Running backup of volume Local Disk(C:), copied (100%).
Backup completed successfully.

Summary of backup:
------------------

Backup of volume Local Disk(C:) completed successfully.
```

> **Note**   Instead of using domain administrator credentials, you can perform backup
> operations using the credentials of a user belonging to the Backup Operators
> group.

Viewing the Status of a Backup Operation Using Wbadmin

You can view the status of a backup operation currently underway by using the
Wbadmin Get Status command as follows:

```
C:\Windows\system32>wbadmin get status
wbadmin 1.0 - Backup command-line tool
(C) Copyright 2004 Microsoft Corp.

Running backup of volume Local Disk(C:), copied (95%).
Running backup of volume Local Disk(C:), copied (97%).
Running backup of volume Local Disk(C:), copied (99%).
Backup of volume Local Disk(C:) completed successfully.
Backup completed successfully.

Summary of backup:
------------------

Backup of volume Local Disk(C:) completed successfully.
```

> **Note**   If you run the previous command when no backup is underway, the
> message "ERROR – No job is currently running" returns.

Performing a Recovery Using Wbadmin

You can use the Wbadmin command to recover files, applications, or volumes from a
previous backup. For example, to recover the Documents folder and its contents for
the domain Administrator from the most recent scheduled backup, perform these
steps:

1. Use the Wbadmin Get Versions command to list all available backups stored on
   the destination volume (in this case the Z: drive):

   ```
   C:\Users\Administrator.FABRIKAM>wbadmin get versions
   -backuptarget:Z:
   wbadmin 1.0 - Backup command-line tool
   ```

```
(C) Copyright 2004 Microsoft Corp.

Backup time: 7/1/2008 02:11 AM
Backup target: Fixed Disk labeled SEA-
SC3 2008_07_02 04:57 DISK_01(\\?\Volume{ce5b2ab7-47bf-11dd-8243-
0003ff57888c})
Version identifier: 07/01/2008-07:11
Can Recover: Volume(s), File(s), Application(s), Bare Metal Recovery,
 System State

Backup time: 7/2/2008 02:12 AM
Backup target: Fixed Disk labeled SEA-SC3 2008_07_02 04:57 DISK_01(Z:)
Version identifier: 07/02/2008-07:12
Can Recover: Volume(s), File(s), Application(s), Bare Metal Recovery,
 System State
```

2. Now use the following command to recover the contents of the Documents folder from the most recent (second) backup listed in step 1. The –recursive switch restores all subfolders and files subordinate to the Documents folder. If this switch is omitted, only the files immediately within the Documents folder will be restored. The –overwrite:skip switch indicates that existing files will be skipped during the recovery process. Other options you can use here are –overwrite:createcopy and –overwrite:overwrite. Here is the command with sample output:

```
C:\Users\Administrator.FABRIKAM>wbadmin start recovery -version:
07/02/2008-07:12  -items:C:\Users\Administrator.FABRIKAM\
Documents -itemtype:File -backuptarget:Z: -recursive -overwrite:skip -quiet
wbadmin 1.0 - Backup command-line tool
(C) Copyright 2004 Microsoft Corp.

Retrieving volume information...

You have chosen to restore the file(s) C:\Users\Administrator.
FABRIKAM\Documents
 from the backup taken on 7/2/2008 11:29 AM to
C:\Users\Administrator.FABRIKAM\.


Restore of C:\Users\Administrator.FABRIKAM\Documents to C:\Users\
Administrator.FABRIKAM\ completed successfully.
Total bytes recovered  - 122664 bytes
Total files recovered  - 54
Total files failed     - 0

Log of files successfully restored
'C:\Windows\Logs\WindowsServerBackup\FileRestore 02-07-2008
11-42-01.log'
```

```
Recovery operation completed.


Summary of recovery:
--------------------

Restore of C:\Users\Administrator.FABRIKAM\Documents to C:\Users\
Administrator.FABRIKAM\ completed successfully.
Total bytes recovered  - 122664 bytes
Total files recovered  - 54
Total files failed     - 0

Log of files successfully restored
'C:\Windows\Logs\WindowsServerBackup\FileRestore 02-07-2008 11-42-01.log'
```

You can also use Wbadmin Start Recovery to recover applications such as the Registry and entire volumes. For more information, type **wbadmin start recovery /?** at the command prompt.

Backing Up the System State Using Wbadmin

You can use Wbadmin to back up only the system state of a Server Core computer. For example, the following command backs up the system state of server SEA-SC3 and stores the backup on the E: drive:

```
C:\Windows\system32>wbadmin start SystemStateBackup -backuptarget:e:
wbadmin 1.0 - Backup command-line tool
(C) Copyright 2004 Microsoft Corp.

Starting System State Backup [7/2/2008 10:47 AM]
Retrieving volume information...

This would backup the system state from volume(s) Local Disk(C:) to e:.
Do you want to start the backup operation?
[Y] Yes [N] No y

Creating the shadow copy of volumes requested for backup.
Creating the shadow copy of volumes requested for backup.
Creating the shadow copy of volumes requested for backup.
Identifying system state files to backup (This may take a few minutes)...
Found (144) files
Found (488) files
Found (897) files
...
Search for system state files complete
Starting backup of files
Overall progress - 0% (Currently backing up files reported by 'System Writer')
Overall progress - 2% (Currently backing up files reported by 'System Writer')
```

```
Overall progress - 5% (Currently backing up files reported by 'System Writer')
...
Backup of files reported by 'System Writer' completed
Backup of files reported by 'Registry Writer' completed
Backup of files reported by 'COM+ REGDB Writer' completed
Backup of files reported by 'WMI Writer' completed
Overall progress -
 99% (Currently backing up additional system state files)

Summary of backup:
------------------

Backup of system state completed successfully [7/2/2008 11:00 AM]

Log of files successfully backed up
'C:\Windows\Logs\WindowsServerBackup\SystemStateBackup 02-07-2008
10-47-44.log'


C:\Windows\system32>
```

You can also use Wbadmin to back up or recover the system state of a domain controller, which includes the contents of the Sysvol folder and the AD DS database file NTDS.dit in addition to the system state files found on a member server or stand-alone computer.

You can use the Wbadmin Start Sysrecovery command to recover system state information from a backup. However, you can run this command only from the Windows Recovery Environment. For more information on recovering system state, see the entry for "Wbadmin start sysrecovery" in the Windows Server 2008 Command Reference, which can be found in the Windows Server 2008 Technical Library on Microsoft TechNet at *http://technet.microsoft.com/en-us/windowsserver/2008/default.aspx*.

> **Note** You cannot back up a system state to a network share—you must back it up to a local volume, which can be either a fixed disk or a removable drive.

For more information about using the Wbadmin command, type **wbadmin /?** at the command prompt.

Installing Software Updates

You can configure Server Core to download and install software updates automatically from the Microsoft Update Web service. For instructions on how to do this, see the section "Configuring Automatic Updates" in Chapter 3, "Initial Configuration." Once Automatic Updates has been configured, you can either let your server automatically download and install updates from the Windows Update site using the default schedule, or you can initiate a manual check for updates at any time by typing **wuauclt /detectnow** at the command prompt.

Tip   To view the current status of update detection, type **notepad %windir%\WindowsUpdate.log** at the command prompt and view the entries towards the end of the log file.

You can also have Server Core download updates using Windows Server Update Services (WSUS) if you have WSUS deployed on your corporate network. The recommended method for configuring WSUS clients is to use Group Policy, and the policy setting for specifying the WSUS server from which your computers should download updates is the following:

Computer Configuration\Policies\Administrative Templates\Windows Components\Windows Update\Specify Intranet Microsoft Update Service Location

For more information on configuring computers to pull updates from a WSUS server, see the technical guidance found at http://technet.microsoft.com/en-us/wsus/default.aspx.

Installing Updates Manually

You can install updates manually from the command line on Server Core if desired. You can use the Microsoft Update Catalog to download security updates and other type updates and to deploy them manually to your Server Core computers. You may also obtain needed hotfixes from the Microsoft Download Center, from links in Microsoft Knowledge Base articles, or directly from Microsoft Customer Support Services.

As an example of downloading and installing an update manually, perform these steps to download updates for Windows Server 2008 and install them on a Server Core computer:

1. From a management workstation, browse to the URL *http://catalog.update.microsoft.com/v7/site/Home.aspx* using Internet Explorer.

2. In the Start Your Search box, enter a description of the type of device for which you are searching for drivers. For example, you could type **Windows Server 2008 update**.

3. Scroll down the list to find the update you want, such as "Update for Windows Server 2008 (KB947562)."

4. Click the name of the update to open a dialog box describing the update, and read the information to determine whether you need to apply the update to Server Core.

5. If you decide that you need the update, click the Add button beside it.

6. If needed, repeat steps 3–5 to download additional updates.

7. Click the View Basket link under the search box and verify that you have found all the updates you need.

8. Click Download, and then browse to and select the folder on your hard drive to which you want to download the updates.

9. Click Continue, and when the progress indicator indicates the download is completed, click Close.

10. Each update is downloaded as a separate subfolder named after the update, and each subfolder generally contains a single Microsoft Update stand-alone Package (.msu) file for the update.

11. Copy the .msu files onto removable storage or a network share, and then copy them to a folder on your Server Core computer. For example, you could create a folder named C:\Updates on your Server Core computer for this purpose.

12. On your Server Core computer, change the current directory to C:\Updates and verify that you have the update you need as follows:

```
C:\Users\administrator>cd C:\Updates

C:\Updates>dir
 Volume in drive C has no label.
 Volume Serial Number is E8B3-3EBE

 Directory of C:\Updates

07/02/2008  12:27 PM    <DIR>          .
07/02/2008  12:27 PM    <DIR>          ..
05/07/2008  07:34 PM         3,588,159 X86-all-windows6.0-kb947562-
x86_6ff6b13433eba0503ffcd8e47e1daefac3dc83b4.msu
               1 File(s)      3,588,159 bytes
               2 Dir(s)  16,718,540,800 bytes free
```

13. Install each update silently using the Windows Update Stand-alone Installer (Wusa.exe) utility. For example, if the .msu file for "Update for Windows Server 2008 (KB947562)" is named X86-all-windows6.0-kb947562-x86_6ff6b13433eba0503ffcd8e47e1daefac3dc83b4.msu, install the update manually using this command:

```
C:\Updates>wusa X86-all-windows6.0-kb947562-x86_6ff6b13433eba0503ffcd
8e47e1daefac3dc83b4.msu /quiet
```

Viewing Installed Updates

You can use the Windows Management Instrumentation Command-line (WMIC) to view the installed updates on your computer. For example, to verify that the update installed in the previous section has been installed on your computer, do this:

```
C:\Updates>wmic qfe list
Caption                                    CSName    Description  FixComments  Ho
tFixID  InstallDate  InstalledBy                                  InstalledOn
    Name  ServicePackInEffect  Status
http://support.microsoft.com/?kbid=947562  SEA-
SC1  Update                   KB
947562            S-1-5-21-940954651-3993729752-4124607334-
500  01c8dc69493ce e0b
```

If the WMIC output is difficult to read, you can use Systeminfo instead, as follows:

```
C:\Updates>systeminfo | find ": KB"
                        [01]: KB947562
```

Uninstalling Updates

To uninstall an update, you must extract the .cab file from the .msu package and then use Package Manager (Pkgmgr.exe) to uninstall the update. For example, to uninstall the "Update for Windows Server 2008 (KB947562)" that you installed previously, perform these steps:

1. Create a temporary directory under the directory where the update package is located as follows:

   ```
   C:\Updates>mkdir Files
   ```

2. Extract all the files from the .msu package into the subdirectory as follows:

   ```
   C:\Updates>expand X86-all-windows6.0-kb947562-x86
   _6ff6b13433eba0503ffcd8e47e1daefac3dc83b4.msu -f:* Files
   Microsoft (R) File Expansion Utility  Version 6.0.6001.18000
   Copyright (c) Microsoft Corporation. All rights reserved.

   Adding Files\WSUSSCAN.cab to Extraction Queue
   Adding Files\Windows6.0-KB947562-x86.cab to Extraction Queue
   Adding Files\Windows6.0-KB947562-x86-
   pkgProperties.txt to Extraction Queue
   Adding Files\Windows6.0-KB947562-x86.xml to Extraction Queue
    Expanding Files ....

   Expanding Files Complete ...
   4 files total.
   ```

3. Change the current directory to your subdirectory and list the files in the directory as follows:

   ```
   C:\Updates>cd Files

   C:\Updates\Files>dir
    Volume in drive C has no label.
    Volume Serial Number is E8B3-3EBE
   ```

```
Directory of C:\Updates\Files

07/02/2008  12:39 PM    <DIR>          .
07/02/2008  12:39 PM    <DIR>          ..
03/10/2008  03:28 PM                490 Windows6.0-KB947562-x86-
pkgProperties.txt

03/10/2008  03:23 PM          3,426,463 Windows6.0-KB947562-x86.cab
03/10/2008  03:28 PM                442 Windows6.0-KB947562-x86.xml
03/10/2008  03:27 PM            166,604 WSUSSCAN.cab
               4 File(s)      3,593,999 bytes
               2 Dir(s) 16,704,724,992 bytes free
```

4. Open the .txt file for the update and confirm that the update should be applied to Server Core. In this example, you do this by typing **notepad Windows6.0-KB947562-x86-pkgProperties.txt** at the command prompt. The following information is displayed:

```
ApplicabilityInfo="Windows Vista SP1;Windows Server 2008;Windows Server
Core;Windows Vista;"
Applies to="Windows 6.0"
Build Date="2008/03/10"
Company="Microsoft Corporation"
File Version="1"
Installation Type="FULL"
Installer Engine="Component Based Servicing - WUSA.exe"
Installer Version="6.0.0.0"
KB Article Number="947562"
Language="ALL"
Package Type="Update"
Processor Architecture="x86"
Product Name="Windows 6.0"
Support Link=http://support.microsoft.com?kbid=947562
```

The first line in this text file confirms that the update does in fact apply to Server Core.

5. Use Pkgmgr to uninstall the update as follows:

```
C:\Updates\Files>pkgmgr /up /m:Windows6.0-KB947562-x86.cab /quiet
```

6. Verify the result as follows:

```
C:\Updates\Files>wmic qfe list
No Instance(s) Available.
```

Note You can delete the temporary directory and its contents when you're finished uninstalling the update.

Installing Applications

Server Core is not intended as a platform for running applications. For example, you can't run Microsoft SQL Server or Microsoft Visual Studio on Server Core. The reason you cannot run most common applications on Server Core is that these applications depend upon components that have been removed from Server Core to minimize its servicing footprint. Specifically, you cannot run any applications on Server Core that depend upon the Windows Desktop shell or any other GUI components that have been removed from the platform. And you cannot run applications that use managed code because the .NET Framework and Common Language Runtime (CLR) are not on Server Core.

As described in Chapter 1, only a few GUI applications like Notepad and Registry Editor are included in Server Core. And even these applications work only because of the application compatibility shim infrastructure present in Server Core. A *shim* is a thin layer of code inserted between an application and a Windows application programming interface (API). The shimming engine stores data in a shim database (Sysmain.sdb) found in the %SystemRoot%\AppPatch directory on x86 architecture systems and in the %SystemRoot%\AppPatch\AppPatch64 directory on x64 architecture systems. The shim database in Server Core is only a small subset of the shim database found on a Full installation of Windows Server 2008. It contains the following two shims:

- **RegEditImportExportLoadHive**   Provides for importing and exporting of registry hives

- **NoExplorerForGetFileName**   Provides the older File Open and File Save dialog boxes used by Notepad on Server Core

These two shims can be applied to other applications that you may want to install on Server Core by using the Application Compatibility Toolkit (ACT), which is available from Microsoft TechNet at *http://technet.microsoft.com/en-us/library/cc507852.aspx.*

> **Note**   The two shims described here are the only in-box shims available on Server Core. You cannot add additional shims to the shim database, but you can use ACT to create a custom shim database if desired.

Supported Types of Applications

While Server Core is not intended as a general application platform, it supports the development of management tools, utilities, and agents. Examples of such applications that can be designed to run on Server Core include network backup agents, antivirus software agents, and system management or monitoring agents. Such agents usually do not have a GUI and typically report to a service running on another server. For a management agent to work on Server Core, it must comply with the following requirements:

- It must have no shell or GUI dependencies.

- It should have no interactive components.

- It should replace any managed code with native code.

- It must not make function calls not supported by Server Core.

- It must use only protocols supported by Server Core, such as Remote Procedure Call (RPC) or Distributed Component Object Model (DCOM).

- It should be thoroughly tested on Server Core before being released.

Tip Developers of management agents can find a list of the DLLs included in Server Core and the functions supported by Server Core on MSDN at *http://msdn.microsoft.com/en-us/library/ms723891(VS.85).aspx*.

Installing and Uninstalling Applications

Server Core supports both the Microsoft Windows Installer (MSI) and Setup.exe installation methods. The following sections illustrate how to install and uninstall MSI-based applications on Server Core.

Installing an Application

You can use the Msiexec command to install an application on Server Core using the .msi package for the application. When using Msiexec, you should always include the /qn (No UI) switch.

For example, to install Computer Associates eTrust Antivirus from C:\MSI\eTrust Antivirus.msi, do the following:

```
C:\Users\administrator>msiexec /i "C:\MSI\eTrust Antivirus.msi" /qn
```

Viewing Installed Applications

To display a quick list of installed applications (and verify the installation in the previous section), you can use WMIC like this:

```
C:\Users\administrator>wmic product get name /value

Name=CA eTrust Antivirus
```

If you want more detailed information concerning each installed application, do this:

```
C:\Users\administrator>wmic product list brief
Caption                 IdentifyingNumber                    Name
  Vendor                                    Version
CA eTrust Antivirus   {99747F0D-D4F8-4877-9CA0-
4AE96D963633}  CA eTrust Antivirus
  Computer Associates International, Inc.  7.1.0192
```

This information provides the Product Code or globally unique identifier (GUID) of the application, which is displayed here as the IdentifyingNumber.

Uninstalling an Application

You can use Msiexec to uninstall applications from Server Core. For example, to uninstall Computer Associates eTrust Antivirus using its .msi file, do this:

```
C:\Users\administrator>msiexec /x "C:\MSI\eTrust Antivirus.msi" /qn
```

If you deleted the .msi file, you can still uninstall the application by specifying its GUID as follows:

```
C:\Users\administrator>msiexec /x {99747F0D-D4F8-4877-9CA0-4AE96D963633}
```

Verify the uninstall:

```
C:\Users\administrator>wmic product get name /value
No Instance(s) Available.
```

Index

Symbols

% (percent sign), 106
& (ampersand), 103
&& (double ampersand), 103
() parentheses, 103
* (asterisks), 53
| (bar), 104
|| (double bar), 103

A

A resource record, 222, 227
AAAA resource record, 227
access control lists (ACLs), 237, 259–263
ACLs (access control lists), 237, 259–263
Active Directory Application Mode (ADAM), 349
Active Directory Domains And Trusts, 171, 174
Active Directory Installation Wizard, 158
Active Directory Sites And Services, 174
Active Directory Users And Computers
  additional information, 71
  changing focus, 129
  configuring password replication, 186
  managing domain controllers, 174
AD CS (Active Directory Certificate Services), 6
AD DS (Active Directory Domain Services)
  creating child domains, 159–160
  creating domain trees, 158–159
  creating forests, 144–158
  DFSN support, 272
  DNS support, 213
  installing, 143
  installing replica domain controllers, 160–165
  managing domain controllers, 172–175
  package names, 80
  performing common management tasks, 175–182
  preparing environment for domain controllers, 169–172
  removing domain controllers, 165–169
  RODC support, 182–188
  role support, 77, 92
  Server Core installation option, 3, 6, 15
AD DS-integrated primary DNS server, 220
AD DS-integrated primary zone, 225
AD DS-integrated zone, 222, 226
AD FS (Active Directory Federation Services), 6
AD LDS (Active Directory Lightweight Directory Services)
  installing, 348–352
  role support, 77, 80, 92
  Server Core installation option, 6, 15

AD LDS instance, 349–352
AD RMS (Active Directory Rights Management Services), 6
ADAM (Active Directory Application Mode), 349
AdamInstall.exe command, 349
Add Features Wizard, 134
Add Or Remove Snap-ins dialog box, 140
Add Printer Wizard, 288
Add Roles Wizard, 83
admin role separation, 184
Adprep command
  functionality, 144
  preparing environment, 169–172
  preparing forests for RODCs, 184
  viewing debug logs, 170
Advanced Encryption Standard (AES) encryption, 172
AeLookupSvc (Application Experience), 11
AES (Advanced Encryption Standard) encryption, 172
ALLUSERSPROFILE environment variable, 104
ampersand (&), 103
answer files
  activating Windows, 67
  additional information, 29–30, 47
  configuring Automatic Updates, 61–62
  configuring CEIP settings, 65
  configuring date/time settings, 58–59
  configuring regional/language settings, 60
  configuring TCP/IP settings, 53, 56–57
  configuring Windows Error Reporting, 64
  creating child domains, 159–160
  creating domain trees, 158–159
  creating for unattended installs, 23–30
  creating new forests, 144–158
  defined, 24
  deploying Server Core, 17
  enabling Remote Desktop, 69, 118
  enabling Windows Firewall remote administration, 70
  installing backup feature, 404–405
  installing DHCP server role, 189–190
  installing DNS servers, 213–218
  installing File Services, 246–247
  installing replica domain controllers, 160–165
  installing RODCs, 185–186
  installing roles/features, 78
  joining domains, 72
  manipulating roles/features, 88–89
  Network Level Authentication, 119–120

About the Author

Mitch Tulloch is lead author for the *Microsoft Windows Vista Resource Kit, Second Edition* (Microsoft Press, 2008) and is a widely recognized expert on Windows administration, networking, and security. Mitch has published almost 300 articles for different IT pro sites and magazines and has written almost two dozen books, including *Introducing Windows Server 2008* (Microsoft Press, 2007). His articles have been widely syndicated on IT sites such as ComputerWorld and TechTarget and have even been featured on news media sites like CNN. Mitch also writes a weekly editorial for IT World's *Windows in the Enterprise* newsletter, which is read by thousands of IT professionals around the world. Mitch has also been the technical reviewer for numerous IT professional titles from Microsoft Press, and he has developed and taught graduate-level courses in Information Security Management (ISM) for the Master of Business Administration (MBA) program of Jones International University.

Mitch has been repeatedly awarded Most Valuable Professional (MVP) status by Microsoft for his outstanding contributions in supporting both his local IT pro user group and the larger global community of IT professionals around the world. The Microsoft MVP Program recognizes individuals who share a deep commitment to building community among IT professionals and show a willingness to help others with their questions and problems. You can find out more about Microsoft's MVP Program at *http://mvp.support.microsoft.com*.

Mitch currently lives in Winnipeg, Canada. Prior to launching his own business in 1998, Mitch worked as a Microsoft Certified Trainer (MCT) for Productivity Point International. For more information about Mitch, see his Web site at *http://www.mtit.com*.

What do you think of this book?

We want to hear from you!

Your feedback will help us continually improve our books and learning resources for you. To participate in a brief online survey, please visit:

microsoft.com/learning/booksurvey

...and enter this book's ISBN-10 or ISBN-13 number (appears above barcode on back cover). As a thank-you to survey participants in the U.S. and Canada, each month we'll randomly select five respondents to win one of five $100 gift certificates from a leading online merchant. At the conclusion of the survey, you can enter the drawing by providing your e-mail address, which will be used for prize notification only.*

Thank you in advance for your input!

Where to find the ISBN on back cover

Example only. Each book has unique ISBN.

Stay in touch!

To subscribe to the *Microsoft Press*® *Book Connection Newsletter*—for news on upcoming books, events, and special offers—please visit:

microsoft.com/learning/books/newsletter